BARRON'S

AP

STATISTICS
ADVANCED PLACEMENT TEST IN STATISTICS

Martin Sternstein, Ph.D.
Professor of Mathematics
Ithaca College
Ithaca, New York

BARRON'S

All inquiries should be addressed to:
Barron's Educational Series, Inc.
250 Wireless Boulevard
Hauppauge, New York 11788
http://www.barronseduc.com

Library of Congress Catalog Card No. 97-37761

International Standard Book No. 0-7641-0221-4

Library of Congress Cataloging-in-Publication Data
Sternstein, Martin.
    How to prepare for the advanced placement examination : statistics
/ Martin Sternstein.
        p.   cm.
    ISBN 0-7641-0221-4
    1. Mathematical statistics—Examinations, questions, etc.
    2. College entrance achievement tests—Study guides.   I. Title.
QA276.2.S74   1998
001.4'22'076–dc21   97-37761
                                                            CIP

PRINTED IN THE UNITED STATES OF AMERICA
9 8 7 6 5

Contents

Author's Note

The number of students who take a statistics course in college will soon surpass the number who take a calculus course. High schools across the country have recognized this trend and are developing and expanding their statistics offerings. The Advanced Placement (AP) Program of the College Entrance Examination Board has lent their thoughtful and powerful support by developing a suggested course outline and by giving an AP examination in statistics for the first time in May 1997.

This Barron's book is intended both as a brush-up text and also to provide additional insights for students enrolled in a high school statistics course equivalent to a one-semester introductory non-calculus-based college course in statistics. Ultimately, the focus of the book is the sample practice questions and step-by-step solutions with detailed explanations.

Special thanks are due to David Bock and his students at Ithaca High School and to Rhonda Weissman and her students at Benjamin Cardozo High School for their many useful suggestions regarding the text and for pretesting and commenting on the practice questions. I extend thanks to my good friends Osman and Ayda, Paul and Linda, and Leonard and Miriam for their always cheerful and heartfelt support. Thanks to Louisa Sandvik for her four drawings. And I thank Linda Turner, project editor at Barron's, for her guidance, and Melody Covington for her expert typesetting skills.

Thanks are also due to my sons, Jonathan and Jeremy, for their love and for the lessons they gave me, teaching me new computer techniques and teaching me humility and the value of keeping in good shape by crushing me on the basketball court. Most thanks of all are due to my wife, Faith, whose warm encouragement and always calm and optimistic perspective on life provide a home environment in which deadlines can be met and goals easily achieved.

Ithaca College   Martin Sternstein
Spring 1998

Introduction

The contents of this book cover the topics recommended by the 1995–96 Development Committee in Statistics of the Advanced Placement Program of the College Entrance Examination Board. A review of each of the 15 topics is followed by multiple-choice and free-response questions on that topic, and detailed explanations are provided for all answers to these questions. Finally there are five full-length practice exams, again with detailed answers. The focus of the book is the practice questions and solutions, and there are 545 of these.

Several points with regard to particular answers should be noted. First, most calculations in this book are performed step by step using the given tables. However, they often can be performed much more quickly using the statistics packages in typical graphing calculators. The calculator answers have less round-off error than the answers based on the tables, and thus there are sometimes very minor differences. Second, some of the solutions given here use z-scores where perfectly reasonable answers can also be obtained using a calculator and t-scores. Again, minor differences in answers may result. Third, calculator packages can easily handle degrees of freedom that are not whole numbers, again sometimes resulting in minor differences in answers. In all these cases, the multiple-choice answers in this book have only one reasonable correct answer, while written explanations are necessary with regard to free-response questions.

Students taking the AP Statistics Examination are furnished with a list of formulas (from descriptive statistics, probability, and inferential statistics), with tables (including standard normal probabilities, t-distribution critical values, and χ^2 critical values), and with a table of random digits. Students are expected to bring a graphing calculator with statistics capabilities to the examination; however, exam questions are designed to not favor students who use more expensive calculators. Students are allowed to bring to the examination calculators containing whichever programs they wish to use and are not required to clear calculator memories. Minicomputers, pocket organizers, electronic writing pads (Newton), and calculators with QWERTY (typewriter) keyboards are not allowed.

There is active ongoing discussion among AP Statistics teachers about the place of calculators in the AP exam, and similar discussions are probably taking place among College Board consultants and policymakers. There are many possible multiple-choice questions that are reasonable and worthwhile under the assumption that students are using calculators with statistics capabilities. For example, both analysis of small samples from raw data and χ^2 testing for goodness of fit or for independence lead to interesting, accessible applications of elementary statistics. However, without appropriate software the resulting calculations can be lengthy and messy. At present, such topics as the above are included in the AP outline, and, furthermore, the AP exam assumes that students have calculators with statistics capabilities and are familiar with their use. Thus, there are some multiple-choice questions in this book that are appropriate for such circumstances but that might be considered unreasonable for students without calculators. It should be noted that after taking the first AP Statistics exam, many students commented that calculator usage was less than they had anticipated.

The examination consists of two parts: a 90-minute section with 35 multiple-choice problems, and a 90-minute free-response section with five open-ended questions and an investigative task to complete. In grading, the two sections of the exam are given equal weight. A correction factor compensates for random guessing in the multiple-choice section, however, students should guess if they can eliminate even one incorrect choice. In the free-response section, students must show all their work. Methods should be clearly indicated, as the problems are graded on the correctness of the methods as well as on the accuracy of the results and explanations. That is, the free-response answers should address *why* a particular test was chosen, not just *how* the test is performed. Even if a statistical test is performed on a calculator such as the TI-83, formulas should still be stated. Points are allotted based on *choosing a test* (justifying by confirming underlying assumptions) and *making a decision* consistent with the results of the test statistic. Each completed AP examination paper receives a grade based on a five-point scale, with 5 high and 1 low. Most colleges and universities accept a grade of 3 or better for credit, advanced placement, or both.

AP exams are given to students at their high schools every May. There is then a mid-June deadline for students to cancel grades, change colleges designated to receive grades, or withhold grades. In July AP grades are sent to students, their high schools, and their designated colleges.

While a review book such as this can be extremely useful in helping prepare students for the AP exam, nothing can substitute for a good high school teacher and a good textbook. I personally recommend the following texts from among the many excellent books recommended by the College Board's Development Committee in Statistics: *Introduction to the Practice of Statistics* by David Moore and George McCabe, *The Basic Practice of Statistics* by David Moore, *Workshop Statistics* by Alan Rossman, *Activity-Based Statistics* by Richard Scheaffer et al., and *Statistics* by David Freedman et al.

The student who uses this book independently should study the text and illustrative examples carefully and try to complete the practice problems before referring to the solution. Simply reading the detailed explanations of the answers without striving to first work through the problems on one's own is not the proper approach. Remember the old adage—Mathematics is not a spectator sport! Teachers can clearly use this book with a class in many profitable ways. All 545 problems can be assigned for practice in the weeks before the AP exam. Alternatively, each individual topic reviewed together with practice problems can be assigned after the topic has been covered in class, with the five full-length practice exams reserved for final review shortly before examination time.

THEME ONE

Exploratory Analysis

ITHACA, N.Y.
Population 29,541
Year incorporated 1,888
Colleges 2
AVERAGE 10,477

TOPIC ONE

Graphical Displays

There are a variety of ways to organize and arrange data. Much information can be put into tables, but these arrays of bare figures tend to be spiritless and sometimes even forbidding. Some form of graphical display is often best for seeing patterns and shapes and for presenting an immediate impression of everything about the data. Among the most common visual representations of data are dotplots, bar charts, histograms, and stemplots.

Dotplots

Dotplots and bar charts are particularly useful with regard to *categorical variables,* that is, variables that note the category to which each individual belongs. This is in contrast to *quantitative variables,* which take on numerical values.

Example 1.1.   Suppose that in a class of 35 students, 10 choose basketball as their favorite sport while 7 pick baseball, 6 pick football, 5 pick tennis, 5 pick soccer, and 2 pick hockey. These data can be displayed in the following *dotplot:*

The *frequency* of each result is indicated by the *number of dots* representing that result.

Bar Charts

Example 1.2. Suppose there are 2000 families in a small town and the distribution of children among them is as follows: 300 families are childless, 400 have 1 child, 700 have 2 children, 300 have 3, 100 have 4, 100 have 5, and 100 have 6. These data can be displayed in the following *bar chart* (or *bar graph*):

The frequencies of different results are indicated by the *heights* of the bars representing these results.

Histograms

A *histogram* can be constructed from the above bar chart by widening each bar until the sides meet at a point halfway between.

Sometimes, instead of labeling the vertical axis with frequencies, it is more convenient or more meaningful to use *relative frequencies,* that is, frequencies divided by the total number in the population.

Number of Children	Frequency	Relative Frequency
0	300	300/2000 = .150
1	400	400/2000 = .200
2	700	700/2000 = .350
3	300	300/2000 = .150
4	100	100/2000 = .050
5	100	100/2000 = .050
6	100	100/2000 = .050

Note that the shape of the histogram is the same whether the vertical axis is labeled with frequencies or with relative frequencies. Sometimes we show both frequencies and relative frequencies on the same graph.

Example 1.3. Consider the following histogram displaying 40 salaries paid to the top-level executives of a large company.

What can we learn from this histogram? For example, none of the executives earned more than $90,000 or less than $20,000. Twelve earned between $50,000 and $60,000. Twenty-five percent earned between $40,000

and $50,000. Note how this histogram shows the number of items (salaries) falling *between* certain values, whereas the preceding histogram showed the number of items (families) falling *at* each value. For example, in Example 1.3 we see that ten salaries fell somewhere between $40,000 and $50,000, while in Example 1.2 we see that 700 families had exactly two children.

Example 1.4. Consider the following histogram where the vertical axis has not been labeled. What can we learn from this histogram?

Answer: It is impossible to determine the actual frequencies; however, we can determine the relative frequencies by noting the fraction of the total *area* that is over any interval:

We can divide the area into ten equal portions, and then note that $\frac{1}{10}$ or 10% of the area is above 25–26, 20% is above 26–27, 40% is above 27–28, and 30% is above 28–29.

Although it is usually not possible to divide histograms so nicely into ten equal areas, the principle of relative frequencies corresponding to relative areas still applies.

Stemplots

Although a histogram may show how many scores fall into each grouping or interval, the exact values of individual scores are often lost. An alternative pictorial display, called a stemplot, retains this individual information.

Example 1.5.   Consider the set {25, 33, 28, 31, 45, 52, 37, 31, 46, 33, 20}. Let 2, 3, 4, and 5 be placeholders for 20, 30, 40, and 50. List the last digit of each value from the original set after the appropriate placeholder.

The result is a *stemplot* (also called a *stem and leaf display*) of these data:

Stems	Leaves
2	5 8 0
3	3 1 7 1 3
4	5 6
5	2

Drawing a continuous line around the leaves results in a horizontal histogram:

Note that the stemplot gives the shape of the histogram and, unlike the histogram, indicates the values of the original data.

Sometimes further structure is shown by rearranging the numbers in each row in ascending order. This ordered display shows a second level of information from the original stemplot.

The revised display of the data in Example 1.5 is as follows:

2	0 5 8
3	1 1 3 3 7
4	5 6
5	2

Example 1.6. Suppose the distribution of 25 advertised home prices (in thousands of dollars) in a certain community is given by the set {56, 89, 165, 73, 83, 145, 90, 189, 127, 77, 110, 112, 132, 120, 94, 130, 84, 65, 99, 154, 86, 120, 122, 103, 130}. One possible stemplot of these data is

50–74	56	65	73					
75–99	77	83	84	86	89	90	94	99
100–124	03	10	12	20	20			
125–149	22	27	30	30	32	45		
150–174	54	65						
175–200	89							

Note that the stems were chosen to be intervals of length 25 and that the 1 in 100 is left out of the leaves so that they align vertically.

Center and Spread

Looking at a graphical display, we see that two important aspects of the overall pattern are

1. the *center,* which separates the values (or area under the curve in the case of a histogram) roughly in half, and
2. the *spread,* that is, the scope of the values from smallest to largest.

In the bar chart in Example 1.2, the center is 2 children while the spread is from 0 to 6 children.

In the histogram in Example 1.3, the center is between 50 and 60, and the spread is from 20 to 90; in the histogram in Example 1.4, the center is between 27 and 28, and the spread is from 25 to 29.

In the stemplot in Example 1.5, the center is 33, and the spread is from 20 to 52; in the stemplot in Example 1.6, the center is 110, and the spread is from 56 to 189.

Clusters and Gaps

Other important aspects of the overall pattern are

1. *clusters,* which show natural subgroups into which the values fall, and
2. *gaps,* which show holes where no values fall.

Example 1.7.   Consider the following histogram:

Simply saying that the center of the distribution is around 42 and the spread is from 31 to 52 clearly misses something. The values fall into two distinct clusters with a gap between.

Outliers

Extreme values, called *outliers,* are found in many distributions. Sometimes they are the result of blunders in measurements and deserve scrutiny; however, outliers can also be the result of natural chance variation.

Shape

Distributions come in an endless variety of shapes; however, certain common patterns are worth special mention:

1. A *symmetric* distribution is one in which the two halves are mirror images of each other.
2. A distribution is *skewed to the right* if it spreads far and thinly toward the higher values.
3. A distribution is *skewed to the left* if it spreads far and thinly toward the lower values.
4. A *bell-shaped* distribution is symmetric with a center mound and two sloping tails.
5. A distribution is *uniform* if its histogram is a horizontal line.

Symmetric   Skewed to the right   Skewed to the left

Bell-shaped   Uniform

Questions on Topic 1: Graphical Displays

Multiple-Choice Questions

> *Directions:* The questions or incomplete statements that follow are each followed by five suggested answers or completions. Choose the response that best answers the question or completes the statement.

1. Following are the SAT math scores for an AP Statistics class of 20 students: 664, 658, 610, 670, 640, 643, 675, 650, 676, 575, 660, 661, 520, 667, 668, 635, 671, 673, 645, and 650. The distribution of scores is
   (A) symmetric.
   (B) skewed to the left.
   (C) skewed to the right.
   (D) uniform.
   (E) bell-shaped.

2. Which of the following statements are true?

    I. Stemplots are useful both for quantitative and categorical data sets.
    II. Stemplots are equally useful for small and very large data sets.
    III. Stemplots can show symmetry, gaps, clusters, and outliers.

    (A) I only
    (B) II only
    (C) III only
    (D) I and II
    (E) I and III

3. Consider the following histogram:

Which of the following statements are true?

I. Total sales in 1995 were two times total sales in 1994, while total sales in 1996 were three times the 1994 total.

II. The choice of labeling for the vertical axis results in a misleading sales picture.

III. A histogram showing the same information, but this time with a vertical axis starting at $78,000, would be less misleading.

(A) I only
(B) II only
(C) III only
(D) II and III
(E) None of the above gives the complete set of true responses.

4. Consider the following histogram:

Which of the following statements are true?

I. Each year from 1977 to 1986 the number of indictments has steadily decreased.

II. While the number of indictments has decreased each year, the amount of decrease has lessened.

III. The labeling of the horizontal axis has resulted in a misleading picture.

(A) I only

(B) II only

(C) III only

(D) I and II

(E) None of the above gives the complete set of true responses.

5. Which of the following are true statements?

    I. Both dotplots and stemplots can show symmetry, gaps, clusters, and outliers.

    II. In histograms, relative areas correspond to relative frequencies.

    III. In histograms, frequencies can be determined from relative heights.

    (A) II only

    (B) I and II

    (C) I and III

    (D) II and III

    (E) I, II, and III

6. Which of the following are true statements?

    I. All symmetric histograms have single peaks.

    II. All symmetric bell-shaped curves are normal.

    III. All normal curves are bell-shaped and symmetric.

    (A) I only

    (B) II only

    (C) III only

    (D) I and II

    (E) None of the above gives the complete set of true responses.

7. Which of the following distributions are more likely to be skewed to the right than skewed to the left?

    I. Household incomes

    II. Home prices

    III. Ages of teenage drivers

    (A) II only

    (B) I and II

    (C) I and III

    (D) II and III

    (E) I, II, and III

8. Which of the following are true statements?

    I. Two students working with the same set of data may come up with histograms that look different.

    II. Displaying outliers is less problematic when using histograms than when using stemplots.

    III. Histograms are more widely used than stemplots or dotplots because histograms display the values of individual observations.

    (A) I only

    (B) II only

    (C) III only

    (D) I and II

    (E) II and III

9. Following is a histogram of test scores.

Which of the following statements are true?

    I. The middle (median) score was 75.

    II. If the passing score was 60, most students failed.

    III. More students scored between 50 and 60 than between 90 and 100.

    (A) I only

    (B) II only

    (C) III only

    (D) II and III

    (E) I, II, and III

10. Which is a histogram for the ages of all family members in households where the parents have been married less than 3 years?

11. A histogram of the educational level (in number of years of schooling) of the adult population of the United States would have which of the following characteristics?

    I. Symmetry

    II. Clusters

    III. Skewness to the left

(A) II only

(B) I and II

(C) I and III

(D) II and III

(E) I, II, and III

12. Following is a stemplot of a data set of size 125.

```
1 | 8
2 | 0 0 1 3 5 6 7 7 8 9
3 | 0 1 1 2 3 3 3 4 4 5 6 6 6 6 7 8 8 9 9
4 | 0 0 0 1 1 1 2 2 2 3 3 3 3 4 4 5 6 6 7 7 8 8
5 | 0 0 0 0 2 2 2 3 3 3 3 4 4 4 4 5 5 5 6 6 6 7 7 7 7 7 8 8 8 8 8 9 9 9 9 9 9 9 9 9 9
6 | 0 0 0 1 1 1 2 2 2 3 4 4 5 5 6 6 7 7 8 8 9 9
7 | 0 1 2 5 6 6 7 9
8 | 1 2
```

What is the middle (median) of this set?

(A) 53

(B) 54

(C) 62

(D) 63

(E) 64

13. The following histogram indicates the relative frequencies of ages of U.S. scientists in 1967.

Approximately what percentage of the scientists are between 25 and 40 years of age?

(A) 10%

(B) 15%

(C) 25%

(D) 40%

(E) 50%

Answer Key

1. **B**	4. **C**	7. **B**	10. **B**	13. **E**
2. **C**	5. **B**	8. **A**	11. **D**	
3. **B**	6. **C**	9. **C**	12. **B**	

Answers Explained

1. **(B)** The low scores of 520, 575, and 610, far from the remaining scores which are all between 635 and 680, make this distribution skewed to the left.
2. **(C)** Stemplots are not used for categorical data sets and are too unwieldy to be used for very large data sets.
3. **(B)** The vertical axis, starting at $77,000, results in a misleading sales picture. It would be better to start at $0, not $78,000.
4. **(C)** Labeling the horizontal axis with different year spans results in a misleading picture. The number of indictments per year is actually increasing.
5. **(B)** In general, histograms give information about relative frequencies, not actual frequencies.
6. **(C)** Symmetric histograms can have any number of peaks. All normal curves are bell-shaped and symmetric, but not all symmetric bell-shaped curves are normal.
7. **(B)** Incomes and home prices tend to have a few very high scores that make the distributions skewed to the right. Teenage drivers mostly have ages in the last teenage years with a scattering of younger drivers, and thus a distribution skewed to the left.
8. **(A)** Choice of width and number of classes changes the appearance of a histogram. Displaying outliers is *more* problematic with histograms. Histograms do not show individual observations.
9. **(C)** The median score splits the area in half, and so the median is not 75. The area between 50 and 60 is greater than the area between 90 and 100 but is less than the area between 60 and 100.
10. **(B)** Most of the families probably have no children, while a few have very young children, hence the small bump on the lower end of (B).
11. **(D)** There will be clusters around 8, 12, and 16 years of schooling. Small segments of the population will have very few years of schooling, and so the distribution will be skewed to the left.
12. **(B)** The 125 scores are already arranged in ascending order. Counting up or down to the sixty-third score shows the median to be 54.

13. **(E)**

If we compare areas (or count small rectangles!), we can conclude that 50% of the scientists are between 25 and 40 years of age.

Free-Response Questions

> *Directions:* You must show all work and indicate the methods you use. You will be graded on the correctness of your methods and on the accuracy of your final answers.

Two Open-Ended Questions

1. According to the *1992 NAEP Trial State Assessment* the average mathematics proficiency scores in eighth grade for 41 states were as follows:

AL	251	IN	269	MO	270	PA	271
AZ	265	IA	283	NE	277	RI	265
AR	255	KY	261	NH	278	SC	260
CA	260	LA	249	NJ	271	TN	258
CO	272	ME	278	NM	259	TX	264
CT	273	MD	264	NY	266	UT	274
DE	262	MA	272	NC	258	VA	267
FL	259	MI	267	ND	283	WV	258
GA	259	MN	282	OH	267	WI	277
HI	257	MS	246	OK	267	WY	274
ID	274						

What does a stemplot show about the shape of this distribution?

2. Consider the following murder rates (per 100,000 people).

AL	13.3	IN	6.2	NE	3.0	SC	11.5
AK	12.9	IA	2.6	NV	15.5	SD	1.9
AZ	9.4	KS	5.7	NH	1.4	TN	9.4
AR	9.1	KY	9.0	NM	10.2	TX	14.2
CA	11.7	LA	15.8	NY	10.3	UT	3.7
CO	7.3	ME	2.7	NC	10.8	VT	3.3
CT	4.2	MD	8.2	ND	1.2	VA	8.8
DE	6.7	MA	3.7	OH	6.9	WA	4.6
FL	11.0	MI	10.6	OK	8.5	WV	6.8
GA	14.4	MN	2.0	OR	5.0	WI	2.5
HI	6.7	MS	12.6	PA	6.2	WY	7.1
ID	5.4	MO	10.4	RI	4.0		
IL	9.9	MT	4.8				

What does a histogram show about the shape of this distribution?

Answers Explained

1.

```
28 | 2 3 3
27 | 0 1 1 2 2 3 4 4 4 7 7 8 8
26 | 0 0 1 2 4 4 5 5 6 7 7 7 7 7 9
25 | 1 5 7 8 8 8 9 9 9
24 | 6 9
```

The data are roughly symmetric and bell-shaped; they are centered in the 260s, with a spread from 246 to 283 and no outliers, clusters, or gaps.

2.

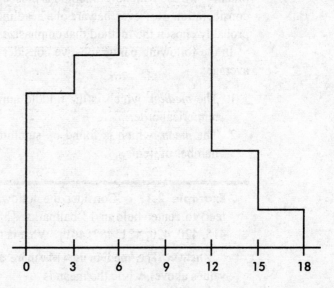

The distribution is not symmetric but rather has a slight skew to the right.

TOPIC TWO

Summarizing Distributions

Given a raw set of data, often we can detect no overall pattern. Perhaps some values occur more frequently, a few extreme values may stand out, and the range of values is usually apparent. The presentation of data, including summarizations and descriptions, and involving such concepts as representative or average values, measures of dispersion, positions of various values, and the shape of a distribution, falls under the broad topic of *descriptive statistics*. This aspect of statistics is in contrast to *statistical analysis,* the process of drawing inferences from limited data, a subject discussed in later topics.

Measuring the Center: Median and Mean

The word *average* is used in phrases common to everyday conversation. People speak of bowling and batting averages or the average life expectancy of a battery or a human being. Actually the word *average* is derived from the French *avarie,* which refers to the money that shippers contributed to help compensate for losses suffered by other shippers whose cargo did not arrive safely (i.e., the losses were shared, with everyone contributing an average amount). In common usage *average* has come to mean a representative score or a typical value or the center of a distribution. Mathematically, there are a variety of ways to define the average of a set of data. In practice, we use whichever method is most appropriate for the particular case under consideration. However, beware of a headline with the word *average;* the writer has probably chosen the method that emphasizes the point he wishes to make.

In the following paragraphs we consider the two primary ways of denoting an average:

1. The *median,* which is the middle number of a set of numbers arranged in numerical order.
2. The *mean,* which is found by summing items in a set and dividing by the number of items.

Example 2.1.   Consider the following set of homerun distances (in feet) to center field in 13 ballparks: {387, 400, 400, 410, 410, 410, 414, 415, 420, 420, 421, 457, 461}. What is the average?

Answer: The median is 414 (there are six values below 414 and six values above), while the mean is

$$\frac{387 + 400 + 400 + 410 + 410 + \cdots + 457 + 461}{13} = 417.3 \text{ feet}$$

Median

The word *median* is derived from the Latin *medius* which means "middle." The values under consideration are arranged in ascending or descending order. If there is an odd number of values, the median is the middle one. If there is an even number, the median is found by adding the two middle values and dividing by 2. Thus the median of a set has the same number of elements above it as below it.

The median is not affected by exactly how large the larger values are or by exactly how small the smaller values are. Thus it is a particularly useful measurement when the extreme values, called *outliers,* are in some way suspicious or when we want to diminish their effect. For example, if ten mice try to solve a maze, and nine succeed in less than 15 minutes while one is still trying after 24 hours, the most representative value is the median (not the mean, which is over 1 hour). Similarly, if the salaries of four executives are each between $240,000 and $245,000 while a fifth is paid less than $20,000, again the most representative value is the median (the mean is under $200,000).

In certain situations the median offers the most economical and quickest way to calculate an average. For example, suppose 10,000 light bulbs of a particular brand are installed in a factory. An average life expectancy for the bulbs can most easily be found by noting how much time passes before exactly one-half of them have to be replaced. The median is also useful in certain kinds of medical research. For example, to compare the relative strengths of different poisons, a scientist notes what dosage of each poison will result in the death of exactly one-half the test animals. If one of the animals proves especially susceptible to a particular poison, the median lethal dose is not affected.

Mean

While the median is often useful in descriptive statistics, the *mean,* or more accurately, the *arithmetic mean,* is most important for statistical inference and analysis. Also, for the layperson, the average is usually understood to be the mean.

The mean of a *whole population* (the complete set of items of interest) is often denoted by the Greek letter μ (mu), while the mean of a *sample* (a part of a population) is often denoted by $\bar{x}$. For example, the mean value of the set of all houses in the United States might be $\mu = \$56,400$, while the mean value of 100 randomly chosen houses might be $\bar{x} = \$52,100$ or perhaps $\bar{x} = \$63,800$ or even $\bar{x} = \$124,000$.

In statistics we learn how to estimate a population mean from a sample mean. Throughout this book, the word *sample* implies a *random sample,* that is, a sample selected in such a way that each element of the population has an equal chance of being included. In the real world, this process of random selection is often very difficult to achieve.

Mathematically, the mean $= \frac{\Sigma x}{n}$, where Σx represents the sum of all the elements of the set under consideration and n is the actual number of elements. Σ is the uppercase Greek letter sigma.

Example 2.2.   Suppose that the numbers of unnecessary procedures recommended by five doctors in a 1-month period are given by the set {2, 2, 8, 20, 33}. Note that the median is 8 and the mean is $\frac{2+2+8+20+33}{5} = 13$. If it is discovered that the fifth doctor also recommended an additional 25 unnecessary procedures, how will the median and mean be affected?

Answer: The set is now {2, 2, 8, 20, 58}. The median is still 8; however, the mean changes to $\frac{2+2+8+20+58}{5} = 18$.

The above example illustrates how the mean, unlike the median, is sensitive to a change in any value.

Example 2.3. Suppose the salaries of six employees are $3000, $7000, $15,000, $22,000, $23,000, and $38,000, respectively.

a. What is the mean salary?
   Answer:

   $$\frac{3000 + 7000 + 15,000 + 22,000 + 23,000 + 38,000}{6} = \$18,000$$

b. What will the new mean salary be if everyone receives a $3000 increase?
   Answer:

   $$\frac{6000 + 10,000 + 18,000 + 25,000 + 26,000 + 41,000}{6} = \$21,000$$

   Note that $18,000 + $3000 = $21,000.

c. What if everyone receives a 10% raise?
   Answer:

   $$\frac{3300 + 7700 + 16,500 + 24,200 + 25,300 + 41,800}{6} = \$19,800$$

   Note that 110% of $18,000 is $19,800.

The above example illustrates how adding the same constant to each value increases the mean by a like amount. Similarly, multiplying each value by the same constant multiplies the mean by a like amount.

Measuring Spread: Range, Interquartile Range, Variance, and Standard Deviation

In describing a set of numbers, not only is it useful to designate an average value but it is also important to be able to indicate the *variability* or the *dispersion* of the measurements. A producer of time bombs aims for small variability—it would not be good for his 30-minute fuses actually to have a range of 10–50 minutes before detonation. On the other hand, a teacher interested in distinguishing better students from poorer students aims to design exams with large variability in results—it would not be helpful if all her students scored exactly the same. The players on two basketball teams may have the same average height, but this observation doesn't tell the whole story. If the dispersions are quite different, one team may have a 7-foot player, whereas the other has no one over 6 feet tall. Two Mediterranean holiday cruises may advertise the same average age for their passengers. One, however, may have only passengers between 20 and 25 years old, while the other has only middle-aged parents in their forties together with their children under age 10.

There are four primary ways of describing variability or dispersion:

1. The *range,* which is the difference between the largest and smallest values
2. The *interquartile range,* which is the difference between the largest and smallest values after removing the lower and upper quarters (i.e., the range of the middle 50%)
3. The *variance,* which is determined by averaging the squared differences of all the values from the mean
4. The *standard deviation,* which is the square root of the variance.

Example 2.4.   The monthly rainfall in Monrovia, Liberia, where May through October is the rainy season and November through April the dry season, is as follows:

Month:	Jan	Feb	Mar	Apr	May	June	July	Aug	Sept	Oct	Nov	Dec
Rain (in.):	1	2	4	6	18	37	31	16	28	24	9	4

The mean is

$$\frac{1+2+4+6+18+37+31+16+28+24+9+4}{12} = 15 \text{ inches}$$

What are the measures of variability?

Answer: Range: The maximum is 37 inches (June), and the minimum is 1 inch (January). Thus the range is $37 - 1 = 36$ inches of rain.

Interquartile range: Removing the lower and upper quarters leaves 4, 6, 9, 16, 18, and 24. Thus the interquartile range is $24 - 4 = 20$. [The interquartile range is sometimes calculated as follows: The median of the lower half is $Q_1 = \frac{4+4}{2} = 4$, the median of the upper half is $Q_3 = \frac{24+28}{2} = 26$, and the interquartile range is $Q_3 - Q_1 = 22$. When there is a large number of values in the set, the two methods give the same answer.]

Variance:

$$\frac{14^2 + 13^2 + 11^2 + 9^2 + 3^2 + 22^2 + 16^2 + 1^2 + 13^2 + 9^2 + 6^2 + 11^2}{12} = 143.7$$

Standard deviation: $\sqrt{143.7} = 12.0$ inches

Range

The simplest, most easily calculated measure of variability is the *range*. The difference between the largest and smallest values can be noted quickly, and the range gives some impression of the dispersion. However, it is entirely dependent on the two extreme values and is insensitive to the ones in the middle.

One use of the range is to evaluate samples with very few items. For example, some quality control techniques involve taking periodic small samples and basing further action on the range found in several such samples.

Interquartile Range

Finding the *interquartile range* is one method of removing the influence of extreme values on the range. It is calculated by arranging the data in numerical order, removing the upper and lower quarters of the values, and noting the range of the remaining values. That is, it is the range of the middle 50% of the values.

Example 2.5.   Suppose that farm sizes in a small community have the following characteristics: the smallest value is 16.6 acres, 10% of the values are below 23.5 acres, 25% are below 41.1 acres, the median is 57.6 acres, 60% are below 87.2 acres, 75% are below 101.9 acres, 90% are below 124.0 acres, and the top value is 201.7 acres.

  a. What is the range?
  Answer: The range is $201.7 - 16.6 = 185.1$ acres.
  b. What is the interquartile range?
  Answer: The interquartile range, with the highest and lowest quarters of the values removed, is $101.9 - 41.1 = 60.8$ acres. Thus, while the largest farm is 185 acres more than the smallest, the middle 50% of the farm sizes range over a 61-acre interval.

Variance

Dispersion is often the result of various chance happenings. For example, consider the motion of microscopic particles suspended in a liquid. The unpredictable motion of any particle is the result of many small movements in various directions caused by random bumps from other particles. If we average the total displacements of all the particles from their starting points, the result will not increase in direct proportion to time. If, however, we average the *squares* of the total displacements of all the particles, this result will increase in direct proportion to time.

The same holds true for the movement of paramecia. Their seemingly random motions as seen under a microscope can be described by the observation that the average of the squares of the displacements from their starting points is directly proportional to time. Also, consider ping-pong balls dropped straight down from a high tower and subjected to chance buffeting in the air. We can measure the deviations from a center spot on the ground to the spots where the balls actually strike. As the height of the tower is increased, the average of the squared deviations increases proportionately.

In a wide variety of cases we are in effect trying to measure dispersion from the mean due to a multitude of chance effects. The proper tool in these cases is the average of the squared deviations from the mean; it is called the *variance* and is denoted by σ^2 (σ is the lowercase Greek letter sigma):

$$\sigma^2 = \frac{\Sigma(x-\mu)^2}{n}$$

For circumstances specified later, the variance of a sample, denoted by s^2, is calculated as

$$s^2 = \frac{\Sigma(x-\bar{x})^2}{n-1}$$

Example 2.6.   During the years 1929–39 of the Great Depression, the weekly average hours worked in manufacturing jobs were 45, 43, 41, 39, 39, 35, 37, 40, 39, 36, and 37, respectively. What is the variance?

Answer: The variance can be quickly found on any calculator with a simple statistical package, or it can be found as follows:

$$\mu = \frac{45+43+41+39+39+35+37+40+39+36+37}{11} = 39.2 \text{ hours}$$

$$\sigma^2 = \frac{(45-39.2)^2 + (43-39.2)^2 + \cdots + (36-39.2)^2 + (37-39.2)^2}{11} = 8.1$$

An arithmetic tool for calculating the variance is

$$\sigma^2 = \frac{\Sigma x^2}{n} - \mu^2$$

In words, the variance can be found by subtracting the square of the mean from the average of the squared scores.

Example 2.7.   Let $X = \{3, 7, 15, 23\}$. What is the variance?

Answer: Again, use the statistical package on your calculator, or

$$\Sigma x = 3+7+15+23 = 48$$
$$\Sigma x^2 = 3^2 + 7^2 + 15^2 + 23^2 = 812$$
$$\mu = \frac{\Sigma x}{n} = \frac{48}{4} = 12$$

The variance can be calculated from its definition:

$$\sigma^2 = \frac{\Sigma(x-\mu)^2}{n} = \frac{(3-12)^2 + (7-12)^2 + (15-12)^2 + (23-12)^2}{4} = 59$$

Or it can be calculated as follows:

$$\sigma^2 = \frac{\Sigma x^2}{n} - \mu^2 = \frac{812}{4} - 12^2 = 203 - 144 = 59$$

Similarly, there is an arithmetic tool for calculating the variance of a sample:

$$s^2 = \frac{\Sigma x^2 - \frac{(\Sigma x)^2}{n}}{n-1}$$

Of course, using the built-in statistical package on your calculator allows you to enter data and then simply read off means and variances.

Standard Deviation

Suppose we wish to pick a representative value for the variability of a certain population. The preceding discussions indicate that a natural choice is the value whose square is the average of the squared deviations from the mean. Thus we are led to consider the square root of the variance. This value is called the *standard deviation*, is denoted by σ, and is calculated on your calculator or as follows:

$$\sigma = \sqrt{\frac{\Sigma(x-\mu)^2}{n}} = \sqrt{\frac{\Sigma x^2}{n} - \mu^2}$$

Similarly, the standard deviation of a sample is denoted by s and is calculated on your calculator or as follows:

$$s = \sqrt{\frac{\Sigma(x-\bar{x})^2}{n-1}} = \sqrt{\frac{\Sigma x^2 - \frac{(\Sigma x)^2}{n}}{n-1}}$$

Example 2.8. Putting the data $\{1, 6, 3, 8\}$ into a calculator such as the TI-83 gives what value for the standard deviation?

Answer: The TI-83 gives

```
1-Var Stats
x̄=4.5
Σx=18
Σx²=110
Sx=3.109126351
σx=2.692582404
```

Thus, if the data are a population, the standard deviation is $\sigma = 2.693$, while if the data are a sample, the standard deviation is $s = 3.109$.

Measuring Position: Simple Ranking, Percentile Ranking, and z-Score

We have seen several ways of choosing a value to represent the center of a distribution. We also need to be able to talk about the *position* of any other values. In some situations, such as wine tasting, simple rankings are of interest. Other cases, for example, evaluating college applications, may involve positioning according to percentile rankings. There are also situations in which position can be specified by making use of measurements of both central tendency and variability.

There are three important, recognized procedures for designating position:

1. *Simple ranking,* which involves arranging the elements in some order and noting where in that order a particular value falls
2. *Percentile ranking,* which indicates what percentage of all values fall below the value under consideration
3. The *z-score,* which states very specifically by how many standard deviations a particular value varies from the mean.

Example 2.9. The water capacities (in gallons) of the 57 major solid-fuel boilers sold in the United States are 6.3, 7.4, 8.6, 10, 12.1, 50, 8.2, 9.8, 11.4, 12.9, 14.5, 16.1, 26, 21, 27, 40, 55, 30, 35, 55, 65, 18.8, 23.3, 28.3, 33.8, 26.4, 33, 50, 35, 21, 21, 18.5, 26.4, 37, 12, 12, 50, 65, 65, 56, 66, 60, 70, 27.7, 34.3, 42, 46.2, 33, 25, 29, 40, 19, 9, 12.5, 15.8, 24.5, and 16.5, respectively (John W. Bartok, *Solid-Fuel Furnaces and Boilers,* Garden Way, Charlotte, Vermont). What is the position of the Passat HO-45, which has a capacity of 46.2 gallons?

Answer: Since there are 12 boilers with higher capacities on the list, the Passat has a simple ranking of thirteenth (out of 57). Forty-four boilers have lower capacities, and so the Passat has a percentile ranking of $\frac{44}{57} = 77.2\%$. The above list has a mean of 30.2 and a standard deviation of 17.8, so the Passat has a z-score of $\frac{46.2-30.3}{17.8} = 0.89$.

Simple Ranking

Simple ranking is easily calculated and easily understood. We know what it means for someone to graduate second in a class of 435, or for a player from a team of size 30 to have the seventh-best batting average. Simple ranking is useful even when no numerical values are associated with the elements. For example, detergents can be ranked according to relative cleansing ability without any numerical measurements of strength.

Percentile Ranking

Percentile ranking, another readily understood measurement of position, is helpful in comparing positions with different bases. We can more easily compare a rank of 176 out of 704 with a rank of 187 out of 935 by noting that the first has a rank of 75%, and the second, a rank of 80%. Percentile rank is also useful when the exact population size is not known or is irrelevant. For example, it is more meaningful to say that Jennifer scored in the 90th percentile on a national exam rather than trying to determine her exact ranking among some large number of test takers.

The *quartiles, Q_1* and Q_3, lie one-quarter and three-quarters of the way up a list, respectively. Their percentile ranks are 25% and 75%, respectively. The interquartile range defined earlier can also be defined to be $Q_3 - Q_1$. The *deciles* lie one-tenth and nine-tenths of the way up a list, respectively, and have percentile ranks of 10% and 90%.

z-Score

The *z-score* is a measure of position that takes into account both the center and the dispersion of the distribution. More specifically, the z-score of a value tells how many standard deviations the value is from the mean. Mathematically, $x - \mu$ gives the raw distance from μ to x; dividing by σ converts this to number of standard deviations. Thus $z = \frac{x-\mu}{\sigma}$, where x is the raw score, μ is the mean, and σ is the standard deviation. If the score x is greater than the mean μ, then z is positive; if x is less than μ, then z is negative.

Given a z-score, we can reverse the procedure and find the corresponding raw score. Solving for x gives $x = \mu + z\sigma$.

Example 2.10. Suppose the average (mean) price of gasoline in a large city is \$1.80 per gallon with a standard deviation of \$0.05. Then \$1.90 has a z-score of $\frac{1.90-1.80}{0.05} = +2$, while \$1.65 has a z-score of $\frac{1.65-1.80}{0.05} = -3$. Alternatively, a z-score of $+2.2$ corresponds to a raw score of $1.80 + 2.2(0.05) = 1.80 + 0.11 = 1.91$, while a z-score of -1.6 corresponds to $1.80 - 1.6(0.05) = 1.72$.

It is often useful to portray integer z-scores and the corresponding raw scores as follows:

Example 2.11. Suppose the attendance at a movie theater averages 780 with a standard deviation of 40. Adding multiples of 40 to and subtracting multiples of 40 from the mean 780 gives

A theater attendance of 835 is converted to a z-score as follows: $\frac{835-780}{40} = \frac{55}{40} = 1.375$. A z-score of -2.15 is converted to a theater attendance as follows: $780 - 2.15(40) = 694$.

Empirical Rule

The *empirical rule* applies specifically to symmetric bell-shaped data. In this case, about 68% of the values lie within 1 standard deviation of the mean, about 95% of the values lie within 2 standard deviations of the mean, and more than 99% of the values lie within 3 standard deviations of the mean.

In the following figure the horizontal axis shows *z*-scores:

Example 2.12.   Suppose that taxicabs in New York City are driven an average of 75,000 miles per year with a standard deviation of 12,000 miles. What information does the empirical rule give us?

Answer: Assuming that the distribution is bell-shaped, we can conclude that approximately 68% of the taxis are driven between 63,000 and 87,000 miles per year, approximately 95% are driven between 51,000 and 99,000 miles, and virtually all are driven between 39,000 and 111,000 miles.

The empirical rule also gives a useful quick estimate of the standard deviation in terms of the range. We can see in the figure above that 95% of the data fall within a span of 4 standard deviations (from −2 to +2 on the *z*-score line) and 99% of the data fall within 6 standard deviations (from −3 to +3 on the *z*-score line). It is therefore reasonable to conclude that for these data the standard deviation is roughly between one-fourth and one-sixth of the range. Since we can find the range of a set almost immediately, the empirical rule technique for estimating the standard deviation is often helpful in pointing out probable arithmetic errors.

Example 2.13.   If the range of a data set is 60, what is an estimate for the standard deviation?

Answer: By the empirical rule, the standard deviation is expected to be between $(\frac{1}{6})60 = 10$ and $(\frac{1}{4})60 = 15$. If the standard deviation is calculated to be 0.32 or 87, there is probably an arithmetic error; a calculation of 12, however, is reasonable.

Histograms and Measures of Central Tendency

Suppose we have a detailed histogram such as

Our measures of central tendency fit naturally into such a diagram.

The *median* divides a distribution in half, so it is represented by a line that divides the area of the histogram in half.

The *mean* is affected by the spacing of all the values. Therefore, if the histogram is considered to be a solid region, the mean corresponds to a line passing through the center of gravity.

The above distribution, spread thinly far to the low side, is said to be *skewed to the left*. Note that in this case the mean is less than the median. Similarly, a distribution spread far to the high side is *skewed to the right*, and its mean is greater than its median.

Example 2.14.   Suppose that the faculty salaries at a college have a median of $32,500 and a mean of $38,700. What does this indicate about the shape of the distribution of the salaries?

Answer: The median is less than the mean, and so the salaries are probably skewed to the right. There are a few highly paid professors, with the bulk of the faculty at the lower end of the pay scale.

Histograms, z-scores, and Percentile Rankings

We have seen that relative frequencies are represented by relative areas, and so labeling the vertical axis is not crucial. If we know the standard deviation, the horizontal axis can be labeled in terms of z-scores. In fact, if we are given the percentile rankings of various z-scores, we can construct a histogram.

Example 2.15.   Suppose we are asked to construct a histogram from these data:

z-score:	−2	−1	0	1	2
Percentile ranking:	0	20	60	70	100

We note that the entire area is less than z-score +2 and greater than z-score −2. Also, 20% of the area is between z-scores −2 and −1, 40% is between −1 and 0, 10% is between 0 and 1, and 30% is between 1 and 2. Thus the histogram is as follows:

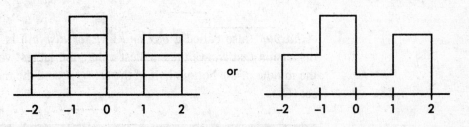

Now suppose we are given four in-between z-scores as well:

z-score	Percentile Ranking
2.0	100
1.5	80
1.0	70
0.5	65
0.0	60
−0.5	30
−1.0	20
−1.5	5
−2.0	0

Then we have:

With 1000 z-scores perhaps the histogram would look like

The height at any point is meaningless; what is important is relative areas. For example, in the final diagram above, what percentage of the area is between z-scores of $+1$ and $+2$?

Answer: Still 30%.

What percent is to the left of 0?

Answer: Still 60%.

Boxplots

A *boxplot* (also called a *box and whisker display*) is a visual representation of dispersion that shows the smallest value, the largest value, the middle (median), the middle of the bottom half of the set (Q_1), and the middle of the top half of the set (Q_3).

Example 2.16.   The total farm product indexes for the years 1919–45 (with 1910–14 as 100) are 215, 210, 130, 140, 150, 150, 160, 150, 140, 150, 150, 125, 85, 70, 75, 90, 115, 120, 125, 100, 95, 100, 130, 160, 200, 200, 210, respectively. (Note the instability of prices received by farmers!) The largest value is 215, the smallest is 70, the middle is 140, the middle of the top half is 160, and the middle of the bottom half is 100. A boxplot of these five numbers is

Note that the display consists of two "boxes" together with two "whiskers"—hence the alternative name. The boxes show the spread of the two middle quarters; the whiskers show the spread of the two outer quarters. This relatively simple display conveys information not immediately available from histograms or stem and leaf displays.

Questions on Topic Two: Summarizing Distributions

Multiple-Choice Questions

Directions: The questions or incomplete statements that follow are each followed by five suggested answers or completions. Choose the response that best answers the question or completes the statement.

1. In the second game of the 1989 World Series between Oakland and San Francisco (played 2 days before the northern California earthquake postponed the series), ten players went hitless, eight players had one hit apiece, and one player (Rickey Henderson) had three hits. What were the mean and median number of hits?

   (A) 11/19, 0
   (B) 11/19, 1
   (C) 1, 1
   (D) 0, 1
   (E) 1, 0

2. Which of the following are true statements?

   I. The range of the sample data set is never greater than the range of the population.
   II. The interquartile range is half the distance between the first quartile and the third quartile.
   III. While the range is affected by outliers, the interquartile range is not.

   (A) I only
   (B) II only
   (C) III only
   (D) I and II
   (E) I and III

3. Which of the following are true statements?

   I. The standard deviation is the square root of the variance.
   II. The standard deviation is zero only when all the values are the same.
   III. The standard deviation is strongly affected by outliers.

   (A) I and II
   (B) I and III
   (C) II and III
   (D) I, II, and III
   (E) None of the above gives the complete set of true responses.

4. A z-score is
   (A) the mean of the distribution.
   (B) the deviation from the mean divided by the standard deviation.
   (C) always positive.
   (D) all of the above.
   (E) none of the above.

5. On August 23, 1994, the 5-day total returns for equal investments in foreign stocks, U.S. stocks, gold, money market funds, and treasury bonds averaged 0.086% (*Business Week,* September 5, 1994, p. 97). If the respective returns for foreign stocks, U.S. stocks, gold, and money market funds were +0.70%, −0.11%, +1.34%, and +0.05%, what was the return for treasury bonds?
   (A) 0.4132%
   (B) 0.43%
   (C) −1.55%
   (D) −1.636%
   (E) −1.77%

6. Suppose the average score on a national test is 500 with a standard deviation of 100. If each score is increased by 25, what are the new mean and standard deviation?
   (A) 500, 100
   (B) 500, 125
   (C) 525, 100
   (D) 525, 105
   (E) 525, 125

7. Suppose the average score on a national test is 500 with a standard deviation of 100. If each score is increased by 25%, what are the new mean and standard deviation?
   (A) 500, 100
   (B) 525, 100
   (C) 625, 100
   (D) 625, 105
   (E) 625, 125

8. In a certain southwestern city the air pollution index averages 62.5 during the year with a standard deviation of 18.0. Assuming that the empirical rule is appropriate, the index falls within what interval 95% of the time?
   (A) (8.5, 116.5)
   (B) (26.5, 98.5)
   (C) (44.5, 80.5)
   (D) (45.4, 79.6)
   (E) There is insufficient information to answer this question.

9. A 1995 poll by the Program for International Policy asked respondents what percentage of the U.S. budget they thought went to foreign aid. The mean response was 18%, and the median was 15%. (The actual amount is less than 1%.) What do these responses indicate about the shape of the distribution of all the responses?

(A) The distribution is skewed to the left.

(B) The distribution is skewed to the right.

(C) The distribution is symmetric around 16.5%.

(D) The distribution is bell-shaped with a standard deviation of 3%.

(E) The distribution is uniform between 15% and 18%.

10. The average cost per ounce for glass cleaner is 7.7 cents with a standard deviation of 2.5 cents. What is the z-score of Windex with a cost of 10.1 cents per ounce?

(A) 0.96

(B) 1.31

(C) 1.94

(D) 4.04

(E) None of these

11. Which of the following are true statements?

I. If the sample has variance zero, the variance of the population is also zero.

II. If the population has variance zero, the variance of the sample is also zero.

III. If the sample has variance zero, the sample mean and the sample median are equal.

(A) I and II

(B) I and III

(C) II and III

(D) I, II, and III

(E) None of the above gives the complete set of true responses.

12. If the range of a data set is 144, which of the following are reasonable values for the standard deviation?

(A) 1.40, 1.42, 1.44

(B) 12, 14, 16

(C) 25, 30, 35

(D) 48, 72, 96

(E) All of the above

13. Suppose the starting salaries of a graduating class are as follows:

Number of Students	Starting Salary ($)
10	15,000
17	20,000
25	25,000
38	30,000
27	35,000
21	40,000
12	45,000

What is the mean starting salary?

(A) $30,000
(B) $30,533
(C) $32,500
(D) $32,533
(E) $35,000

14. When a set of data has suspect outliers, which of the following are preferred measures of central tendency and of variability?

    (A) mean and standard deviation
    (B) mean and variance
    (C) mean and range
    (D) median and range
    (E) median and interquartile range

15. If the standard deviation of a set of observations is 0, you can conclude

    (A) that there is no relationship between the observations.
    (B) that the average value is 0.
    (C) that all observations are the same value.
    (D) that a mistake in arithmetic has been made.
    (E) none of the above.

16. A teacher is teaching two AP Statistics classes. On the final exam, the 20 students in the first class averaged 92 while the 25 students in the second class averaged only 83. If the teacher combines the classes, what will the average final exam score be?

    (A) 87
    (B) 87.5
    (C) 88
    (D) None of the above
    (E) More information is needed to make this calculation.

17. The 60 longest rivers in the world have lengths distributed as follows:

Length (mi):	1000–1499	1500–1999	2000–2499	2500–2999	3000–3499	3500–3999	4000–4499
Number of rivers:	21	22	4	8	2	2	1

(The Nile is the longest with a length of 4145 miles, and the Amazon is the second longest at 3900 miles.)

Which of the following best describes these data?

    (A) Skewed distribution, mean greater than median
    (B) Skewed distribution, median greater than mean
    (C) Symmetric distribution, mean greater than median
    (D) Symmetric distribution, median greater than mean
    (E) Symmetric distribution with outliers on high end

18. In 1993 the seven states with the fewest business bankruptcies were Vermont (900), Alaska (1000), North Dakota (1100), Wyoming (1300), South Dakota (1400), Hawaii (1500), and Delaware (1600).

    Which of the following are reasonable conclusions about the distribution of bankruptcies throughout the 50 states in 1993?

    I. The total number of bankruptcies in the United States in 1993 was approximately 50(1300) = 65,000.
    II. Because of these low values, the distribution was skewed to the left.
    III. The range of the distribution was approximately 50(1600 − 1000) = 30,000.

    (A) I only
    (B) II only
    (C) III only
    (D) All are reasonable.
    (E) None are reasonable.

19. The *1992 NAEP Trial State Assessment* calculated a state-by-state average mathematics proficiency score for students in the eighth grade. The resulting boxplot is

    Which of the following statements are true?
    I. The state score 273 has a percentile rank of 75.
    II. The mean state score is 267.
    III. The lowest state score is 246.

    (A) III only
    (B) I and II
    (C) I and III
    (D) II and III
    (E) I, II, and III

20. A stemplot for the 1988 per capita personal income (in hundreds of dollars) for the 50 states is

```
11 | 0  7
12 | 6  2  7  8  2  7  5  7  8  5  0
13 | 3  7  7
14 | 9  7  8  1  6
15 | 0  9  0  5  2  5  0  4  4
16 | 4  5  9  4  8  2  8  6
17 | 7  6  4  6
18 | 9
19 | 5  3  0  3
20 | 7
21 | 9
22 | 8
```

Which of the following best describes these data?

(A) Skewed distribution, mean greater than median
(B) Skewed distribution, median greater than mean
(C) Symmetric distribution, mean greater than median
(D) Symmetric distribution, median greater than mean
(E) Symmetric distribution with outliers on high end

21. Which of the following statements are true?

I. If the right and left sides of a histogram are mirror images of each other, the distribution is symmetric.
II. A distribution spread far to the right side is said to be skewed to the right.
III. If a distribution is skewed to the right, its mean is greater than its median.

(A) I only
(B) I and II
(C) I and III
(D) II and III
(E) None of the above gives the complete set of true responses.

22. Which of the following statements are true?

I. In a stemplot the number of leaves equals the size of the set of data.
II. Both the dotplot and the stemplot are useful in identifying outliers.
III. Histograms do not retain the identity of individual scores; however, dotplots, stemplots, and boxplots all do.

(A) I and II
(B) I and III
(C) II and III
(D) I, II, and III
(E) None of the above gives the complete set of true responses.

23. The 70 highest dams in the world have an average height of 206 meters with a standard deviation of 35 meters. The Hoover and Grand Coulee dams have heights of 221 and 168 meters, respectively. The Russian dams, the Nurek and Charvak, have heights with z-scores of $+2.69$ and -1.13, respectively. List the dams in order of ascending size.

(A) Charvak, Grand Coulee, Hoover, Nurek
(B) Charvak, Grand Coulee, Nurek, Hoover
(C) Grand Coulee, Charvak, Hoover, Nurek
(D) Grand Coulee, Charvak, Nurek, Hoover
(E) Grand Coulee, Hoover, Charvak, Nurek

24. According to *Consumer Reports* magazine, the costs per pound of protein for 20 major-brand beef hot dogs are $14.23, $21.70, $14.49, $20.49, $14.47, $15.45, $25.25, $24.02, $18.86, $18.86, $30.65, $25.62, $8.12, $12.74, $14.21, $13.39, $22.31, $19.95, $22.90, and $19.78, respectively. If the least expensive is considered the top-ranked, what is the position in terms of a z-score of Thorn Apple Valley beef hot dogs at $14.23 per pound of protein?

(A) -2.67
(B) -0.85
(C) 0.85
(D) 1.42
(E) 2.67

Answer Key

1. **A**	6. **C**	11. **C**	16. **A**	21. **E**
2. **E**	7. **E**	12. **C**	17. **A**	22. **A**
3. **D**	8. **B**	13. **B**	18. **E**	23. **A**
4. **B**	9. **B**	14. **E**	19. **C**	24. **B**
5. **C**	10. **A**	15. **C**	20. **A**	

Answers Explained

1. **(A)** The set is $\{0,0,0,0,0,0,0,0,0,0,0,1,1,1,1,1,1,1,1,3\}$, so the mean is $\frac{11}{19}$ and the median is 0.

2. **(E)** All elements of the sample are taken from the population, and so the smallest value in the sample cannot be less than the smallest value in the population; similarly, the largest value in the sample cannot be greater than the largest value in the population. The interquartile range is the full distance between the first quartile and the third quartile. Outliers are extreme values, and while they may affect the range, they do not affect the interquartile range when the lower and upper quarters have been removed before calculation.

3. **(D)** The standard deviation is defined to be the square root of the variance. Because of the squaring operation in the definition, the standard deviation (and also the variance) can be zero only if all the values in the set are equal and thus equal to the mean.

4. **(B)** The z-score tells specifically by how many standard deviations a particular value varies from the mean or, in other words, the deviation from the mean divided by the standard deviation.

5. **(C)** From $\frac{0.70-0.11+1.34+0.05+x}{5} = 0.086$, the return was -1.55%.

6. **(C)** Adding the same constant to every value increases the mean by that same constant; however, the distances between the increased values and the increased mean stay the same, and so the standard deviation is unchanged. Graphically, you should picture the whole distribution as moving over by a constant; the mean moves, but the standard deviation (which measures spread) doesn't change.

7. **(E)** Multiplying every value by the same constant multiplies both the mean and the standard deviation by that constant. Graphically, increasing each value by 25% (multiplying by 1.25) both moves and spreads out the distribution.

8. **(B)** The empirical rule gives that about 95% of the values lie within two standard deviations of the mean, and so we calculate $62.5 \pm 2(18.0) = 62.5 \pm 36.0$ or $(26.5, 98.5)$.

9. **(B)** The median is less than the mean, and so the responses are probably skewed to the right; there are a few high guesses, with most of the responses on the lower end of the scale.

10. **(A)** The z-score is the number of standard deviations the value is from the mean: $\frac{10.1-7.7}{2.5} = 0.96$.

11. **(C)** If the variance of a set is zero, all the values in the set are equal. If all the values of the population are equal, the same holds true for any subset; however, if all the values of a subset are the same, this may not be true of the whole population. If all the values in a set are equal, the mean and the median both equal this common value and so equal each other.

12. **(C)** By the empirical rule (if it applies), the standard deviation is expected to be between $\left(\frac{1}{6}\right)144 = 24$ and $\left(\frac{1}{4}\right)144 = 36$.

13. **(B)** There are a total of $10 + 17 + 25 + 38 + 27 + 21 + 12 = 150$ students. Their total salary is $10(15,000) + 17(20,000) + 25(25,000) + 38(30,000) + 27(35,000) + 21(40,000) + 12(45,000) = \$4,580,000$. The mean is $\frac{4,580,000}{150} = \$30,533$.

14. **(E)** The mean, standard deviation, variance, and range are all affected by outliers; the median and interquartile range are not.

15. **(C)** Because of the squaring operation in the definition, the standard deviation (and also the variance) can be zero only if all the values in the set are equal.

16. **(A)** The sum of the scores in one class is $20 \times 92 = 1840$, while the sum in the other is $25 \times 83 = 2075$. The total sum is $1840 + 2075 = 3915$. There are $20 + 25 = 45$ students, and so the average score is $\frac{3915}{45} = 87$.

17. **(A)** A distribution spread thinly on the high end is a skewed distribution with the mean greater than the median.

18. **(E)** None are reasonable because we are not looking at a random sample of states but rather only at the seven lowest values, that is, at the very low end of the tail of the whole distribution. (The distribution was actually skewed to the right, with California having 159,700 bankruptcies, followed by New York with 51,300, and all other states below 50,000.)

19. **(C)** The smallest state score is 246, and the largest is 283; 259 has a percentile rank of 25, and 273 has a percentile rank of 75; and the median, not the mean, is 267.

20. **(A)** A distribution spread thinly on the high end is a skewed distribution with

the mean greater than the median.

21. **(E)** All three statements are true.

22. **(A)** Dotplots and stemplots retain the identity of individual scores; however, histograms and boxplots do not.

23. **(A)** $206 + 2.69(35) = 300$; $206 - 1.13(35) = 166$.

24. **(B)** A calculator gives a mean of 18.875 with a standard deviation of 5.472, and so the z-score is $\frac{14.23 - 18.875}{5.472} = -0.85$.

Free-Response Questions

> *Directions:* You must show all work and indicate the methods you use. You will be graded on the correctness of your methods and on the accuracy of your final answers.

Two Open-Ended Questions

1. According to a 1988 *New York Times* article, the ten car models with the highest theft rates were as follows:

Vehicle Model	Thefts per 1000 Cars
Pontiac Firebird	30.14
Chevrolet Camaro	26.02
Chevrolet Monte Carlo	20.28
Toyota MR2	19.25
Buick Regal	14.70
Mitsubishi Starion	14.70
Ferrari Mondial	13.60
Mitsubishi Mirage	12.80
Pontiac Fiero	12.68
Oldsmobile Cutlass	11.73

What are the mean, range, and standard deviation of these theft rates? Explain how each of these values changes if each theft rate increases by 1.5 and if each increases by 15%.

2. In 1977 the 88 quarterbacks on National Football League (NFL) rosters earned a mean average salary of either $58,750 or $89,354. The number that is not the mean is the median. Which number is the mean salary? Justify your answer.

Answers Explained

1. Use your calculator to obtain a mean of 17.59 and a standard deviation of 5.94. The range is $30.14 - 11.73 = 18.41$. Increasing each value by 1.5 increases the mean by 1.5 to 19.09 and leaves the range and standard deviation unchanged. Increasing each value by 15% increases the mean, range, and standard deviation each by 15% to 20.23, 21.17, and 6.83, respectively.

2. If the median were greater than the mean, the salaries would be skewed to the left with a few very low salaries dragging the mean down while the bulk of the salaries would be above the mean. However, it would be difficult to

construct a data set where reasonable, but low, salaries dragged the mean down to $58,750 while half the salaries were above $89,354. It is much more likely that the median was less than the mean and the salary distribution was skewed to the right with a few high salaries dragging the mean up while the bulk of the salaries were below the mean. We conclude that the mean was $89,354 (and that the median was $58,750).

An Investigative Task

1. In situations where outliers are suspect, it is often more appropriate to use the median instead of the mean to describe the center or representative score of a distribution. In such cases it is proper to use the interquartile range to describe variability. It is also meaningful to describe variability by averaging the absolute values of the deviations from the median; that is,

$$\frac{\Sigma|x - M|}{n}$$

where M is the median and n is the size of the set. Investigate, as follows, whether $\Sigma|x - K|$ is smallest when K equals the median M.

Consider the set $\{1, 4, 7, 13, 19, 23\}$.

   a. Find the median M and calculate $\Sigma|x - M|$.
   b. What is the value of $\Sigma|x - K|$ for $K = 11$? 12? 9?
   c. What happens to $\Sigma|x - K|$ when K passes one of the x values, for example, when $K = 14$? 15? 6? 5?
   d. What happens to $\Sigma|x - K|$ when K passes another of the x values, for example, when $K = 20$? 3?

Consider the set of test scores from a class of ten students: $\{15, 85, 85, 86, 87, 87, 90, 92, 93, 95\}$.

   e. Find the mean and the standard deviation.
   f. Find the median M and calculate $\frac{\Sigma|x-M|}{n}$.
   g. Comment on the answers to parts e and f above.

Solution

1. a. The median is $M = \frac{7+13}{2} = 10$. $\Sigma|x - M| = 9+6+3+3+9+13 = 43$.
    b. $\Sigma|x - 11| = \Sigma|x - 12| = \Sigma|x - 9| = 43$.
    c. The sum increases: $\Sigma|x - 14| = \Sigma|x - 6| = 45$, and $\Sigma|x - 15| = \Sigma|x - 5| = 47$.
    d. The sum increases more: $\Sigma|x - 3| = 53$, and $\Sigma|x - 20| = 59$.
    e. The mean $= 81.5$, and the standard deviation $= 22.4$.
    f. The median $= 87$, and $\frac{\Sigma|x-M|}{n} = 9.9$.
    g. The values 87 and 9.9 appear to be more appropriate representations of a representative score and the variability than 81.5 and 22.4.

TOPIC THREE

Comparing Distributions

Many real-life applications of statistics involve comparisons of *two* populations. Such comparisons can involve modifications of graphical displays such as dotplots, bar charts, stemplots, and boxplots to portray both sets simultaneously. Alternatively, a new set, the set of differences, can be formed and analyzed.

Dotplots

Example 3.1. The caloric intakes of 25 people on each of two weight loss programs are recorded as follows:

Program A: 1000, 1000, 1100, 1100, 1100, 1200, 1200, 1200, 1200, 1300, 1300, 1300, 1300, 1300, 1400, 1400, 1400, 1400, 1400, 1500, 1500, 1600, 1600, 1700, 1900

Program B: 1000, 1100, 1100, 1200, 1200, 1200, 1300, 1300, 1300, 1400, 1400, 1400, 1400, 1500, 1500, 1500, 1500, 1500, 1600, 1600, 1600, 1700, 1700, 1800, 1800

These data can be compared with dotplots, one above the other, using the same horizontal scale.

We see that both sets of data are roughly bell-shaped (the empirical rule applies), Program A shows an outlier at 1900 calories, and Program A seems to be associated with a lower average caloric intake than Program B.

41

Double Bar Charts

Example 3.2. A study tabulated the percentages of young adults who recognized various photographs as follows: Joe Stalin (10%), Joe Camel (95%), Senator Simpson of Wyoming (5%), Bart Simpson (80%), Al Gore (30%), Al Bundy (60%), Mickey Mantle (20%), Mickey Mouse (100%), Charlie Chaplin (25%), Charlie the Tuna (90%). These data can be illustrated with a bar chart appropriately displayed in pairs of bars.

The pairs of bar graphs visually indicate the reason for concern felt by some educators.

Back-to-back Stemplots

Example 3.3. In a 40-year study, survival years were measured for cancer patients undergoing one of two different chemotherapy treatments. The data for 25 patients on the first drug and 30 on the second were as follows:

Drug A: 5, 10, 17, 39, 29, 25, 20, 4, 8, 31, 21, 3, 12, 11, 19, 10, 4, 22, 17, 18, 13, 28, 11, 14, 21.

Drug B: 19, 12, 20, 28, 22, 35, 1, 21, 21, 26, 18, 28, 29, 20, 15, 32, 31, 24, 22, 26, 18, 20, 22, 35, 30, 18, 25, 24, 19, 21.

In drawing a back-to-back stemplot of the above data, we place a vertical line on each side of the column of stems and then arrange one set of leaves extending out to the right while the other extends out to the left.

Drug B		Drug A
1	0	3 4 4 5 8
9 9 8 8 8 5 2	1	0 0 1 1 2 3 4 7 7 8 9
9 8 8 6 6 5 4 4 2 2 2 1 1 1 0 0 0	2	0 1 1 2 5 8 9
5 5 2 1 0	3	1 9

Note that even though drug A showed the longest-surviving patient (39 years) and drug B showed the shortest-surviving patient (1 year), the back-to-back stemplot indicates that the bulk of patients on drug B survived longer than the bulk of patients on drug A.

Parallel Boxplots

Example 3.4. Mail-order labs and 1-hour minilabs were compared with regard to price for developing and printing one 24-exposure roll of 35-millimeter color-print film. Prices included shipping and handling charges where applicable. Following is a computer output describing the results:

For mail-order labs:
```
Mean = 5.37   Standard deviation = 1.92   Min = 3.51
Max = 8.00   N = 18   Median = 4.77   Quartiles = 3.92,
6.45
```

For 1-hour minilabs:
```
Mean = 10.11   Standard deviation = 1.32   Min = 8.58
Max = 11.95   N = 15   Median = 10.08   Quartiles = 8.97,
11.51
```

In drawing parallel boxplots (also called side-by-side boxplots) of the above data, we place both on the same diagram:

Boxplots show the minimum, maximum, median, and quartile values. The distribution of mail-order lab prices is lower and more spread out than that of prices of 1-hour minilabs. Both are slightly skewed toward the upper end (the skewness can also be noted from the computer output showing the mean to be greater than the median in both cases.)

Parallel boxplots are useful in presenting a picture of the comparison of several distributions.

Example 3.5.   Following are parallel boxplots showing the daily price fluctuations of a certain common stock over the course of 5 years. What trends do the boxplots show?

The parallel boxplots show that from year to year the median daily stock price has steadily risen 20 points from about $58 to about $78, the third quartile value has been roughly stable at about $84, the yearly low has never decreased from that of the previous year, and the interquartile range has never increased from one year to the next.

Questions on Topic Three: Comparing Distributions

Multiple-Choice Questions

> *Directions:* The questions or incomplete statements that follow are each followed by five suggested answers or completions. Choose the response that best answers the question or completes the statement.

1. The following double bar graph shows the choice of heating fuel for new homes completed during the indicated years. In each pair the top bar indicates electricity while the lower bar indicates gas.

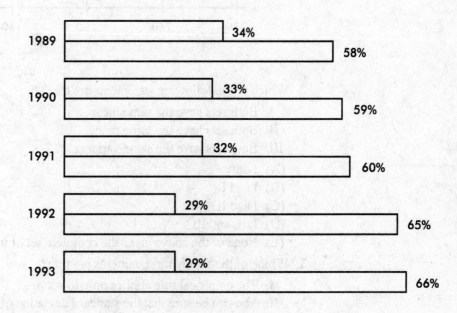

Which of the following are true statements?

   I. The percentage of new homes using electricity has never risen from one year to another.
   II. The percentage of new homes using gas has increased every year.
   III. The percentage of new homes using fuels other than electricity and gas has never risen from one year to another.

   (A) I and II
   (B) II and III
   (C) I and III
   (D) I, II, and III
   (E) None of the above gives the complete set of true responses.

For Questions 2 and 3 consider the following two histograms:

2. Which of the following statements are true?

   I. Both sets have the same mean.

   II. Both sets have the same range.

   III. Both sets have the same variance.

  (A) I only

  (B) I and II

  (C) I and III

  (D) I, II, and III

  (E) None of the above gives the complete set of true responses.

3. Which of the following statements are true?

   I. The empirical rule applies only to set A.

   II. You can be sure that the standard deviation of set A is greater than 5.

   III. You can be sure that the standard deviation of set B is greater than 5.

  (A) I only

  (B) II only

  (C) I and II

  (D) I and III

  (E) II and III

4. Consider the following back-to-back stemplots comparing car battery lives (in months) of samples of two popular brands.

Brand A		Brand B
	3	7
7	4	2 3 4 8 8
3 2	5	1 4 5 6 7 8 9 9
8 7 5 4	6	3 4 6 6 8
9 6 5 3 3 0	7	6
6 5 4 3 3 3 1	8	

Which of the following are true statements?

    I. The sample sizes are the same.
   II. The ranges are the same.
  III. The variances are the same.
  IV. The means are the same.
   V. The medians are the same.

(A) I and II
(B) I and IV
(C) II and V
(D) III and V
(E) I, II, and III

5. Consider the following parallel boxplots illustrating the daily temperatures (in degrees Fahrenheit) of an upstate New York city during January and July.

Which of the following are true statements?

    I. The ranges are the same.
   II. The interquartile ranges are the same.
  III. Because of symmetry, the medians are the same.

(A) I only
(B) II only
(C) I and II
(D) I and III
(E) II and III

For Questions 6 and 7 consider the following parallel boxplots of gasoline mileage for three car makes:

6. Which of the following are true statements?

   I. All three have the same range.

   II. All three have the same interquartile range.

   III. The difference in the medians between the first and third distributions is equal to the interquartile range of the second distribution.

  (A) I and II

  (B) I and III

  (C) II and III

  (D) I, II, and III

  (E) None of the above gives the complete set of true responses.

7. Which of the following are true statements?

   I. All three are symmetric.

   II. The first is skewed to the left while the third is skewed to the right.

   III. The second is skewed on both sides.

  (A) I only

  (B) II only

  (C) III only

  (D) II and III

  (E) None of the above gives the complete set of true responses.

8. Consider the following back-to-back stemplot:

73	2	
642	3	37
7	4	246
9300	5	7
9920	6	0039
943	7	0299
8	8	349
	9	8

Which of the following are true statements?

   I. The distributions have the same mean.

   II. The distributions have the same range.

   III. The distributions have the same variance.

  (A) II only

  (B) I and II

  (C) I and III

  (D) II and III

  (E) I, II, and III

Answer Key

1. **D**	3. **E**	5. **A**	7. **B**
2. **B**	4. **A**	6. **B**	8. **D**

Answers Explained

1. **(D)** The percentage of homeowners choosing electricity has gone done from 34% to 33% to 32% to 29%, where it has settled for another year. The percentage of homeowners using gas has risen steadily from 58% to 66%. Together, electricity and gas have captured from 92% to 95% of the market, leaving 8%, 8%, 8%, 6%, and 5% of the market for other heating fuels such as oil.

2. **(B)** Both sets are symmetric about 150 and so have the same mean. Both sets have the range $170 - 130 = 40$. Set A is much more spread out than set B, and so set A has the greater variance.

3. **(E)** The empirical rule applies to bell-shaped data like those found in set B, not in set A. For bell-shaped data, 95% of the values fall within two standard deviations of the mean, and 99% within three. However, in the histogram for set B one sees that 95% of the data are not between 140 and 160 and 99% are not between 135 and 165. Thus the standard deviation for set B must be greater than 5. The standard deviation for set A is even larger, and so it too must be greater than 5.

4. **(A)** Both sets have 20 elements. The ranges, $76 - 37 = 39$ and $86 - 47 = 39$, are equal. Brand A clearly has the larger mean and median, and with its skewness it also has the larger variance.

5. **(A)** Both ranges are 30. January has an interquartile range of 25, while July has an interquartile range of 20 (but to compare the interquartile ranges, you need only visually compare the lengths of the boxes). The median temperatures for January and July are 20 and 80, respectively.

6. **(B)** The range is the distance between the tips of the two whiskers, and so all three ranges are equal. The interquartile range is the length of the box, and so these three values are not all equal. The median of the first distribution is equal to Q_3 of the second, while the median of the third distribution is equal to Q_1 of the second, and so the difference of the medians is $Q_3 - Q_1$, which is the interquartile range of the second.

7. **(B)** In the first distribution the median is far to the right, and so the scores are concentrated there, while both the lower whisker and between the median and first quartile are spread out; thus it is skewed to the left. Similarly the third distribution is skewed to the right. Only the middle distribution looks symmetric around its median. There is no such thing as being skewed to both sides.

8. **(D)** The two sets of data have different means, but they have identical shapes and thus the same variability, including both range and variance (and standard deviation). Note that adding 10 to each score in the left set results in the right set. Thus the means differ by 10, but the measures of variability remain the same.

Free-Response Questions

> *Directions:* You must show all work and indicate the methods you use. You will be graded on the correctness of your methods and on the accuracy of your final answers.

Two Open-Ended Questions

1. Is it easier for the best National Basketball Association (NBA) players to get a rebound or an assist? During the 1994–95 season the top 20 rebounding leaders averaged the following numbers of rebounds per game: 16.8 (Rodman), 12.6, 11.4, 11.1, 11.0, 10.9, 10.9, 10.9, 10.8, 10.8, 10.6, 10.6, 10.6, 10.4, 10.3, 9.9, 9.7, 9.7, 9.6, and 9.4. The top 20 assist leaders averaged the following numbers of assists per game: 12.3 (Stockton), 9.4, 9.3, 8.8, 8.7, 8.3, 8.2, 7.9, 7.7, 7.7, 7.6, 7.5, 7.3, 7.2, 7.1, 6.9, 6.4, 6.2, 6.1, and 5.7. Compare these data using back-to-back stemplots. Comment on shape and outliers.

2. In 1980 automobile registrations by states ranged from a low of 262,000 (Alaska) to a high of 16,873,000 (California) with a median of 2,329,000 (Iowa), a 25th percentile of 834,000, and a 75th percentile of 3,749,000. In 1990 the registrations ranged from 462,000 (Vermont) to 21,926,000 (California) with a median of 2,649,000 (Oklahoma), a 25th percentile of 1,054,000, and a 75th percentile of 4,444,000. Draw parallel boxplots and compare the distributions.

Answers Explained

1.

Assists per game		Rebounds per game
7	5	
9421	6	
97765321	7	
8732	8	
43	9	46779
	10	3466688999
	11	014
3	12	6
	13	
	14	
	15	
	16	8

(where 16 | 8 represents 16.8)

Both distributions are very slightly skewed to the upper end, but when the outliers (Rodman and Stockton) are discarded, both are roughly symmetric and bell-shaped (the empirical rule will then apply). Clearly the best rebounders get more rebounds per game than the best assist leaders get assists per game.

2.

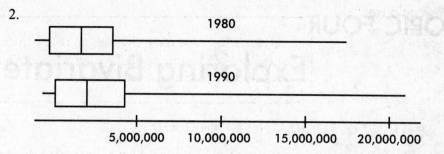

There was an increase in all the data from 1980 to 1990; however, the most striking aspect is how skewed to the right both sets of data appear to be. The difference between the lowest value and the median changed very little between 1980 and 1990, while the upper-half spread increased substantially. It would be interesting to note various upper values to see how much of an outlier the California number is each year.

An Investigative Task

1. Draw a back-to-back stemplot of two sets of data whose parallel boxplots are the following:

Solution

Both sets appear to be roughly symmetric with median 50, low score 10, and high score 90. Set A is concentrated at the extremes, with 25% of its scores between 10 and 20 and 25% between 80 and 90. Set B is concentrated in the middle, with 50% of its scores between 40 and 60. Some care has to be taken in the choice of scores. One of many possible stemplots is

Set A		Set B
9876543210	1	012
321	2	3456
7654	3	789
998	4	1234567899
211	5	1123456789
6543	6	123
987	7	456
987654321	8	789
0	9	0

TOPIC FOUR

Exploring Bivariate Data

Our studies so far have been concerned with measurements of a single variable. However, many important applications of statistics involve examining whether two or more variables are related to one another. For example, is there a relationship between the smoking histories of pregnant women and the birth weights of their children? Between SAT scores and success in college? Between amount of fertilizer used and amount of crop harvested?

Two questions immediately arise. First, how can the strength of an apparent relationship be measured? Second, how can an observed relationship be put into functional terms? For example, a real estate broker might not only wish to determine whether a relationship exists between the prime rate and the number of new homes sold in a month but might also find useful an expression with which to predict the number of home sales given a particular value of the prime rate.

Scatterplots

Suppose a relationship is perceived between two variables X and Y, and we graph the pairs (x, y). The result, called a *scatterplot,* gives a visual impression of the existing relationship between the variables. In this topic we examine whether the relationship can be reasonably explained in terms of a linear function, that is, one whose graph is a straight line.

For example, we might be looking at a plot such as

52

We need to know what the term *best-fitting straight line* means and how we can find this line. Furthermore, we want to be able to gauge whether the relationship between the variables is strong enough so that finding and making use of this straight line is meaningful.

Patterns in Scatterplots

When larger values of one variable are associated with larger values of a second variable, the variables are called *positively associated*. When larger values of one are associated with smaller values of the other, the variables are called *negatively associated*.

Example 4.1.

Positively associated   Negatively associated

The strength of the association is gauged by how close the plotted points are to a straight line.

Example 4.2.

Stronger positive association   Weaker positive association

Sometimes different dots in a scatterplot are labeled with different symbols or different colors to show a categorical variable. The resulting *labeled scatterplot* might distinguish between men and women, between stocks and bonds, and so on.

Example 4.3.

The above diagram is a labeled scatterplot distinguishing men with plus signs and women with square dots to show a categorical variable.

Correlation and Linearity

Although a scatter diagram usually gives an intuitive visual indication when a linear relationship is strong, in most cases it is quite difficult to visually judge the specific strength of a relationship. For this reason there is a mathematical measure called *correlation*. Important as correlation is, we always need to keep in mind that significant correlation does not necessarily indicate *causation* and that correlation measures the strength only of a *linear* relationship.

Correlation, designated by r, has the formula

$$r = \frac{1}{n-1} \sum \left(\frac{x_i - \bar{x}}{s_x}\right) \left(\frac{y_i - \bar{y}}{s_y}\right)$$

in terms of the means and standard deviations of the two sets. We note that the formula is actually the sum of the products of the corresponding z-scores divided by 1 less than the sample size. However, you should be able to quickly calculate correlation using the statistical package on your calculator.

Note from the formula that correlation does not distinguish between which variable is called x and which is called y. The formula is also based on standardized scores (z-scores), and so changing units does not change the correlation. Finally, since means and standard deviations can be strongly influenced by outliers, correlation is also strongly affected by extreme values.

The value of r always falls between -1 and $+1$, with -1 indicating perfect negative correlation and $+1$ indicating perfect positive correlation.

Example 4.4.

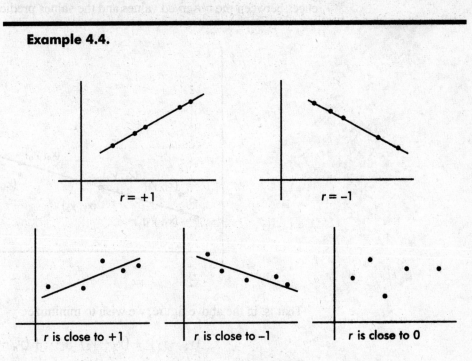

r = +1   r = -1

r is close to +1   r is close to -1   r is close to 0

It can be shown that r^2, called the *coefficient of determination,* is the ratio of the variance of the predicted values y' to the variance of the observed values y. That is, there is a partition of the y-variance, and r^2 is the proportion of this variance that is predictable from a knowledge of x. Alternatively, we can say that r^2 gives the percentage of variation in y that is explained by the variation in x.

Least Squares Regression Line

What is the best-fitting straight line that can be drawn through a set of points?

?
?
?

On the basis of our experience with measuring variances, by *best-fitting straight line* we mean the straight line that minimizes the sum of the squares of the differences between the observed values and the values predicted by the line.

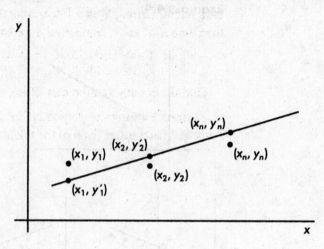

That is, in the above figure, we wish to minimize

$$(y_1 - y'_1)^2 + (y_2 - y'_2)^2 + \cdots + (y_n - y'_n)^2$$

It is reasonable, intuitive, and correct that the best-fitting line will pass through $(\bar{x}, \bar{y})$ where $\bar{x}$ and $\bar{y}$ are the means of the variables X and Y. Then, from the basic expression for a line with a given slope through a given point, we have

$y' - \bar{y} = b_1(x - \bar{x})$
or $y' = \bar{y} + b_1(x - \bar{x})$,
where b_1 is the slope
of the line

The slope b_1 can be determined from the formula

$$b_1 = r\frac{s_y}{s_x}$$

where r is the correlation and s_x and s_y are the standard deviations of the two sets.

This best-fitting straight line, that is, the line that minimizes the sum of the squares of the differences between the observed values and the values predicted by the line, is called the *least squares regression line* or simply the *regression line*. It can be calculated directly by entering the two data sets and using the statistics package on your calculator.

Example 4.5.   An insurance company conducts a survey of 15 of its life insurance agents. The average number of minutes spent with each potential customer and the number of policies sold in a week are noted for each agent. Letting X and Y represent the average number of minutes and the number of sales, respectively, we have

$$X: 25\ 23\ 30\ 25\ 20\ 33\ 18\ 21\ 22\ 30\ 26\ 26\ 27\ 29\ 20$$
$$Y: 10\ 11\ 14\ 12\ \ 8\ 18\ \ 9\ 10\ 10\ 15\ 11\ 15\ 12\ 14\ 11$$

Find the equation of the best-fitting straight line for the data.

Answer: Plotting the 15 points $(25, 10), (23, 11), \ldots, (20,11)$ gives an intuitive visual impression of the relationship:

This scatter diagram indicates the existence of a relationship that appears to be *linear;* that is, the points lie roughly on a straight line. Furthermore, the linear relationship is *positive;* that is, as one variable increases, so does the other (the straight line slopes upward).

Using a calculator, we find the correlation to be $r = .8836$, the coefficient of determination to be $r^2 = .78$ (indicating that 78% of the variation in the number of policies is explained by the variation in the number of minutes spent), and the regression line to be

$$\begin{aligned} y' &= \bar{y} + b_1(x - \bar{x}) \\ &= 12 + 0.5492(x - 25) \\ &= 0.5492x - 1.73 \end{aligned}$$

Adding this to our scatterplot yields

Thus, for example, we might predict that agents who average 24 minutes per customer will average $0.5492(24) - 1.73 = 11.45$ sales per week. We also note that each additional minute spent seems to produce an average 0.5492 extra sale.

Example 4.6. Following are advertising expenditures and total sales for six detergent products:

| Advertising ($1000) ($x$): | 2.3 | 5.7 | 4.8 | 7.3 | 5.9 | 6.2 |
| Total sales ($1000) ($y$): | 77 | 105 | 96 | 118 | 102 | 95 |

Predict the total sales if $5000 is spent on advertising and interpret the slope of the regression line. What if $100,000 is spent on advertising?

Answer: With your calculator, the equation of the regression line is found to be

$$y' = 98.833 + 7.293(x - 5.367) = 7.293x + 59.691$$

(A calculator like the TI-83, with less round-off error, directly gives $y' = 7.295x + 59.683$.)

It is also worthwhile to replace the x and y with more appropriately named variables, resulting, for example, in

$$\text{Sales} = 7.293 \, \text{Advcost} + 59.691$$

The regression line predicts that if $5000 is spent on advertising, the resulting total sales will be $7.293(5) + 59.691 = 96.156$ thousands of dollars ($96,156).

The slope of the regression line indicates that every extra $1000 spent on advertising will result in $7293 of added sales.

If $100,000 is spent on advertising, we calculate $7.293(100) + 59.691 = 788.991$ thousands of dollars ($\approx \$789,000$). How much confidence should we have in this answer? Not much! We are trying to use the regression line to predict a value far outside the range of the data values. This procedure is called *extrapolation* and must be used with great care.

Residual Plots, Outliers, and Influential Points

The difference between an observed and predicted value is called the *residual*. When the regression line is graphed on the scatterplot, the residual of a point is the vertical distance the point is from the regression line.

Example 4.7.   We calculate the predicted values from the regression line in Example 4.6 and subtract from the observed values to obtain the residuals:

x	2.3	5.7	4.8	7.3	5.9	6.2
y	77	105	96	118	102	95
y'	76.5	101.3	94.7	112.9	102.7	104.9
$y-y'$	0.5	3.7	1.3	5.1	−0.7	−9.9

Note that the sum of the residuals is

$$0.5 + 3.7 + 1.3 + 5.1 - 0.7 - 9.9 = 0.0$$

The above equation is true in general; that is, the sum and thus the mean of the residuals is always zero.

Points with large residuals are called *outliers*, as they fall outside the straight-line pattern indicated by the regression line. A residual plot with definite pattern is an indication that a nonlinear model will show a better fit to the data than the straight regression line.

Example 4.8. Suppose the drying time of a paint product varies depending on the amount of a certain additive it contains.

Additive (oz), x:	1	2	3	4	5	6	7	8	9	10
Drying time (hr), y:	4	2.1	1.5	1	1.2	1.7	2.5	3.6	4.9	6.1

Using a calculator, we find the regression line $y = 0.327x + 1.062$, and we find the residuals:

x:	1	2	3	4	5	6	7	8	9	10
$y - y'$:	2.61	0.38	−0.54	−1.37	−1.5	−1.32	−0.85	−0.08	0.89	1.77

The resulting residual plot shows a strong pattern:

This pattern indicates that a nonlinear model will be a better fit than a straight-line model. A scatterplot of the original data shows clearly what is happening:

Scores with large residuals are called *outliers*. In a scatterplot, outliers are indicated by points falling far away, either above or below, from the straight-line pattern.

Example 4.9.   A scatterplot of grade point average (GPA) versus weekly television time for a group of high school seniors is as follows:

By direct observation of the scatterplot, we note that there are two outliers: one person who watches 5 hours of television weekly yet has only a 1.5 GPA, and another person who watches 25 hours weekly yet has a 3.0 GPA. Note also that while the value of 30 weekly hours of television may be considered an outlier for the television hours variable and the 0.5 GPA may be considered an outlier for the GPA variable, the point (30, 0.5) is *not* an outlier in the regression context because it does not fall off the straight-line pattern.

Scores whose removal would sharply change the regression line are called *influential scores*. Sometimes this description is restricted to points with extreme *x*-values. An influential score may have a small residual but still have a greater effect on the regression line than scores with possibly larger residuals but average *x*-values.

Example 4.10. Consider the following scatterplot and regression line for starting salaries versus years of education:

The dotted lines below show what happens if the points (15, 40,000) and (24, 76,000) are removed, respectively.

Note that the regression line is greatly affected by the removal of (24, 76,000) but not by the removal of (15, 40,000). Thus (24, 76,000) is an influential score, while (15, 40,000) is not. This is true in spite of the fact that (24, 76,000) is closer to the original regression line than (15, 40,000).

Transformations to Achieve Linearity

Often a straight-line pattern is not the best model for depicting a relationship between two variables. A clear indication of this problem is when the scatterplot shows a distinctive curved pattern. Another indication is when the residuals show a distinctive pattern rather than a random scattering. In such a case, the nonlinear model can sometimes be revealed by transforming one or both of the variables and then noting a linear relationship. Useful transformations often result from using the *log* button on your calculator to create new variables.

Example 4.11.   Consider the following years and corresponding populations:

Year, x:	1950	1960	1970	1980	1990
Population (1000s), y:	51	62	77	113	173

On a calculator, the correlation is seen to be $r = .944$. However, the scatterplot indicates that a nonlinear relationship would be an even stronger model.

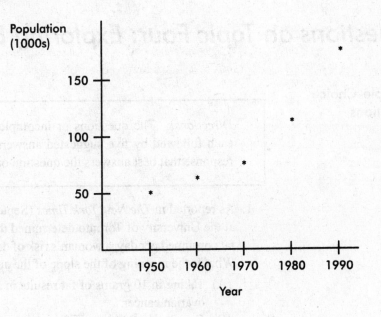

Letting log y be a new variable, we obtain

x:	1950	1960	1970	1980	1990
log y:	1.71	1.79	1.89	2.05	2.24

A calculator shows the correlation between these variables to be $r = .984$, and the scatterplot now indicates a stronger linear relationship.

Questions on Topic Four: Exploring Bivariate Data

Multiple-Choice Questions

> *Directions:*   The questions or incomplete statements that follow are each followed by five suggested answers or completions. Choose the response that best answers the question or completes the statement.

1. As reported in *The New York Times* (September 21, 1994, page C10), a study at the University of Toronto determined that, for every 10 grams of saturated fat consumed per day, a woman's risk of developing ovarian cancer rises 20%. What is the meaning of the slope of the appropriate regression line?

   (A) Taking in 10 grams of fat results in a 20% increased risk of developing ovarian cancer.

   (B) Consuming 0 grams of fat per day results in a zero increase in the risk of developing ovarian cancer.

   (C) Consuming 50 grams of fat doubles the risk of developing ovarian cancer.

   (D) Increased intake of fat causes higher rates of developing ovarian cancer.

   (E) A woman's risk of developing ovarian cancer rises 2% for every gram of fat consumed per day.

Questions 2 and 3 are based on the following: Jay Bennett (*Chance,* Winter 1995, page 38) calculated the regression line for average 1991 SAT scores (total math plus verbal) versus number of dollars spent per student in 1991 for New Jersey school districts and obtained a slope of 0.0227 and a *y*-intercept of 707.

2. What average SAT result does this regression line predict for students in a district that spends $10,000 per student?

   (A) 467
   (B) 480
   (C) 730
   (D) 934
   (E) More information is needed to make this calculation.

3. According to this analysis, how much should a district spend per student in order for its students to average 1000 on the SAT exam?

   (A) $6,651
   (B) $12,907
   (C) $16,049
   (D) $44,053
   (E) More information is needed to make this calculation.

4. Consider the following three scatterplots:

   Which has the greatest correlation coefficient?

   (A) I
   (B) II
   (C) III
   (D) They all have the same correlation coefficient.
   (E) This question cannot be answered without additional information.

5. Suppose the correlation is negative. Given two points from the scatterplot, which of the following is possible?

   I. The first point has a larger x-value and a smaller y-value than the second point.
   II. The first point has a larger x-value and a larger y-value than the second point.
   III. The first point has a smaller x-value and a larger y-value than the second point.

   (A) I only
   (B) II only
   (C) III only
   (D) I and III
   (E) I, II, and III

6. Which of the following would you expect to be true about the correlation between distances and tolls on the New York State Thruway?

    (A) Strong and positive
    (B) Weak and positive
    (C) Strong and negative
    (D) Weak and negative
    (E) Zero

7. Suppose the regression line for a set of data, $y = 3x + b$, passes through the point $(2, 5)$. If $\bar{x}$ and $\bar{y}$ are the sample means of the x- and y-values, respectively, then $\bar{y} =$

    (A) $\bar{x}$.
    (B) $\bar{x} - 2$.
    (C) $\bar{x} + 5$.
    (D) $3\bar{x}$.
    (E) $3\bar{x} - 1$.

8. Suppose a study finds that the correlation coefficient relating family income to SAT scores is $r = +1$. Which of the following are proper conclusions?

    I. Poverty causes low SAT scores.
    II. Wealth causes high SAT scores.
    III. There is a very strong association between family income and SAT scores.

    (A) I only
    (B) II only
    (C) III only
    (D) I and II
    (E) I, II, and III

9. A study of department chairperson ratings and student ratings of the performance of high school statistics teachers reports a correlation of $r = 1.15$ between the two ratings. From this information we can conclude that

    (A) chairpersons and students tend to agree on who is a good teacher.
    (B) chairpersons and students tend to disagree on who is a good teacher.
    (C) there is little relationship between chairperson and student ratings of teachers.
    (D) there is strong association between chairperson and student ratings of teachers, but it would be incorrect to infer causation.
    (E) a mistake in arithmetic has been made.

10. Which of the following statements about the correlation coefficient r are true?

    I. A correlation coefficient of .2 means that 20% of the points are highly correlated.
    II. The square of the correlation coefficient measures the proportion of the y-variance that is predictable from a knowledge of x.
    III. Perfect correlation, that is, when the points lie exactly on a straight line, results in $r = 0$.

(A) I only
(B) II only
(C) III only
(D) None of these statements is true.
(E) None of the above gives the complete set of true responses.

11. Which of the following statements about the correlation coefficient r are true?

    I. It is not affected by changes in the measurement units of the variables.

    II. It is not affected by which variable is called x and which is called y.

    III. It is not affected by extreme values.

(A) I and II
(B) I and III
(C) II and III
(D) I, II, and III
(E) None of the above gives the complete set of true responses.

12. With regard to regression, which of the following statements about outliers are true?

    I. Outliers have large residuals.

    II. A point may not be an outlier even though its x-value is an outlier in the x-variable and its y-value is an outlier in the y-variable.

    III. Removal of an outlier sharply affects the regression line.

(A) I and II
(B) I and III
(C) II and III
(D) I, II, and III
(E) None of the above gives the complete set of true responses.

13. Which of the following statements about influential scores are true?

    I. Influential scores have large residuals.

    II. Removal of an influential score sharply affects the regression line.

    III. An x-value that is an outlier in the x-variable is more indicative that a point is influential than a y-value that is an outlier in the y-variable.

(A) I and II
(B) I and III
(C) II and III
(D) I, II, and III
(E) None of the above gives the complete set of true responses.

14. Which of the following statements about residuals are true?

    I. The mean of the residuals is always zero.

    II. The regression line for a residual plot is a horizontal line.

    III. A definite pattern in the residual plot is an indication that a nonlinear model will show a better fit to the data than the straight regression line.

(A) I and II
(B) I and III
(C) II and III
(D) I, II, and III
(E) None of the above gives the complete set of true responses.

15. Data are obtained for a group of college freshmen examining their SAT scores (math plus verbal) from their senior year of high school and their GPAs during their first year of college. The resulting regression equation is

$$y = 0.00161x + 1.35 \quad \text{with } r = .632$$

What percentage of the variation in GPAs can be explained by looking at SAT scores?

(A) 0.161%

(B) 16.1%

(C) 39.9%

(D) 63.2%

(E) This value cannot be computed from the information given.

Questions 16 and 17 are based on the following: The heart disease death rates per 100,000 people in the United States for certain years, as reported by the National Center for Health Statistics, were

Year:	1950	1960	1970	1975	1980
Death rate:	307.6	286.2	253.6	217.8	202.0

16. Which one of the following is a correct interpretation of the slope of the best-fitting straight line for the above data?

(A) The heart disease rate per 100,000 people has been dropping about 3.627 per year.

(B) The baseline heart disease rate is 7386.87.

(C) The regression line explains 96.28% of the variation in heart disease death rates over the years.

(D) The regression line explains 98.12% of the variation in heart disease death rates over the years.

(E) Heart disease will be cured in the year 2036.

17. Based on the regression line, what is the predicted death rate for the year 1983?

(A) 145.8 per 100,000 people

(B) 192.5 per 100,000 people

(C) 196.8 per 100,000 people

(D) 198.5 per 100,000 people

(E) None of the above

18. Consider the following scatterplot of midterm and final exam scores for a class of 15 students.

Which of the following are true statements?

I. The same number of students scored 100 on the midterm exam as scored 100 on the final exam.

II. Students who scored higher on the midterm exam tended to score higher on the final exam.

III. The scatterplot shows a moderate negative correlation between midterm and final exam scores.

(A) I and II
(B) I and III
(C) II and III
(D) I, II, and III
(E) None of the above gives the complete set of true responses.

19. If every woman married a man who was exactly 2 inches taller than she, what would the correlation between the heights of married men and women be?

(A) Somewhat negative
(B) 0
(C) Somewhat positive
(D) Nearly 1
(E) 1

20. Which of the following statements about the correlation coefficient r are true?

I. The correlation coefficient and the slope of the regression line have the same sign.

II. A correlation of $-.35$ and a correlation of $+.35$ show the same degree of clustering around the regression line.

III. A correlation of .75 indicates a relationship that is 3 times as linear as one for which the correlation is only .25.

(A) I and II
(B) I and III
(C) II and III
(D) I, II, and III
(E) None of the above gives the complete set of true responses.

21. Suppose the correlation between two variables is $r = .23$. What will the new correlation be if .14 is added to all values of the x-variable, every value of the y-variable is doubled, and the two variables are interchanged?

    (A) .23
    (B) .37
    (C) .74
    (D) −.23
    (E) −.74

22. As reported in the *Journal of the American Medical Association* (June 13, 1990, page 3031), for a study of ten nonagenarians (subjects were age 90 ± 1), the following tabulation shows a measure of strength (heaviest weight subject could lift using knee extensors) versus a measure of functional mobility (time taken to walk 6 meters).

Strength (kg):	7.5	6	11.5	10.5	9.5	18	4	12	9	3
Walk time (s):	18	46	8	25	25	7	22	12	10	48

    What is the sign of the slope of the regression line and what does it signify?
    (A) The sign is positive, signifying a direct cause-and-effect relationship between strength and functional mobility.
    (B) The sign is positive, signifying that the greater the strength, the greater the functional mobility.
    (C) The sign is negative, signifying that the relationship between strength and functional mobility is weak.
    (D) The sign is negative, signifying that the greater the strength, the less the functional mobility.
    (E) The slope is close to zero, signifying that the relationship between strength and functional mobility is weak.

23. Suppose the correlation between two variables is −.57. If each of the y-scores is multiplied by −1, which of the following is true about the new scatterplot?

    (A) It slopes up to the right, and the correlation is −.57.
    (B) It slopes up to the right, and the correlation is +.57.
    (C) It slopes down to the right, and the correlation is −.57.
    (D) It slopes down to the right, and the correlation is +.57.
    (E) None of the above is true.

24. A study of 100 elementary school children showed a strong positive correlation between weight and reading speed. Which of the following are proper conclusions?

    I. Heavier elementary school children tend to have higher reading speeds.
    II. Among elementary school children, faster readers tend to be heavier.
    III. If you want to improve the reading speed of elementary school children, you should feed them more.

(A) I only
(B) I and II
(C) I, II, and III
(D) None of the three statements is a proper conclusion.
(E) None of the above gives the complete set of proper conclusions.

25. Consider the set of points $\{(2, 5), (3, 7), (4, 9), (5, 12), (10, n)\}$. What should n be so that the correlation between the x- and y-values is 1?

  (A) 21
  (B) 24
  (C) 25
  (D) A value different from any of the above.
  (E) No value for n can make $r = 1$.

26. A study is conducted relating GPA to number of study hours per week, and the correlation is found to be .5. Which of the following are true statements?

  I. On the average, a 30% increase in study time per week results in a 15% increase in GPA.
  II. Fifty percent of a student's GPA can be explained by the number of study hours per week.
  III. Higher GPAs tend to be associated with higher numbers of study hours.

  (A) I and II
  (B) I and III
  (C) II and III
  (D) I, II, and III
  (E) None of the above gives the complete set of true responses.

27. Consider the following three scatterplots:

Which of the following is a true statement about the correlation coefficients for the three scatterplots?

  (A) None are 0.
  (B) One is 0, one is negative, and one is positive.
  (C) One is 0, and both of the others are positive.
  (D) Two are 0, and the other is 1.
  (E) Two are 0, and the other is close to 1.

28. Consider the three points (2, 11), (3, 17), and (4, 29). Given any straight line, we can calculate the sum of the squares of the three vertical distances from these points to the line. What is the smallest possible value this sum can be?

    (A) 6
    (B) 9
    (C) 29
    (D) 57
    (E) None of these values

29. Suppose that the scatterplot of $\log X$ and $\log Y$ shows a strong positive correlation close to 1. Which of the following is true?

    I. The variables X and Y also have a correlation close to 1.
    II. A scatterplot of the variables X and Y shows a strong nonlinear pattern.
    III. The residual plot of the variables X and Y shows a random pattern.

    (A) I only
    (B) II only
    (C) III only
    (D) I and II
    (E) I, II, and III

30. Which of the following statements about the correlation coefficient r are true?

    I. When $r = 0$, there is no relationship between the variables.
    II. When $r = .5$, 50% of the variables are closely related.
    III. When $r = 1$, there is a perfect cause-and-effect relationship between the variables.

    (A) I only
    (B) II only
    (C) III only
    (D) I, II, and III
    (E) All the statements are false.

Answer Key

1. **E**	7. **E**	13. **C**	19. **E**	25. **E**
2. **D**	8. **C**	14. **D**	20. **A**	26. **E**
3. **B**	9. **E**	15. **C**	21. **A**	27. **E**
4. **D**	10. **B**	16. **A**	22. **D**	28. **A**
5. **E**	11. **A**	17. **E**	23. **B**	29. **B**
6. **A**	12. **A**	18. **B**	24. **B**	30. **E**

Answers Explained

1. **(E)** The slope is 20/10 = 2; that is, a woman's risk of developing ovarian cancer rises 2% for every gram of fat consumed per day. The other statements may be true, but they do not answer the question.

2. **(D)** We have $y = 0.0227x + 707$, where x represents dollars spent per student and y represents average SAT total score. Thus $0.0227(10,000) + 707 = 934$.

3. **(B)** We have $0.0227x + 707 = 1000$, which gives $x = \$12,907$.

4. **(D)** The correlation coefficient is not changed by adding the same number to each value of one of the variables or by multiplying each value of one of the variables by the same positive number.

5. **(E)** A negative correlation shows a tendency for higher values of one variable to be associated with lower values of the other; however, given any two points, anything is possible.

6. **(A)** Tolls on the thruway correspond almost exactly with distance.

7. **(E)** Since $(2, 5)$ is on the line $y = 3x + b$, we have $5 = 6 + b$ and $b = -1$. Thus the regression line is $y = 3x - 1$. The point $(\bar{x}, \bar{y})$ is always on the regression line, and so we have $\bar{y} = 3\bar{x} - 1$.

8. **(C)** The correlation r measures association, not causation.

9. **(E)** The correlation r cannot take a value greater than 1.

10. **(B)** It can be shown that r^2, called the coefficient of determination, is the ratio of the variance of the predicted values y' to the variance of the observed values y. Alternatively, we can say that there is a partition of the y-variance and that r^2 is the proportion of this variance that is predictable from a knowledge of x. In the case of perfect correlation, $r = \pm 1$.

11. **(A)** Correlation has the formula

$$r = \frac{1}{n-1} \sum \left(\frac{x_i - \bar{x}}{s_x} \right) \left(\frac{y_i - \bar{y}}{s_y} \right)$$

We see that x and y are interchangeable, and so the correlation does not distinguish between which variable is called x and which is called y. The formula is also based on standardized scores (z-scores), and so changing units does not change the correlation. Finally, since means and standard deviations can be strongly influenced by outliers, the correlation is also strongly affected by extreme values.

12. **(A)** Removal of scores with large residuals but average x values may not have a great effect on the regression line.

13. **(C)** An influential score may have a small residual but still have a greater effect on the regression line than scores with possibly larger residuals but average x-values.

14. **(D)** The sum and thus the mean of the residuals are always zero. In a good straight-line fit, the residuals show a random pattern.

15. **(C)** The coefficient of determination r^2 gives the proportion of the y-variance that is predictable from a knowledge of x. In this case $r^2 = (.632)^2 = .399$ or 39.9%.

16. **(A)** The regression equation is $y = -3.627x + 7386.87$, and so its slope is -3.627 and the y-value drops 3.627 for every unit increase in the x-value. Answer (C) is a true statement but doesn't pertain to the question.

17. **(E)** $-3.627(1983) + 7386.87 = 194.5$

18. **(B)** On each exam, two students had scores of 100. There is a general negative slope to the data showing a moderate negative correlation.

19. **(E)** On the scatterplot all the points lie perfectly on a line sloping up to the right, and so $r = 1$.

20. **(A)** The slope and the correlation are related by the formula

$$b_1 = r \frac{s_y}{s_x}$$

The standard deviations are always positive, and so b_1 and r have the same sign. Positive and negative correlations with the same absolute value indicate data having the same degree of clustering around their respective regression lines, one of which slopes up to the right and the other of which slopes down to the right. While $r = .75$ indicates a better fit with a linear model than $r = .25$ does, we cannot say that the linearity is threefold.

21. **(A)** The correlation coefficient is not changed by adding the same number to every value of one of the variables, by multiplying every value of one of the variables by the same positive number, or by interchanging the x- and y-variables.

22. **(D)** Surprisingly, the slope is negative (-2.4348); that is, the regression line slopes down to the right, indicating that nonagenarians with greater strength have less functional mobility.

23. **(B)** The slope and the correlation coefficient have the same sign. Multiplying every y-value by -1 changes this sign.

24. **(B)** Correlation shows association, not causation. In this example, older school children both weigh more and have faster reading speeds.

25. **(E)** A scatterplot readily shows that while the first three points lie on a straight line, the fourth point does not lie on this line. Thus no matter what the fifth point is, all the points cannot lie on a straight line, and so r cannot be 1.

26. **(E)** Only III is true. A positive correlation indicates that higher values of x tend to be associated with higher values of y.

27. **(E)** All three scatterplots show very strong nonlinear patterns; however, the correlation coefficient r measures the strength of only a linear association. Thus $r = 0$ in the first two scatterplots and is close to 1 in the third.

28. **(A)** Using your calculator, find the regression line to be $y = 9x - 8$. The regression line, also called the least squares regression line, minimizes the sum of the squares of the vertical distances between the points and the line. In this case $(2, 10)$, $(3, 19)$, and $(4, 28)$ are on the line, and so the minimum sum is $(10 - 11)^2 + (19 - 17)^2 + (28 - 29)^2 = 6$.

29. **(B)** When transforming the variables leads to a linear relationship, the original variables have a nonlinear relationship, their correlation (which measures linearity) is not close to 1, and the residuals do not show a random pattern.

30. **(E)** These are all misconceptions about correlation. Correlation measures only linearity, and so when $r = 0$, there still may be a nonlinear relationship. Correlation shows association, not causation.

Free-Response Questions

> *Directions:* You must show all work and indicate the methods you use. You will be graded on the correctness of your methods and on the accuracy of your final answers.

Five Open-Ended Questions

1. According to *The New York Times* (April 2, 1993, page A1), the average monthly rate for basic television cable service has increased as follows:

Year:	1986	1987	1988	1989	1990	1991	1992
Rate ($):	11.00	13.20	13.90	15.20	16.80	18.00	20.00

a. Find the equation of the best-fitting straight line.
b. Interpret the slope.
c. Predict the average monthly rate in 1993 (actually, it was $21.00).
d. Predict in what year the rate will reach $50.00.
e. Comment on the accuracy of the predictions in parts *c* and *d*.

2. The shoe sizes and the number of ties owned by ten corporate vice presidents are as follows.

Shoe size, x:	8	9.5	9	11	9	9.5	8.5	9	9	9.5
Number of ties, y:	10	10	8	15	12	13	16	7	12	4

a. Draw a scatterplot for these data.
b. Find the correlation r.
c. Can we find the best-fitting straight-line approximation to the above data? Does it make sense to use this equation to predict the number of ties owned by a corporate executive who wears size 10 shoes? Explain.

3. Following is a scatterplot of the average life expectancies and per capita incomes (in thousands of dollars) for people in a sample of 50 countries.

a. Estimate the mean for the set of 50 life expectancies and for the set of 50 per capita incomes.
b. Estimate the standard deviation for the set of life expectancies and for the set of per capita incomes. Explain your reasoning.
c. Does the scatterplot show a correlation between per capita income and life expectancy? Is it positive or negative? Is it weak or strong?

4. *a.* Find the correlation coefficient *r* for each of the three sets:
   A = {(5, 5), (5, 10), (10, 5), (10, 10)}
   B = {(50, 50), (50, 55), (55, 50), (55, 55)}
   C = {(90, 90), (90, 95), (95, 90), (95, 95)}
   b. Find the correlation coefficient for the set consisting of the 12 scores from A, B, and C.
   c. Comment on the above results.

5. An outlier can have a striking effect on the correlation coefficient *r*. For example, comment on the following three scatterplots:

Answers Explained

1. *a.* A calculator readily gives $y = 1.4107x - 2790.47$.
   b. The average monthly rate for basic television cable service has increased by about $1.41 per year.
   c. $1.4107 (1993) - 2790.47 = \$21.06$
   d. $1.4107x - 2790.47 = 50$ gives 2014 as the year when the rate will reach $50.00.
   e. It is expected that the 1993 prediction is close to the actual rate; however, the extrapolation resulting in 2014 is far from the given values and cannot be relied on.

2. *a.*

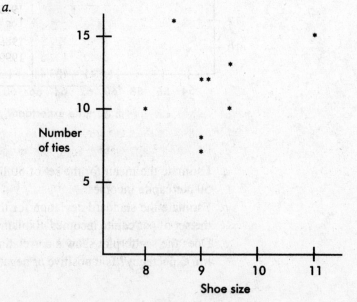

    b. A calculator gives $r = .1568$.

    c. The correlation r is low for this number of data scores, and the scatterplot shows no linear pattern whatsoever. Although theoretically we could use our techniques to find the best-fitting straight-line approximation, the result would be meaningless and should not be used for predictions.

3.   *a.* By visual inspection $\bar{x} \approx 68$ and $\bar{y} \approx 21$.

    b. The range of the life expectancies is $80 - 54 = 26$, and so the standard deviation is roughly $\frac{26}{4} = 6.5$. Similarly the standard deviation of the per capita incomes is roughly $\frac{30-10}{4} = 5$.

    c. While the points generally fall from the lower left to the upper right, they are still widely scattered. Thus the scatterplot shows a weak positive correlation between per capita income and life expectancy.

4.   *a.* The correlation for each of the three sets is 0.

    b. The correlation for the set consisting of all 12 scores is .9948.

    c. The data from each set taken separately show no linear pattern. However, together they show a strong linear fit. Note the positions of the data from the separate sets in the complete scatterplot.

5. In the first scatterplot, the points fall exactly on a downward sloping straight line, so $r = -1$. In the second scatterplot, the outlier is an influential point, and r is close to $+1$. In the third scatterplot, the outlier is also influential, and r is close to 0.

Three Investigative Tasks

1. The following table *(Statistical Abstract of the United States)* gives the U.S. population (in millions) for various years of the twentieth century.

1900	76.1	1950	151.9
1905	83.8	1955	165.1
1910	92.4	1960	180.0
1915	100.5	1965	193.5
1920	106.5	1970	204.0
1925	115.8	1975	215.5
1930	123.1	1980	227.2
1935	127.3	1985	237.9
1940	132.5	1990	249.4
1945	133.4		

    a. Find the equation of the regression line of population y in terms of year x and calculate the correlation.

    b. To find an alternative nonlinear model, make a table of years t since 1900 versus the natural log of the above population values. Find the equation of the regression line of $\log y$ in terms of t and calculate the correlation.

    c. Use each model to predict what the population will be in the year 2100 and to predict when the population will reach 300 million.

    d. Comment on your answers in part *c.*

2. Following are the average distances from the sun and the times of revolution for the nine planets in our solar system:

Planet	Average Distance from Sun (million miles)	Time for Revolution (days)
Mercury	36	88
Venus	67	275
Earth	93	365
Mars	141	687
Jupiter	484	4,332
Saturn	888	10,826
Uranus	1,764	30,676
Neptune	2,790	59,911
Pluto	3,654	90,824

a. Letting x be the average distance and y the revolution time, find the equation of the regression line of $\log y$ in terms of $\log x$ and calculate the correlation.

b. Suppose a new planet is discovered at a distance of 5000 million miles from the sun. Using your regression line, extrapolate and predict the time of revolution.

c. Suppose a new planet is discovered with a revolution time of 45,000 days. Using your regression line, predict its average distance from the sun.

3. The 23 shuttle launches before *Challenger* each experienced from zero to three O-ring failures. There was some speculation that the number of O-ring failures was related to the temperature at liftoff. Find the correlation r and the regression equation given the following data:

Temperature at Liftoff	Number of O-Ring Failures	Temperature at Liftoff	Number of O-Ring Failures
66	0	67	0
70	1	53	3
69	0	67	0
68	0	75	0
67	0	70	0
72	0	81	0
73	0	76	0
70	0	79	0
57	1	75	2
63	1	76	0
70	1	58	1
78	0		

a. *Challenger* was launched at 31 degrees Fahrenheit. What would have been predicted for the number of O-ring failures using a linear model?

What is the correlation r?

b. A scatterplot indicates a nonlinear model. Replace the y-values with $\log(y+1)$ and predict the number of O-ring failures. Why can't you simply use $\log y$? What is the correlation r?

c. Unfortunately, National Aeronautical and Space Administration (NASA) scientists made their calculations using only data from the seven prior launches that had had at least one O-ring failure. What correlation r did they calculate? What do you think was their conclusion?

Answers Explained

1. a. $y = 1.926x - 3593$; $r = .989$.

b. On your calculator you can replace the y-list with $\log y$ and the x-list with $x - 1900$. Then the regression calculation gives $\log y = 0.005637t + 1.905$, $r = .996$.

c. Using the linear model, we calculate $1.926(2100) - 3593 = 452$ (million); and $1.926x - 3593 = 300$ gives $x = 2021$. Using the nonlinear model, we calculate $\log y = 0.005637(200) + 1.905 = 3.0324$, and so $y = 1077$ (million); and $\log 300 = 0.005637t + 1.905$, and so $t = 101$ and the year is $1900 + 101 = 2001$.

d. The nonlinear model showed a higher correlation and so should be more accurate. Predicting the year when the population will reach 300 million gives an answer not too far from the range of the given data. However, predicting the population in the year 2100 is a substantial extrapolation and must be viewed with some suspicion.

2. a. Replacing list X with $\log X$ and list Y with $\log Y$ and then running a linear regression program on a calculator yields $\log y = -0.788 + 1.486 \log x$, with $r = .9997$

b. $\log y = -0.788 + 1.486 \log 5000 = 11.87$, and so $y = 142,700$ days.

c. $\log 45,000 = -0.788 + 1.486 \log x$, which gives $\log x = 7.741$ and $x = 2300$ million miles.

(The above calculations were done with natural logs. Using common logs would have given $\log y = -0.342 + 1.486 \log x$ with the same correlation and the same answers for parts b and c.)

3. a. Using the linear regression feature of your calculator, find $y = -0.063t + 4.8$, with $r = -.561$. At 31 degrees Fahrenheit this gives $-0.063(31) + 4.8 = 2.8$.

b. We need to use $\log(y+1)$ because $\log 0$ is not defined. Replacing the y-values with $\log(y+1)$ and performing the linear regression calculation results in $\log(y+1) = -0.015t + 1.15$, with $r = -.570$. At 31 degrees Fahrenheit, $\log(y+1) = -0.015(31) + 1.15 = 0.685$, so $y + 1 = 10^{0.685} = 4.8$ and $y = 3.8$.

c. Using only data from the seven prior launches that had had O-ring failures results in $r = -.263$. Looking at a correlation of only $-.263$, the scientists allowed *Challenger* to be launched. (Looking at a correlation of $-.570$, they might have decided differently!)

TOPIC FIVE

Exploring Categorical Data: Frequency Tables

While many variables such as age, income, and years of education are quantitative or numerical in nature, others such as gender, race, brand preference, mode of transportation, and type of occupation are qualitative or categorical. Quantitative variables are sometimes grouped into categorical classes.

Marginal Frequencies for Two-way Tables

Qualitative data often encompass two categorical variables that may or may not have a dependent relationship. These data can be displayed in a *two-way contingency table*.

Example 5.1. A 4-year study, reported in *The New York Times*, on men more than 70 years old analyzed blood cholesterol and noted how many men with different cholesterol levels suffered nonfatal or fatal heart attacks.

	Low cholesterol	Medium cholesterol	High cholesterol
Nonfatal heart attacks	29	17	18
Fatal heart attacks	19	20	9

Severity of heart attacks is the *row variable,* while cholesterol level is the *column variable.*

One method of analyzing these data involves first calculating the totals for each row and each column:

	Low cholesterol	Medium cholesterol	High cholesterol	Total
Nonfatal heart attacks	29	17	18	64
Fatal heart attacks	19	20	9	48
Total	48	37	27	112

These totals are placed in the right and bottom margins of the table and thus are called *marginal frequencies*.

These marginal frequencies are often put in the form of proportions or percentages. The *marginal distribution* of the cholesterol level is

Low: $\frac{48}{112} = .429 = 42.9\%$

Medium: $\frac{37}{112} = .330 = 33.0\%$

High: $\frac{27}{112} = .241 = 24.1\%$.

This distribution can also be displayed in a bar graph as follows:

Cholesterol levels
(of elderly men who suffered heart attacks)

Similarly we can determine the marginal distribution for the severity of heart attacks:

Nonfatal: $\frac{64}{112} = .571 = 57.1\%$

Fatal: $\frac{48}{112} = .429 = 42.9\%$.

The representative bar graph is

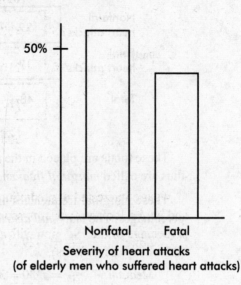

Severity of heart attacks
(of elderly men who suffered heart attacks)

Conditional Relative Frequencies and Association

The marginal distributions described and calculated above do not describe or measure the relationship between the two categorical variables. For this we must consider the information in the body of the table, not just the sums in the margins.

Example 5.2. Is hair loss pattern related to body mass index? One study (*Journal of the American Medical Association*, February 24, 1993, page 1000) of 769 men showed the following numbers:

		Hair loss pattern		
		None	Frontal	Vertex
Body mass index	<25	137	22	40
	25–28	218	34	67
	>28	153	30	68

The analysis first involves finding the row and column totals as we did before.

Hair loss pattern

Body mass index		None	Frontal	Vertex	
	<25	137	22	40	199
	25–28	218	34	67	319
	>28	153	30	68	251
		508	86	175	769

We are interested in predicting hair loss pattern from body mass index, and so we look at each row separately. For example, what proportion or percentage of the 199 men with a body mass index less than 25 have each of the hair loss patterns?

None: $\quad \frac{137}{199} = .688 = 68.8\%$

Frontal: $\quad \frac{22}{199} = .111 = 11.1\%$

Vertex: $\quad \frac{40}{199} = .201 = 20.1\%.$

These *conditional relative frequencies* can be displayed in a segmented bar chart where each segment has a length corresponding to its relative frequency:

Similarly, the conditional relative frequencies for the 319 men with a body mass index between 25 and 28 are

None: $\quad \frac{218}{319} = .683 = 68.3\%$

Frontal: $\quad \frac{34}{319} = .107 = 10.7\%$

Vertex: $\quad \frac{67}{319} = .210 = 21.0\%.$

For the 251 men with a body mass index of more than 28 we have

None: $\frac{153}{251} = .610 = 61.0\%$

Frontal: $\frac{30}{251} = .120 = 12.0\%$

Vertex: $\frac{68}{251} = .271 = 27.1\%$.

The segmented bar charts give a visual picture:

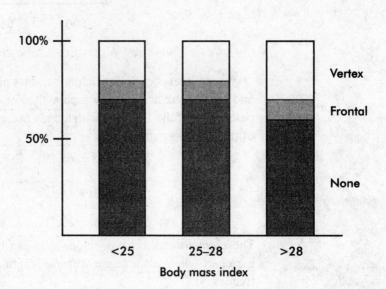

Segmented bar charts indicate a slight relationship between higher vertex pattern baldness and a body mass index of more than 28.

Example 5.3. A study was made to compare year in high school with preference for vanilla or chocolate ice cream with the following results:

	Vanilla	Chocolate
Freshman	20	10
Sophomore	24	12
Junior	18	9
Senior	22	11

What are the conditional relative frequencies for each class?

Freshmen: $\frac{20}{30} = .667$ prefer vanilla and $\frac{10}{30} = .333$ prefer chocolate.

Sophomores: $\frac{24}{36} = .667$ prefer vanilla and $\frac{12}{36} = .333$ prefer chocolate.

Juniors: $\frac{18}{27} = .667$ prefer vanilla and $\frac{9}{27} = .333$ prefer chocolate.

Seniors: $\frac{22}{33} = .667$ prefer vanilla and $\frac{11}{33} = .333$ prefer chocolate.

In such a case, where all the conditional relative frequency distributions are identical, we say that the two variables show *perfect independence*. (However, it should be noted that even if the two variables are completely independent, the chance is very slim that a resulting contingency table will show perfect independence.)

Example 5.4.   Suppose you need heart surgery and are trying to decide between two surgeons, Dr. Fixit and Dr. Patch. You find out that each operated 250 times last year with the following results:

	Dr. F	Dr. P
Died	60	50
Survived	190	200

Whom should you go to? Among Dr. Fixit's 250 patients 190 survived, for a survival rate of $\frac{190}{250} = .76$ or 76%, while among Dr. Patch's 250 patients 200 survived, for a survival rate of $\frac{200}{250} = .80$ or 80%. Your choice seems clear.

However, everything may not be so clear-cut. Suppose that on further investigation you determine that the surgeons operated on patients who were in either good or poor condition with the following results:

	Good condition			Poor condition	
	Dr. F	Dr. P		Dr. F	Dr. P
Died	8	17	Died	52	33
Survived	60	120	Survived	130	80

Note that adding corresponding boxes from these two tables gives the original table above.

How do the surgeons compare when operating on patients in good health? Dr. Fixit's 68 patients in good condition have a survival rate of $\frac{60}{68} = .882$ or 88.2%, while Dr. Patch's 137 patients in good condition have a survival rate of $\frac{120}{137} = .876$ or 87.6%. Similarly, we note that Dr. Fixit's 182 patients in poor condition have a survival rate of $\frac{130}{182} = .714$ or 71.4%, while Dr. Patch's 113 patients in poor condition have a survival rate of $\frac{80}{113} = .708$ or 70.8%.

Thus Dr. Fixit does better with patients in good condition (88.2% versus Dr. Patch's 87.6%) and also does better with patients in poor condition (71.4% versus Dr. P's 70.8%). However, Dr. Fixit has a lower overall patient survival rate (76% versus Dr. Patch's 80%)! How can this be?

This problem is an example of *Simpson's paradox,* where a comparison can be reversed when more than one group is combined to form a single group. The effect of another variable, sometimes called a *lurking variable,* is masked when the groups are combined. In this particular example, closer scrutiny reveals that Dr. Fixit operates on many more patients in poor condition than Dr. Patch, and these patients in poor condition are precisely the ones with lower survival rates. Thus even though Dr. Fixit does better with all patients, his overall rating is lower. Our original table hid the effect of the lurking variable related to the condition of the patients.

Questions on Topic Five: Exploring Categorical Data

Multiple-Choice Questions

Directions: The questions or incomplete statements that follow are each followed by five suggested answers or completions. Choose the response that best answers the question or completes the statement.

Questions 1–5 are based on the following: To study the relationship between party affiliation and support for a balanced budget amendment, 500 registered voters were surveyed with the following results:

	For	Against	No opinion
Democrat	50	150	50
Republican	125	50	25
Independent	15	10	25

1. What percentage of those surveyed were Democrats?
   (A) 10%
   (B) 20%
   (C) 30%
   (D) 40%
   (E) 50%

2. What percentage of those surveyed were for the amendment and were Republicans?

   (A) 25%
   (B) 38%
   (C) 40%
   (D) 62.5%
   (E) 65.8%

3. What percentage of Independents had no opinion?

   (A) 5%
   (B) 10%
   (C) 20%
   (D) 25%
   (E) 50%

4. What percentage of those against the amendment were Democrats?

   (A) 30%
   (B) 42%
   (C) 50%
   (D) 60%
   (E) 71.4%

5. Voters of which affiliation were most likely to have no opinion about the amendment?

   (A) Democrat
   (B) Republican
   (C) Independent
   (D) Republican and Independent, equally
   (E) Democrat, Republican, and Independent, equally

Questions 6–10 are based on the following: A study of music preferences in three geographic locations resulted in the following segmented bar chart:

6. What percentage of those surveyed from the Northeast prefer country music?
   (A) 20%
   (B) 30%
   (C) 40%
   (D) 50%
   (E) 70%

7. Which of the following is greatest?
   (A) Percentage of those from the Northeast who prefer classical
   (B) Percentage of those from the West who prefer country
   (C) Percentage of those from the South who prefer pop or rock
   (D) The above are all equal.
   (E) It is impossible to determine the answer without knowing the actual numbers of people involved.

8. Which of the following is greatest?
   (A) The number of people in the Northeast who prefer pop or rock
   (B) The number of people in the West who prefer classical
   (C) The number of people in the South who prefer country
   (D) The above are all equal.
   (E) It is impossible to determine the answer without knowing the actual numbers of people involved.

9. All three bars have a height of 100%.
   (A) This is a coincidence.
   (B) This happened because each bar shows a complete distribution.
   (C) This happened because there are three bars each divided into three segments.
   (D) This happened because of the nature of musical patterns.
   (E) None of the above is true.

10. Based on the given segmented bar chart, does there seem to be a relationship between geographic location and music preference?
    (A) Yes, because the corresponding segments of the three bars have different lengths.
    (B) Yes, because the heights of the three bars are identical.
    (C) Yes, because there are three segments and three bars.
    (D) No, because the heights of the three bars are identical.
    (E) No, because summing the corresponding segments for classical, summing the corresponding segments for country, and summing the corresponding segments for pop or rock all give approximately the same total.

11. In the following table, what value for n results in a table showing perfect independence?

20	50
30	n

(A) 10
(B) 40
(C) 60
(D) 75
(E) 100

12. A company employs both men and women in its secretarial and executive positions. In reports filed with the government, the company shows that the percentage of female employees who receive raises is higher than the percentage of male employees who receive raises. A government investigator claims that the percentage of male secretaries who receive raises is higher than the percentage of female secretaries who receive raises, and that the percentage of male executives who receive raises is higher than the percentage of female executives who receive raises. Is this possible?

   (A) No, either the company report is wrong or the investigator's claim is wrong.

   (B) No, if the company report is correct, then either a greater percentage of female secretaries than of male secretaries receive raises or a greater percentage of female executives than of male executives receive raises.

   (C) No, if the investigator is correct, then by summation of the corresponding numbers, the total percentage of male employees who receive raises would have to be greater than the total percentage of female employees who receive raises.

   (D) All of the above are true.

   (E) It is possible for both the company report to be true and the investigator's claim to be correct.

Answer Key

1. **E**	4. **E**	7. **B**	10. **A**
2. **A**	5. **C**	8. **E**	11. **D**
3. **E**	6. **A**	9. **B**	12. **E**

Answers Explained

1. **(E)** Of the 500 people surveyed, $50 + 150 + 50 = 250$ were Democrats, and $\frac{250}{500} = .5$ or 50%.

2. **(A)** Of the 500 people surveyed, 125 were both for the amendment and were Republicans, and $\frac{125}{500} = .25$ or 25%.

3. **(E)** There were $15 + 10 + 25 = 50$ Independents; 25 of them had no opinion, and $\frac{25}{50} = .5$ or 50%.

4. **(E)** There were $150 + 50 + 10 = 210$ people against the amendment; 150 of them were Democrats, and $\frac{150}{210} = .714$ or 71.4%.

5. **(C)** The percentages of Democrats, Republicans, and Independents with no opinion are 20%, 12.5%, and 50%, respectively.

6. **(A)** In the bar corresponding to the Northeast, the segment corresponding to country music stretches from the 50% level to the 70% level, indicating a length of 20%.

7. **(B)** Based on lengths of indicated segments, the percentage from the West who prefer country is the greatest.

8. **(E)** The given bar chart shows percentages, not actual numbers.

9. **(B)** In a complete distribution, the probabilities sum to 1, and the relative frequencies total 100%.

10. **(A)** The different lengths of corresponding segments show that in different geographic regions different percentages of people prefer each of the music categories.

11. **(D)** Relative frequencies must be equal. Either looking at rows gives $\frac{20}{70} = \frac{30}{30+n}$ or looking at columns gives $\frac{20}{50} = \frac{50}{50+n}$. We could also set up a proportion $\frac{n}{30} = \frac{50}{20}$ or $\frac{n}{50} = \frac{30}{20}$. Solving any of these equations gives $n = 75$.

12. **(E)** It is possible for both to be correct, for example, if there were 11 secretaries (10 women, 3 of whom receive raises, and 1 man who receives a raise) and 11 executives (10 men, 1 of whom receives a raise, and 1 woman who does not receive a raise). Then 100% of the male secretaries receive raises while only 30% of the female secretaries do; and 10% of the male executives receive raises while 0% of the female executives do. However, overall 3 out of 11 women receive raises, while only 2 out of 11 men receive raises. This is an example of Simpson's paradox.

Free-Response Questions

> *Directions:* You must show all work and indicate the methods you use. You will be graded on the correctness of your methods and on the accuracy of your final answers.

Two Open-Ended Questions

1. Suppose that in a telephone survey of 800 registered voters, the data are cross-classified both by gender of respondent and by respondent's opinion on an environmental bond issue.

	Bond issue	
	For	Against
Men	450	150
Women	160	40

Analyze this table looking both at marginal distributions and conditional distributions.

2. Following are the results of a study (*New England Journal of Medicine*, Vol. 319, No. 17, p. 1108, 1988) to determine whether taking an aspirin every other day reduces the risk of a heart attack in men:

	Aspirin	Placebo
Fatal attack	5	18
Nonfatal attack	99	171
No heart attack	10,933	10,845

Analyze this table by looking both at marginal distributions and conditional distributions.

Answers Explained

1. First we find the row and column totals:

	Bond issue		
	For	Against	
Men	450	150	600
Women	160	40	200
	610	190	800

We calculate the following marginal distributions:

Of the 800 people interviewed, $\frac{600}{800}$ or 75% are men and $\frac{200}{800}$ or 25% are women.

Of the 800 people interviewed, $\frac{610}{800}$ or 76.25% are for the bond issue and $\frac{190}{800}$ or 23.75% are against the bond issue.

Looking at the body of the table, we calculate the following conditional distributions:

Of the 600 men interviewed, $\frac{450}{600}$ or 75% are for the bond issue and $\frac{150}{600}$ or 25% are against it.

Of the 200 women interviewed, $\frac{160}{200}$ or 80% are for the bond issue and $\frac{40}{200}$ or 20% are against it.

Of the 610 people for the bond issue, $\frac{450}{610}$ or 73.77% are men and $\frac{160}{610}$ or 26.23% are women.

Of the 190 people against the bond issue, $\frac{150}{190}$ or 78.95% are men and $\frac{40}{190}$ or 21.05% are women.

There doesn't seem to be much of a relationship between the gender of a respondent and the respondent's opinion on the environmental bond issue.

2. First we find the row and column totals:

	Aspirin	Placebo	
Fatal attack	5	18	23
Nonfatal attack	99	171	270
No heart attack	10,933	10,845	21,778
	11,037	11,034	22,071

We calculate the following marginal distributions:

Of the 22,071 men in the study, $\frac{11,037}{22,071}$ or 50% took aspirin, and $\frac{11,034}{22,071}$ or 50% took the placebo.

Of the 22,071 men in the study, $\frac{23}{22,071}$ or .10% had a fatal heart attack, $\frac{270}{22,071}$ or 1.22% had a nonfatal attack, and $\frac{21,778}{22,071}$ or 98.67% had no heart attack.

Looking at the body of the table, we calculate the following conditional distributions:

Of the 11,037 men taking aspirin, $\frac{5}{11,037}$ or .045% had a fatal heart attack, $\frac{99}{11,037}$ or .897% had a nonfatal attack, and $\frac{10,933}{11,037}$ or 99.058% had no heart attack.

Of the 11,034 men taking the placebo, $\frac{18}{11,034}$ or .163% had a fatal heart attack, $\frac{171}{11,034}$ or 1.550% had a nonfatal attack, and $\frac{10,845}{11,034}$ or 98.287% had no heart attack.

Of the 23 men who had a fatal heart attack, $\frac{5}{23}$ or 21.74% had taken aspirin, while $\frac{18}{23}$ or 78.26% had taken the placebo.

Of the 270 men who had a nonfatal heart attack, $\frac{99}{270}$ or 36.67% had taken aspirin, while $\frac{171}{270}$ or 63.33% had taken the placebo.

Of the 21,778 men who had no heart attack, $\frac{10,933}{21,778}$ or 50.2% had taken aspirin, while $\frac{10,845}{21,778}$ or 49.8% had taken the placebo.

It seems clear that in men there is a relationship between taking an aspirin every other day and the risk of having a heart attack.

Two Investigative Tasks

1. The graduate school at the University of California at Berkeley reported that in 1973 they accepted 44% of 8442 male applicants and 35% of 4321 female applicants. Concerned that one of their programs was guilty of gender bias, the graduate school analyzed admissions to the six largest graduate programs and obtained the following results:

Program	Men Accepted	Men Rejected	Women Accepted	Women Rejected
A	511	314	89	19
B	352	208	17	8
C	120	205	202	391
D	137	270	132	243
E	53	138	95	298
F	22	351	24	317

   a. Find the percentage of men and the percentage of women accepted by each program. Comment on any pattern or bias you see.

   b. Find the percentage of men and the percentage of women accepted overall by these six programs. Does this appear to contradict the results from part *a*?

   c. If you worked in the Graduate Admissions Office, what would you say to an inquiring reporter who is investigating gender bias in graduate admissions?

2. Suppose you are a baseball scout and are interested in comparing two relief pitchers, Curver and Knuckler, both of whom play college ball. In particular you are interested in their strikeout ability. A quick glance at their records shows you that each came in to relieve in a similar number of games and that each faced 150 batters during his last season. However, Curver struck out 95 batters, while Knuckler struck out only 85 batters. When you tell their coaches that you're probably going to pick Curver, Knuckler's coach asks you to please look at their separate records against right- and left-handed batters. You do the required calculations and are surprised to find out that Knuckler has a higher strikeout rate against right-handed batters than does Curver, and that Knuckler also has a higher strikeout rate against left-handed batters than does Curver!

   Construct a set of hypothetical data to show how this is possible and explain the apparent paradox. *Hint:* One way of doing this involves having one pitcher face many more right-handed batters than the second, while the second faces many more left-handed batters than the first.

Answers Explained

1. *a.*

Program	Percentage of Men Accepted (%)	Percentage of Women Accepted (%)
A	62	82
B	63	68
C	37	34
D	33	35
E	28	24
F	6	7

There doesn't appear to be any real pattern; however, women seem to be favored in four of the programs, while men seem to be slightly favored in the other two programs.

b. Overall, 1195 out of 2691 male applicants were accepted, for a 44% acceptance rate, while 559 out of 1835 female applicants were accepted, for a 30% acceptance rate. This appears to contradict the results from part *a.*

c. You should tell the reporter that while it is true that the overall acceptance rate for women is 30% compared to the 44% acceptance rate for men, program by program women have either higher acceptance rates or only slightly lower acceptance rates than men. The reason behind this apparent paradox is that most men applied to programs A and B, which are easy to get into and have high acceptance rates. However, most women applied to programs C, D, E, and F, which are much harder to get into and have low acceptance rates.

2. One possible set of data is

Against right-handed batters

	Curver	Knuckler
Strikeout	80	45
Non-strikeout	20	5

Against left-handed batters

	Curver	Knuckler
Strikeout	15	40
Non-strikeout	35	60

Note that Knuckler struck out $\frac{45}{50}$ or 90% of the right-handed batters he faced, while Curver struck out only $\frac{80}{100}$ or 80% of the right-handed batters he faced. Similarly, Knuckler struck out $\frac{40}{100}$ or 40% of the left-handed batters he faced, while Curver struck out only $\frac{15}{50}$ or 30% of the left-handed batters he faced. So Knuckler did better against right-handed and against left-handed batters than Curver did, even though Curver seemed to do better overall. The reason for the apparent paradox is that both pitchers seem to have more trouble against left-handed batters, and Knuckler faced many more of these than Curver did. Curver was able to fatten up his overall strikeout percentage by pitching more often against the easier right-handed batters!

THEME TWO

Planning a Study

"Think carefully...your opinion will represent 1,000,000 people."

Overview of Methods of Data Collection

In the real world, time and cost considerations usually make it impossible to analyze an entire population. Does the government question you and your parents before announcing the monthly unemployment rates? Does a television producer check every household's viewing preferences before deciding whether a pilot program will be continued? In studying statistics we learn how to estimate *population* characteristics by considering a *sample*. For example, later in this book we will see how to estimate population means and proportions by looking at sample means and proportions.

To derive conclusions about the larger population, we need to be confident that the sample we have chosen represents that population fairly. Analyzing the data with computers is often easier than gathering the data, but the frequently quoted "Garbage in, garbage out" applies here. Nothing can help if the data are badly collected. Unfortunately, many of the statistics with which we are bombarded by newspapers, radio, and television are based on poorly designed data collection procedures.

Census

A *census* is a complete enumeration of an entire population. In common use, it is often thought of as an official attempt to contact every member of the population, usually with details regarding age, marital status, race, gender, occupation, income, years of school completed, and so on. Every 10 years the U.S. Bureau of the Census divides the nation into nine regions and attempts to gather information about everyone in the country. A massive amount of data is obtained, but even with the resources of the U.S. government, the census is not complete. For example, many homeless people are always missed, and there are always households that do not respond even after repeated requests for information. It was estimated that the 1990 census missed about 1.6% of the population as a whole and may have missed up to 5.0% of Hispanics and 4.6% of African Americans.

Sample Survey

The census tries to count everyone; it is not a sample. A sample survey aims to obtain information about a whole population by studying a part of it, that is, a sample. The goal is to gather information without disturbing or changing the population. Numerous procedures are used to collect data through sampling, and much of the statistical information distributed to us comes from sample surveys. Often, controlled experiments are later undertaken to demonstrate relationships suggested by sample surveys.

Experiment

In a controlled study, called an *experiment,* the researcher can randomly divide subjects into appropriate groups. Some action is taken on one or more of the groups, and the response is observed. For example, patients may be randomly given unmarked capsules of either aspirin or acetaminophen and the effects of the medication measured. Experiments often have a *treatment group* and a *control group;* in the ideal situation, neither the subjects nor the researcher knows which group is which. The Salk vaccine experiment of the 1950s, in which half the children received the vaccine and half were given a placebo, with not even their doctors knowing who received what, is a classic example of this *double-blind* approach. Controlled experiments can indicate cause-and-effect relationships.

Observational Study

Sample surveys are one example of what are called *observational studies*. In observational studies there is no choice in regard to who goes into the treatment and control groups. For example, a researcher cannot ethically tell 100 people to smoke three packs of cigarettes a day and 100 others to smoke only one pack per day; he can only observe people who habitually smoke these amounts. In observational studies the researcher strives to determine which variables affect the noted response. While results may suggest relationships, it is difficult to conclude cause and effect.

Questions on Topic Six: Overview of Methods of Data Collection

Multiple-Choice Questions

> *Directions:* The questions or incomplete statements that follow are each followed by five suggested answers or completions. Choose the response that best answers the question or completes the statement.

1. When travelers change airlines during connecting flights, each airline receives a portion of the fare. Several years ago, the major airlines used a sample trial period to determine what percentage of certain fares each should collect. Using these statistical results to determine fare splits, the airlines now claim huge savings over previous clerical costs. Which of the following is true?

   I. The airlines ran an experiment using a trial period for the control group.
   II. The airlines ran an observational study using the calculations from a trial period as a sample.
   III. The airlines feel that any monetary error in fare splitting resulting from using a statistical sample is smaller than the previous clerical costs necessary to calculate exact fare splits.

   (A) I only
   (B) II only
   (C) III only
   (D) I and III
   (E) II and III

2. Which of the following are true statements?

   I. In an experiment some treatment is intentionally forced on one group to note the response.
   II. In an observational study information is gathered on an already existing situation.
   III. Sample surveys are observational studies, not experiments.

   (A) I and II
   (B) I and III
   (C) II and III
   (D) I, II, and III
   (E) None of the above gives the complete set of true responses.

3. Which of the following are true statements?

   I. In an experiment researchers decide how people are placed in different groups.
   II. In an observational study, the people themselves select which group they are in.
   III. A control group is most often a self-selected grouping in an experiment.

(A) I and II

(B) I and III

(C) II and III

(D) I, II, and III

(E) None of the above gives the complete set of true responses.

4. In one study on the effect of niacin on cholesterol level, 100 subjects who acknowledged being long-time niacin takers had their cholesterol levels compared with those of 100 people who had never taken niacin. In a second study, 50 subjects were randomly chosen to receive niacin and 50 were chosen to receive a placebo.

(A) The first study was a controlled experiment, while the second was an observational study.

(B) The first study was an observational study, while the second was a controlled experiment.

(C) Both studies were controlled experiments.

(D) Both studies were observational studies.

(E) Each study was part controlled experiment and part observational study.

5. In one study subjects were randomly given either 500 or 1000 milligrams of vitamin C daily, and the number of colds they came down with during a winter season was noted. In a second study people responded to a questionnaire asking about the average number of hours they sleep per night and the number of colds they came down with during a winter season.

(A) The first study was an experiment without a control group, while the second was an observational study.

(B) The first study was an observational study, while the second was a controlled experiment.

(C) Both studies were controlled experiments.

(D) Both studies were observational studies.

(E) None of the above is a correct statement.

6. In a 1992 London study, 12 out of 20 migraine sufferers were given chocolate whose flavor was masked by peppermint, while the remaining eight sufferers received a similar-looking, similar-tasting tablet that had no chocolate. Within 1 day, five of those receiving chocolate complained of migraines, while no complaints were made by any of those who did not receive chocolate. Which of the following is a true statement?

(A) This study was an observational study of 20 migraine sufferers in which it was noted how many came down with migraines after eating chocolate.

(B) This study was a sample survey in which 12 out of 20 migraine sufferers were picked to receive peppermint-flavored chocolate.

(C) A census of 20 migraine sufferers was taken, noting how many were given chocolate and how many developed migraines.

(D) A study was performed using chocolate as a placebo to study one cause of migraines.

(E) An experiment was performed comparing a treatment group that was given chocolate to a control group that was not.

7. Suppose you wish to compare the average class size of mathematics classes to the average class size of English classes in your high school. Which is the most appropriate technique for gathering the needed data?

   (A) Census
   (B) Sample survey
   (C) Experiment
   (D) Observational study
   (E) None of these methods is appropriate.

8. Which of the following are true statements?

   I. Based on careful use of control groups, experiments can often indicate cause-and-effect relationships.
   II. While observational studies may suggest relationships, great care must be taken in concluding that there is cause and effect because of the lack of control over lurking variables.
   III. A complete census is the only way to establish a cause-and-effect relationship absolutely.

   (A) I and II
   (B) I and III
   (C) II and III
   (D) I, II, and III
   (E) None of the above gives the complete set of true responses.

9. Two studies are run to compare the experiences of families living in high-rise public housing to those of families living in townhouse subsidized rentals. The first study interviews 25 families who have been in each government program for at least 1 year, while the second randomly assigns 25 families to each program and interviews them after 1 year. Which of the following is a true statement?

   (A) Both studies are observational studies because of the time period involved.
   (B) Both studies are observational studies because there are no control groups.
   (C) The first study is an observational study, while the second is an experiment.
   (D) The first study is an experiment, while the second is an observational study.
   (E) Both studies are experiments.

10. Two studies are run to determine the effect of low levels of wine consumption on cholesterol level. The first study measures the cholesterol levels of 100 volunteers who have not consumed alcohol in the past year and compares these values with their cholesterol levels after 1 year, during which time each volunteer drinks one glass of wine daily. The second study measures the cholesterol levels of 100 volunteers who have not consumed alcohol in the past year, randomly picks half the group to drink one glass of wine daily for a year while the others drink no alcohol for the year, and finally measures their levels again. Which of the following is a true statement?

(A) The first study is an observational study, while the second is an experiment.

(B) The first study is an experiment, while the second is an observational study.

(C) Both studies are observational studies, but only one uses both randomization and a control group.

(D) The first study is a census of 100 volunteers, while the second study is an experiment.

(E) Both studies are experiments.

Answer Key

1. **E**	3. **A**	5. **A**	7. **A**	9. **C**
2. **D**	4. **B**	6. **E**	8. **A**	10. **E**

Answers Explained

1. **(E)** This study is not an experiment in which responses are being compared. It is an observational study in which the airlines use split fare calculations from a trial period as a sample to indicate the pattern of all split fare transactions. They claim that this leads to "huge savings."

2. **(D)** I and II can be considered part of the definitions of *experiment* and *observational study*. A sample survey does not impose any treatment; it simply counts a certain outcome, and so it is an observational study, not an experiment.

3. **(A)** In an experiment a control group is the untreated group picked by the researchers. It is usually best when the selection process involves chance.

4. **(B)** The first study was observational because the subjects were not chosen for treatment.

5. **(A)** The first study was an experiment with two treatment groups and no control group. The second study was observational; the researcher did not randomly divide the subjects into groups and have each group sleep a designated number of hours per night.

6. **(E)** This study was an experiment in which the researchers divided the subjects into treatment and control groups. A census would involve a study of all migraine sufferers, not a sample of 20. The response of the treatment group receiving chocolate was compared to the response of the control group receiving a placebo. The peppermint tablet with no chocolate was the placebo.

7. **(A)** The main office at your school should be able to give you the class sizes of every math and English class. If need be, you can check with every math and English teacher.

8. **(A)** A complete census can provide much information about a population, but it doesn't necessarily establish a cause-and-effect relationship among seemingly related population parameters.

9. **(C)** In the first study the families were already in the housing units, while in the second study one of two treatments was applied to each family.

10. **(E)** Both studies apply treatments and measure responses, and so both are experiments.

Planning and Conducting Surveys

Most data collection involves observational studies, not controlled experiments. Furthermore, while most data collection has some purpose, many studies come to mind after the data have been assembled and examined. For data collection to be useful, the resulting sample must be representative of the population under consideration.

Simple Random Sampling

How can a good, that is, a representative, sample be chosen? The most accurate technique would be to write the name of each member of the population on a card, mix the cards thoroughly in a large box, and pull out a specified number of cards. This method would give everyone in the population an equal chance of being selected as part of the sample. Unfortunately, this method is usually too time-consuming and too costly, and bias might still creep in if the mixing is not thorough. A *simple random sample,* that is, one in which every possible sample of the desired size has an equal chance of being selected, can more easily be obtained by assigning a number to everyone in the population and using a random number table or having a computer generate random numbers to indicate choices.

Example 7.1.　Suppose 80 students are taking an AP Statistics course and the teacher wants to randomly pick out a sample of 10 students to try out a practice exam. She first assigns the students numbers 01, 02, 03, ..., 80. Reading off two digits at a time from a random number table, she ignores any over 80 and ignores repeats, stopping when she has a set of ten. If the table began 75425 56573 90420 48642 27537 61036 15074 84675, she would choose the students numbered 75, 42, 55, 65, 73, 04, 27, 53, 76, and 10. Note that 90 and 86 are ignored because they are over 80, and the second and third occurrences of 42 are ignored because they are repeats.

Characteristics of a Well-Designed, Well-Conducted Survey

A well-designed survey always incorporates chance, such as using random numbers from a table or a computer. However, the use of probability techniques is not enough to ensure a representative sample. Often we don't have a complete listing of the population, and so we have to be careful about exactly how we are applying "chance." Even when subjects are picked by chance, they may choose not to respond to the survey or they may not be available to respond, thus calling into question how representative the final sample really is. The wording of the questions must be neutral—subjects give different answers depending on the phrasing.

Example 7.2. Suppose we are interested in determining the percentage of adults in a small town who eat a nutritious breakfast. How about randomly selecting 100 numbers out of the telephone book, calling each one, and asking whether the respondent is intelligent enough to eat a nutritious breakfast every morning?

Answer: Random selection is good, but a number of questions should be addressed. For example, are there many people in the town without telephones or with unlisted numbers? How will the time of day the calls are made affect whether the selected people are reachable? If people are unreachable, will replacements be randomly chosen in the same way or will this lead to a certain class of people being underrepresented? Finally, even if these issues are satisfactorily addressed, the wording of the question is clearly not neutral—unless the phrase *intelligent enough* is dropped, answers will be almost meaningless.

Sampling Error: The Variation Inherent in a Survey

No matter how well-designed and well-conducted a survey is, it still gives a sample *statistic* as an estimate for a population *parameter*. Different samples give different sample statistics, all of which are estimates for the same population parameter, and so error is naturally present. This error can be described using probability; that is, we can say how likely we are to have a certain size error. Generally, the chance of this error occurring is smaller when the sample size is larger. However, the way the data are obtained is crucial—a large sample size cannot make up for a poor survey design or faulty collection techniques.

Example 7.3. Each of four major news organizations surveys likely voters and separately reports that the percentage favoring the incumbent candidate is 53.4%, 54.1%, 52.0%, and 54.2%, respectively. What is the correct percentage? Did three or more of the news organizations make a mistake?

Answer: There is no way of knowing the correct population percentage from the information given. The four surveys led to four statistics, each an estimate of the population parameter. No one made a mistake unless there was a bad survey, for example, one without the use of chance, or not representative of the population, or with poor wording of the question. Sampling differences are natural.

Sources of Bias in Surveys

Poorly designed sampling techniques result in *bias,* that is, in a tendency to favor the selection of certain members of a population. An often-cited example of *selection bias* is the *Literary Digest* opinion poll that predicted a landslide victory for Alfred Landon over Franklin D. Roosevelt in the 1936 presidential election. The *Digest* surveyed people with cars and telephones, but in 1936 only the wealthy minority, who mainly voted Republican, had cars and telephones. Examples of *nonresponse bias* are present in most mailed questionnaires. They tend to have very low response percentages, and it is often unclear which part of the population is responding. *Unintentional bias* often creeps in when the surveyor tries to systematically pick people representative of the whole population. For example, in the 1948 presidential election, the *Chicago Tribune* incorrectly called Thomas E. Dewey the winner over Harry S. Truman. Here the mistake was partly due to misleading polls based on quota sampling that left the interviewers too much free choice in picking people to fill their quotas.

Two common sampling techniques that often result in flawed conclusions are voluntary response samples and convenience samples. *Voluntary response samples,* based on individuals who offer to participate, typically give too much emphasis to persons with strong opinions. For example, radio call-in programs about controversial topics such as gun control, abortion, and school segregation do not produce meaningful data on what proportion of the population favor or oppose related issues. *Convenience samples,* based on choosing individuals who are easy to reach, are also suspect. For example, interviews at shopping malls tend to produce data highly unrepresentative of the entire population.

The wording of questions or the very questions themselves can lead to *response bias*. People often don't want to be perceived as having unpopular, unsavory, or illegal views and so may respond untruthfully when face to face with an interviewer or when filling out a questionnaire that is not anonymous. Sometimes people chosen for a survey simply refuse to respond or are unreachable or too difficult to contact. These situations lead to *nonresponse bias*. At other times certain people are left out of consideration, which results in *undercoverage bias*. For example, telephone surveys simply ignore all those possible subjects who don't have telephones, and door-to-door surveys ignore the homeless.

Example 7.4.   In response to student protests over the firing of Coach Niceguy, the university public relations spokesperson released the following statement: "A questionnaire mailed to 120,000 alumni produced over 5000 responses, 60% of which were unfavorable to Coach Niceguy. Furthermore, these respondents contributed an average gift of over $200 last year, including Mr. Mon E. Bags' contribution of a million dollars for a new luxury box on the fifty yard line. Finally, 30% of the faculty have expressed unhappiness with Niceguy, so that a total of 90% of the alumni and faculty want him to go. We had no choice but to fire him." What do you think of the university's explanation of the firing?

Answer: There are so many examples of improper reasoning above that it is hard to know where to begin. Only 5000 of 120,000 alumni responded (nonresponse bias). The survey was unrepresentative, as most respondents seem to have been contributors (voluntary response survey). The average contribution of $200 is meaningless if one of the contributions was $1 million. You can't add 60% of one group and 30% of another group and come up with 90% of anything.

Stratifying to Reduce Variation

Time- and cost-saving modifications are needed to implement sampling procedures. *Systematic sampling* involves randomly listing the population in order and then picking every tenth, hundredth, thousandth, and so on, person from the list. In *stratified sampling* the population is divided into representative groups called *strata,* and random samples of persons from all strata are chosen. *Multistage sampling* involves dividing the population into groupings, subdividing each grouping, selecting a random sampling of the subdivisions, and finally picking a random sample of people from the selected subdivisions. What is crucial in all these techniques is the presence of a methodical procedure that involves the use of chance and leaves no freedom of choice to the interviewers.

Example 7.5.   Suppose a sample of 100 high school students from a school of size 5000 is to be chosen to determine their views on the death penalty. One method would be to have each student write his or her name on a slip of paper, put the papers in a box, and have the principal reach in and pull out 100 of the papers. However, questions could arise regarding how well the papers are mixed up in the box. For example, how might the outcome be affected if all students in one homeroom toss in their names at the same time so that their papers are clumped together? Another method would be to assign each student a number from 1 to 5000 and then use a random number table, picking out four digits at a time and tossing out repeats and numbers over 5000. What are other cost- or time-saving alternatives?

Answer: From a list of the students, the surveyor could simply note every fiftieth name (systematic sampling). Since students in each class have certain characteristics in common, the surveyor could use a random selection method to pick 25 students from each of the separate lists of freshmen, sophomores, juniors, and seniors (stratified sampling). The researcher could separate the homerooms by classes; then randomly pick five freshmen homerooms, five sophomore homerooms, five junior homerooms, and five senior homerooms; and then randomly pick five students from each of the homerooms (multistage sampling).

It should be noted that none of the alternative procedures in the above example result in a *simple random sample* because every possible sample of size 100 does not have an equal chance of being selected.

Questions on Topic Seven: Planning and Conducting Surveys

Multiple-Choice Questions

Directions: The questions or incomplete statements that follow are each followed by five suggested answers or completions. Choose the response that best answers the question or completes the statement.

1. Ann Landers, who writes a daily advice column appearing in newspapers across the country, once asked her readers, "If you had it to do over again, would you have children?" Of the more than 10,000 readers who responded, 70% said no. What does this show?

   (A) The survey is meaningless because of voluntary response bias.
   (B) No meaningful conclusion is possible without knowing something more about the characteristics of her readers.
   (C) The survey would have been more meaningful if she had picked a random sample of the 10,000 readers who responded.
   (D) The survey would have been more meaningful if she had used a control group.
   (E) This was a legitimate sample, randomly drawn from her readers and of sufficient size to allow the conclusion that most of her readers who are parents would have second thoughts about having children.

2. Which of the following are true statements?

   I. If bias is present in a sampling procedure, it can be overcome by dramatically increasing the sample size.
   II. There is no such thing as a "bad sample."
   III. Sampling techniques that use probability techniques effectively eliminate bias.

(A) I only

(B) II only

(C) III only

(D) None of the statements are true.

(E) None of the above gives the complete set of true responses.

3. Two possible wordings for a questionnaire on gun control are as follows:

I. The United States has the highest rate of murder by handguns among all countries. Most of these murders are known to be crimes of passion or crimes provoked by anger between acquaintances. Are you in favor of a 7-day cooling-off period between the filing of an application to purchase a handgun and the resulting sale?

II. The United States has one of the highest violent crime rates among all countries. Many people want to keep handguns in their homes for self-protection. Fortunately, U.S. citizens are guaranteed the right to bear arms by the Constitution. Are you in favor of a 7-day waiting period between the filing of an application to purchase a needed handgun and the resulting sale?

One of these questions showed that 25% of the population favored a 7-day waiting period between application for purchase of a handgun and the resulting sale, while the other question showed that 70% of the population favored the waiting period. Which produced which result and why?

(A) The first question probably showed 70% and the second question 25% because of the lack of randomization in the choice of pro-gun and anti-gun subjects as evidenced by the wording of the questions.

(B) The first question probably showed 25% and the second question 70% because of a placebo effect due to the wording of the questions.

(C) The first question probably showed 70% and the second question 25% because of the lack of a control group.

(D) The first question probably showed 25% and the second question 70% because of response bias due to the wording of the questions.

(E) The first question probably showed 70% and the second question 25% because of response bias due to the wording of the questions.

4. Which of the following are true statements?

I. Voluntary response samples often underrepresent people with strong opinions.

II. Convenience samples often lead to undercoverage bias.

III. Questionnaires with nonneutral wording are likely to have response bias.

(A) I and II

(B) I and III

(C) II and III

(D) I, II, and III

(E) None of the above gives the complete set of true responses.

5. Each of the 29 NBA teams has 12 players. A sample of 58 players is to be chosen as follows. Each team will be asked to place 12 cards with their players' names into a hat and randomly draw out two names. The two names from each team will be combined to make up the sample. Will this method result in a simple random sample of the 348 basketball players?

   (A) Yes, because each player has the same chance of being selected.
   (B) Yes, because each team is equally represented.
   (C) Yes, because this is an example of stratified sampling, which is a special case of simple random sampling.
   (D) No, because the teams are not chosen randomly.
   (E) No, because not each group of 58 players has the same chance of being selected.

6. To survey the opinions of bleacher fans at Wrigley Field, a surveyor plans to select every one-hundredth fan entering the bleachers one afternoon. Will this result in a simple random sample of Cub fans who sit in the bleachers?

   (A) Yes, because each bleacher fan has the same chance of being selected.
   (B) Yes, but only if there is a single entrance to the bleachers.
   (C) Yes, because the 99 out of 100 bleacher fans who are not selected will form a control group.
   (D) Yes, because this is an example of systematic sampling, which is a special case of simple random sampling.
   (E) No, because not every sample of the intended size has an equal chance of being selected.

7. Which of the following are true statements about sampling error?

   I. Sampling error can be eliminated only if a survey is both extremely well designed and extremely well conducted.
   II. Sampling error concerns natural variation between samples, is always present, and can be described using probability.
   III. Sampling error is generally smaller when the sample size is larger.

   (A) I and II
   (B) I and III
   (C) II and III
   (D) I, II, and III
   (E) None of the above gives the complete set of true responses.

8. What fault do all these sampling designs have in common?

   I. The *Wall Street Journal* plans to make a prediction for a presidential election based on a survey of its readers.
   II. A radio talk show asks people to phone in their views on whether the United States should pay off its huge debt to the United Nations.
   III. A police detective, interested in determining the extent of drug use by teenagers, randomly picks a sample of high school students and interviews each one about any illegal drug use by the student during the past year.

(A) All the designs make improper use of stratification.

(B) All the designs have errors that can lead to strong bias.

(C) All the designs confuse *association* with *cause and effect*.

(D) None of the designs satisfactorily controls for sampling error.

(E) None of the designs makes use of chance in selecting a sample.

9. A state auditor is given an assignment to choose and audit 26 companies. She lists all companies whose name begins with *A,* assigns each a number, and uses a random number table to pick one of these numbers and thus one company. She proceeds to use the same procedure for each letter of the alphabet and then combines the 26 results into a group for auditing. Which of the following are true statements?

   I. Her procedure makes use of chance.

   II. Her procedure results in a simple random sample.

   III. Each company has an equal probability of being audited.

   (A) I and II

   (B) I and III

   (C) II and III

   (D) I, II, and III

   (E) None of the above gives the complete set of true responses.

10. A researcher planning a survey of heads of households in a particular state has census lists for each of the 23 counties in that state. The procedure will be to obtain a random sample of heads of households from each of the counties rather than grouping all the census lists together and obtaining a sample from the entire group. Which of the following is a true statement about the resulting stratified sample.

    I. It is not a simple random sample.

    II. It is easier and less costly to obtain than a simple random sample.

    III. It gives comparative information that a simple random sample wouldn't give.

    (A) I only

    (B) I and II

    (C) I and III

    (D) I, II, and III

    (E) None of the above gives the complete set of true responses.

11. To find out the average occupancy size of student-rented apartments, a researcher picks a simple random sample of 100 such apartments. Even after one follow-up visit, the interviewer is unable to make contact with anyone in 27 of these apartments. Concerned about nonresponse bias, the researcher chooses another simple random sample and instructs the interviewer to continue this procedure until contact is made with someone in a total of 100 apartments. The average occupancy size in the final 100-apartment sample is 2.78. Is this estimate probably too low or too high?

(A) Too low, because of undercoverage bias.

(B) Too low, because convenience samples overestimate average results.

(C) Too high, because of undercoverage bias.

(D) Too high, because convenience samples overestimate average results.

(E) Too high, because voluntary response samples overestimate average results.

12. To conduct a survey of long-distance calling patterns, a researcher opens a telephone book to a random page, closes his eyes, puts his finger down on the page, and then reads off the next 50 names. Which of the following are true statements?

   I. The survey design incorporates chance.

   II. The procedure results in a simple random sample.

   III. The procedure could easily result in selection bias.

   (A) I and II

   (B) I and III

   (C) II and III

   (D) I, II, and III

   (E) None of the above gives the complete set of true responses.

13. Which of the following are true statements about sampling?

   I. Careful analysis of a given sample will indicate whether or not it is random.

   II. Sampling error implies an error, possibly very small but still an error, on the part of the surveyor.

   III. Data obtained while conducting a census are always more accurate than data obtained from a sample, no matter how careful the design of the sample.

   (A) I only

   (B) II only

   (C) III only

   (D) None of these statements are true.

   (E) None of the above gives the complete set of true responses.

14. Consider the following three events:

   I. Although 18% of the student body are minorities, in a random sample of 20 students, 5 are minorities.

   II. In a survey about sexual habits, an embarrassed student deliberately gives the wrong answers.

   III. A surveyor mistakenly records answers to one question in the wrong space.

   Which of the following correctly characterizes the above?

   (A) I, sampling error; II, response bias; III, human mistake

   (B) I, sampling error; II, nonresponse bias; III, hidden error

   (C) I, hidden bias; II, voluntary sample bias; III, sampling error

   (D) I, undercoverage error; II, voluntary error; III, unintentional error

   (E) I, small sample error; II, deliberate error; III, mistaken error

15. A researcher plans a study to examine the depth of belief in God among the adult population. He obtains a simple random sample of 100 adults as they leave church one Sunday morning. All but one of them agree to participate in the survey. Which of the following are true statements?

I. Proper use of chance as evidenced by the simple random sample makes this a well-designed survey.

II. The high response rate makes this a well-designed survey.

III. Selection bias makes this a poorly designed survey.

(A) I only
(B) II only
(C) III only
(D) I and II
(E) None of these statements is true.

Answer Key

1. **A**	4. **C**	7. **C**	10. **D**	13. **D**
2. **D**	5. **E**	8. **B**	11. **C**	14. **A**
3. **E**	6. **E**	9. **E**	12. **B**	15. **C**

Answers Explained

1. **(A)** This survey provides a good example of voluntary response bias, which often overrepresents negative opinions. The people who chose to respond were most likely parents who were very unhappy, and so there is very little chance that the 10,000 respondents were representative of the population. Knowing more about her readers, or taking a sample of the sample would not have helped.

2. **(D)** If there is bias, taking a larger sample just magnifies the bias on a larger scale. If there is enough bias, the sample can be worthless. Even when the subjects are chosen randomly, there can be bias due, for example, to non-response or to the wording of the questions.

3. **(E)** The wording of the questions can lead to response bias. The neutral way of asking this question would simply have been: Are you in favor of a 7-day waiting period between the filing of an application to purchase a handgun and the resulting sale?

4. **(C)** Voluntary response samples, like radio call-in surveys, are based on individuals who offer to participate, and they typically overrepresent persons with strong opinions. Convenience samples, like shopping mall surveys, are based on choosing individuals who are easy to reach, and they typically miss a large segment of the population. Nonneutral wording can readily lead to response bias, and if surveyors want a particular result, they deliberately build bias into the wording.

5. **(E)** In a simple random sample, every possible group of the given size has to be equally likely to be selected, and this is not true here. For example, with this procedure it will be impossible for all the Bulls to be together in the final sample. This procedure is an example of stratified sampling, but stratified sampling does not result in simple random samples.

6. **(E)**   In a simple random sample, every possible group of the given size has to be equally likely to be selected, and this is not true here. For example, with this procedure it will be impossible for all the early arrivals to be together in the final sample. This procedure is an example of systematic sampling, but systematic sampling does not result in simple random samples.

7. **(C)**   Different samples give different sample statistics, all of which are estimates of a population parameter. Sampling error relates to natural variation between samples, can never be eliminated, can be described using probability, and is generally smaller if the sample size is larger.

8. **(B)**   The *Wall Street Journal* survey has strong selection bias; that is, people who read the *Journal* are not very representative of the general population. The talk show survey results in a *voluntary response sample,* which typically gives too much emphasis to persons with strong opinions. The police detective's survey has strong response bias in that students may not give truthful responses to a police detective about their illegal drug use.

9. **(E)**   Only I is a true statement. While the auditor does use chance, each company will have the same chance of being audited only if the same number of companies have names starting with each letter of the alphabet. This will not result in a simple random sample because each possible set of 26 companies does not have the same chance of being picked as the sample. For example, a group of companies whose names all start with *A* will not be chosen.

10. **(D)**   This is not a simple random sample because all possible sets of the required size do not have the same chance of being picked. For example, a set of households all from just half the counties has no chance of being picked to be the sample. Stratified samples are often easier and less costly to obtain and also make comparative data available. In this case responses can be compared among various counties.

11. **(C)**   It is most likely that the apartments at which the interviewer had difficulty finding someone home were apartments with fewer students living in them. Replacing these with other randomly picked apartments most likely replaces smaller-occupancy apartments with larger-occupancy ones.

12. **(B)**   While the procedure does use some element of chance, all possible groups of size 50 do not have the same chance of being picked, and so the result is not a simple random sample. There is a very real chance of selection bias. For example, a number of relatives with the same name and similar long-distance calling patterns might be selected.

13. **(D)**   To determine if a sample is random, one must analyze the procedure by which it was obtained. Sampling error is natural variation among samples; it is not an error committed by any person. If a census is poorly run, it will provide less information and be less accurate than a well-designed survey. For example, having the principal ask every single student in the school whether or not he or she regularly cheats on exams produces less useful data than a carefully worded anonymous questionnaire filled out by a randomly selected sample of the student body.

14. **(A)**   The natural variation in samples is called sampling error. Embarrassing questions and resulting untruthful answers are an example of response bias. Inaccuracies and mistakes due to human error are one of the real concerns of researchers.

15. **(C)**   Surveying people coming out of church results in a very unrepresentative sample of the adult population, especially given the question under consideration. Using chance and obtaining a high response rate will not change the selection bias and make this into a well-designed survey.

Free-Response Questions

Directions: You must show all work and indicate the methods you use. You will be graded on the correctness of your methods and on the accuracy of your final answers.

Four Open-Ended Questions

1. A questionnaire is being designed to determine whether most people are or are not in favor of legislation protecting the habitat of the spotted owl. Give two examples of poorly worded questions, one biased toward each response.

2. To obtain a sample of 25 students from among the 500 students present in school one day, a surveyor decides to pick every twentieth student waiting on line to attend a required assembly in the gym.

   a. Explain why this procedure will not result in a simple random sample of the students present that day.

   b. Describe a procedure that will result in a simple random sample of the students present that day.

3. A hot topic in government these days is welfare reform. Suppose a congresswoman wishes to survey her constituents concerning their opinions on whether the federal government should turn welfare over to the states. Discuss possible sources of bias with regard to the following four options: (1) conducting a survey via random telephone dialing into her district, (2) sending out a mailing using a registered voter list, (3) having a pollster interview everyone who walks past her downtown office, and (4) broadcasting a radio appeal urging interested citizens in her district to call in their opinions to her office.

4. You and nine friends go to a restaurant and check your coats. You all forget to pick up the ticket stubs, and so when you are ready to leave, Hilda, the hatcheck girl, randomly gives each of you one of the ten coats. You are surprised that one person actually receives the correct coat. You would like to explore this further and decide to use a random number table to simulate the situation. Describe how the random number table can be used to simulate one trial of the coat episode. Explain what each of the digits 0 through 9 will represent.

Answers Explained

1. There are many possible examples, such as Are you in favor of protecting the habitat of the spotted owl, which is almost extinct and desperately in need of help from an environmentally conscious government? and Are you in favor of protecting the habitat of the spotted owl no matter how much unemployment and resulting poverty this causes among hard-working loggers?

there are 40 students who always rush to be first in line, this procedure will allow for only 2 of them to be in the sample. Or if each homeroom of size 20 arrives as a unit, this procedure will allow for only 1 person from each homeroom to be in the sample.

   b. A simple random sample of the students can be obtained by numbering them from 001 to 500 and then picking three digits at a time from a random number table, ignoring numbers over 500 and ignoring repeats, until a group of 25 numbers is obtained. The students corresponding to these 25 numbers will be a simple random sample.

3. The direct telephone and mailing options will both suffer from undercoverage bias. For example, especially affected by the legislation under discussion are the homeless, and they do not have telephones or mailing addresses. The pollster interviews will result in a convenience sample, which can be highly unrepresentative of the population. In this case, there might be a real question concerning which members of her constituency spend any time in the downtown area where her office is located. The radio appeal will lead to a voluntary response sample, which typically gives too much emphasis to persons with strong opinions.

4. In numbering the people 0 through 9, each digit stands for whose coat someone receives. Pick the digits, omitting repeats, until a group of ten different digits is obtained. Check for a match (1 appearing in the first position corresponding to person 1, or 2 appearing in the next position corresponding to person 2, and so on, up to 0 appearing in the last position corresponding to person 10).

An Investigative Task

1. Suppose that in your statistics class of 30 students, 2 students discover they have the same birthday (month and date). You decide to test whether this is an unusual occurrence by using a random number table to simulate picking 30 randomly selected birth dates.

   a. Clearly explain how to perform this test and then do so, showing your procedure step by step and your result.
   b. Do you feel justified in making some conclusion based on the result of your test? Explain.
   c. Can you make any definite conclusion about the probability of finding two students with the same birth month? Explain.

```
84177 06757 17613 15582 51506 81435 41050 92031 06449 05059
59884 31180 53115 84469 94868 57967 05811 84514 75011 13006
63395 55041 15866 06589 13119 71020 85940 91932 06488 74987
54355 52704 90359 02649 47496 71567 94268 08844 26294 64759
08989 57024 97284 00637 89283 03514 59195 07635 03309 72605
29357 23737 67881 03668 33876 35841 52869 23114 15864 38942
```

Answers Explained

1. *a.* Let the birth dates correspond to the numbers 001 (January 1) through 365 (December 31). Go through the random number table, picking three digits at a time, and throwing away any numbers over 365. After listing a group of 30 such numbers, check for duplicates.

   Looking at groups of three digits, and throwing away numbers over 365 gives {155, 150, 203, 106, 050, 180, 158, 184, 111, 300, 131, 197, 102, 085, 320, 270, 359, 026, 294, 024, 063, 283, 035, 145, 024, 097, 260, 357, 237, 103}. Note that there is a duplicate, namely, 024.

   b. There happens to be a number (birthday) that is duplicated among the sample of 30 numbers from the random number table. Clearly there won't always be duplicates. Before we can draw any conclusion, we should repeat this procedure, picking groups of 30 random numbers between 001 and 365 many more times. Only then might we be able to estimate the probability of finding a duplicate birthday in a room of 30 people.

   c. The probability is 1 that 2 of the 30 students will have the same birth month because there is no way of spreading 30 students among 12 months without having duplicates.

Planning and Conducting Experiments

There are several primary principles dealing with the proper planning and conducting of experiments. First, possible confounding variables must be controlled for, usually through the use of comparison. Second, chance should be used in assigning which subjects are to be placed in which groups for which treatment. Third, natural variation in outcomes can be lessened by using more subjects.

Experiments Versus Observational Studies Versus Surveys

In an experiment we impose some change or treatment and measure the result or response. In an observational study we simply observe and measure something that has taken place or is taking place, while trying not to cause any changes by our presence. A sample survey is an observational study in which we draw conclusions about an entire population by considering an appropriately chosen sample to look at. An experiment often suggests a causal relationship, while an observational study may show only the existence of associations.

Example 8.1. A study is to be designed to determine whether daily calcium supplements benefit women by increasing bone mass. How can an observational study be performed? An experiment? Which is more appropriate here?

Answer: An observational study might interview and run tests on women seen purchasing calcium supplements in a pharmacy. Or perhaps all patients hospitalized during a particular time period could be interviewed with regard to taking calcium and then their bone mass measured. The bone mass measurements of those taking calcium supplements could then be compared to that of those not taking supplements.

An experiment could be performed by selecting some number of subjects, using chance to pick half to receive calcium supplements while the other half receives similar-looking placebos, and noting the difference in bone mass before and after treatment for each group.

The experimental approach is more appropriate here. With the observational study there could be many explanations for any bone mass difference noted between patients who take calcium and those who don't. For example, women who have voluntarily been taking calcium supplements might be precisely those who take better care of themselves in general and thus have higher bone mass for other reasons. The experiment tries to control for lurking variables by randomly giving half the subjects calcium.

Example 8.2.   A study is to be designed to examine the life expectancies of tall people versus those of short people. Which is more appropriate, an observational study or an experiment?

Answer: An observational study, examining medical records of heights and ages at time of death, seems straightforward. An experiment where subjects are randomly chosen to be made short or tall, followed by recording age at death, would be groundbreaking (and, of course, nonsensical).

Example 8.3.   A study is to be designed to examine the GPAs of students who take marijuana regularly and those who don't. Which is more appropriate, an observational study or an experiment?

Answer: As much as some researchers might want to randomly require half the subjects to take an illegal drug, this would be unethical. The proper procedure here is an observational study, having students anonymously fill out questionnaires asking about marijuana usage and GPA.

Experiments involve *explanatory variables* that are believed to have an effect on *response variables*. A group is treated with some level of the explanatory variable, and the outcome on the response variable is measured.

Example 8.4.   To test the value of help sessions outside the classroom, students could be divided into three groups, with one group receiving 4 hours of help sessions per week outside the classroom, a second group receiving 2 hours of help sessions outside the classroom, and a third group receiving no help outside the classroom. What are the explanatory and response variables and what are the levels?

Answer: The explanatory variable, help sessions outside the classroom, is being given at three levels: 4 hours weekly, 2 hours weekly, and 0 hours weekly. The response variable is not specified but might be a final exam score or performance on a particular test.

Confounding, Control Groups, Placebo Effects, and Blinding

When there is uncertainty with regard to which variable is causing an effect, we say the variables are *confounded*. That is, when comparing two groups with regard to their response to some variable, if there is a lurking variable in regard to which the two groups also differ, this lurking variable may very well be confounded with the variable under consideration. Confounding is easier to control for when doing experiments than when doing observational studies.

In an experiment there is a group that receives the treatment, and there is a *control group* that doesn't. The experiment compares the responses in the treatment group to the responses in the control group.

It is a fact that many people respond to any kind of perceived treatment. This is called the *placebo effect*. For example, when given a sugar pill after surgery but told that it is a strong pain reliever, many patients feel immediate relief from their pain. In many studies, subjects appear to consciously or subconsciously want to help the researcher prove a point. Thus when responses are noticed in any experiment, there is concern whether real physical responses are being caused by the psychological placebo effect. *Blinding* occurs when the subjects or the response evaluators don't know which subjects are receiving different treatments such as placebos.

Example 8.5.   A study is intended to test the effects of vitamin E and beta carotene on heart attack rates. How should it be set up?

Answer: Using randomization, the subjects should be split into four groups: those who will be given just vitamin E, just beta carotene, both vitamin E and beta carotene, and neither vitamin E nor beta carotene. For example, as each subject joins the test, the next digit in a random number table can be read off, ignoring 0 and 5–9, and with 1, 2, 3, and 4 designating which group the subject is placed in. Or if the total number of subjects is known and available, for example, 800, then each can be assigned a number and three digits at a time be read off the random number table. With repeats and numbers over 800 thrown away, the first 200 numbers picked represent one group, the next 200 another, and so on. More meaningful results will be obtained if the study is double-blind, that is, if not only are the subjects unaware of what kind of tablets they are taking but neither are the doctors evaluating whether or not they have heart problems. Many diagnoses are not clear-cut, and doctors can be influenced if they know exactly which potential preventative their patients are taking.

Treatments, Experimental Units, and Randomization

An experiment is performed on objects called *experimental units,* and if the units are people, they are called *subjects*. The experimental units or subjects are typically divided into two groups. One group receives a *treatment* and is called the *treatment group*. A comparison is made between the response noted in the treatment group and the response noted in the *control group,* the group that receives no treatment.

To help minimize the effect of lurking variables, it is important to use *randomization,* that is, to use chance in deciding which subjects go into which group. It is not sufficient to try to systematically match characteristics between the two groups. It seems reasonable, for example, to hand-sort subjects so that both the treatment group and the control group have the same number of women, the same number of Catholics, the same number of Hispanics, the same number of short people, and so on, but this method does not work well. There are always other variables that one might not think of considering until after the results of the experiment start coming in. The best method to use is randomization employing a computer, a hat with names in it, or a random number table.

Completely Randomized Design for Two Treatments

Comparing two treatments using randomization is often the design of choice. To help minimize hidden bias, it is best if subjects do not know which treatment they are receiving. This is called *single-blinding*. Another precaution is the use of *double-blinding,* in which neither the subjects nor those evaluating their responses know who is receiving which treatment.

Example 8.6.   There is a pressure point on the wrist that some doctors believe can be used to help control the nausea experienced following certain medical procedures. The idea is to place a band containing a small marble firmly on a patient's wrist so that the marble is located directly over the pressure point. Describe how an experiment might be run on 50 postoperative patients.

Answer: Assign each patient a number from 01 to 50. From a random number table read off two digits at a time, throwing away repeats and numbers over 50, until 25 numbers have been selected. Put wristbands with marbles over the pressure point on the patients with these assigned numbers. Put wristbands with marbles on the remaining patients also, but *not* over the pressure point. Have a researcher check by telephone with all 50 patients at designated time intervals to determine the degree of nausea being experienced. Neither the patients nor the researcher on the telephone should know which patients have the marbles over the correct pressure point.

Example 8.7.   A chemical fertilizer company wishes to test whether using their product results in superior vegetables. After dividing a large field into small plots, how might the experiment proceed?

Answer: If the company has one recommended fertilizer application level, half the plots can be randomly selected (assigning the plots numbers and using a random number table) to receive the prescribed dosage of fertilizer. This random selection of plots is to ensure that neither fertilized plants nor unfertilized plants are inadvertently given land with better rainfall, sunshine, soil type, and so on. To avoid possible bias on the part of employees who will weed and water the plants, they should not know which plots have received the fertilizer. It might be necessary to have containers, one for each plot, of a similar-looking, similar-smelling substance, half of which contain the fertilizer while the rest contain a chemically inactive material. Finally, if the vegetables are to be judged by quantity and size, the measurements will be less subject to bias. However, if they are to be judged qualitatively, for example, by taste, the judges should not know which vegetables were treated with the fertilizer and which were not.

If the researchers also wish to consider level, that is, the amount of fertilizer, randomization should be used for more groupings. For example, if there are 60 plots on which to test four levels of fertilizer, the first 12 different two-digit numbers in the range 01–60 appearing on a random number table might receive one level, the next 12 new two-digit numbers a second level, and so on, with the last 12 plots receiving the "placebo" treatment.

Randomized Paired Comparison Design

Two treatments can be compared based on the responses of paired subjects, one of whom receives one treatment while the other receives the second treatment. Often the paired subjects are really single subjects who are given both treatments, one at a time.

Example 8.8.　The famous Pepsi-Coke tests had subjects compare the taste of samples of each drink. How could such a paired comparison test be set up?

Answer:　It is crucial that such a test be blind, that is, that the subjects not know which cup contains which drink. Furthermore, to help avoid hidden bias, which drink the subjects taste first should be decided by chance. For example, as each subject arrives, the researcher could read off the next digit from a random number table, with the subject receiving Pepsi or Coke first depending on whether the digit is odd or even.

Example 8.9.　Does seeing pictures of accidents caused by drunk drivers influence one's opinion on penalties for drunk drivers? How could a comparison test be designed?

Answer:　The subjects could be asked questions about drunk driving penalties before and then again after seeing the pictures, and any change in answers noted. This would be a poor design because there is no control group, there is no use of randomization, and subjects might well change their answers because they realize that that is what is expected of them after seeing the pictures.

A better design is to use randomization to split the subjects into two groups, half of whom simply answer the questions while the other half first see the pictures and then answer the questions.

Another possibility is to use a group of twins as subjects. One of each set of twins is randomly picked (e.g., based on choosing an odd or even digit from a random number table) to answer the questions without seeing the pictures, while the others first see the pictures and then answer the questions. The answers could be compared from each set of twins. This is a paired comparison test that might help minimize lurking variables due to family environment, heredity, and so on.

Replication, Blocking, and Generalizability of Results

When differences are observed in a comparison test, the researcher must decide whether these differences are *statistically significant* or whether they can be explained by natural variation. One important consideration is the size of the sample —the larger the sample, the more significant the observation. This is the principle of *replication;* that is, the treatment should be repeated on a sufficient number of subjects so that real response differences are more apparent.

Just as stratification in sampling design first divides the population into representative groups called strata, *blocking* in experiment design first divides the subjects into representative groups called blocks. This technique helps control certain lurking variables by bringing them directly into the picture and helps make conclusions more specific. The paired comparison design is a special case of blocking in which each pair (or each subject if the subjects serve as their own controls) can be considered a block.

Example 8.10.   There is a rising trend for star college athletes to turn professional without finishing their degrees. A study is performed to assess whether reading an article about professional salaries has an impact on such decisions. Randomization can be used to split the subjects into two groups, and those in one group given the article before answering questions. How can a block design be incorporated into the design of this experiment?

Answer: The subjects can be split into two blocks, underclass and upperclass, before using randomization to assign some to read the article before questioning. With this design, the impact of the salary article on freshmen and sophomores can be distinguished from the impact on juniors and seniors.

Similarly, blocking can be used to separately analyze men and women, those with high GPAs and those with low GPAs, those in different sports, those with different majors, and so on.

A major goal of experiments is to be able to *generalize* the results to broader populations. Often an experiment must be repeated in a variety of settings. For example, it is hard to generalize from the effect a television commercial has on students at a private midwestern high school to the effect the same commercial has on retired senior citizens in Florida. Generally, comparison and randomization are important, blinding is sometimes critical, and taking care to avoid hidden bias as much as possible is always indicative of a well-designed experiment. However, knowledge of the subject so that realistic situations can be created in testing should also be emphasized. Testing and experimenting on people does not put them in natural states, and this situation can lead to artificial responses.

Questions on Topic Eight: Planning and Conducting Experiments

Multiple-Choice Questions

> *Directions:* The questions or incomplete statements that follow are each followed by five suggested answers or completions. Choose the response that best answers the question or completes the statement.

1. A study is made to determine whether studying Latin helps students achieve higher scores on the verbal section of the SAT exam. In comparing records of 200 students, half of whom have taken at least 1 year of Latin, it is noted that the average SAT verbal score is higher for those 100 students who have taken Latin than for those who have not. Based on this study, guidance counselors begin to recommend Latin for students who want to do well on the SAT exam. Which of the following are true statements?

   I. While this study indicates a relation, it does not prove causation.
   II. There could well be a confounding variable responsible for the seeming relationship.
   III. Self-selection here makes drawing the counselors' conclusion difficult.

   (A) I and II
   (B) I and III
   (C) II and III
   (D) I, II, and III
   (E) None of the above gives the complete set of true responses.

2. In a 1927–32 Western Electric Company study on the effect of lighting on worker productivity, productivity increased with each increase in lighting but then also increased with every decrease in lighting. If it is assumed that the workers knew a study was in progress, this is an example of

   (A) the effect of a treatment unit.
   (B) the placebo effect.
   (C) the control group effect.
   (D) sampling error.
   (E) voluntary response bias.

3. When the estrogen-blocking drug tamoxifen was first introduced to treat breast cancer, there was concern that it would cause osteoporosis as a side effect. To test this concern, cancer subjects were randomly selected and given tamoxifen, and their bone density was measured before and after treatment. Which of the following is a true statement?

   I. This study was an observational study.
   II. This study was a sample survey of randomly selected cancer patients.
   III. This study was an experiment in which the subjects were used as their own controls.

    (A) I only

    (B) II only

    (C) III only

    (D) I and II

    (E) None of the above gives the complete set of true responses.

4. In designing an experiment, blocking is used

    (A) to reduce bias.

    (B) to reduce variation.

    (C) as a substitute for a control group.

    (D) as a first step in randomization.

    (E) to control the level of the experiment.

5. Which of the following are true statements about blocking?

    I. Blocking is to experiment design as stratification is to sampling design.

    II. By controlling certain variables, blocking can make conclusions more specific.

    III. The paired comparison design is a special case of blocking.

    (A) I and II

    (B) I and III

    (C) II and III

    (D) I, II, and III

    (E) None of the above gives the complete set of true responses.

6. Consider the following studies being run by three different nursing home establishments.

    I. One nursing home has pets brought in for an hour every day to see if patient morale is improved.

    II. One nursing home allows hourly visits every day by kindergarten children to see if patient morale is improved.

    III. One nursing home administers antidepressants to all patients to see if patient morale is improved.

Which of the following is true?

    (A) None of these studies uses randomization.

    (B) None of these studies uses control groups.

    (C) None of these studies uses blinding.

    (D) Important information can be obtained from all these studies, but none will be able to establish causal relationships.

    (E) All of the above

7. A consumer product agency tests miles per gallon for a sample of automobiles using each of four different octanes of gasoline. Which of the following is true?

    (A) There are four explanatory variables and one response variable.

    (B) There is one explanatory variable with four levels of response.

    (C) Miles per gallon is the only explanatory variable, but there are four response variables corresponding to the different octanes.

    (D) There are four levels of a single explanatory variable.

    (E) Each explanatory level has an associated level of response.

8. Which of the following are true statements?

    I. In general, strong association implies causation.

    II. In well-designed, well-conducted experiments, strong association implies causation.

    III. Causation and association are unrelated concepts.

  (A) I only

  (B) II only

  (C) III only

  (D) I and II

  (E) I, II, and III

9. Which of the following are true statements?

    I. In well-designed observational studies, responses are systematically influenced during the collection of data.

    II. In well-designed experiments, the treatments result in responses that are as similar as possible.

    III. A well-designed experiment always has a single treatment but may test that treatment at different levels.

  (A) I only

  (B) II only

  (C) III only

  (D) II and III

  (E) None of these statements is true.

10. Which of the following are important in the design of experiments?

    I. Control of confounding variables

    II. Randomization in assigning subjects to different treatments

    III. Replication of the experiment using sufficient numbers of subjects

  (A) I and II

  (B) I and III

  (C) II and III

  (D) I, II, and III

  (E) None of the above gives the complete set of true responses.

11. Which of the following are true about the design of matched-pair experiments?

    I. Each subject might receive both treatments.

    II. Each pair of subjects receives the identical treatment, and differences in their responses are noted.

    III. Blocking is one form of matched-pair design.

  (A) I only

  (B) II only

  (C) III only

  (D) I and III

  (E) II and III

12. A nutritionist believes that having each player take a vitamin pill before a game enhances the performance of the football team. During the course of one season, each player takes a vitamin pill before each game, and the team

achieves a winning season for the first time in several years. Is this an experiment or an observational study?

(A) An experiment, but with no reasonable conclusion possible about cause and effect

(B) An experiment, thus making cause and effect a reasonable conclusion

(C) An observational study, because there was no use of a control group

(D) An observational study, but a poorly designed one because randomization was not used

(E) An observational study, thus allowing a reasonable conclusion of association but not of cause and effect

13. Some researchers believe that too much iron in the blood can raise the level of cholesterol. The iron level in the blood can be lowered by making periodic blood donations. A study is performed by randomly selecting half of a group of volunteers to give periodic blood donations while the rest do not. Is this an experiment or an observational study?

(A) An experiment with control group and blinding

(B) An experiment with blocking

(C) An observational study with comparison and randomization

(D) An observational study with little if any bias

(E) None of the above

Answer Key

1. **D**	4. **B**	7. **D**	10. **D**	13. **E**
2. **B**	5. **D**	8. **B**	11. **A**	
3. **C**	6. **E**	9. **E**	12. **A**	

Answers Explained

1. **(D)** It may well be that very bright students are the same ones who both take Latin and do well on the SAT verbal exam. If students could be randomly assigned to take or not take Latin, the results would be more meaningful. Of course, ethical considerations might make it impossible to isolate the confounding variable in this way.

2. **(B)** The desire of the workers for the study to be successful led to a placebo effect.

3. **(C)** In experiments on people, the subjects can be used as their own controls, with responses noted before and after the treatment. However, with such designs there is always the danger of a placebo effect. Thus the design of choice would involve a separate control group to be used for comparison.

4. **(B)** Blocking divides the subjects into groups, such as men and women, or political affiliations, and thus reduces variation.

5. **(D)** Blocking in experiment design first divides the subjects into representative groups called blocks, just as stratification in sampling design first divides the population into representative groups called strata. This procedure can control certain variables by bringing them directly into the picture, and thus conclusions are more specific. The paired comparison design is a special case of blocking in which each pair can be considered a block.

6. **(E)**   None of the studies has any controls, such as randomization, control groups, or blinding, and so while they may give valuable information, they cannot establish cause and effect.

7. **(D)**   Octane is the only explanatory variable, and it is being tested at four levels. Miles per gallon is the single response variable.

8. **(B)**   Well-designed experiments can show cause and effect.

9. **(E)**   In good observational studies, the responses are not influenced during the collecting of data. In good experiments, treatments are compared as to differences in responses. In an experiment, there can be many treatments, each at a different level.

10. **(D)**   Control, randomization, and replication are all important aspects of well-designed experiments.

11. **(A)**   Each subject might receive both treatments, as, for example, in the Pepsi-Coke taste comparison study. The point is to give each subject in a matched pair a different treatment and note any difference in responses. Matched-pair experiments are a particular example of blocking, not vice versa.

12. **(A)**   This study was an experiment because a treatment (vitamin pills) was imposed on the subjects. However, it was a poorly designed experiment with no use of randomization and no control over lurking variables, and so the results are meaningless.

13. **(E)**   This study is an experiment because a treatment (periodic removal of a pint of blood) is imposed. There is no blinding because the subjects clearly know whether or not they are giving blood. There is no blocking because the subjects are not divided into blocks before random assignment to treatments. For example, blocking would have been used if the subjects had been separated by gender or age before random assignment to give or not give blood donations.

Free-Response Questions

Directions: You must show all work and indicate the methods you use. You will be graded on the correctness of your methods and on the accuracy of your final answers.

Five Open-Ended Questions

1. Some health care professionals recommend the use of melatonin to promote better sleep patterns. To test this idea the manufacturer has 100 of its employees fill out a questionnaire about their sleeping patterns, once at the beginning of the study and then again after taking a 3-milligram melatonin capsule every night at bedtime for a week. Comment on the design of this experiment.

2. Suppose a new drug is developed that appears in laboratory settings to completely prevent people who test positive for human immunodeficiency virus (HIV) from ever developing full-blown acquired immunodeficiency syndrome (AIDS). Putting all ethical considerations aside, design an experiment to test the drug. What ethical considerations might arise during the testing that would force an early end to the experiment?

3. A new weight-loss supplement is to be tested at three different levels (once, twice, and three times a day). Design an experiment, including a control group and including blocking for gender, for 80 overweight volunteers, half of whom are men. Explain carefully how you will use randomization.

4. Two studies are run to measure the health benefits of long-time use of daily high doses of vitamin C. Researchers in the first study send a questionnaire to all 50,000 subscribers to a health magazine, asking whether they have taken large doses of vitamin C for at least a 2-year period and what they perceive to be the health benefits, if any. The response rate is 80%. The 10,000 people who did not respond to the first mailing receive follow-up telephone calls, and eventually responses are registered from 98% of the magazine subscribers. Researchers in a second study take a group of 200 volunteers and randomly select 100 to receive high doses of vitamin C while the others receive a similar-looking, similar-tasting placebo. The volunteers are not told whether they are receiving the vitamin, but their doctors know and are asked to note health changes during a 2-year period. Comment on the designs of the two studies, remarking on their good points and on possible sources of error.

5. Explain how you would design an experiment to evaluate whether subliminal advertising (flashing "BUY POPCORN" on the screen for a fraction of a second) results in more popcorn being sold in a movie theater. Show how you will incorporate comparison, randomization, and blinding.

Answers Explained

1. Any conclusions would probably be meaningless. There is a substantial danger that the placebo effect will occur here; that is, real physical responses can be caused by the psychological effect of knowing the intent of the research. The experiment would be considerably strengthened by using a control group taking a look-alike capsule. Any conclusions would be further suspect because of the choice of subjects. Rather than making some random selection from the intended population, the company is using its own employees, a sample almost guaranteed to have concerns, interests, and backgrounds that will confound the responses or limit the generalizability of the results.

2. Ask doctors, hospitals, or blood testing laboratories to make known that you are looking for HIV-positive volunteers. As the volunteers arrive, use a random number table to give each one the drug or a placebo (e.g., if the next digit in the table is odd, the volunteer gets the drug, while if the next digit is even, the volunteer gets a placebo). Use double-blinding; that is, both the volunteers and their doctors should not know if they are receiving the drug or the placebo. Ethical considerations will arise, for example, if the drug is very successful. If volunteers on the placebo are steadily developing full-blown AIDS while no one on the drug is, then ethically the test should be stopped and everyone put on the drug. Or if most of the volunteers on the drug are dying from an unexpected fatal side effect, the test should be stopped and everyone taken off the drug.

3. To achieve blocking by gender, first separate the men and women. Label the 40 men 01 through 40. Use a random number table to pick two digits at a time, ignoring numbers larger than 40 and ignoring repeats, until a group of ten such numbers is obtained. These men will receive the supplement at

the once-a-day level. Relabel the remaining men 01 though 30. Following along in the table, pick two digits at a time, ignoring numbers larger than 30 and ignoring repeats, until another group of ten is selected. These men will receive the supplement at the twice-a-day level. Relabel the remaining men 01 through 20. Again following along in the table, pick two digits at a time, ignoring numbers larger than 20 and ignoring repeats, until another group of ten is selected. These men will receive the supplement at the three-times-a-day level, while the remaining men will be a control group. Now repeat the entire procedure, starting by labeling the women 01 through 40.

4. The first study, an observational study, does not suffer from nonresponse bias, as do most mailed questionnaires, because it involved follow-up telephone calls and achieved a high response rate. However, this study suffers terribly from selection bias because people who subscribe to a health magazine are not representative of the general population. One would expect most of them to strongly believe that vitamins improve their health. The second study, a controlled experiment, used comparison between a treatment group and a control group, used randomization in selecting who went into each group, and used blinding to control for a placebo effect on the part of the volunteers. However, it did not use double-blinding; that is, the doctors knew whether their patients were receiving the vitamin, and this could have introduced hidden bias when they made judgments regarding their patients' health.

5. Every day for some specified period of time, look at the next digit on a random number table. If it is odd, flash the subliminal message all day on the screen, while if it is even, don't flash the message that day (randomization). Don't let the customers know what is happening (blinding) and don't let the clerks selling the popcorn know what is happening (double-blinding). Compare the quantity of popcorn bought by the treatment group, that is, by the people who receive the subliminal message, to the quantity bought by the control group, the people who don't receive the message (comparison).

Two Investigative Tasks

1. A high school offers two precalculus courses, one that uses a traditional lecture and drill method, and a second that divides students into small groups to work on open-ended problems. To compare the effectiveness of the two methods, the administration proposes to compare average SAT math scores for the students in the two courses.

   a. What is wrong with the administration's proposal?

   b. Suppose a group of 50 students are willing to take either course. Explain how you would use a random number table to set up an experiment comparing the effectiveness of the two courses.

   c. Apply your setup procedure to the given random number table:

84177 06757 17613 15582 51506 81435 41050 92031 06449
05059 59884 31180 53115 84469 94868 57967 05811 84514
75011 13006 63395 55041 15866 06589 13119 71020 85940
91932 06488 74987 54355 52704 90359 02649 47496 71567
94268 08844 26294 64759 08989 57024 97284 00637 89283
03514 59195 07635 03309 72605 29357 23737 67881 03668
33876 35841 52869 23114 15864 38942

   d. Discuss any lurking variables that your setup doesn't consider.

2. Suppose you are head of admissions at a college. Two of your employees come up with ideas for distributing recruiting brochures, and you would like to see which idea results in more follow-up contacts. You print test quantities of version A and version B and must decide how to distribute them as requests come in.

   a. Design an experiment with instructions to a secretary explaining how to decide which brochure should be sent out as each individual request comes in.

   b. Design an experiment with instructions to a secretary explaining how to evenly distribute brochures to each set of 20 requests that come in.

   c. Suppose that 20 people (Jones, Smith, Black, Berry, Stein, Gold, West, Tomas, Johns, Little, Jagne, Hurd, Tastle, Novak, Bass, Yolt, Cross, Nash, Dole, and Uvay) request brochures. Using the random number table, list who will receive each version of the brochure under the experimental design in part a. Then do the same for the experimental design in part b.

84177 06757 17613 15582 51506 81435 41050 92031 06449
05059 59884 31180 53115 84469 94868 57967 05811 84514
75011 13006 63395 55041 15866 06589 13119 71020 85940
91932 06488 74987 54355 52704 90359 02649 47496 71567

Answers Explained

1.   a. There is no reason to believe that there was anything random about which students took which course. Perhaps all the weaker students self-selected or were advised to choose the traditional course.

   b. The students could be labeled 01 through 50. Pairs of digits could then be read off a random number table, ignoring numbers over 50 and ignoring duplicates, until a set of 25 numbers is obtained. The students corresponding to these numbers could be enrolled in the traditional course, and the remaining students in the other.

   c. Applying the above procedure results in {17, 31, 14, 35, 41, 05, 09, 20, 06, 44, 50, 43, 11, 18, 45, 01, 13, 33, 04, 19, 02, 08, 40, 49, 03}. Enroll the students with these numbers in the traditional course.

   d. Which teachers teach which courses is not considered. Perhaps the more interesting, exciting teachers teach the new version. Even though a control group is selected, there is no blinding, and so students in the new version might work harder because they realize they are part of an experiment.

2.   *a.* As each request comes in, the secretary looks at the next digit in the random number table. If the digit is odd, the person is sent version A, while if the digit is even, the person is sent version B.

    b. The secretary gives each person a number from 01 to 20. Two digits at a time are then read off the random number table, and he copies down all resulting pairs between 01 and 20, ignoring those larger than 20 and ignoring repeats, until ten such numbers have been selected. The people corresponding to these ten numbers are sent version A, while the remaining ten people are sent version B. For the next set of 20 people, the secretary resumes reading numbers where he left off the previous time.

    c. With the first procedure, 8 is even and so Jones gets version B, 4 is even and so Smith gets version B, 1 is odd and so Black gets version A, and so on, resulting in

Version A: Black, Berry, Stein, Tomas, Johns, Little, Jagne, Hurd, Novak, Bass, Yolt, Cross, Nash

Version B: Jones, Smith, Gold, West, Tastle, Dole, Uvay

With the second procedure, each person is first assigned a number between 01 and 20: Jones (01), Smith (02), Black (03), Berry (04), Stein (05), Gold (06), West (07), Tomas (08), Johns (09), Little (10), Jagne (11), Hurd (12), Tastle (13), Novak (14), Bass (15), Yolt (16), Cross (17), Nash (18), Dole (19), and Uvay (20). Reading pairs of digits from the table, ignoring those larger than 20 and ignoring repeats, and underlining the selections give

```
84177 06757 17613 15582 51506 81435 41050 92031 06449
05059 59884 31180 53115 84469 94868 57967 05811 84514
75011 13006 63395 55041 15866 06589 13119 71020 85940
91932 06488 74987 54355 52704 90359 02649 47496 71567
```

The resulting set, {17, 14, 05, 09, 20, 06, 11, 18, 01, 15}, corresponds to those receiving version A, while the rest receive version B:

Version A: Cross, Novak, Stein, Johns, Uvay, Gold, Jagne, Nash, Jones, Bass

Version B: Smith, Black, Berry, West, Tomas, Little, Hurd, Tastle, Yolt, Dole

THEME THREE

Probability

The jury reaches an impartial verdict.

TOPIC NINE

Probability as Relative Frequency

In the world around us, unlikely events sometimes take place. At other times, events that seem inevitable do not occur. Because of the myriad and minute origins of various happenings, it is often impracticable, or simply impossible, to predict exact outcomes. However, while we may not be able to foretell a specific result, we can sometimes assign what is called a *probability* to indicate the likelihood that a particular event will occur.

The Law of Large Numbers

The *relative frequency* of an event is the proportion of times the event happened, that is, the number of times the event happened divided by the total number of trials.

Example 9.1.   If there were 12 cloudy days during a 30-day period, the relative frequency of cloudy days was $\frac{12}{30} = .4$.

Relative frequencies may change every time an experiment is performed. However, when an experiment is performed a large number of times, the relative frequency of an event tends to become closer to what is called the probability of the event. (In some cases, *probability* can be defined as long-term relative frequency.)

Example 9.2.   A nurse notes that on one day 23 out of 50 new patients had a fever, while on another day 28 out of 56 had a fever. The two relative frequencies, $\frac{19}{50} = .38$ and $\frac{28}{56} = .50$, are different. However, summing up these numbers day after day for many days, she might be able to conclude that the probability of a patient arriving with a fever is, for example, about .412.

Example 9.3.   Suppose the numbers in the following random number table correspond to people arriving for work at a large factory. Let 0, 1, and 2 be smokers and 3–9 be nonsmokers. After each ten arrivals, calculate the total relative frequency of smokers and graph the results.

84177 06757 17613 15582 51506 81435 41050 92031 06449 05059
59884 31180 53115 84469 94868 57967 05811 84514 75011 13006
63395 55041 15866 06589 13119 71020 85940 91932 06488 74987
54355 52704 90359 02649 47496 71567 94268 08844 26294 64759
08989 57024 97284 00637 89283 03514 59195 07635 03309 72605
29357 23737 67881 03668 33876 35841 52869 23114 15864 38942

Answer: The cumulative relative frequencies are $\frac{2}{10} = .2$, $\frac{6}{20} = .3$, $\frac{9}{30} = .3$, $\frac{15}{40} = .375$, $\frac{18}{50} = .36$, $\frac{21}{60} = .35$, $\frac{23}{70} = .329$, $\frac{23}{80} = .288$, $\frac{27}{90} = .3$, $\frac{33}{100} = .33$, and so on. Graphing these and further values gives

Note how the cumulative relative frequency at first fluctuates considerably but then seems to level off. The concept that the relative frequency tends closer and closer to a certain number (the probability) as an experiment is repeated more and more times is called the *law of large numbers*.

The *probability* of a particular outcome of an experiment is a mathematical statement about the likelihood of that event occurring. Probabilities are always between 0 and 1, with a probability close to 0 meaning that an event is unlikely to occur and a probability close to 1 meaning that the event is likely to occur. The sum of the probabilities of all the separate outcomes of an experiment is always 1.

Addition Rule, Multiplication Rule, Conditional Probabilites, and Independence

Complementary Events

The probability that an event will not occur, that is, the probability of its complement, is equal to 1 minus the probability that the event will occur:

$$P(X') = 1 - P(X)$$

Example 9.4.   If the probability that a company will win a contract is .3, what is the probability that it will not win the contract?

Answer: $1 - .3 = .7$

Addition Principle

If two events are mutually exclusive, that is, they cannot occur simultaneously, the probability that at least one event will occur is equal to the sum of the respective probabilities of the two events:

$$\text{If } P(X \cap Y) = 0 \quad \text{then} \quad P(X \cup Y) = P(X) + P(Y)$$

where $X \cap Y$, (read "X intersect Y") means that both X and Y occur, while $X \cup Y$, (read "X union Y") means that either X or Y or both occur.

Example 9.5.   If the probabilities that Jane, Tom, and Mary will be chosen chairperson of the board are .5, .3, and .2, respectively, the probability that the chairperson will be either Jane or Mary is $.5 + .2 = .7$.

When two events are not mutually exclusive, the sum of their probabilities counts their shared occurrence twice. This leads to the following rule.

General Addition Rule

For any pair of events X and Y,

$$P(X \cup Y) = P(X) + P(Y) - P(X \cap Y)$$

Example 9.6.   Suppose the probability that a construction company will be awarded a certain contract is .25, the probability that it will be awarded a second contract is .21, and the probability that it will get both contracts is .13. What is the probability that the company will win at least one of the two contracts?

Answer: $.25 + .21 - .13 = .33$

Multiplication Rule

If the chance that one event will happen is not influenced by whether or not a second event happens, the probability that *both* events will occur is the product of their separate probabilities.

Example 9.7. The probability that a student will receive a state grant is $\frac{1}{3}$, while the probability that she will be awarded a federal grant is $\frac{1}{2}$. If whether or not she receives one grant is not influenced by whether or not she receives the other, what is the probability of her receiving both grants?

Answer: $\frac{1}{3} \times \frac{1}{2} = \frac{1}{6}$

The multiplication rule can be extended to more than two events; that is, given a sequence of *independent* events, the probability that *all* will happen is equal to the product of their individual probabilities.

Example 9.8. Suppose a reputed psychic in an extrasensory perception (ESP) experiment has called heads or tails correctly on ten successive tosses of a coin. What is the probability that guessing would have yielded this perfect score?

Answer: $\left(\frac{1}{2}\right)\left(\frac{1}{2}\right)\cdots\left(\frac{1}{2}\right) = \left(\frac{1}{2}\right)^{10} = \frac{1}{1024}$

To best understand independence as mentioned above, we first examine the idea of *conditional probability,* that is, the probability of an event given that another event has occurred.

Example 9.9. The table below gives the results of a survey of the drinking and smoking habits of 1200 college students. Rows and columns have also been summed.

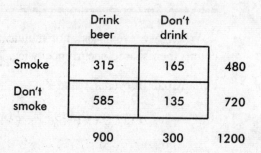

	Drink beer	Don't drink	
Smoke	315	165	480
Don't smoke	585	135	720
	900	300	1200

What is the probability that someone in this group smokes?

Answer: $P(\text{smokes}) = \frac{480}{1200} = .4$

What is the probability a student smokes given that she is a beer drinker?

Answer: We now narrow our attention to the 900 beer drinkers, and thus we calculate $\frac{315}{900} = .35$. We use the following notation: $P(\text{smoke}|\text{drink})$ (read "the probability that people smoke given that they drink").

What is the probability that someone drinks?

Answer: $P(\text{drink}) = \frac{900}{1200} = .75$

What is the probability that students drink given that they smoke?

Answer: $P(\text{drink}|\text{smoke}) = \frac{315}{480} = .65625$

A formula for conditional probability is given by

$$P(E|F) = \frac{P(E \cap F)}{P(F)}$$

Example 9.10.   If 90% of the households in a certain region have answering machines and 50% have both answering machines and call waiting, what is the probability that a household chosen at random and found to have an answering machine also has call waiting?

Answer:

$P(\text{call waiting}|\text{answering machine})$

$= \dfrac{P(\text{call waiting} \cap \text{answering machine})}{P(\text{answering machine})} = \dfrac{.5}{.9} = \dfrac{5}{9}$

Example 9.11.   A psychologist interested in right-handedness versus left-handedness and in IQ scores collected the following data from a random sample of 2000 high school students.

	Right-handed	Left-handed	
High IQ	190	10	200
Normal IQ	1710	90	1800
	1900	100	2000

What is the probability that a student from this group has a high IQ?

Answer: $P(\text{high IQ}) = \frac{200}{2000} = .1$

What is the probability that a student has a high IQ given that she is left-handed?

Answer: $P(\text{high IQ}|\text{left-handed}) = \frac{10}{100} = .1$

Note that the probability of having a high IQ is not affected by the fact that the student is left-handed. We say that the two events, high IQ and left-handed, are *independent*.

That is, E and F are independent if $P(E|F) = P(E)$, and earlier it was noted that in this case we also have

$$P(E \cap F) = P(E)P(F)$$

Multistage Probability Calculations

Example 9.12.   A videocassette recorder (VCR) manufacturer receives 70% of his parts from factory F1 and the rest from factory F2. Suppose that 3% of the output from F1 are defective, while only 2% of the output from F2 are defective. What is the probability a received part is defective?

Answer: In such problems it is helpful to draw a tree diagram like the following.

We then have

$$P(F1 \cap def) = P(F1)P(def|F1) = (.7)(.03) = .021$$

$$P(F2 \cap def) = P(F2)P(def|F2) = (.3)(.02) = .006$$

At this stage a Venn diagram is helpful in finishing the problem:

$$P(def) = P(F1 \cap def) + P(F2 \cap def) = .021 + .006 = .027$$

We can take the above analysis one stage further and answer such questions as: If a randomly chosen part is defective, what is the probability it came from factory F1? From factory F2?

$$P(F1|def) = \frac{P(F1 \cap def)}{P(def)} = \frac{.021}{.027} \approx .778$$

$$P(F2|\text{def}) = \frac{P(F2 \cap \text{def})}{P(\text{def})} = \frac{.006}{.027} \approx .222$$

Example 9.13. Suppose that three branches of a local bank average, respectively, 120, 180, and 100 clients per day. Suppose further that the probabilities that a client will transact business involving more than $100 during a visit are, respectively, .5, .6, and .7. A client is chosen at random. What is the probability that the client will transact business involving over $100? What is the probability that the client went to the first branch given that she transacted business involving over $100?

Answer: $P(B1) = \frac{120}{400} = .3$, $P(B2) = \frac{180}{400} = .45$, and $P(B3) = \frac{100}{400} = .25$. Then we have

Now $P(> \$100) = .15 + .27 + .175 = .595$, and $P(B1| > \$100) = \frac{.3}{.595} \approx .504$.

Discrete Random Variables and Their Probability Distributions

Often each outcome of an experiment has not only an associated probability but also an associated *real number*. For example, the probability may be $\frac{1}{2}$ that there are five defective batteries, the probability may be .01 that a company receives seven contracts, or the probability may be .95 that three people recover from a disease. If X represents the different numbers associated with the potential outcomes of some chance situation, we call X a *random variable*.

Example 9.14. A prison official knows that $\frac{1}{2}$ of the inmates he admits stay only 1 day, $\frac{1}{4}$ stay 2 days, $\frac{1}{5}$ stay 3 days, and $\frac{1}{20}$ stay 4 days before they are either released or are sent on to the county jail. If X represents the number of days, then X is a random variable that takes the value 1 with probability $\frac{1}{2}$, the value 2 with probability $\frac{1}{4}$, the value 3 with probability $\frac{1}{5}$, and the value 4 with probability $\frac{1}{20}$.

The random variable in Example 9.14 is called *discrete* because it can assume only a countable number of values. The random variable in Example 9.15, however, is said to be *continuous* because it can assume values associated with a whole line interval.

Example 9.15. Let X be a random variable whose values correspond to the speeds at which a jet plane can fly. The jet may be traveling at 623.478 ... miles per hour or at any other speed in some whole interval. We might ask what the probability is that the plane is flying at between 300 and 400 miles per hour.

A *probability distribution* for a discrete variable is a listing or formula giving the probability for each value of the random variable.

In many applications, such as coin tossing, there are only *two* possible outcomes. For example, on each toss either the psychic guesses correctly or she guesses incorrectly, either a radio is defective or it is not defective, either the workers will go on strike or they will not walk out, either the manager's salary is above $50,000 or it does not exceed $50,000. In some applications such two-outcome situations are repeated many times. For example, we can ask about the chances that at most one out of four tires is defective, that at least three out of five unions will vote to go on strike, or that exactly two out of three executives have salaries above $50,000. For applications in which a two-outcome situation is repeated a certain number of times and the probability of each of the two outcomes remains the same for each repetition, the resulting calculations involve what are known as *binomial probabilities*.

Example 9.16. Suppose the probability that a light bulb is defective is .1. What is the probability that four light bulbs are all defective?

Answer: Because of independence (i.e., whether one light bulb is defective is not influenced by whether any other light bulb is defective), we can multiply individual probabilities of being defective to find the probability that all the bulbs are defective:

$$(.1)(.1)(.1)(.1) = (.1)^4 = .0001$$

Example 9.17. Again suppose the probability that a light bulb is defective is .1. What is the probability that exactly two out of three light bulbs are defective?

Answer: We subdivide the problem as follows: The probability that the first two bulbs are defective and the third is good is $(.1)(.1)(.9) = .009$. (Note that if the probability of being defective is .1, the probability of being good is .9.) The probability that the first bulb is good and the other two are defective is $(.9)(.1)(.1) = .009$. Finally, the probability that the second bulb is good and the other two are defective is $(.1)(.9)(.1) = .009$. Summing, we find that the probability that exactly two out of three bulbs are defective is $.009 + .009 + .009 = .027$.

Example 9.18.   If the probability that a light bulb is defective is .1, what is the probability that exactly three out of eight light bulbs are defective?

Answer: Again we can subdivide the problem. For example, the probability that the first, third, and seventh bulbs are defective and the rest are good is

$$(.1)(.9)(.1)(.9)(.9)(.9)(.1)(.9) = (.1)^3(.9)^5 = .00059049$$

The probability that the second, third, and fifth bulbs are defective and the rest are good is

$$(.9)(.1)(.1)(.9)(.1)(.9)(.9)(.9) = (.1)^3(.9)^5 = .00059049$$

As can be seen, the probability of any particular arrangement of three defective and five good bulbs is $(.1)^3(.9)^5 = .00059049$. How many such arrangements are there? In other words, in how many ways can we pick three of eight positions for the defective bulbs (the remaining five positions are for good bulbs)? The answer is given by *combinations:*

$$\binom{8}{3} = \frac{8!}{5!3!} = \frac{8 \times 7 \times 6}{3 \times 2} = 56$$

Each of these 56 arrangements has a probability of .00059049. Thus, the probability that exactly three out of eight light bulbs are defective is $56 \times .00059049 = .03306744$:

$$\binom{8}{3}(.1)^3(.9)^5 = \frac{8!}{3!5!}(.1)^3(.9)^5 = .03306744$$

Example 9.19.   Suppose 30% of the employees in a large factory are smokers. What is the probability that there will be exactly two smokers in a randomly chosen five-person work group?

Answer: We reason as follows. The probability that a person smokes is $30\% = .3$, and so the probability that he or she does not smoke is $1 - .3 = .7$. The probability of a particular arrangement of two smokers and three nonsmokers is $(.3)^2(.7)^3 = .03087$. The number of such arrangements is

$$\binom{5}{2} = \frac{5!}{2!3!} = 10$$

Each such arrangement has probability .03087, and so the final answer is $10 \times .03087 = .3087$.

$$\binom{5}{2}(.3)^2(.7)^3 = \frac{5!}{2!3!}(.3)^2(.7)^3 = .3087$$

We can state the general principle as follows.

Binomial formula Suppose an experiment has two possible outcomes, called *success* and *failure,* with the probability of success equal to p and the probability of failure equal to q (of course, $p + q = 1$). Suppose further that the experiment is repeated n times and that the outcome at any particular time has no influence over the outcome at any other time. Then the probability of exactly k successes (and thus $n - k$ failures) is

$$\binom{n}{k} p^k q^{n-k} = \frac{n!}{k!(n-k)!} p^k q^{n-k}$$

Example 9.20. A manager notes that there is a .125 probability that any employee will arrive late for work. What is the probability that exactly one person in a six-person department will arrive late?

Answer: If the probability of being late is .125, the probability of being on time is $1 - .125 = .875$. If one person out of six is late, $6 - 1 = 5$ will be on time. Thus the desired probability is

$$\binom{6}{1}(.125)^1(.875)^5 = 6(.125)(.875)^5 = .385$$

Many, perhaps most, applications of probability involve such phrases as *at least, at most, less than,* and *more than.* In these cases, solutions involve summing two or more cases.

Example 9.21. A manufacturer has the following quality control check at the end of a production line: If at least eight of ten randomly picked articles meet all specifications, the whole shipment is approved. If, in reality, 85% of a particular shipment meet all specifications, what is the probability that the shipment will make it through the control check?

Answer: The probability of an item meeting specifications is .85, and so the probability of it not meeting specifications must be .15. We want to determine the probability that at least eight out of ten articles will meet specifications, that is, the probability that exactly eight or exactly nine or exactly ten articles will meet specifications. We sum the three binomial probabilities:

Exactly 8 of 10 meet specifications	Exactly 9 of 10 meet specifications	Exactly 10 of 10 meet specifications

$$\binom{10}{8}(.85)^8(.15)^2 \ + \ \binom{10}{9}(.85)^9(.15)^1 \ + \ \binom{10}{10}(.85)^{10}(.15)^0$$

$$= \frac{10!}{8!2!}(.85)^8(.15)^2 + 10(.85)^9(.15) + (.85)^{10} \approx .820$$

Example 9.22. For the problem in Example 9.21, what is the probability that a shipment in which only 70% of the articles meet specifications will make it through the control check?

Answer:

$$\binom{10}{8}(.7)^8(.3)^2 + \binom{10}{9}(.7)^9(.3)^1 + \binom{10}{10}(.7)^{10}(.3)^0$$
$$= 45(.7)^8(.3)^2 + 10(.7)^9(.3) + (.7)^{10}$$
$$\approx .383$$

In some situations it is easier to calculate the probability of the complementary event and subtract this value from 1.

Example 9.23. Joe DiMaggio had a career batting average of .325. What was the probability that he would get at least one hit in five official times at bat?

Answer: We could sum the probabilities of exactly one hit, two hits, three hits, four hits, and five hits. However, the complement of "at least one hit" is "zero hits." The probability of no hit is

$$\binom{5}{0}(.325)^0(.675)^5 = (.675)^5 \approx .140$$

and thus the probability of at least one hit in five times at bat is $1 - .140 = .860$.

Example 9.24. A grocery store manager notes that 35% of customers who buy a particular product make use of a store coupon to receive a discount. If seven people purchase the product, what is the probability that fewer than four will use a coupon?

Answer: In this situation, "fewer than four" means zero, one, two, or three.

$$\binom{7}{0}(.35)^0(.65)^7 + \binom{7}{1}(.35)^1(.65)^6 + \binom{7}{2}(.35)^2(.65)^5 + \binom{7}{3}(.35)^3(.65)^4$$
$$= (.65)^7 + 7(.35)(.65)^6 + 21(.35)^2(.65)^5 + 35(.35)^3(.65)^4$$
$$\approx .800$$

Sometimes we are asked to calculate the probability of each of the possible outcomes (the results should sum to 1).

Example 9.25. If the probability that a male birth will occur is .51, what is the probability that a five-child family will have all boys? Exactly four boys? Exactly three boys? Exactly two boys? Exactly one boy? All girls?

Answer:

$$P(5 \text{ boys}) = \binom{5}{5}(.51)^5(.49)^0 = (.51)^5 = .0345$$

$$P(4 \text{ boys}) = \binom{5}{4}(.51)^4(.49)^1 = 5(.51)^4(.49) = .1657$$

$$P(3 \text{ boys}) = \binom{5}{3}(.51)^3(.49)^2 = 10(.51)^3(.49)^2 = .3185$$

$$P(2 \text{ boys}) = \binom{5}{2}(.51)^2(.49)^3 = 10(.51)^2(.49)^3 = .3060$$

$$P(1 \text{ boy}) = \binom{5}{1}(.51)^1(.49)^4 = 5(.51)(.49)^4 = .1470$$

$$P(0 \text{ boys}) = \binom{5}{0}(.51)^0(.49)^5 = (.49)^5 = .0283$$

$$\overline{ 1.0000}$$

A list such as the one in Example 9.25 shows the entire *probability distribution,* which in this case refers to a listing of all outcomes and their probabilities.

Simulation of Probability Distributions, Including Binomial and Geometric

Instead of algebraic calculations, sometimes we can use simulation to answer probability questions.

Example 9.26. A study reported by Liu and Schutz states that in hockey the better team has a 65% chance of scoring the first goal in overtime. If a team is considered the better team in all five of its overtime games, is it reasonable to believe that it will score the first goal in at least four of these games? Answer the question using simulation.

Answer: Since the team will score first 65% of the time, let the digits 01–65 represent this outcome. To simulate five games select ten digits from the random number table and look at them two at a time. Among the five pairs, note how many times 01–65 appear. Underlining these pairs gives

8417706757	1761315582	5150681435	4105092031	0644905059
5988431180	5311584469	9486857967	0581184514	7501113006
6339555041	1586606589	1311971020	8594091932	0648874987
5435552704	9035902649	4749671567	9426808844	2629464759
0898957024	9728400637	8928303514	5919507635	0330972605
2935723737	6788103668	3387635841	5286923114	1586438942

For example, in the first group of five pairs, two (17 and 57) out of five are between 01 and 65. In the second group, four (17, 61, 31, and 55) out of five are in the range. Tabulating the frequencies of each result gives

Number of First Goals	Frequency
0	1
1	0
2	4
3	8
4	13
5	4

In this simulation we see that the better team will score the first goal in at least four of the five overtime games 17 out of 30 times. Thus the answer to the original question is that it is not unreasonable to believe that the better team will win at least four of the five games.

It is easy to confuse *number of samples* with *sample size*. Note that above we have simulated 30 samples of five games each.

In Example 9.26 simulation is used with regard to a binomial distribution, while in the example below it is used with regard to what is called a geometric distribution. A *geometric distribution* shows the number of trials needed until a success is achieved.

Example 9.27.   Suppose the probability that a company will land a contract is .3. Use simulation to find the probability that the company will first land a contract on the first bid, on the second, on the third, and so on.

Answer: Let 0, 1, and 2 represent landing a contract, while 3–9 represent not getting the contract. Read the random number table, one digit at a time, noting how many digits must be read until a 0, 1, or 2 is encountered. Using the table in Example 9.24 results in

> 841(first success in third try)
> 770(first success in third try)
> 67571(first success in fifth try)
> 761(first success in third try)
> 31(first success in second try).

Continuing in this fashion and tabulating the results, we have

Number of Tries Before First Success	Frequency
1	21
2	19
3	16
4	7
5	9
Over 5	12

Thus we estimate the probabilities as follows:

Number of Tries Before First Success	Estimated Probability
1	$\frac{21}{84} = .25$
2	$\frac{19}{84} = .23$
3	$\frac{16}{84} = .19$
4	$\frac{7}{84} = .08$
5	$\frac{9}{84} = .11$
Over 5	$\frac{12}{84} = .14$

One example of simulating a nonbinomial distribution is the following.

Example 9.28.   If a two-person committee is chosen at random from a group consisting of three supervisors and six employees, what is the probability that the committee will have exactly one supervisor and one employee? Use simulation to estimate the answer.

Answer: Let the digits 1, 2, and 3 represent the supervisors, and the digits 4, 5, 6, 7, 8, and 9 represent the employees. Our procedure is to pick digits one at a time from a random number table, ignoring repeats and ignoring 0's, until two different digits have been chosen. Reading from the random number table in Exercise 9.26 results in the committees (8, 4) with two employees, (1, 7) with one of each, (7, 6) with two employees, (7, 5) with two employees, (7, 1) with one of each, (7, 6) with two employees, (1, 3) with two supervisors, and so on. Tabulating from the table gives

    Two supervisors: 11
    One of each: 53
    Two employees: 66.

Thus an estimate of the probability that the committee will consist of one supervisor and one employee is $\frac{53}{130} = .41$.

Mean (Expected Value) and Standard Deviation of a Random Variable, Including Binomial

A bettor placing a chip on a number in roulette has a small chance of winning a lot and a large chance of losing a little. To determine whether the bet is "fair," we must be able to calculate the *expected value* of the game to the bettor. An insurance company in any given year pays out a large sum of money to each of a relatively small number of people, while collecting a small sum of money from each of many other individuals. To determine policy premiums an actuary must calculate the expected values relating to deaths in various age groups of policyholders.

Example 9.29.   Concessionaires know that attendance at a football stadium will be 60,000 on a clear day, 45,000 if there is light snow, and 15,000 if there is heavy snow. Furthermore, the probability of clear skies, light snow, or heavy snow on any particular day is $\frac{1}{2}$, $\frac{1}{3}$, and $\frac{1}{6}$, respectively. (Here we have a random variable X that takes the values 60,000, 45,000, and 15,000.)

Outcome:	Clear skies	Light snow	Heavy snow
Probability:	$\frac{1}{2}$	$\frac{1}{3}$	$\frac{1}{6}$
Random variable:	60,000	45,000	15,000

What average attendance should be expected for the season?

Answer: We reason as follows. Suppose on, say, 12 game days we have clear skies $\frac{1}{2}$ of the time (6 days), a light snow $\frac{1}{3}$ of the time (4 days), and a heavy snow $\frac{1}{6}$ of the time (2 days). Then the average attendance will be

$$\frac{(6 \times 60,000) + (4 \times 45,000) + (2 \times 15,000)}{12} = 47,500$$

Note that we could have divided the 12 into each of the three terms in the numerator to obtain

$$\left(\frac{6}{12} \times 60,000\right) + \left(\frac{4}{12} \times 45,000\right) + \left(\frac{2}{12} \times 15,000\right)$$

or, equivalently,

$$\left(\frac{1}{2} \times 60,000\right) + \left(\frac{1}{3} \times 45,000\right) + \left(\frac{1}{6} \times 15,000\right) = 47,500$$

Actually, there was no need to consider 12 days. We could have simply multiplied probabilities by corresponding attendances and summed the resulting products.

The final calculation in Example 9.29 motivates our definition of expected value. The *expected value* (or *average* or *mean*) of a random variable X is the sum of the products obtained by multiplying each value x_i by the corresponding probability p_i:

$$E(X) = \mu_x = \sum x_i p_i$$

Example 9.30. In a lottery, 10,000 tickets are sold at \$1 each with a prize of \$7500 for one winner. What is the average result for each bettor?

Answer: The actual winning payoff is \$7499 because the winner paid \$1 for a ticket, so we have

Outcome:	Win	Lose
Probability:	$\frac{1}{10,000}$	$\frac{9,999}{10,000}$
Random variable:	7499	−1

$$\text{Expected Value} = 7499\left(\frac{1}{10,000}\right) + (-1)\left(\frac{9999}{10,000}\right) = -0.25$$

Thus the *average* result for each person betting on the lottery is a \$0.25 loss. Alternatively, we can say that the expected payoff to the lottery system is \$0.25 for each ticket sold.

Example 9.31. A manager must choose among three options. Option A has a 10% chance of resulting in a \$250,000 gain but otherwise will result in a \$10,000 loss. Option B has a 50% chance of gaining \$40,000 and a 50% chance of losing \$2000. Finally, option C has a 5% chance of gaining \$800,000 but otherwise will result in a loss of \$20,000. Which option should the manager choose?

Answer: Calculate the expected values of the three options:

	Option A		**Option B**		**Option C**	
Outcome	Gain	Loss	Gain	Loss	Gain	Loss
Probability	.10	.90	.50	.50	.05	.95
Random variable	250,000	−10,000	40,000	−2,000	800,000	−20,000

$$
\begin{aligned}
E(A) &= .10(250,000) + .90(-10,000) = \$16,000 \\
E(B) &= .50(40,000) + .50(-2000) = \$19,000 \\
E(C) &= .05(800,000) + .95(-20,000) = \$21,000
\end{aligned}
$$

The manager should choose option C! However, although option C has the greatest mean (expected value), the manager may well wish to consider the relative riskiness of the various options. If, for example, a \$5000 loss would be disastrous for the company, the manager might well decide to choose option B with its maximum possible loss of $2000. (It should be intuitively clear that some concept of variance would be helpful here in measuring the risk; later in this topic the variance of a random variable will be defined.)

Suppose we have a *binomial random variable,* that is, a random variable whose values are the numbers of "successes" in some binomial probability distribution.

Example 9.32.   Of the automobiles produced at a particular plant, 40% had a certain defect. Suppose a company purchases five of these cars. What is the expected value for the number of cars with defects?

Answer: We might guess that the average or mean or expected value is 40% of $5 = .4 \times 5 = 2$, but let's calculate from the definition. Letting X represent the number of cars with the defect, we have

$$P(0) = \binom{5}{0}(.4)^0(.6)^5 = \quad (.6)^5 \quad = .07776$$

$$P(1) = \binom{5}{1}(.4)^1(.6)^4 = 5(.4)(.6)^4 = .25920$$

$$P(2) = \binom{5}{2}(.4)^2(.6)^3 = 10(.4)^2(.6)^3 = .34560$$

$$P(3) = \binom{5}{3}(.4)^3(.6)^2 = 10(.4)^3(.6)^2 = .23040$$

$$P(4) = \binom{5}{4}(.4)^4(.6)^1 = 5(.4)^4(.6) = .07680$$

$$P(5) = \binom{5}{5}(.4)^5(.6)^0 = \quad (.4)^5 \quad = .01024$$

Outcome (no. of cars):	0	1	2	3	4	5
Probability:	.07776	.25920	.34560	.23040	.07680	.01024
Random variable:	0	1	2	3	4	5

$$
\begin{aligned}
E(X) &= 0(.07776) + 1(.25920) + 2(.34560) + 3(.23040) \\
&\quad + 4(.07680) + 5(.01024) \\
&= 2
\end{aligned}
$$

Thus the answer turns out to be the same as would be obtained by simply multiplying the probability of a "success" by the number of cases.

The following is true: If we have a binomial probability situation with the probability of a success equal to p and the number of trials equal to n, the expected value or mean number of successes for the n trials is np.

Example 9.33. An insurance salesperson is able to sell policies to 15% of the people she contacts. Suppose she contacts 120 people during a 2-week period. What is the expected value for the number of policies she sells?

Answer: We have a binomial probability with the probability of a success .15 and the number of trials 120, and so the mean or expected value for the number of successes is $120 \times .15 = 18$.

We have seen that the mean of a random variable is $\Sigma x_i p_i$. However, not only is the mean important, but also we would like to measure the variability for the values taken on by a random variable. Since we are dealing with chance events, the proper tool is variance. *Variance* was defined in Topic Two to be the mean average of the squared deviations $(x - \mu)^2$. If we regard the $(x - \mu)^2$ terms as the values of some random variable (whose probability is the same as the probability of x), the mean of this new random variable is $\Sigma(x_i - \mu_x)^2 p_i$, which is precisely how we define the variance σ^2 of a random variable:

$$\text{var}(X) = \sigma_x^2 = \sum(x_i - \mu_x)^2 p_i$$

As before, the standard deviation σ is the square root of the variance.

Example 9.34. A highway engineer knows that his crew can lay 5 miles of highway on a clear day, 2 miles on a rainy day, and only 1 mile on a snowy day. Suppose the probabilities are as follows:

Outcome:	Clear	Rain	Snow
Probability:	.6	.3	.1
Random variable (miles of highway):	5	2	1

What are the mean (expected value) and the variance?

Answer:

$$\mu_x = \sum x_i p_i = 5(.6) + 2(.3) + 1(.1) = 3.7$$

$$\begin{aligned} \sigma_x^2 &= \sum(x_i - \mu_x)^2 p_i = (5 - 3.7)^2(.6) + (2 - 3.7)^2(.3) \\ &\quad + (1 - 3.7)^2(.1) \\ &= 2.61 \end{aligned}$$

Example 9.35. Look again at Example 9.32. We calculated the mean to be 2. What is the variance?

Answer: $\sigma^2 = (0-2)^2(.07776) + (1-2)^2(.2592) + (2-2)^2(.3456) + (3-2)^2(.2304) + (4-2)^2(.0768) + (5-2)^2(.01024) = 1.2$

Could we have calculated the above result more easily? In this case, we have a binomial random variable and the variance can be simply calculated as $npq = np(1-p)$.

Example 9.36.   How can we use this method to calculate the variance in Example 9.35 more simply?

Answer: $np(1-p) = 5(.4)(.6) = 1.2$

Thus, for a random variable X,

Mean or expected value: $\mu_x = \sum x_i p_i$

Variance: $\sigma_x^2 = \sum (x_i - \mu_x)^2 p_i$

Standard deviation: $\sigma_x = \sqrt{\sum (x_i - \mu_x)^2 p_i}.$

In the case of a binomial probability distribution with probability of a success equal to p and number of trials equal to n, if we let X be the number of successes in the n trials, the above equations become

Mean or expected value: $\mu_x = np$

Variance: $\sigma_x^2 = npq = np(1-p)$

Standard deviation: $\sigma_x = \sqrt{npq} = \sqrt{np(1-p)}.$

Example 9.37.   Sixty percent of all buyers of new cars choose automatic transmissions. For a group of five buyers of new cars, calculate the mean and standard deviation for the number of buyers choosing automatic transmissions.

Answer:

$$\begin{aligned}
\mu_x &= np = 5(.6) = 3.0 \\
\sigma_x &= \sqrt{np(1-p)} = \sqrt{5(.6)(.4)} \approx 1.1
\end{aligned}$$

Questions on Topic Nine: Probability as Relative Frequency

Multiple-Choice Questions

> *Directions:*   The questions or incomplete statements that follow are each followed by five suggested answers or completions. Choose the response that best answers the question or completes the statement.

1. Of the coral reef species on the Great Barrier Reef off Australia, 73% are poisonous. If a tourist boat taking divers to different points off the reef encounters an average of 25 coral reef species, what are the mean and standard deviation for the expected number of poisonous species seen?

    (A) $\mu_x = 6.75$, $\sigma_x = 4.93$
    (B) $\mu_x = 18.25$, $\sigma_x = 2.22$
    (C) $\mu_x = 18.25$, $\sigma_x = 4.93$
    (D) $\mu_x = 18.25$, $\sigma_x = 8.88$
    (E) None of the above gives a set of correct answers.

2. In the November 27, 1994, issue of *Parade* magazine, the "Ask Marilyn" section contained this question: "Suppose a person was having two surgeries performed at the same time. If the chances of success for surgery A are 85%, and the chances of success for surgery B are 90%, what are the chances that both would fail?" What do you think of Marilyn's solution: $(.15)(.10) = .015$ or 1.5%?

    (A) Her solution is mathematically correct but not explained very well.
    (B) Her solution is both mathematically correct and intuitively obvious.
    (C) Her use of complementary events is incorrect.
    (D) Her use of the general addition formula is incorrect.
    (E) She assumed independence of events, which is most likely wrong.

3. In November 1994, Intel announced that a "subtle flaw" in its Pentium chip would affect 1 in 9 billion division problems. Suppose a computer performs 20 million divisions (a not unreasonable number) in the course of a particular program. What is the probability of no error? Of at least one error?

    (A) .99778, .00222
    (B) .000000000111, .00222
    (C) .000000000111, .999999999889
    (D) .999999999889, .000000000111
    (E) .999999999889, .00222

4. According to a CBS/*New York Times* poll taken in 1992, 15% of the public have responded to a telephone call-in poll. In a random group of five people, what is the probability that exactly two have responded to a call-in poll?

    (A) .138
    (B) .165
    (C) .300
    (D) .835
    (E) .973

5. In a 1974 "Dear Abby" letter a woman lamented that she had just given birth to her eighth child, and all were girls! Her doctor had assured her that the chance of the eighth child being a girl was only 1 in 100.

   a. What was the real probability that the eighth child would be a girl?
   b. Before the birth of the first child, what was the probability that the woman would give birth to eight girls in a row?

   (A) .5, .0039
   (B) .0039, .0039
   (C) .5, .5
   (D) .0039, .4
   (E) .5, .01

6. The yearly mortality rate for American men from prostate cancer has been constant for decades at about 25 of every 100,000 men. (This rate has not changed in spite of new diagnostic techniques and new treatments.) In a group of 100 American men, what is the probability that at least 1 will die from prostate cancer in a given year?

   (A) .00025
   (B) .0247
   (C) .025
   (D) .9753
   (E) .99975

7. Alan Dershowitz, one of O. J. Simpson's lawyers, has stated that only 1 out of every 1000 abusive relationships ends in murder each year. If he is correct, and if there are approximately 1.5 million abusive relationships in the United States, what is the expected value for the number of people who are killed each year by an abusive partner?

   (A) 1
   (B) 500
   (C) 1000
   (D) 1500
   (E) None of the above

8. A television game show has three payoffs with the following probabilities:

Payoff ($):	0	1000	10,000
Probability:	.6	.3	.1

   What are the mean and standard deviation for the payoff variable?

   (A) $\mu_x = 1300$, $\sigma_x = 2934$
   (B) $\mu_x = 1300$, $\sigma_x = 8802$
   (C) $\mu_x = 3667$, $\sigma_x = 4497$
   (D) $\mu_x = 3667$, $\sigma_x = 5508$
   (E) None of the above gives a set of correct answers.

9. Suppose that among the 6000 students at a high school, 1500 are taking honors courses and 1800 prefer watching basketball to watching football. If taking honors courses and preferring basketball are independent, how many students are both taking honors courses and prefer basketball to football?

(A) 300

(B) 330

(C) 450

(D) 825

(E) There is insufficient information to answer this question.

10. As reported in *The New York Times* (February 19, 1995, p. 12), the Russian Health Ministry announced that one-quarter of the country's hospitals had no sewage system and one-seventh had no running water. What is the probability that a Russian hospital will have at least one of these problems

    a. if the two problems are independent?

    b. if hospitals with a running water problem are a subset of those with a sewage problem?

(A) 11/28, 1/4

(B) 11/28, 1/7

(C) 9/28, 1/4

(D) 9/28, 1/7

(E) 5/14, 1/4

11. An inspection procedure at a manufacturing plant involves picking three items at random and then accepting the whole lot if at least two of the three items are in perfect condition. If in reality 90% of the whole lot are perfect, what is the probability that the lot will be accepted?

(A) .600

(B) .667

(C) .729

(D) .810

(E) .972

12. Suppose that, in a certain part of the world, in any 50-year period the probability of a major plague is .39, the probability of a major famine is .52, and the probability of both a plague and a famine is .15. What is the probability of a famine given that there is a plague?

(A) .240

(B) .288

(C) .370

(D) .385

(E) .760

13. Suppose that, for any given year, the probabilities that the stock market declines, that women's hemlines are lower, and that both events occur are, respectively, .4, .35, and .3. Are the two events independent?

(A) Yes, because $(.4)(.35) \neq .3$.

(B) No, because $(.4)(.35) \neq .3$.

(C) Yes, because $.4 > .35 > .3$.

(D) No, because $.5(.3 + .4) = .35$.

(E) There is insufficient information to answer this question.

14. If $P(A) = .2$ and $P(B) = .1$, what is $P(A \cup B)$ if A and B are independent?

   (A) .02
   (B) .28
   (C) .30
   (D) .32
   (E) There is insufficient information to answer this question.

15. The following data are from *The Commissioner's Standard Ordinary Table of Mortality:*

Age	Number Surviving
0	10,000,000
20	9,664,994
40	9,241,359
70	5,592,012

   What is the probability that a 20-year-old will survive to be 70?

   (A) .407
   (B) .421
   (C) .559
   (D) .579
   (E) .966

16. At a warehouse sale 100 customers are invited to choose one of 100 identical boxes. Five boxes contain $700 color television sets, 25 boxes contain $540 camcorders, and the remaining boxes contain $260 cameras. What should a customer be willing to pay to participate in the sale?

   (A) $260
   (B) $352
   (C) $500
   (D) $540
   (E) $699

17. There are two games involving flipping a coin. In the first game you win a prize if you can throw between 40% and 60% heads. In the second game you win if you can throw more than 75% heads. For each game would you rather flip the coin 50 times or 500 times?

   (A) 50 times for each game
   (B) 500 times for each game
   (C) 50 times for the first game, and 500 for the second
   (D) 500 times for the first game, and 50 for the second
   (E) The outcomes of the games do not depend on the number of flips

18. Which of the following are true statements?

   I. The probability of an event is always at least 0 and at most 1.
   II. The probability that an event will happen is always 1 minus the probability that it won't happen.
   III. If two events cannot occur simultaneously, the probability that at least one event will occur is the sum of the respective probabilities of the two events.

(A) I and II

(B) I and III

(C) II and III

(D) I, II, and III

(E) None of the above gives the complete set of true responses.

19. Suppose there are five outcomes to an experiment and a computer calculates the respective probabilities of the outcomes to be .4, .5, .3, 0, and −.2. The proper conclusion is that

(A) the sum of the individual probabilities is 1.

(B) one of the outcomes will never occur.

(C) one of the outcomes will occur 50% of the time.

(D) all of the above are true.

(E) there is a bug in the computer program.

20. The average annual incomes of high school and college graduates in a midwestern town are $21,000 and $35,000, respectively. If a company hires only personnel with at least a high school diploma and 20% of its employees have been through college, what is the mean income of the company employees?

(A) $23,800

(B) $27,110

(C) $28,000

(D) $32,200

(E) $56,000

21. An insurance company charges $800 annually for car insurance. The policy specifies that the company will pay $1000 for a minor accident and $5000 for a major accident. If the probability of a motorist having a minor accident during the year is .2, and of having a major accident, .05, how much can the insurance company expect to make on a policy?

(A) $200

(B) $250

(C) $300

(D) $350

(E) $450

22. Which of the following are true statements?

I. By the law of large numbers, the mean of a random variable will get closer and closer to a specific value.

II. The standard deviation of a random variable is never negative.

III. The standard deviation of a random variable is 0 only if the random variable takes a lone single value.

(A) I and II

(B) I and III

(C) II and III

(D) I, II, and III

(E) None of the above gives the complete set of true responses.

23. You can choose one of three boxes. Box A has four $5 bills and a single $100 bill, box B has 400 $5 bills and 100 $100 bills, and box C has 24 $1 bills. You can have all of box C or blindly pick one bill out of either box A or box B. Which offers the greatest expected winning?

(A) Box A
(B) Box B
(C) Box C
(D) Either A or B, but not C
(E) All offer the same expected winning.

24. Given that 52% of the U.S. population are female and 15% are older than age 65, can we conclude that $(.52)(.15) = 7.8\%$ are women older than age 65?

(A) Yes, by the multiplication rule.
(B) Yes, by conditional probabilities.
(C) Yes, by the law of large numbers.
(D) No, because the events are not independent.
(E) No, because the events are not mutually exclusive.

25. Companies proved to have violated pollution laws are being fined various amounts with the following probabilities:

Fine ($):	1000	10,000	50,000	100,000
Probability:	.4	.3	.2	.1

What are the mean and standard deviation for the fine variable?

(A) $\mu_x = 40,250, \sigma_x = 39,118$
(B) $\mu_x = 40,250, \sigma_x = 45,169$
(C) $\mu_x = 23,400, \sigma_x = 31,350$
(D) $\mu_x = 23,400, \sigma_x = 85,185$
(E) None of the above gives a set of correct answers.

Questions 26–30 refer to the following study: One thousand students at a city high school were classified both according to GPA and whether or not they consistently skipped classes.

	GPA <2.0	GPA 2.0–3.0	GPA >3.0	
Many skipped classes	80	25	5	110
Few skipped classes	175	450	265	890
	255	475	270	

26. What is the probability that a student has a GPA between 2.0 and 3.0?

(A) .025
(B) .227
(C) .450
(D) .475
(E) .506

27. What is the probability that a student has a GPA under 2.0 and has skipped many classes?

(A) .080

(B) .281

(C) .285

(D) .314

(E) .727

28. What is the probability that a student has a GPA under 2.0 or has skipped many classes?

(A) .080

(B) .281

(C) .285

(D) .314

(E) .727

29. What is the probability that a student has a GPA under 2.0 given that he has skipped many classes?

(A) .080

(B) .281

(C) .285

(D) .314

(E) .727

30. Are "GPA between 2.0 and 3.0" and "skipped few classes" independent?

(A) No, because .475 ≠ .506.

(B) No, because .475 ≠ .890.

(C) No, because .450 ≠ .475.

(D) Yes, because of conditional probabilities.

(E) Yes, because of the product rule.

31. Mathematically speaking, casinos and life insurance companies make a profit because of

(A) their understanding of sampling error and sources of bias.

(B) their use of well-designed, well-conducted surveys and experiments.

(C) their use of simulation of probability distributions.

(D) the central limit theorem.

(E) the law of large numbers.

32. Consider the following table of ages of U.S. senators:

Age (yr):	<40	40–49	50–59	60–69	70–79	>79
Number of senators:	5	30	36	22	5	2

What is the probability that a senator is under 70 years old given that he is at least 50 years old?

(A) .580

(B) .624

(C) .643

(D) .892

(E) .969

Questions 33–36 refer to the following study: Five hundred people used a home test for HIV, and then all underwent more conclusive hospital testing. The accuracy of the home test was evidenced in the following table.

	HIV	Healthy	
Positive test	35	25	60
Negative test	5	435	440
	40	460	

33. What is the *predictive value* of the test? That is, what is the probability that a person has HIV and tests positive?

(A) .070
(B) .130
(C) .538
(D) .583
(E) .875

34. What is the *false-positive* rate? That is, what is the probability of testing positive given that the person does not have HIV?

(A) .054
(B) .050
(C) .130
(D) .417
(E) .875

35. What is the *sensitivity* of the test? That is, what is the probability of testing positive given that the person has HIV?

(A) .070
(B) .130
(C) .538
(D) .583
(E) .875

36. What is the *specificity* of the test? That is, what is the probability of testing negative given that the person does not have HIV?

(A) .125
(B) .583
(C) .870
(D) .950
(E) .946

37. Suppose that 2% of a clinic's patients are known to have cancer. A blood test is developed that is positive in 98% of patients with cancer but is also positive in 3% of patients who do not have cancer. If a person who is chosen at random from the clinic's patients is given the test and it comes out positive, what is the probability that the person actually has cancer?

(A) .02
(B) .4
(C) .5
(D) .6
(E) .98

38. Suppose the probability that you will receive an A in AP Statistics is .35, the probability that you will receive A's in both AP Statistics and AP Biology is .19, and the probability that you will receive an A in AP Statistics but not in AP Biology is .17. Which of the following is a proper conclusion?

    (A) The probability that you will receive an A in AP Biology is .36.
    (B) The probability that you didn't take AP Biology is .01.
    (C) The probability that you will receive an A in AP Biology but not in AP Statistics is .18.
    (D) The given probabilities are impossible.
    (E) None of the above

39. Suppose you are one of 7.5 million people who send in their name for a drawing with 1 top prize of $1 million, 5 second-place prizes of $10,000, and 20 third-place prizes of $100. Is it worth the $0.32 postage it cost you to send in your name?

    (A) Yes, because $\frac{1,000,000}{0.32} = 3,125,000$, which is less than 7,500,000.
    (B) No, because your expected winnings are only $0.14.
    (C) Yes, because $\frac{7,500,000}{(1+5+20)} = 288,462$.
    (D) No, because $1,052,000 < 7,500,000$.
    (E) Yes, because $\frac{1,052,000}{26} = 40,462$.

40. You have a choice of three investments, the first of which gives you a 10% chance of making $1 million, otherwise you lose $25,000; the second of which gives you a 50% chance of making $500,000, otherwise you lose $345,000; and the third of which gives you an 80% chance of making $50,000, otherwise you make only $1,000. Assuming you will go bankrupt if you don't show a profit, which option should you choose for the best chance of avoiding bankruptcy?

    (A) First choice
    (B) Second choice
    (C) Third choice
    (D) Either the first or the second choice
    (E) All the choices give an equal chance of avoiding bankruptcy.

41. Can the function $f(x) = \frac{x+6}{24}$, for $x = 1, 2,$ and 3, be the probability distribution for some random variable?

    (A) Yes.
    (B) No, because probabilities cannot be negative.
    (C) No, because probabilities cannot be greater than 1.
    (D) No, because the probabilities do not sum to 1.
    (E) Not enough information is given to answer the question.

42. Sixty-five percent of all divorce cases cite incompatibility as the underlying reason. If four couples file for a divorce, what is the probability that exactly two will state incompatibility as the reason?

    (A) .104
    (B) .207
    (C) .254
    (D) .311
    (E) .423

43. Suppose we have a random variable X where the probability associated with the value k is $\binom{10}{k}(.37)^k(.63)^{10-k}$ for $k = 0, \ldots, 10$. What is the mean of X?

   (A) 0.37
   (B) 0.63
   (C) 3.7
   (D) 6.3
   (E) None of the above

44. A computer technician notes that 40% of computers fail because of the hard drive, 25% because of the monitor, 20% because of a disk drive, and 15% because of the microprocessor. If the problem is not in the monitor, what is the probability that it is in the hard drive?

   (A) .150
   (B) .400
   (C) .417
   (D) .533
   (E) .650

45. Suppose you toss a coin ten times and it comes up heads every time. Which of the following is a true statement?

   (A) By the law of large numbers, the next toss is more likely to be tails than another heads.
   (B) By the properties of conditional probability, the next toss is more likely to be heads given that ten tosses in a row have been heads.
   (C) Coins actually do have memories, and thus what comes up on the next toss is influenced by the past tosses.
   (D) The law of large numbers tells how many tosses will be necessary before the percentages of heads and tails are again in balance.
   (E) The probability that the next toss will again be heads is .5.

46. Which of the following lead to binomial distributions?

   I. An inspection procedure at an automobile manufacturing plant involves selecting a sample of cars from the assembly line and noting for each car whether there are no defects, at least one major defect, or only minor defects.

   II. As students study more and more during their AP Statistics class, their chances of getting an A on any given test continue to improve. The teacher is interested in the probability of any given student receiving various numbers of A's on the class exams.

   III. A committee of two is to be selected from among the five teachers and ten students attending a meeting. What are the probabilities that the committee will consist of two teachers, of two students, or of exactly one teacher and one student?

   (A) I only
   (B) II only
   (C) III only
   (D) II and III
   (E) None of the above gives the complete set of true responses.

47. Which of the following are true statements?

I. The histogram of a binomial distribution with $p = .5$ is always symmetric no matter what n, the number of trials, is.

II. The histogram of a binomial distribution with $p = .9$ is skewed to the right.

III. The histogram of a binomial distribution with $p = .9$ is almost symmetric if n is very large.

(A) I and II
(B) I and III
(C) II and III
(D) I, II, and III
(E) None of the above gives the complete set of true responses.

48. Suppose that 60% of students who take the AP Statistics exam score 4 or 5, 25% score 3, and the rest score 1 or 2. Suppose further that 95% of those scoring 4 or 5 receive college credit, 50% of those scoring 3 receive such credit, and 4% of those scoring 1 or 2 receive credit. If a student who is chosen at random from among those taking the exam receives college credit, what is the probability that she received a 3 on the exam?

(A) .125
(B) .178
(C) .701
(D) .813
(E) .822

Answer Key

1. **B**	11. **E**	21. **D**	31. **E**	41. **A**
2. **E**	12. **D**	22. **C**	32. **D**	42. **D**
3. **A**	13. **B**	23. **E**	33. **A**	43. **C**
4. **A**	14. **B**	24. **D**	34. **A**	44. **D**
5. **A**	15. **D**	25. **C**	35. **E**	45. **E**
6. **B**	16. **B**	26. **D**	36. **E**	46. **E**
7. **D**	17. **D**	27. **A**	37. **B**	47. **B**
8. **A**	18. **D**	28. **C**	38. **D**	48. **B**
9. **C**	19. **E**	29. **E**	39. **B**	
10. **E**	20. **A**	30. **A**	40. **C**	

Answers Explained

1. **(B)** $\mu = 25(.73) = 18.25$, $\sigma^2 = 25(.73)(.27) = 4.9275$, and $\sigma = 2.22$.

2. **(E)** The probability that *both* events will occur is the product of their separate probabilities only if the events are independent, that is, only if the chance that one event will happen is not influenced by whether or not the second event happens. In this case the probability of different surgeries failing are probably closely related.

3. **(A)** If $p = \frac{1}{9,000,000,000}$, then $P(0 \text{ errors}) = (1-p)^{20,000,000} = .99778$ and $P(\text{at least 1 error}) = 1 - .99778 = .00222$.

4. **(A)** $10(.15)^2(.85)^3 = .138$

5. **(A)**   The probability of the next child being a girl is independent of the gender of the previous children. The probability of having eight girls in a row is $(.5)^8 = .0039$.

6. **(B)** $1 - (.99975)^{100} = .0247$

7. **(D)** $.001(1,500,000) = 1500$

8. **(A)** $\mu = 0(.6) + 1000(.3) + 10,000(.1) = \$1300$, $\sigma^2 = (0 - 1300)^2(.6) + (1000 - 1300)^2(.3) + (10,000 - 1300)^2(.1) = 8,610,000$, and $\sigma = \$2934$.

9. **(C)** $\frac{1500}{6000} = .25$ are honors students, and $\frac{1800}{6000} = .3$ prefer basketball. Because of independence, their intersection is $(.25)(.3) = .075$ of the students, and $.075(6000) = 450$.

10. **(E)** $\frac{1}{4} + \frac{1}{7} - (\frac{1}{4})(\frac{1}{7}) = \frac{5}{14}$. If X is a subset of Y, then $P(X \cup Y) = P(Y)$.

11. **(E)** $(.9)^3 + 3(.9)^2(.1) = .972$

12. **(D)** $P(\text{famine|plague}) = \dfrac{P(\text{famine} \cap \text{plague})}{P(\text{plague})} = \dfrac{.15}{.39} = .385$

13. **(B)**   If E and F are independent, then $P(E \cap F) = P(E)P(F)$; however, in this problem, $(.4)(.35) \ne .3$.

14. **(B)**   Because A and B are independent, we have $P(A \cap B) = P(A)P(B)$, and thus $P(A \cup B) = .2 + .1 - (.2)(.1) = .28$.

15. **(D)** $\dfrac{5,592,012}{9,664,994} = .579$

16. **(B)** $E(X) = \mu_x = \sum x_i p_i = 700(.05) + 540(.25) + 260(.7) = 352$

17. **(D)**   The probability of throwing heads is .5. By the law of large numbers, the more times you flip the coin, the more the relative frequency tends to become closer to this probability. With fewer tosses there is a greater chance of wide swings in the relative frequency.

18. **(D)**   These are all true facts about probability. Note that the more general statement $P(X \cup Y) = P(X) + P(Y) - P(X \cap Y)$ reduces to $P(X \cup Y) = P(X) + P(Y)$ when the two events cannot occur simultaneously.

19. **(E)**   Probabilities are never less than 0.

20. **(A)** $E(X) = \mu_x = \sum x_i p_i = 21,000(.8) + 35,000(.2) = 23,800$

21. **(D)** $1000(.2) + 5000(.05) = 450$, and $800 - 450 = 350$.

22. **(C)**   The mean is an unchanging, fixed number; the law of large numbers gives that the average of observed X values tends to be closer and closer to this mean after more and more repetitions.

23. **(E)** $5(\frac{4}{5}) + 100(\frac{1}{5}) = 24$, and $5(\frac{400}{500}) + 100(\frac{100}{500}) = 24$

24. **(D)** $P(E \cap F) = P(E)P(F)$ only if the events are independent. In this case, women live longer than men and so the events are not independent.

25. **(C)** $\mu = 1000(.4) + 10,000(.3) + 50,000(.2) + 100,000(.1) = 23,400$, $\sigma^2 = (1000 - 23,400)^2(.4) + (10,000 - 23,400)^2(.3) + (50,000 - 23,400)^2(.2) + (100,000 - 23,400)^2(.1) = 982,840,000$, and $\sigma = \$31,350$.

For questions 26–30, we first sum the rows and columns:

	GPA			
	<2.0	2.0–3.0	>3.0	
Many skipped classes	80	25	5	110
Few skipped classes	175	450	265	890
	255	475	270	1000

26. **(D)** $\frac{25+450}{1000} = .475$

27. **(A)** $\frac{80}{1000} = .080$ (probability of an intersection)

28. **(C)** $\frac{80+25+5+175}{1000} = .285$ (probability of a union)

29. **(E)** $\frac{80}{80+25+5} = .727$ (conditional probability)

30. **(A)** $P(2.0\text{–}3.0\ \text{GPA}) = \frac{475}{1000} = .475$; however, $P(2.0\text{–}3.0\ \text{GPA}|\text{few skips}) = \frac{450}{890} = .506$. If independent, these would have been equal.

31. **(E)** While the outcome of any single play on a roulette wheel or the age at death of any particular person is uncertain, the law of large numbers gives that the relative frequencies of specific outcomes in the long run tend to become closer to numbers called probabilities.

32. **(D)** $\frac{36+22}{36+22+5+2} = .892$

33. **(A)** $\frac{35}{500} = .070$

34. **(A)** $\frac{25}{460} = .054$

35. **(E)** $\frac{35}{40} = .875$

36. **(E)** $\frac{435}{460} = .946$

37. **(B)**

$$P(\text{positive test}) = P(\text{cancer} \cap \text{positive test})$$
$$+ P(\text{no cancer} \cap \text{positive test})$$
$$= .0196 + .0294$$
$$= .0490$$

$$P(\text{cancer}|\text{positive test}) = \frac{P(\text{cancer} \cap \text{positive test})}{P(\text{positive test})}$$
$$= \frac{.0196}{.0490}$$
$$= .4$$

38. **(D)** The probability that you will receive an A in AP Statistics but not in AP Biology must be $.35 - .19 = .16$, not $.17$.

39. **(B)** Your expected winnings are only

$$\frac{1}{7,500,000}(1,000,000) + \frac{5}{7,500,000}(10,000) + \frac{20}{7,500,000}(100) = 0.14$$

40. **(C)** Even though the first two choices have a higher expected value than the third choice, the third choice gives a 100% chance of avoiding bankruptcy.

41. **(A)** The probabilities $\frac{7}{24}$, $\frac{8}{24}$, and $\frac{9}{24}$ are all nonnegative, and they sum to 1.

42. **(D)** $6(.65)^2(.35)^2 = .311$

43. **(C)** This is a binomial with $n = 10$ and $p = .37$, and so the mean is $np = 10(.37) = 3.7$.

44. **(D)** $\frac{.40}{.40+.20+.15} = .533$

45. **(E)** Coins have no memory, and so the probability that the next toss will be heads is .5 and the probability that it will be tails is .5. The law of large numbers says that as the number of tosses becomes larger, the percentage of heads tends to become closer to .5.

46. **(E)** None of them lead to binomial distributions. The first has three outcomes, not two. In the second, p increases from test to test. In the third, there is a lack of independence in choosing the first and second people to be on the committee; for example, if the first person chosen is a teacher, the probability that the second will also be a teacher is $\frac{4}{14}$, not $\frac{5}{15}$.

47. **(B)** If $p > .5$, the more likely numbers of successes are to the right and the lower numbers of successes have small probabilities, and so the histogram is skewed to the left. No matter what p is, if n is sufficiently large, the histogram will look almost symmetric.

48. **(B)**

$$P(\text{credit}) = .57 + .125 + .006 = .701$$

$$P(3|\text{credit}) = \frac{P(3 \cap \text{credit})}{P(\text{credit})} = \frac{.125}{.701} = .178$$

Free-Response Questions

> *Directions:* You must show all work and indicate the methods you use. You will be graded on the correctness of your methods and on the accuracy of your final answers.

Six Open-Ended Questions

1. Suppose you will be taking exams in English, statistics, and chemistry tomorrow, and from past experience you know that for each exam you have a 50% chance of receiving an A. List all eight possibilities for receiving A's on the various exams. Letting X represent the number of A's you will receive, show the distribution of X, that is, the values and associated probabilities.

2. A sample of applicants for a management position yields the following numbers with regard to age and experience:

	Years of experience		
	0–5	6–10	>10
Less than 50 years old	80	125	20
More than 50 years old	10	75	50

   a. What is the probability that an applicant is less than 50 years old? Has more than 10 years' experience? Is more than 50 years old and has five or fewer years' experience?

   b. What is the probability that an applicant is less than 50 years old given that she has between 6 and 10 years' experience?

   c. Are the two events "less than 50 years old" and "more than 10 years' experience" independent events? How about the two events "more than 50 years old" and "between 6 and 10 years' experience"? Explain.

3. *The New York Times* (September 21, 1994, p. C10) reported that an American woman diagnosed with ovarian cancer has a 37.5% chance of survival and that approximately 20,000 American women are diagnosed with ovarian cancer each year. Discuss these observations with regard to expected number of deaths and also reference some measure of variability.

4. Suppose USAir accounts for 20% of all U.S. domestic flights. As of mid-1994, USAir was involved in four of the previous seven major disasters. "That's enough to begin getting suspicious but not enough to hang them," said Dr. Brad Efton in *The New York Times* (September 11, 1994, Sec. 4, p.4). Using a binomial distribution, comment on Dr. Efton's remark.

5. Assume there is no overlap between the 56% of the population who wear glasses and the 4% who wear contacts. If 55% of those who wear glasses are women and 63% of those who wear contacts are women, what is the probability that the next person you encounter on the street will be a woman with glasses? A woman with contacts? A man with glasses? A man with contacts? A person not wearing glasses or contacts? Explain your reasoning.

6. Explain what is wrong with each of the following statements:

   a. The probability that a student will score high on the AP Statistics exam is .43, while the probability that she will not score high is .47.

   b. The probability that a student plays tennis is .18, while the probability that he plays basketball is six times as great.

   c. The probability that a student enjoys her English class is .64, while the probability that she enjoys both her English and her social studies classes is .71.

   d. The probability that a student will be accepted by his first choice for college is .38, while the probability that he will be accepted by his first or second choice is .32.

   e. The probability that a student fails AP Statistics and will still be accepted by an Ivy League school is −.17.

Answers Explained

1. The eight possible ways of scoring A's are

English	A	A	A	A	—	—	—	—
Statistics	A	A	—	—	A	A	—	—
Chemistry	A	—	A	—	A	—	A	—

The values and probabilities for X, the number of A's, are found by noting there is one way of receiving no A's, three ways of receiving one A, three ways of receiving two A's, and one way of receiving all A's. Each of the eight ways has probability $\frac{1}{8} = .125$.

Value of X:	0	1	2	3
Probability:	.125	.375	.375	.125

2. It's easiest to first sum the rows and columns:

	Years of experience			
	0–5	6–10	>10	
Less than 50 years old	80	125	20	225
More than 50 years old	10	75	50	135
	90	200	70	360

a. $P(\text{age} < 50) = \frac{225}{360} = .625$

$P(\text{experience} > 10) = \frac{70}{360} = .194$

$P(\text{age} > 50 \cap \text{experience } 6\text{–}10) = \frac{75}{360} = .208$

b. $P(\text{age} < 50 | \text{experience } 6\text{–}10) = \frac{125}{200} = .6$

  c. $P(\text{age} < 50) = \frac{225}{360} = .625$; however, $P(\text{age} < 50 | \text{experience} > 10) = \frac{20}{70} = .286$, and so they are not independent.

   $P(\text{age} > 50) = \frac{135}{360} = .375$ and also $P(\text{age} > 50 | \text{experience } 6\text{–}10) = \frac{75}{200} = .375$, and so these two are independent.

3. The probability of death for a woman diagnosed with ovarian cancer is $1 - .375 = .625$. Thus we are considering a binomial with $n = 20,000$ and $p = .625$. For this we can calculate:

$$\mu_x = 20,000(.625) = 12,500$$
$$\sigma_x = \sqrt{20,000(.625)(.375)} = 68.5$$

Thus one can expect an average of 12,500 deaths per year with a standard deviation of 68.5 deaths among American women diagnosed with ovarian cancer.

4. If USAir accounted for 20% of the major disasters, the chance that it would be involved in at least four of seven such disasters is

$$\binom{7}{4}(.2)^4(.8)^3 + \binom{7}{5}(.2)^5(.8)^2 + \binom{7}{6}(.2)^6(.8)^1 + (.2)^7$$
$$= .029 + .004 + .000 + 000$$
$$= .033$$

Mathematically, if USAir accounted for only 20% of the major disasters, there is only a .033 chance of it being involved in four of seven such disasters. This seems more than enough evidence to be suspicious!

5.
$$P(E|F) = \frac{P(E \cap F)}{P(F)} \quad \text{or} \quad P(E \cap F) = P(E|F)P(F),$$

and so

$$
\begin{aligned}
P(\text{woman} \cap \text{glasses}) &= (.55)(.56) \\
&= .308 \\
P(\text{woman} \cap \text{contacts}) &= (.63)(.04) \\
&= .0252
\end{aligned}
$$

If 55% of those who wear glasses are women, 45% of those who wear glasses must be men, and if 63% of those who wear contacts are women, 37% of those who wear contacts must be men. Thus we have

$$
\begin{aligned}
P(\text{man} \cap \text{glasses}) &= (.45)(.56) \\
&= .252 \\
P(\text{man} \cap \text{contacts}) &= (.37)(.04) \\
&= .0148
\end{aligned}
$$

The probability that you will encounter a person not wearing glasses or contacts is $1 - (.308 + .0252 + .252 + .0148) = .4$.

6.   a. The probability of the complement is 1 minus the probability of the event, but $1 - .43 \neq .47$.

     b. Probabilities are never greater than 1, but $6(.18) = 1.08$.

     c. The probability of an intersection cannot be greater than the probability of one of the separate events.

     d. The probability of a union cannot be less than the probability of one of the separate events.

     e. Probabilities are never negative.

Four Investigative Tasks

1. Suppose the probability that someone will make a major mistake on an income tax return is .23. One day, an Internal Revenue Service (IRS) agent plans to audit as many returns as necessary until she finds one with a major mistake.

     a. Use simulation to estimate the probability that a major mistake will be found before the fifth return.

     b. Use probability to calculate the probability that a major mistake will be found before the fifth return.

2. A new antibiotic is tested on six patients in each of 125 hospitals. The number of positive responses among the patients in each hospital is noted with the following results:

Number of positive responses:	0	1	2	3	4	5	6
Actual number of hospitals:	0	0	5	36	51	20	13

     a. How many patients had a positive response?

     b. What is the probability that a patient will have a positive response?

     c. What is the binomial probability distribution with this probability and with $n = 6$?

     d. What is the expected number of hospitals reporting each number of positive responses?

     e. Do the expected and actual numbers of hospitals seem to be close? (If the actual numbers are close to the numbers predicted by the binomial distribution, we can be more confident in concluding that the results are due solely to the antibiotic and not to differences in the hospitals and other factors.)

3. A well-known paradox runs as follows: Suppose every couple continues having children until they have a boy and then they stop. What percentage of male births will result? No couple can have more than one boy, while many can have numerous girls, so it appears that the population will become overwhelmingly female. Test using simulation. What conclusion do you reach? In looking at your simulation outcomes, what do you see is wrong with the reasoning above that led to the conclusion about an increasingly female population?

4. In a championship chess match suppose the probability that player A will win a game is .2, the probability that player B will win is .4, and the probability of a draw is .4. Players receive one point for a win and one-half point for a draw,

and the first to reach three points is the winner. If both reach three points at the same time, they keep playing until one wins another game.

a. Run a simulation to predict the probability of each player winning the championship.

b. Will the probabilities be the same if no points are given for a draw? Test using simulation.

Answers Explained

1. a. Let the numbers 01–23 represent a major mistake, while 24–99 and 00 represent no major mistake. Read off pairs of digits from the random number table until a major mistake is found and note whether it is found before the fifth return. Underlining major mistakes gives

84<u>17</u>706757	<u>17</u>6<u>13</u>15582	5<u>15</u>0681435	4<u>10</u>5092031	0644905059
5988431<u>18</u>0	53<u>11</u>584469	9486857967	<u>05</u>8<u>11</u>845<u>14</u>	75<u>01</u>113006
6339555041	<u>15</u>8660658<u>9</u>	13<u>11</u>971020	8594<u>09</u>1932	0648874987
54355527<u>04</u>	9035902649	4749671567	9426808844	2629464759
<u>08</u>98957<u>024</u>	9728400637	8928303514	5919507635	0330972605
2935723737	6788<u>10</u>3668	3387635841	5286923<u>114</u>	<u>15</u>86438942

The first major mistake (17) is found on the second return, the next major mistake (again 17) is found on the fourth return, the next (14) on the eighth return, and so on. Tabulating gives

Return on Which Major Mistake Is Found	Frequency
1	7
2	11
3	3
4	3
5 or beyond	12

The probability that a major mistake will be found before the fifth return is estimated to be $\frac{7+11+3+3}{36} = \frac{24}{36} = .67$.

b. The probability of the first return having a major mistake is .23. The probability of the first return having no major mistake but the second one having one is $(.23)(.77) = .1771$. The probability of the first return with a major mistake being the third return is $(.23)(.77)^2 = .1364$, and being the fourth return is $(.23)(.77)^3 = .1050$. The probability of the first major mistake being found before the fifth return is thus $.23 + .1771 + .1364 + .1050 = .6485$.

2. a. $5(2) + 36(3) + 51(4) + 20(5) + 13(6) = 500$

b. There were $125(6) = 750$ patients; $\frac{500}{750} = .667$.

c.

$$P(0) = 1(.667)^0(.333)^6 = .001$$
$$P(1) = 6(.667)^1(.333)^5 = .016$$
$$P(2) = 15(.667)^2(.333)^4 = .082$$
$$P(3) = 20(.667)^3(.333)^3 = .219$$
$$P(4) = 15(.667)^4(.333)^2 = .330$$
$$P(5) = 6(.667)^5(.333)^1 = .264$$
$$P(6) = 1(.667)^6(.333)^0 = .088$$
$$\overline{1.000}$$

d. $.001(125) = 1.25$, $.016(125) = 2$, $.082(125) = 10.25$, $.219(125) = 27.375$, $.330(125) = 41.25$, $.264(125) = 33$, and $.088(125) = 11$, and so we have

Number of positive responses:	0	1	2	3	4	5	6
Expected number of hospitals:	1	2	10	27	41	33	11

e. (0, 0, 5, 36, 51, 20, 13) and (1, 2, 10, 27, 41, 33, 11) seem to differ significantly, indicating that the results are not due solely to the antibiotic. (A chi-square test of significance is indicated—see Topic 14.)

3. Let even numbers represent male births and odd numbers represent female births. Read off digits from the random number table, recording the results every time there is a male birth (even number). We have

8 4 1770 6 757176 131558 2 5150 6 8 14 354 10 50 92 0 310 6 4
4 90 50 59598 8 4 3118 0 531158 4 4 6 994 8 6 8 5796 70 58 118
4 514 750 11130 0 6 6 3395550 4 1158 6 6 0 6 58 913119710 2 0
8 594 0 91932 0 6 4 8 8 74 98 754 35552 70 4 90 3590 2 6 4 94
74 96 7156 794 2 6 8 0 8 8 4 4 2 6 2 94 6 4 7590 8 98 9570 2
4 972 8 4 0 0 6 378 92 8 30 3514 591950 76 350 330 972 6 0 52
93572 37376 78 8 10 36 6 8 338 76 358 4 152 8 6 92 3114 158 6
4 38 94 2

Tabulating the numbers of each size family:

1 boy, 0 girls:	74
1 boy, 1 girl:	29
1 boy, 2 girls:	18
1 boy, 3 girls:	11
1 boy, 4 girls:	6
1 boy, 5 girls:	4
1 boy, 6 girls:	1
1 boy, 8 girls:	1

Totaling the numbers of boys and girls yields 144 boys (48%), 156 girls (52%). The results appear to be close to 50% for each. The reasoning that concludes there will be an increasingly female population fails to take into account the largest group, which is the many families that have no girls.

4.   *a.* Let 0 and 1 represent a game win for player A; 2, 3, 4, and 5 represent a game win for player B; and 6, 7, 8, and 9 represent a drawn game. Reading off digits from the random number table, awarding points for wins and draws, and stopping when a player reaches three points (or as soon as either player wins if they reach three at the same time) yields

841770 67571761 3155 82515 0681 435 41050 920310 6449
050595 98843 1180 53115 8446 99486 85796 70581 184514
75011 1300 6633 9555 0411 5866065 89131 1971 0208594 0919
32064 88749 8754 355 52704 90359 02649 4749 67156794
2680884 4262 9464 759089895 70249 7284 00637 89283 03514
59195 07635 0330972 60529 3572 3737 67881 036683 38763
58415 28692 31141 5864 3894 2

Summing wins gives $P(\text{A wins}) = \frac{16}{60} = .27$, while $P(\text{B wins}) = \frac{44}{60} = .73$.

  b. Repeating the procedure giving no points for a draw yields

84177067571 7613155 82515 0681435 41050 920310 644905
05959884 31180 53115 8446994 8685796705811 84514 75011
1300 663395 5504 1158660 65891311 971020 859409193
20648874 987543 555 2704903 590264 947496715 67942680884
4262 946475 90898957024 972840063 78928303 5145 919507635
0330972 605293 5723 73767881036683 387635 84152 86923114
158643 8942

Summing wins gives $P(\text{A wins}) = \frac{10}{43} = .23$, while $P(\text{B wins}) = \frac{33}{43} = .77$.

Combining Independent Random Variables

In many experiments a pair of numbers is associated with each outcome. This situation leads to a study of pairs of random variables. When the random variables are independent, there is an easy calculation for finding both the mean and standard deviation of the sum (and difference) of the two random variables.

Independence Versus Dependence

Example 10.1.   An automobile salesperson sells three models of vans with selling prices of $20,000, $25,000, and $30,000, respectively. For each sale, the salesperson receives a bonus of either $500 or $750. The probabilities of the various outcomes are given by the following table:

		Bonus	
		$500	$750
	$20,000	.30	.05
Amount of sale	$25,000	.20	.20
	$30,000	.05	.20

If X is the "amount of sale" random variable, what is the probability distribution of X?

Answer: Summing each row gives

x ($):	20,000	25,000	30,000
$P(x)$:	.35	.40	.25

If Y is the "bonus" random variable, what is the probability distribution of Y?

Answer: Summing each column gives

$$
\begin{array}{lcc}
y\ (\$): & 500 & 750 \\
P(y): & .55 & .45
\end{array}
$$

What is the probability of a $500 bonus given that the sale was $30,000?

Answer:

$$
P(\$500\ \text{bonus}|\$30,000\ \text{sale}) = \frac{P(\$500\ \text{bonus} \cap \$30,000\ \text{sale})}{P(\$30,000\ \text{sale})}
$$

$$
= \frac{.05}{.25} = .2
$$

However, $P(\$500\ \text{bonus}) = .55$, and so $P(\$500\ \text{bonus}|\$30,000\ \text{sale}) \neq P(\$500\ \text{bonus})$. We say that the amount of sale random variable and the bonus random variable are not independent.

We say that the two random variables X and Y are independent if $P(x|y) = P(x)$ for all values of x and y. Equivalently, X and Y are independent if $P(x \cap y) = P(x)P(y)$ for all values of x and y. [This expression is also written $P(X = x, Y = y) = P(X = x)P(Y = y)$.]

Example 10.2.   In a study on vitamin C and the common cold, people were randomly assigned to take either no vitamin C or 500 milligrams daily, and it was noted whether or not they came down with a cold. Letting X, the "vitamin C" random variable, take the values 0 and 500, and Y, the "colds" random variable, take the values 0 (no colds) and 1 (at least one cold), the following table gives the observed probabilities:

Are the vitamin C random variable and the colds random variable independent?

Answer: Summing rows and columns gives

$$
\begin{aligned}
P(X = 0) &= .10 + .30 = .40 \\
P(X = 500) &= .15 + .45 = .60 \\
P(Y = 0) &= .10 + .15 = .25 \\
P(Y = 1) &= .30 + .45 = .75
\end{aligned}
$$

Now checking the conditional probabilities,

$$P(X = 0|Y = 0) \quad = \frac{.10}{.25} = .4 = P(X = 0)$$

$$P(X = 0|Y = 1) \quad = \frac{.30}{.75} = .4 = P(X = 0)$$

$$P(X = 500|Y = 0) \quad = \frac{.15}{.25} = .6 = P(X = 500)$$

$$P(X = 500|Y = 1) \quad = \frac{.45}{.75} = .6 = P(X = 500)$$

Thus we conclude that X and Y are independent.

Note that an alternative check for independence is the following: $P(X = 0, Y = 0) = .10$ and $P(X = 0)P(Y = 0) = (.40)(.25) = .10$. Similarly, $P(X = 0, Y = 1) = P(X = 0)P(Y = 1) = .30$, $P(X = 500, Y = 0) = P(X = 500)P(Y = 0) = .15$, and $P(X = 500, Y = 1) = P(X = 500)P(Y = 1) = .45$.

Mean and Standard Deviation for Sums and Differences of Independent Random Variables

One way of comparing two populations is to analyze their set of differences.

Example 10.3. Suppose set $X = \{2, 9, 11, 22\}$ and set $Y = \{5, 7, 15\}$. Note that the mean of set X is $\mu_x = \frac{2+9+11+22}{4} = 11$ and the mean of set Y is $\mu_y = \frac{5+7+15}{3} = 9$. Form the set Z of differences by subtracting each element of Y from each element of X:

$$
\begin{aligned}
Z &= \{2-5, 2-7, 2-15, 9-5, 9-7, 9-15, 11-5, 11-7, \\
&\quad\; 11-15, 22-5, 22-7, 22-15\} \\
&= \{-3, -5, -13, 4, 2, -6, 6, 4, -4, 17, 15, 7\}
\end{aligned}
$$

What is the mean of Z?

Answer:

$$\mu = \frac{-3-5-13+4+2-6+6+4-4+17+15+7}{12} = \frac{24}{12} = 2$$

Note that $\mu_z = \mu_x - \mu_y$.

In general, the mean of a set of differences is equal to the difference of the means of the two original sets. Even more generally, if a sum is formed by picking one element from each of several sets, the mean of such sums is simply the sum of the means of the various sets.

How is the variance of Z related to the variances of the original sets?

Answer:

$$\mu_x = 11 \qquad \sigma_x^2 = \frac{(2-11)^2 + (9-11)^2 + (11-11)^2 + (22-11)^2}{4}$$

$$= \frac{206}{4} = 51.5$$

$$\mu_y = 9 \qquad \sigma_y^2 = \frac{(5-9)^2 + (7-9)^2 + (15-9)^2}{3}$$

$$= \frac{56}{3} = 18.67$$

$$\mu_z = 2 \qquad \sigma_z^2 = \frac{(-3-2)^2 + (-5-2)^2 + (-13-2)^2 + \cdots + (7-2)^2}{12}$$

$$= \frac{842}{12} = 70.17$$

Note that in the above example $\sigma_z^2 = \sigma_x^2 + \sigma_y^2$. This is true for the variance of any set of differences. More generally, if a total is formed by a procedure that adds or subtracts one element from each of several sets, the variance of the resulting totals is simply the sum of the variances of the several sets.

Not only can we sum variances as shown above to calculate total variance, but we can also reverse the process and determine how the total variance is split up among its various sources. For example, we can find what portion of the variance in numbers of sales made by a company's sales representatives is due to the individual salesperson, what portion is due to the territory, what portion is due to the particular products sold by each salesperson, and so on.

The above principles extend more broadly to random variables.

Example 10.4. Suppose two random variables X and Y have the following joint probability distribution table:

		Y		
		5	8	9
	3	.10	.05	.15
X	4	.20	.10	.00
	6	.05	.20	.15

What are the expected values (means) of the random variables X, Y, and $X+Y$?

Answer:

$$E(X) = \sum x_i p_i$$
$$= 3(.10+.05+.15)+4(.20+.10+.00)+6(.05+.20+.15)$$
$$= 4.50$$

$$E(Y) = \sum y_i p_i$$
$$= 5(.10+.20+.05)+8(.05+.10+.20)+9(.15+.00+.15)$$
$$= 7.25$$

$$E(X+Y) = (3+5)(.10)+(3+8)(.05)+(3+9)(.15)+(4+5)(.20)$$
$$+(4+8)(.10)+(4+9)(.00)+(6+5)(.05)+(6+8)(.20)$$
$$+(6+9)(.15)$$
$$= 11.75$$

Note that $E(X+Y) = E(X)+E(Y)$. This is true in general for expected values of sums of random variables. It is also true that $E(X-Y) = E(X) - E(Y)$.

What are the variances of the random variables X, Y, and $X+Y$?

Answer:

$$\text{var}(X) = (3-4.50)^2(.30)+(4-4.50)^2(.30)+(6-4.50)^2(.40)$$
$$= 1.65$$

$$\text{var}(Y) = (5-7.25)^2(.35)+(8-7.25)^2(.35)+(9-7.25)^2(.30)$$
$$= 2.8875$$

$$\text{var}(X+Y) = (8-11.75)^2(.10)+(11-11.75)^2(.05)$$
$$+(12-11.75)^2(.15)+(9-11.75)^2(.20)$$
$$+(12-11.75)^2(.10)+(13-11.75)^2(.00)$$
$$+(11-11.75)^2(.05)+(14-11.75)^2(.20)$$
$$+(15-11.75)^2(.15)$$
$$= 5.5875$$

Note that var $(X+Y) \neq$ var $(X)+$ var (Y).

Do the variances ever sum like the means do? Consider the following example of independent random variables X and Y.

Example 10.5.   Suppose that two random variables X and Y have the following joint probability distribution table:

	Y			
	2	**5**	**10**	
5	.07	.05	.08	.20
7	.28	.20	.32	.80
	.35	.25	.40	

If one computes all the conditional probabilities, it can be shown that $P(x|y) = P(x)$ for all values of x and y, and thus X and Y are independent. What are the variances of the random variables X, Y, and $X+Y$?

Answer: First we calculate

$$E(X) = 5(.20)+7(.80) = 6.60$$

$$E(Y) = 2(.35)+5(.25)+10(.40) = 5.95$$

$$E(X+Y) = E(X)+E(Y) = 12.55$$

Then we calculate the variances

$$\text{var}(X) = (5-6.60)^2(.20)+(7-6.60)^2(.80) = 0.64$$

$$\begin{aligned}\text{var}(Y) &= (2-5.95)^2(.35)+(5-5.95)^2(.25)\\ &\quad +(10-5.95)^2(.40)\\ &= 12.2475\end{aligned}$$

$$\begin{aligned}\text{var}(X+Y) &= (7-12.55)^2(.07)+(10-12.55)^2(.05)\\ &\quad +(15-12.55)^2(.08)+(9-12.55)^2(.28)\\ &\quad +(12-12.55)^2(.20)+(17-12.55)^2(.32)\\ &= 12.8875\end{aligned}$$

Note that $0.64+12.2475 = 12.8875$; that is, $\text{var}(X+Y) = \text{var}(X) + \text{var}(Y)$.

More generally, *if two random variables are independent,* the variance of the sum (or the difference) of the two random variables is equal to the *sum* of the two individual variances.

Example 10.6.   Suppose the mean SAT verbal score is 425 with standard deviation 100, while the mean SAT math score is 475 with standard deviation 100. What can be said about the mean and standard deviation of the combined math and verbal scores?

Answer: The mean is $425 + 475 = 900$. Can we add the two variances to obtain $100^2 + 100^2 = 20,000$ and then take the square root to obtain 141.4? No, because we don't have independence—students with high math scores tend to have high verbal scores, and those with low math scores tend to have low verbal scores. The standard deviation of the combined scores cannot be calculated from the given information.

For random variables X and Y the generalizations for transforming X and for combining X and Y are sometimes written as

$$\text{Transforming } X: \qquad \mu_{a \pm bx} = a \pm b\mu_x \qquad \sigma^2_{a \pm bx} = b^2 \sigma^2_x$$
$$\text{Combining } X \text{ and } Y: \qquad \mu_{x \pm y} = \mu_x \pm \mu_y \qquad \sigma^2_{x \pm y} = \sigma^2_x + \sigma^2_y$$

Questions on Topic Ten: Combining Independent Random Variables

Multiple-Choice Questions

Directions: The questions or incomplete statements that follow are each followed by five suggested answers or completions. Choose the response that best answers the question or completes the statement.

Questions 1–4 refer to the following: Students are classified by television usage (unending, average, and infrequent) and how often they exercise (regular, occasional, and never), resulting in the following joint probability table.

TV usage	Exercise Regular $(Y = 1)$	Occasional $(Y = 2)$	Never $(Y = 3)$
Unending $(X = 1)$	.05	.05	.10
Average $(X = 2)$	.20	.15	.10
Infrequent $(X = 3)$	.15	.15	.05

1. What is the probability distribution for X?

   (A) $P(X = 1) = .05, P(X = 2) = .20, P(X = 3) = .15$
   (B) $P(X = 1) = .10, P(X = 2) = .35, P(X = 3) = .30$
   (C) $P(X = 1) = .20, P(X = 2) = .45, P(X = 3) = .35$
   (D) $P(X = 1) = .40, P(X = 2) = .35, P(X = 3) = .25$
   (E) It cannot be determined from the given information.

2. What is the probability $P(X = 2, Y = 3)$, that is, the probability that a student has average television usage but never exercises?

   (A) .10
   (B) .1125
   (C) .22
   (D) .40
   (E) .60

3. What is the probability $P(X = 2|Y = 3)$, that is, the probability that a student has average television usage given that he never exercises?

   (A) .10
   (B) .17
   (C) .22
   (D) .40
   (E) .60

4. Are X and Y independent?

   (A) Yes, because the conditional probabilities $P(X = x|Y = y)$ equal the corresponding unconditional probabilities $P(X = x)$.
   (B) Yes, because the joint probabilities are equal to the product of the respective probabilities.
   (C) Yes, because of either of the above answers.
   (D) No.
   (E) The answer cannot be determined from the given information.

5. Following are parts of the probability distributions for the random variables X and Y.

x	$P(x)$		y	$P(y)$
1	?		1	.4
2	.2		2	?
3	.3		3	.1
4	?			

   If X and Y are independent and the joint probability $P(X = 1, Y = 2) = .1$, what is $P(X = 4)$?

   (A) .1
   (B) .2
   (C) .3
   (D) .4
   (E) .5

6. Following are parts of the probability distributions for the random variables X and Y.

x	P(x)
1	?
2	.4
3	?

y	P(y)
1	.3
2	?
3	?

If X and Y are independent and the joint probabilities $P(X = 1, Y = 1) = .06$ and $P(X = 2, Y = 2) = .1$, what is $P(X = 3, Y = 3)$?

(A) .16
(B) .18
(C) .25
(D) .4
(E) .425

7. Following are parts of the probability distributions for the random variables X and Y.

x	P(x)
1	?
2	?
3	?
4	?

y	P(y)
1	?
2	?

If X and Y are independent and the joint probabilities $P(X = 1, Y = 1) = .14$ and $P(X = 1, Y = 2) = .06$, what is $P(Y = 2)$?

(A) .08
(B) .2
(C) .3
(D) .7
(E) It cannot be determined from the given information.

8. Following are parts of the probability distributions for the random variables X and Y.

x	P(x)
1	.3
2	?
3	.5

y	P(y)
1	.3
2	?
3	.1

If $P(X = 2, Y = 2) = .1$, is it still possible that X and Y are independent?

(A) Yes, but only if $P(X = 1, Y = 1) = .09$.
(B) Yes, but only if $P(X = 3, Y = 3) = .05$.
(C) Yes, but only if both of the above hold.
(D) No.
(E) There is insufficient information to answer this question.

9. Suppose X and Y are random variables with $E(X) = 25$, var $(X) = 3$, $E(Y) = 30$, and var $(Y) = 4$. What are the expected value and variance of the random variable $X + Y$?

   (A) $E(X + Y) = 55$, var $(X + Y) = 3.5$
   (B) $E(X + Y) = 55$, var $(X + Y) = 5$
   (C) $E(X + Y) = 55$, var $(X + Y) = 7$
   (D) $E(X + Y) = 27.5$, var $(X + Y) = 7$
   (E) There is insufficient information to answer this question.

10. Suppose X and Y are random variables with $\mu_x = 10$, $\sigma_x = 3$, $\mu_y = 15$, and $\sigma_y = 4$. Given that X and Y are independent, what are the mean and standard deviation of the random variable $X + Y$?

   (A) $\mu_{x+y} = 25$, $\sigma_{x+y} = 3.5$
   (B) $\mu_{x+y} = 25$, $\sigma_{x+y} = 5$
   (C) $\mu_{x+y} = 25$, $\sigma_{x+y} = 7$
   (D) $\mu_{x+y} = 12.5$, $\sigma_{x+y} = 7$
   (E) There is insufficient information to answer this question.

11. Suppose X and Y are random variables with $E(X) = 500$, var $(X) = 50$, $E(Y) = 400$, and var $(Y) = 30$. Given that X and Y are independent, what are the expected value and variance of the random variable $X - Y$?

   (A) $E(X - Y) = 100$, var $(X - Y) = 20$
   (B) $E(X - Y) = 100$, var $(X - Y) = 80$
   (C) $E(X - Y) = 900$, var $(X - Y) = 20$
   (D) $E(X - Y) = 900$, var $(X - Y) = 80$
   (E) There is insufficient information to answer this question.

12. Suppose the average height of policemen is 71 inches with a standard deviation of 4 inches, while the average for policewomen is 66 inches with a standard deviation of 3 inches. If a committee looks at all ways of pairing up one male with one female officer, what will be the mean and standard deviation for the difference in heights for the set of possible partners?

   (A) Mean of 5 inches with a standard deviation of 1 inch
   (B) Mean of 5 inches with a standard deviation of 3.5 inches
   (C) Mean of 5 inches with a standard deviation of 5 inches
   (D) Mean of 68.5 inches with a standard deviation of 1 inch
   (E) Mean of 68.5 inches with a standard deviation of 3.5 inches

13. Consider the set of scores of all students taking the AP Statistics exam. What is true about the variance of this set?

   (A) Given a boxplot of this distribution, if the whisker lengths are equal, the variance will equal the interquartile range.
   (B) If the distribution of scores is bell-shaped, the variance will be between -3 and $+3$.
   (C) If there are a few high scores with the bulk of the scores less than the mean, the variance will be skewed to the right.
   (D) If the distribution is symmetric, the variance will equal the standard deviation.
   (E) The variance is the sum of variances coming from a variety of factors such as study time, course grade, IQ, and so on.

Answer Key

1. **C**	4. **D**	7. **C**	10. **B**	13. **E**
2. **A**	5. **C**	8. **D**	11. **B**	
3. **D**	6. **B**	9. **E**	12. **C**	

Answers Explained

1. **(C)** Summing each row gives $P(X = 1) = .20$, $P(X = 2) = .45$, and $P(X = 3) = .35$.

2. **(A)** This question asks for the probability of an intersection, and the answer is found in the second row, third column.

3. **(D)** $P(X = 2|Y = 3) = \frac{P(X=2, Y=3)}{P(Y=3)} = \frac{.10}{.10+.10+.05} = .40$

4. **(D)** For example, $P(X = 2|Y = 3) = .40$, but $P(X = 2) = .45$. For independence this has to hold for all values of x and y.

5. **(C)** $P(Y = 2) = 1 - (.4 + .1) = .5$. By independence, $P(X = 1, Y = 2) = P(X = 1)P(Y = 2)$, and so $.1 = P(X = 1)(.5)$ and $P(X = 1) = .2$. Then $P(X = 4) = 1 - (.2 + .2 + .3) = .3$.

6. **(B)** By independence, $P(X = 1)(.3) = .06$, and so $P(X = 1) = .2$. Similarly, $.4P(Y = 2) = .1$, and so $P(Y = 2) = .25$. Now $P(X = 3) = 1 - (.2 + .4) = .4$, and $P(Y = 3) = 1 - (.3 + .25) = .45$. Finally, $P(X = 3, Y = 3) = (.4)(.45) = .18$.

7. **(C)** By independence we have $P(X = 1)P(Y = 1) = .14$ and $P(X = 1)P(Y = 2) = .06$. Adding the two equations gives $P(X = 1)P(Y = 1) + P(X = 1)P(Y = 2) = .14 + .06 = .2$. Factoring gives $P(X = 1)[P(Y = 1) + P(Y = 2)] = .2$, but $P(Y = 1) + P(Y = 2) = 1$, and so $P(X = 1) = .2$. Thus $(.2)P(Y = 2) = .06$, and $P(Y = 2) = .3$.

8. **(D)** $P(X = 2) = 1 - (.5 + .3) = .2$
$P(Y = 2) = 1 - (.3 + .1) = .6$
$P(X = 2)P(Y = 2) = (.2)(.6) = .12 \neq P(X = 2, Y = 2)$

9. **(E)** Without independence we cannot determine var $(X + Y)$ from the information given.

10. **(B)** The means and the variances add. Thus the new variance is $3^2 + 4^2 = 25$, and the new standard deviation is 5.

11. **(B)** If two random variables are independent, the mean of the difference of the two random variables is equal to the difference of the two individual means; however, the variance of the difference of the two random variables is equal to the sum of the two individual variances.

12. **(C)** The mean of a set of differences is the difference of the means of the two sets, while the variance is the sum of the two variances. Thus $71 - 66 = 5$, while $4^2 + 3^2 = 25$ and $\sqrt{25} = 5$.

13. **(E)** The total variance can be split up among its various sources. Also, the alternative choices are all nonsense.

Free-Response Questions

> *Directions:* You must show all work and indicate the methods you use. You will be graded on the correctness of your methods and on the accuracy of your final answers.

An Open-Ended Question

1. Following are the probability distributions for the random variables X and Y.

x	$P(x)$
1	.3
2	.7

y	$P(y)$
1	.6
2	.4

  a. If X and Y are independent random variables, what is their joint probability table?

  b. Give a possible joint probability table for which X and Y are not independent.

Answers Explained

1. a. If X and Y are independent random variables, $P(X = x, Y = y) = P(X = x)P(Y = y)$ for all values of x and y. Multiplying probabilities thus leads to

	Y = 1	Y = 2
X = 1	.18	.12
X = 2	.42	.28

  b. There are many possible answers as long as the first row sums to .3, the second row to .7, the first column to .6, and the second column to .4. So start with anything less than .3 (but not .18) in the upper left corner. For example, if $P(X = 1, Y = 1) = .1$, the complete table is

	Y = 1	Y = 2
X = 1	.1	.2
X = 2	.5	.2

TOPIC ELEVEN
The Normal Distribution

Some of the most useful probability distributions are symmetric and bell-shaped:

In this topic we study one such distribution called the *normal distribution*. The normal distribution is valuable in describing various natural phenomena, especially those involving growth or decay. However, the real importance of the normal distribution in statistics is that it can be used to describe the results of sampling procedures.

The normal distribution can be viewed as a limiting case of the binomial. More specifically, we start with any fixed probability of success p and consider what happens as n becomes arbitrarily large. To obtain a visual representation of the limit, we draw histograms using an increasingly large n for each fixed p.

Histograms for p = .5 and for n = 4, 10, and 25, respectively

Histograms for $p = .1$ and for $n = 4$, 10, and 25, respectively

Histograms for $p = .7$ and for $n = 4$, 10, and 25, respectively

For greater clarity, different scales have been used for the histograms associated with different values of n. From the diagrams above it is reasonable to accept that as n becomes larger without bound, the resulting histograms approach a smooth bell-shaped curve. This is the curve associated with the normal distribution.

Properties of the Normal Distribution

The normal distribution curve is bell-shaped and symmetric and has an infinite base. Long, flat-looking tails cover many values but only a small proportion of the area. The flat appearance of the tails is deceptive. Actually, far out in the tails, the curve drops proportionately at an ever-increasing rate. In other words, when two intervals of equal length are compared, the one closer to the center may experience a greater numerical drop, but the one further out in the tail experiences a greater drop when measured as a proportion of the height at the beginning of the interval.

The mean here is the same as the median and is located at the center. We want a unit of measurement that applies equally well to any normal distribution, and we choose a unit that arises naturally out of the curve's shape. There is a point on each side where the slope is steepest. These two points are called *points of inflection*, and the distance from the mean to either point is precisely equal to one standard deviation. Thus, it is convenient to measure distances under the normal curve in terms of z-scores (recall from Topic 2 that z-scores are fractions or multiples of standard deviations from the mean).

Normal curves with the same mean but different standard deviations

Normal curves with the same standard deviation but different means

Mathematically, the formula for the normal curve turns out to be $y = e^{-z^2/2}$, where y is the relative height above a z-score. (By *relative height* we mean proportion of the height above the mean.) However, our interest is not so much in relative heights under the normal curve as it is in *proportionate areas*. The probability associated with any interval under the normal curve is equal to the proportionate area found under the curve and above the interval.

A useful property of the normal curve is that approximately 68% of the area (and thus 68% of the observations) falls within one standard deviation of the mean, approximately 95% of the area falls within two standard deviations of the mean, and approximately 99.7% of the area falls within three standard deviations of the mean.

Using Tables of the Normal Distribution

Table A in the Appendix shows areas under the normal curve. Specifically, this table shows the area to the left of a given point. It shows, for example, that to the left of a z-score of 1.2 there is .8849 of the area:

Because the total area is 1, the area to the right of a point can be calculated by calculating 1 minus the area to the left of the point. For example, the area to the right of a z-score of −2.13 is $1 - .0166 = .9834$. (Alternatively, by symmetry, we could have said that the area to the right of −2.13 is the same as that to the left of +2.13 and then read the answer directly from Table A.)

The area between two points can be found by subtraction. For example, the area between the z-scores of 1.23 and 2.71 is equal to $.9966 - .8907 = .1059$.

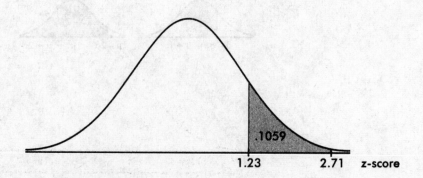

Given a probability, we can use Table A in reverse to find the appropriate z-score. For example, to find the z-score that has an area of .8982 to the left of it, we search for the probability closest to .8982 in the bulk of the table and read off the corresponding z-score. In this case we find .8980 with the z-score 1.27.

To find the z-score with an area of .72 to the right of it, we look for $1 - .72 = .28$ in the bulk of the table. The probability .2810 corresponds to the z-score -0.58.

The Normal Distribution as a Model for Measurement

In solving a problem using the normal distribution as a model, drawing a picture of a normal curve with horizontal lines showing raw scores and z-scores is usually helpful.

Example 11.1. The life expectancy of a particular brand of light bulb is normally distributed with a mean of 1500 hours and a standard deviation of 75 hours.

a. What is the probability that a light bulb will last less than 1410 hours?
Answer: The z-score of 1410 is $\frac{1410-1500}{75} = -1.2$, and from Table A the probability to the left of -1.2 is .1151.

b. What is the probability that a light bulb will last between 1563 and 1648 hours?
Answer: The z-score of 1563 is $\frac{1563-1500}{75} = 0.84$, and the z-score of 1648 is $\frac{1648-1500}{75} = 1.97$. In Table A, 0.84 and 1.97 give probabilities of .7995 and .9756, respectively. Thus between 1563 and 1648 there is a probability of $.9756 - .7995 = .1761$.

c. What is the probability that a light bulb will last between 1416 and 1677 hours?
Answer: The z-score of 1416 is $\frac{1416-1500}{75} = -1.12$, and the z-score of 1677 is $\frac{1677-1500}{75} = 2.36$. In Table A, -1.12 gives a probability of .1314, and 2.36 gives a probability of .9909. Thus between 1416 and 1677 there is a probability of $.9909 - .1314 = .8595$.

Example 11.2.   A packing machine is set to fill a cardboard box with a mean average of 16.1 ounces of cereal. Suppose the amounts per box form a normal distribution with a standard deviation equal to 0.04 ounce.

a. What percentage of the boxes will end up with at least 1 pound of cereal?

Answer: The z-score of 16 is $\frac{16-16.1}{0.04} = -2.5$, and -2.5 in Table A gives a probability of .0062. Thus the probability of having more than 1 pound in a box is $1 - .0062 = .9938$ or 99.38%.

b. Ten percent of the boxes will contain more than what number of ounces?

Answer: In Table A, we note that .1 area (actually .1003) is found to the left of a −1.28 z-score. Converting the z-score of −1.28 into a raw score yields $-1.28 = \frac{x-16.1}{0.04}$ or $16.1 - 1.28(0.04) = 16.049$ ounces.

c. Eighty percent of the boxes will contain more than what number of ounces?

Answer: In Table A, we note that $1 - .8 = .2$ area (actually .2005) is found to the left of a z-score of −0.84, and so to the right of a −0.84 z-score must be 80% of the area. Converting the z-score of −0.84 into a raw score yields $16.1 - 0.84(0.04) = 16.066$ ounces.

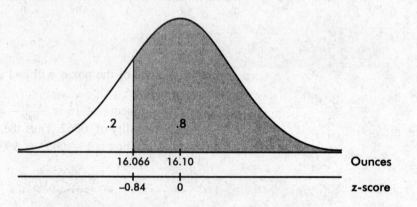

d. The middle 90% of the boxes will be between what two weights?

Answer: Ninety percent in the middle leaves five percent in each tail. In Table A, we note that .0505 area is found to the left of a z-score of −1.64, while .0495 area is found to the left of a z-score of −1.65, and so we use the z-score of −1.645. Then 90% of the area is between z-scores of −1.645 and 1.645. Converting z-scores to raw scores yields $16.1 - 1.645(0.04) = 16.034$ ounces and $16.1 + 1.645(0.04) = 16.166$ ounces, respectively, for the two weights between which we will find the middle 90% of the boxes.

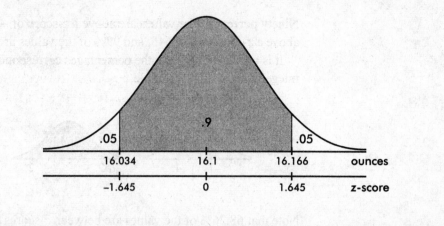

Commonly Used Probabilities and z-scores

As can be seen from Example 11.2*d*, there is often an interest in the limits enclosing some specified middle percentage of the data. For future reference, the limits most frequently asked for are noted below in terms of *z*-scores.

Ninety percent of the values are between *z*-scores of -1.645 and $+1.645$, 95% of the values are between *z*-scores of -1.96 and $+1.96$, and 99% of the values are between *z*-scores of -2.576 and $+2.576$.

Sometimes the interest is in values with particular percentile rankings. For example,

Ninety percent of the values are below a *z*-score of 1.282, 95% of the values are below a *z*-score of 1.645, and 99% of the values are below a *z*-score of 2.326.

There are corresponding conclusions for negative *z*-scores:

Ninety percent of the values are above a z-score of −1.282, 95% of the values are above a z-score of −1.645, and 99% of the values are above a z-score of −2.326.

It is also useful to note the percentages corresponding to values falling between integer z-scores. For example,

Note that 68.26% of the values are between z-scores of −1 and +1, 95.44% of the values are between z-scores of −2 and +2, and 99.74% of the values are between z-scores of −3 and +3.

Example 11.3.   Suppose that the average height of adult males in a particular locality is 70 inches with a standard deviation of 2.5 inches.

a. If the distribution is normal, the middle 95% of males are between what two heights?
   Answer: As noted above, the critical z-scores in this case are ±1.96, and so the two limiting heights are 1.96 standard deviations from the mean. Therefore, $70 \pm 1.96(2.5) = 70 \pm 4.9$, or from 65.1 to 74.9 inches.
b. Ninety percent of the heights are below what value?
   Answer: The critical z-score is 1.282, and so the value in question is $70 + 1.282(2.5) = 73.205$ inches.
c. Ninety-nine percent of the heights are above what value?
   Answer: The critical z-score is −2.326, and so the value in question is $70 - 2.326(2.5) = 64.185$ inches.
d. What percentage of the heights are between z-scores of ±1? Of ±2? Of ±3?
   Answer: 68.26%, 95.44%, and 99.74%, respectively.

Finding Means and Standard Deviations

If we know that a distribution is normal, we can calculate the mean μ and the standard deviation σ using percentage information from the population.

Example 11.4.   Given a normal distribution with a mean of 25, what is the standard deviation if 18% of the values are above 29?

Answer: Looking for a .82 probability in Table A, we note that the corresponding z-score is 0.92. Thus $29 - 25 = 4$ is equal to a standard deviation of 0.92, that is, $0.92\sigma = 4$, and $\sigma = \frac{4}{0.92} = 4.35$.

Example 11.5. Given a normal distribution with a standard deviation of 10, what is the mean if 21% of the values are below 50?

Answer: Looking for a .21 probability in Table A leads us to a z-score of -0.81. Thus 50 is -0.81 standard deviation from the mean, and so $\mu = 50 + 0.81(10) = 58.1$.

Example 11.6. Given a normal distribution with 80% of the values above 125 and 90% of the values above 110, what are the mean and standard deviation?

Answer: Table A gives critical z-scores of -0.84 and -1.28. Thus we have $\frac{125-\mu}{\sigma} = -0.84$ and $\frac{110-\mu}{\sigma} = -1.28$. Solving the system $\{125 - \mu = -0.84\sigma,\ 110 - \mu = -1.28\sigma\}$ simultaneously gives $\mu = 153.64$ and $\sigma = 34.09$.

Normal Approximation to the Binomial

Many practical applications of the binomial involve examples in which n is large. However, for large n, binomial probabilities can be quite tedious to calculate. Since the normal can be viewed as a limiting case of the binomial, it is natural to use the normal to approximate the binomial in appropriate situations.

The binomial takes values only at integers, while the normal is continuous with probabilities corresponding to areas over intervals. Therefore, we establish a technique for converting from one distribution to the other. For approximation purposes we do as follows. Each binomial probability corresponds to the normal probability over a unit interval centered at the desired value. Thus, for example, to approximate the binomial probability of eight successes we determine the normal probability of being between 7.5 and 8.5.

Example 11.7. Suppose that 15% of the cars coming out of an assembly plant have some defect. In a delivery of 40 cars what is the probability that exactly 5 cars have defects?

Answer: The actual answer is $\left(\frac{40!}{35!5!}\right)(.15)^5(.85)^{35}$, but clearly this involves a nontrivial calculation. To approximate the answer using the normal, we first calculate the mean μ and the standard deviation σ as follows:

$$\mu = np = 40(.15) = 6$$
$$\sigma = \sqrt{np(1-p)} = \sqrt{40(.15)(.85)} = 2.258$$

We then calculate the appropriate z-scores: $\frac{4.5-6}{2.258} = -0.66$, and $\frac{5.5-6}{2.258} = -0.22$. Looking up the corresponding probabilities in Table A, we obtain a final answer of $.4129 - .2546 = .1583$. (The actual answer is .1692.)

Cars with defect

z-score

Even more useful are approximations relating to probabilities over intervals.

Example 11.8.   If 60% of the population support massive federal budget cuts, what is the probability that in a survey of 250 people at most 155 people support such cuts?

Answer: The actual answer is the sum of 156 binomial expressions:

$$(.4)^{250} + \cdots + \frac{250!}{155!95!}(.6)^{155}(.4)^{95}$$

However, a good approximation can be obtained quickly and easily by using the normal. We calculate μ and σ:

$$\mu = np = 250(.6) = 150$$
$$\sigma = \sqrt{np(1-p)} = \sqrt{250(.6)(.4)} = 7.746$$

The binomial of at most 155 successes corresponds to the normal probability of ≤ 155.5. The z-score of 155.5 is $\frac{155.5 - 150}{7.746} = 0.71$. Using Table A leads us to a final answer of .7611.

Is the normal a good approximation? The answer, of course, depends on the error tolerances in particular situations. A general rule of thumb is that the normal is a good approximation to the binomial whenever both np and $n(1-p)$ are greater than 5. (Some authors use 10 instead of 5 here.)

Questions on Topic Eleven: The Normal Distribution

Multiple-Choice Questions

> *Directions:* The questions or incomplete statements that follow are each followed by five suggested answers or completions. Choose the response that best answers the question or completes the statement.

1. Which of the following are true statements?

   I. The area under a normal curve is always equal to 1, no matter what the mean and standard deviation are.

   II. The smaller the standard deviation of a normal curve, the higher and narrower the graph.

   III. Normal curves with different means are centered around different numbers.

   (A) I and II
   (B) I and III
   (C) II and III
   (D) I, II, and III
   (E) None of the above gives the complete set of true responses.

2. Which of the following are true statements?

   I. The area under the standard normal curve between 0 and 2 is twice the area between 0 and 1.

   II. The area under the standard normal curve between 0 and 2 is half the area between −2 and 2.

III. For the standard normal curve, the interquartile range is approximately 3.

(A) I and II
(B) I and III
(C) II and III
(D) I, II, and III
(E) None of the above gives the complete set of true responses.

3. Populations P1 and P2 are normally distributed and have identical means. However, the standard deviation of P1 is twice the standard deviation of P2. What can be said about the percentage of observations falling within two standard deviations of the mean for each population?

(A) The percentage for P1 is twice the percentage for P2.
(B) The percentage for P1 is greater, but not twice as great, as the percentage for P2.
(C) The percentage for P2 is twice the percentage for P1.
(D) The percentage for P2 is greater, but not twice as great, as the percentage for P1.
(E) The percentages are identical.

4. Consider the following two normal curves:

Which has the larger mean and which has the larger standard deviation?

(A) Larger mean, a; larger standard deviation, a
(B) Larger mean, a; larger standard deviation, b
(C) Larger mean, b; larger standard deviation, a
(D) Larger mean, b; larger standard deviation, b
(E) Larger mean, b; same standard deviation

5. Which of the following are true statements?

I. In all normal distributions, the mean and median are equal.
II. All bell-shaped curves are normal distributions for some choice of μ and σ.
III. Virtually all the area under a normal curve is within three standard deviations of the mean, no matter what the particular mean and standard deviation are.

(A) I and II
(B) I and III

(C) II and III

(D) I, II, and III

(E) None of the above gives the complete set of true responses.

6. A trucking firm determines that its fleet of trucks averages a mean of 12.4 miles per gallon with a standard deviation of 1.2 miles per gallon on cross-country hauls. What is the probability that one of the trucks averages fewer than 10 miles per gallon?

(A) .0082

(B) .0228

(C) .4772

(D) .5228

(E) .9772

7. A factory dumps an average of 2.43 tons of pollutants into a river every week. If the standard deviation is 0.88 tons, what is the probability that in a week more than 3 tons are dumped?

(A) .2578

(B) .2843

(C) .6500

(D) .7157

(E) .7422

8. An electronic product takes an average of 3.4 hours to move through an assembly line. If the standard deviation is 0.5 hour, what is the probability that an item will take between 3 and 4 hours?

(A) .2119

(B) .2295

(C) .3270

(D) .3811

(E) .6730

9. The mean score on a college placement exam is 500 with a standard deviation of 100. Ninety-five percent of the test takers score above what?

(A) 260

(B) 336

(C) 405

(D) 414

(E) 664

10. The average noise level in a restaurant is 30 decibels with a standard deviation of 4 decibels. Ninety-nine percent of the time it is below what value?

(A) 20.7

(B) 32.0

(C) 33.4

(D) 37.8

(E) 39.3

11. The mean income per household in a certain state is $9500 with a standard deviation of $1750. The middle 95% of incomes are between what two values?

(A) $5422 and $13,578

(B) $6070 and $12,930
(C) $6621 and $12,379
(D) $7260 and $11,740
(E) $8049 and $10,951

12. Jay Olshansky from the University of Chicago was quoted in *Chance News* as arguing that for the average life expectancy to reach 100, 18% of people would have to live to 120. What standard deviation is he assuming for this statement to make sense?

    (A) 21.7
    (B) 24.4
    (C) 25.2
    (D) 35.0
    (E) 111.1

13. Cucumbers grown on a certain farm have weights with a standard deviation of 2 ounces. What is the mean weight if 85% of the cucumbers weigh less than 16 ounces?

    (A) 13.92
    (B) 14.30
    (C) 14.40
    (D) 14.88
    (E) 15.70

14. If 75% of all families spend more than $75 weekly for food, while 15% spend more than $150, what is the mean weekly expenditure and what is the standard deviation?

    (A) $\mu = 83.33$, $\sigma = 12.44$
    (B) $\mu = 56.26$, $\sigma = 11.85$
    (C) $\mu = 118.52$, $\sigma = 56.26$
    (D) $\mu = 104.39$, $\sigma = 43.86$
    (E) $\mu = 139.45$, $\sigma = 83.33$

15. A coffee machine can be adjusted to deliver any fixed number of ounces of coffee. If the machine has a standard deviation in delivery equal to 0.4 ounce, what should be the mean setting so that an 8-ounce cup will overflow only 0.5% of the time?

    (A) 6.97 ounces
    (B) 7.22 ounces
    (C) 7.34 ounces
    (D) 7.80 ounces
    (E) 9.03 ounces

16. Assume that a baseball team has an average pitcher, that is, one whose probability of winning any decision is .5. If this pitcher has 30 decisions in a season, what is the probability that he will win at least 20 games?

    (A) .0505
    (B) .2514
    (C) .2743
    (D) .3333
    (E) .4300

Answer Key

1. **D**	5. **B**	9. **B**	13. **A**
2. **E**	6. **B**	10. **E**	14. **D**
3. **E**	7. **A**	11. **B**	15. **A**
4. **C**	8. **E**	12. **A**	16. **A**

Answers Explained

1. **(D)** The area under any probability distribution is equal to 1. The mean of a normal curve determines the value around which the curve is centered, while the standard deviation determines the height and spread.

2. **(E)** Statement II is true by symmetry of the normal curve, but .4772 is not 2 times .3413, and $0.67 - (-0.67)$ is not 3.

3. **(E)** All normal distributions have about 95% of their observations within two standard deviations of the mean.

4. **(C)** Curve a has mean 6 and standard deviation 2, while curve b has mean 18 and standard deviation 1.

5. **(B)** Because of symmetry, the mean and median are identical for normal distributions. Many bell-shaped curves are *not* normal curves, and we don't *choose* μ and σ. For all normal curves, 99.7% of the area is within three standard deviations of the mean.

6. **(B)** The z-score of 10 is $\frac{10-12.4}{1.2} = -2$. From Table A, to the left of -2 is an area of .0228.

7. **(A)** The z-score of 3 is $\frac{3-2.43}{0.88} = 0.65$. From Table A, to the left of 0.65 is an area of .7422, and so to the right must be $1 - .7422 = .2578$.

8. **(E)** The z-scores of 3 and 4 are $\frac{3-3.4}{0.5} = -0.8$ and $\frac{4-3.4}{0.5} = 1.2$, respectively. From Table A, to the left of -0.8 is an area of .2119, and to the left of 1.2 is an area of .8849. Thus between 3 and 4 is an area of $.8849 - .2119 = .6730$.

9. **(B)** If 95% of the area is to the right of a score, 5% is to the left. Looking for .05 in the body of Table A, we note the z-score of -1.645. Converting this to a raw score gives $500 - 1.645(100) = 336$.

10. **(E)** The critical z-score associated with 99% to the left is 2.326, and $30 + 2.326(4) = 39.3$.

11. **(B)** The critical z-scores associated with the middle 95% are ± 1.96, and $9500 \pm 1.96(1750) = 6070$ and 12,930.

12. **(A)** The critical z-score associated with 18% to the right or 82% to the left is 0.92. Then $100 + 0.92\sigma = 120$ gives $\sigma = 21.7$.

13. **(A)** The critical z-score associated with 85% to the left is 1.04. Then $\mu + 1.04(2) = 16$ gives $\mu = 13.92$.

14. **(D)** The critical z-scores associated with 75% to the right (25% to the left) and with 15% to the right (85% to the left) are -0.67 and 1.04, respectively. Then $\{\mu - 0.67\sigma = 75,\ \mu + 1.04\sigma = 150\}$ gives $\mu = 104.39$ and $\sigma = 43.86$.

15. **(A)** The critical z-score associated with .5% to the right (99.5% to the left) is 2.576. Then $c + 2.576(0.4) = 8$ gives $c = 6.97$.

16. (A)   Using the normal as an approximation to the binomial, we have $\mu = 30(.5) = 15$, $\sigma^2 = 30(.5)(.5) = 7.5$, $\sigma = 2.739$, $\frac{19.5-15}{2.739} = 1.64$, and $1 - .9495 = .0505$.

Free-Response Questions

Directions: You must show all work and indicate the methods you use. You will be graded on the correctness of your methods and on the accuracy of your final answers.

Three Open-Ended Questions

1. Explain why each of the following are not normal curves.

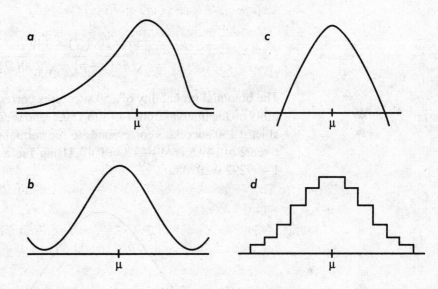

2. Consider two normal curves, one whose mean is larger than the other's mean.
   a. What can be said about which standard deviation is larger?
   b. What can be said about the percentage of area to the left of the mean for the curve with the smaller mean compared to the percentage for the curve with the larger mean?
   c. When drawn above the same axis, must each normal curve extend as far as the mean of the other curve? Explain.

3. A particular form of cancer is fatal within 1 year in 30% of all diagnosed cases. A new drug is tried on 200 patients with this disease. Researchers will judge the new medication effective if at least 150 of the patients survive for longer than 1 year. If the medication has no effect, what is the probability that at least 150 patients will survive for longer than 1 year?

Answers Explained

1. *a.* Normal curves are symmetric.
   b. The tails of a normal curve continue to become closer and closer to the axis.

    c. Normal curves do not cross the axis.

    d. Normal curves are smooth.

2.   *a.* Knowing which mean is larger does not give any information about which standard deviation is larger.

    b. For all normal curves 50% of the area is to the left of the mean.

    c. Yes, because normal curves extend infinitely in both directions.

3. The actual answer is the sum of 51 binomial expressions:

$$\frac{200!}{150!50!}(.7)^{150}(.3)^{50} + \frac{200!}{151!49!}(.7)^{151}(.3)^{49} + \cdots + (.7)^{200}$$

which would be very tedious to calculate. However, an approximate answer using the normal is readily calculated:

$$\mu = np = 200(.7) = 140$$
$$\sigma = \sqrt{np(1-p)} = \sqrt{200(.7)(.3)} = 6.48$$

The binomial probability of 150 successes corresponds to the normal probability on the interval from 149.5 to 150.5, and thus the binomial probability of at least 150 successes corresponds to the normal probability of ≥ 149.5. The z-score of 149.5 is $\frac{149.5-140}{6.48} = 1.47$. Using Table A gives us a final answer of $1 - .9292 = .0708$.

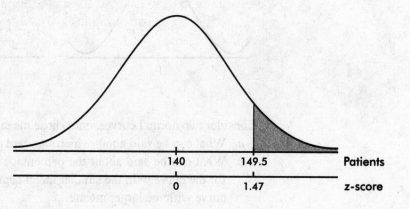

TOPIC TWELVE
Sampling Distributions

The *population* is the complete set of items of interest. A *sample* is a part of a population used to represent the population. The population mean μ and population standard deviation σ are examples of *population parameters*. The sample mean $\bar{x}$ and the sample standard deviation s are examples of *statistics*. Statistics are used to make inferences about population parameters. While a population parameter is a fixed quantity, statistics vary depending on the particular sample chosen. The probability distribution showing how a statistic varies is called a *sampling distribution*. The sampling distribution is *unbiased* if its mean is equal to the associated population parameter.

Sampling Distribution of a Sample Proportion

Whereas the mean is basically a quantitative measurement, the proportion represents essentially a qualitative approach. The interest is simply in the presence or absence of some attribute. We count the number of yes responses and form a proportion. For example, what proportion of drivers wear seat belts? What proportion of SCUD missiles can be intercepted? What proportion of new stereo sets have a certain defect?

This separation of the population into "haves" and "have-nots" suggests that we can make use of our earlier work on binomial distributions. We also keep in mind that, when n (trials, or in this case sample size) is large enough, the binomial can be approximated by the normal.

In this topic we are interested in estimating a population proportion p by considering a single sample proportion $\hat{p}$. This sample proportion is just one of a whole universe of sample proportions, and to judge its significance we must know how sample proportions vary. Consider the set of proportions from all possible samples of a specified size n. It seems reasonable that these proportions will cluster around the population proportion (the sample proportion is an unbiased statistic of the population proportion) and that the larger the chosen sample size, the tighter the clustering.

How do we calculate the mean and standard deviation of the set of population proportions? Suppose the sample size is n and the actual population proportion is p. From our work on binomial distributions, we remember that the mean and standard deviation for the number of successes in a given sample are pn and $\sqrt{np(1-p)}$, respectively, and for large n the complete distribution begins to look "normal."

Here, however, we are interested in the proportion rather than in the number of successes. From Topic Two we remember that when we multiply or divide every element by a constant, we multiply or divide both the mean and the standard deviation by the same constant. In this case, to change number of successes to proportion of successes, we divide by n:

$$\mu_{\hat{p}} = \frac{pn}{n} = p \quad \text{and} \quad \sigma_{\hat{p}} = \frac{\sqrt{np(1-p)}}{n} = \sqrt{\frac{p(1-p)}{n}}$$

Furthermore, if each element in an approximately normal distribution is divided by the same constant, it is reasonable that the result will still be an approximately normal distribution.

Thus the principle forming the basis of the following discussion is

---

Start with a population with a given proportion p. Take all samples of size n. Compute the proportion in each of these samples. Then

1. the set of all sample proportions is approximately normally distributed.
2. the mean $\mu_{\hat{p}}$ of the set of sample proportions equals p, the population proportion.
3. the standard deviation $\sigma_{\hat{p}}$ of the set of sample proportions is approximately equal to $\sqrt{\frac{p(1-p)}{n}}$.

Example 12.1.   Suppose that 70% of all dialysis patients will survive for at least 5 years. If 100 new dialysis patients are selected at random, what is the probability that the proportion surviving for at least 5 years will exceed 80%?

Answer: The set of sample proportions is approximately normally distributed with mean .70 and standard deviation

$$\sigma_{\hat{p}} = \sqrt{\frac{(.7)(.3)}{100}} = .0458$$

With a z-score of $\frac{.80-.70}{.0458} = 2.18$, the probability that the sample proportion will exceed 80% is $1 - .9854 = .0146$.

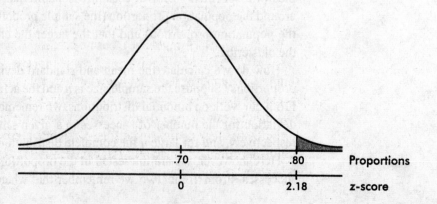

Example 12.2.   It is estimated that 48% of all motorists use their seat belts. If a police officer observes 400 cars go by in an hour, what is the probability that the proportion of drivers wearing seat belts is between 45% and 55%?

Answer: The set of sample proportions is approximately normally distributed with mean .48 and standard deviation

$$\sigma_{\hat{p}} = \sqrt{\frac{(.48)(.52)}{400}} = .0250$$

The z-scores of .45 and .55 are $\frac{.45-.48}{.0250} = -1.2$ and $\frac{.55-.48}{.0250} = 2.8$, respectively. From Table A, the area between .45 and .55 is $.9974 - .1151 = .8823$. Thus there is a .8823 probability that between 45% and 55% of the drivers are wearing seat belts.

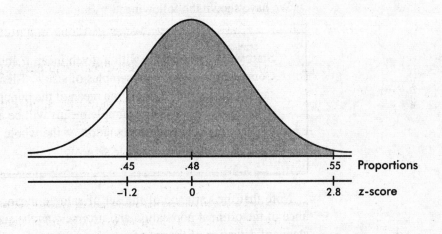

Sampling Distribution of a Sample Mean

Suppose we are interested in estimating the mean μ of a population. For our estimate we could simply randomly pick a single element of the population, but then we would have little confidence in our answer. Suppose instead that we pick 100 elements and calculate their average. It is intuitively clear that the resulting sample mean has a greater chance of being closer to the mean of the whole population than the value for any individual member of the population does.

When we pick a sample and measure its mean $\bar{x}$, we are finding exactly one sample mean out of a whole universe of sample means. To judge the significance of a single sample mean, we must know how sample means vary. Consider the set of means from all possible samples of a specified size. It is both apparent and reasonable that the sample means are clustered around the mean of the whole population; furthermore, these sample means have a tighter clustering than the elements of the original population. In fact, we might guess that the larger the chosen sample size, the tighter the clustering.

How do we calculate the standard deviation $\sigma_{\bar{x}}$ of the set of sample means? Suppose the variance of the population is σ^2 and we are interested in samples of size n. Sample means are obtained by first summing together n elements and then dividing by n. A set of sums has a variance equal to the sum of the variances associated with the original sets. In our case, $\sigma^2_{\text{sums}} = \sigma^2 + \cdots + \sigma^2 = n\sigma^2$. When each element of a set is divided by some constant, the new variance is the old one divided by the square of the constant. Since the sample means are obtained by dividing the sums by n, the variance of the sample means is obtained by dividing the variance of the sums by n^2. Thus if $\sigma_{\bar{x}}$ symbolizes the standard deviation of the sample means, we find that

$$\sigma^2_{\bar{x}} = \frac{\sigma^2_{\text{sums}}}{n^2} = \frac{n\sigma^2}{n^2} = \frac{\sigma^2}{n}$$

In terms of standard deviations, we have $\sigma_{\bar{x}} = \frac{\sigma}{\sqrt{n}}$.

We have shown the following:

> Start with a population with a given mean μ and standard deviation σ. Compute the mean of all samples of size n. Then the mean of the set of sample means will equal μ, the mean of the population, and the standard deviation $\sigma_{\bar{x}}$ of the set of sample means will be approximately equal to $\frac{\sigma}{\sqrt{n}}$, that is, the standard deviation of the whole population divided by the square root of the sample size.

Note that the variance of the set of sample means varies directly as the variance of the original population and inversely as the size of the samples, while the standard deviation of the set of sample means varies directly as the standard deviation of the original population and inversely as the square root of the size of the samples.

Example 12.3. Suppose that tomatoes weigh an average of 10 ounces with a standard deviation of 3 ounces and a store sells boxes containing 12 tomatoes each. If customers determine the average weight of the tomatoes for each box they buy, what will be the mean and standard deviation of these averages?

Answer: The mean of these sample means will equal the population mean, 10 ounces. The standard deviation of these sample means will equal $\frac{3}{\sqrt{12}} = 0.866$ ounces.

Note that while giving the mean and standard deviation of the set of sample means, we did not describe the shape of the distribution. If we are also given that the original population is normal, then we can conclude that the set of sample means has a normal distribution.

Example 12.4.   Suppose that the distribution for total amounts spent by students vacationing for a week in Florida is normally distributed with a mean of $650 and a standard deviation of $120. What is the probability that a group of 10 students will spend an average of between $600 and $700?

Answer: The mean and standard deviation of the set of all sample means of size 10 are:

$$\mu_{\bar{x}} = 650 \quad \text{and} \quad \sigma_{\bar{x}} = \frac{120}{\sqrt{10}} = 37.95$$

The z-scores of 600 and 700 are $\frac{600-650}{37.95} = -1.32$ and $\frac{700-650}{37.95} = 1.32$, respectively. Using Table A, we find the desired probability is .9066 − .0934 = .8132.

Central Limit Theorem

We assumed above that the original population had a normal distribution. Unfortunately, few populations are normal, let alone exactly normal. However, it can be shown mathematically that no matter how the original population is distributed, if *n* is large enough, then the set of sample means is approximately normally distributed. For example, there is no reason to suppose that the amounts of money that different people spend in grocery stores are normally distributed. However, if each day we survey 30 people leaving a store and determine the average grocery bill, these daily averages will have a nearly normal distribution.

The following principle forms the basis of much of what we discuss in this topic and in those following. It is a simplified statement of the *central limit theorem* of statistics.

Start with a population with a given mean μ, a standard deviation σ, and any shape distribution whatsoever. Pick n sufficiently large (at least 30) and take all samples of size n. Compute the mean of each of these samples. Then

1. the set of all sample means is approximately normally distributed.
2. the mean of the set of sample means equals μ, the mean of the population.
3. the standard deviation $\sigma_{\bar{x}}$ of the set of sample means is approximately equal to $\frac{\sigma}{\sqrt{n}}$, that is, equal to the standard deviation of the whole population divided by the square root of the sample size.

Example 12.5. Suppose that the average outstanding credit card balance for young couples is \$650 with a standard deviation of \$420. If 100 couples are selected at random, what is the probability that the mean outstanding credit card balance exceeds \$700?

Answer: The sample size is over 30, and so by the central limit theorem the set of sample means is approximately normally distributed with mean 650 and standard deviation $\frac{420}{\sqrt{100}} = 42$. With a z-score of $\frac{700-650}{42} = 1.19$, the probability that the sample mean exceeds 700 is $1 - .8830 = .1170$.

Example 12.6. The strength of paper coming from a manufacturing plant is known to be 25 pounds per square inch with a standard deviation of 2.3. In a random sample of 40 pieces of paper, what is the probability that the mean strength is between 24.5 and 25.5 pounds per square inch?

Answer: $\mu_{\bar{x}} = 25$ and $\sigma_{\bar{x}} = \frac{2.3}{\sqrt{40}} = 0.364$. The z-scores of 24.5 and 25.5 are $\frac{24.5-25}{0.364} = -1.37$ and $\frac{25.5-25}{0.364} = 1.37$, respectively. The probability that the mean strength in the sample is between 24.5 and 25.5 pounds per square inch is $.9147 - .0853 = .8294$.

	24.5	25	25.5	Pounds per square inch
	−1.37	0	1.37	z-score

Sampling Distribution of a Difference Between Two Independent Sample Proportions

Numerous important and interesting applications of statistics involve the comparison of two population proportions. For example, is the proportion of satisfied purchasers of American automobiles greater than that of buyers of Japanese cars? How does the percentage of surgeons recommending a new cancer treatment compare with the corresponding percentage of oncologists? What can be said about the difference between the proportion of single parents on welfare and the proportion of two-parent families on welfare?

Our procedure involves comparing two sample proportions. When is a difference between two such sample proportions significant? Note that we are dealing with one difference from the set of all possible differences obtained by subtracting sample proportions of one population from sample proportions of a second population. To judge the significance of one particular difference, we must first determine how the differences vary among themselves. Remember that the variance of a set of differences is equal to the sum of the variances of the individual sets; that is,

$$\sigma_d^2 = \sigma_1^2 + \sigma_2^2$$

Now if

$$\sigma_1 = \sqrt{\frac{p_1(1-p_1)}{n_1}} \quad \text{and} \quad \sigma_2 = \sqrt{\frac{p_2(1-p_2)}{n_2}}$$

then

$$\sigma_d^2 = \frac{p_1(1-p_1)}{n_1} + \frac{p_2(1-p_2)}{n_2} \quad \text{and} \quad \sigma_d = \sqrt{\frac{p_1(1-p_1)}{n_1} + \frac{p_2(1-p_2)}{n_2}}$$

Then we have the following about the sampling distribution of $\hat{p}_1 - \hat{p}_2$:

Start with two populations with given proportions p_1 and p_2. Take all samples of sizes n_1 and n_2, respectively. Compute the difference $\hat{p}_1 - \hat{p}_2$ of the two proportions in each pair of samples. Then

1. the set of all differences of sample proportions is approximately normally distributed.
2. the mean of the set of differences of sample proportions equals $p_1 - p_2$, the difference of population proportions.
3. the standard deviation σ_d of the set of differences of sample proportions is approximately equal to

$$\sqrt{\frac{p_1(1-p_1)}{n_1} + \frac{p_2(1-p_2)}{n_2}}$$

Example 12.7. A promoter knows that 23% of males enjoy watching boxing matches; however, only 12% of females enjoy watching this sport. In a random sample of 100 men and 125 women, what is the probability that the difference in the percentages of men and women who enjoy watching boxing is more than 10%?

Answer: For the sampling distribution of $\hat{p}_1 - \hat{p}_2$, the mean is $.23 - .12 = .11$ and the standard deviation is

$$\sqrt{\frac{(.23)(.77)}{100} + \frac{(.12)(.88)}{125}} = .0511$$

The z-score of .10 is $\frac{.10-.11}{.0511} = -0.20$. Using Table A, we find $1 - .4207 = .5793$ for the probability that the difference is more than 10%.

Example 12.8. In urban America 43% of married couples own their own homes while only 19% of single people own their own homes. In a

survey of 200 married couples and 180 single people, the probability is .90 that the difference in percentages of married couples and single people who are homeowners is greater than what percentage?

Answer: For the sampling distribution of $\hat{p}_1 - \hat{p}_2$, the mean is $.43 - .19 = .24$ and the standard deviation is

$$\sqrt{\frac{(.43)(.57)}{200} + \frac{(.19)(.81)}{180}} = .0456$$

The .90 area to the right corresponds to a z-score of -1.282 and thus a difference of $.24 - 1.282(.0456) = .182$. Thus there is a .90 probability that the difference in percentages is greater than 18.2%.

Sampling Distribution of a Difference Between Two Independent Sample Means

Many real-life applications of statistics involve comparisons of two population means. For example, is the average weight of laboratory rabbits receiving a special diet greater than that of rabbits on a standard diet? Which of two accounting firms pays a higher mean starting salary? Is the life expectancy of a coal miner less than that of a school teacher?

First we consider how to compare the means of samples, one from each population. When is a difference between two such sample means significant? The answer is more apparent when we realize that what we are looking at is one difference from a set of differences. That is, there is the set of all possible differences obtained by subtracting sample means from one set from sample means from a second set. To judge the significance of one particular difference we must first determine how the differences vary among themselves. The necessary key is the fact that the variance of a set of differences is equal to the sum of the variances of the individual sets. Thus,

$$\sigma^2_{\bar{x}_1 - \bar{x}_2} = \sigma^2_{\bar{x}_1} + \sigma^2_{\bar{x}_2}$$

Now if

$$\sigma_{\bar{x}_1} = \frac{\sigma_1}{\sqrt{n_1}} \quad \text{and} \quad \sigma_{\bar{x}_2} = \frac{\sigma_2}{\sqrt{n_2}}$$

then

$$\sigma^2_{\bar{x}_1 - \bar{x}_2} = \frac{\sigma_1^2}{n_1} + \frac{\sigma_2^2}{n_2} \quad \text{and} \quad \sigma_{\bar{x}_1 - \bar{x}_2} = \sqrt{\frac{\sigma_1^2}{n_1} + \frac{\sigma_2^2}{n_2}}$$

Then we have the following about the sampling distribution of $\bar{x}_1 - \bar{x}_2$:

Start with two normal populations with given means μ_1 and μ_2. Take all samples of sizes n_1 and n_2, respectively. Compute the difference $\bar{x}_1 - \bar{x}_2$ of the two means in each pair of these samples. Then

1. the set of all differences of sample means is approximately normally distributed.
2. the mean of the set of differences of sample means equals $\mu_1 - \mu_2$, the difference of population means.
3. the standard deviation $\sigma_{\bar{x}_1 - \bar{x}_2}$ of the set of differences of sample means is approximately equal to $\sqrt{\frac{\sigma_1^2}{n_1} + \frac{\sigma_2^2}{n_2}}$.

Example 12.9.   When fertilizer A is used, the vegetable yield is 4.5 tons per acre with a standard deviation of 0.7 tons, while the yield when fertilizer B is used is 4.3 tons per acre with a standard deviation of 0.4 tons. In 45 sample plots using fertilizer A and 50 plots using fertilizer B, what is the probability that the difference in average yields will be negative, that is, that the average yield for the plots using fertilizer A will be less than the average yield for the plots using fertilizer B?

Answer: The mean of the differences is $4.5 - 4.3 = 0.2$, while the standard deviation is $\sqrt{\frac{(0.7)^2}{45} + \frac{(0.4)^2}{50}} = 0.119$. The z-score of a difference of 0 is $\frac{0 - 0.2}{0.119} = -1.68$. From Table A, the area to the left of -1.68 is .0465. Thus there is a 4.65% chance that the average yield for the sample plots using fertilizer A will be less than the average yield for the sample plots using fertilizer B.

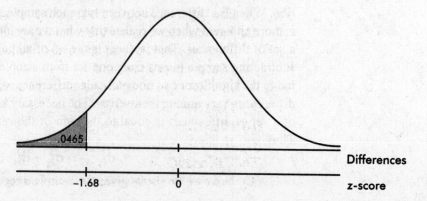

.0465

-1.68	0

Differences

z-score

Example 12.10.   The average number of missed school days for students going to public schools is 8.5 with a standard deviation of 4.1, while students going to private schools miss an average of 5.3 with a standard deviation of 2.9. In a sample of 200 public school students and 150 private school students, with a probability of .95 the difference in average missed days (public average minus private average) is above what number?

Answer: The mean of the differences is $8.5 - 5.3 = 3.2$, while the standard deviation is $\sqrt{\frac{(4.1)^2}{200} + \frac{(2.9)^2}{150}} = 0.374$. An area of .95 to the right corresponds to a z-score of -1.645. The difference in days is $3.2 - 1.645(0.374) = 2.6$. Thus there is a .95 probability that the difference in average missed days between public and private school samples is over 2.6 days.

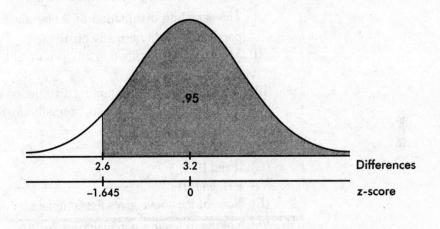

Questions on Topic Twelve: Sampling Distributions

Multiple-Choice Questions

Directions: The questions or incomplete statements that follow are each followed by five suggested answers or completions. Choose the response that best answers the question or completes the statement.

1. Which of the following statements are true?

    I. The larger the sample, the larger the spread in the sampling distribution.

    II. Provided that the population size is significantly greater than the sample size, the spread of a sampling distribution is about the same no matter what the population size.

    III. Bias has to do with the center, not the spread, of a sampling distribution.

    (A) I and II
    (B) I and III
    (C) II and III
    (D) I, II, and III
    (E) None of the above gives the complete set of true responses.

2. Which of the following statements are true?

I. Sample parameters are used to make inferences about population statistics.

II. Statistics from smaller samples have more variability.

III. Parameters are fixed, while statistics vary depending on which sample is chosen.

(A) I and II

(B) I and III

(C) II and III

(D) I, II, and III

(E) None of the above gives the complete set of true responses.

3. Which of the following statements are true?

I. The sampling distribution of $\bar{x}$ has standard deviation $\frac{\sigma}{\sqrt{n}}$ even if the population is not normally distributed.

II. The sampling distribution of $\bar{x}$ is normal if the population has a normal distribution.

III. When n is large, the sampling distribution of $\bar{x}$ is approximately normal even if the population is not normally distributed.

(A) I and II

(B) I and III

(C) II and III

(D) I, II, and III

(E) None of the above gives the complete set of true responses.

4. Which of the following statements are true?

I. The mean of the set of sample means varies inversely as the square root of the size of the samples.

II. The variance of the set of sample means varies directly as the size of the samples and inversely as the variance of the original population.

III. The standard deviation of the set of sample means varies directly as the standard deviation of the original population and inversely as the square root of the size of the samples.

(A) I only

(B) II only

(C) III only

(D) I and II

(E) I and III

5. Which of the following statements are true?

I. The sampling distribution of $\hat{p}$ has a mean equal to the population proportion p.

II. The sampling distribution of $\hat{p}$ has a standard deviation equal to $\sqrt{np(1-p)}$.

III. The sampling distribution of $\hat{p}$ is considered close to normal provided that $n \geq 30$.

(A) I and II

(B) I and III

(C) II and III

(D) I, II, and III

(E) None of the above gives the complete set of true responses.

6. Which of the following statements are true?

   I. The sampling distribution of the difference $\bar{x}_1 - \bar{x}_2$ has a mean equal to the difference of the population means.
   II. The sampling distribution of the difference $\bar{x}_1 - \bar{x}_2$ has a standard deviation equal to the sum of the population standard deviations.
   III. The sampling distribution of the difference $\bar{x}_1 - \bar{x}_2$ has a standard deviation equal to the difference of the population standard deviations.

   (A) I only
   (B) II only
   (C) III only
   (D) I and II
   (E) I and III

7. Which of the following are unbiased estimators for the corresponding population parameters?

   I. Sample means
   II. Sample proportions
   III. Difference of sample means
   IV. Difference of sample proportions

   (A) None are unbiased.
   (B) I and II
   (C) I and III
   (D) III and IV
   (E) All are unbiased.

8. Suppose that 35% of all business executives are willing to switch companies if offered a higher salary. If a headhunter randomly contacts 100 executives, what is the probability that over 40% will be willing to switch companies if offered a higher salary?

   (A) .1469
   (B) .1977
   (C) .4207
   (D) .8023
   (E) .8531

9. Given that 58% of all gold dealers believe next year will be a good one to speculate in South African gold coins, in a random sample of 150 dealers, what is the probability that between 55% and 60% believe that it will be a good year to speculate?

   (A) .0500
   (B) .1192
   (C) .3099
   (D) .4619
   (E) .9215

10. The average outstanding bill for delinquent customer accounts for a national department store chain is $187.50 with a standard deviation of $54.50. In a random sample of 50 delinquent accounts, what is the probability that the mean outstanding bill is over $200?

(A) .0526

(B) .0667

(C) .4090

(D) .5910

(E) .9474

11. The average number of daily emergency room admissions at a hospital is 85 with a standard deviation of 37. In a random sample of 30 days, what is the probability that the mean number of daily emergency admissions is between 75 and 95?

(A) .1388

(B) .2128

(C) .8612

(D) .8990

(E) .9970

12. Two companies offer classes designed to improve students' SAT scores. Suppose that 83% of students enrolling in the first program improve their scores, while 74% of those signing up for the second program also raise their scores. In a random sample of 60 students taking the first program and 50 taking the second, what is the probability that the difference between the percentages of students improving their scores (first program minus second) is more than 15%?

(A) .0281

(B) .2236

(C) .2764

(D) .3632

(E) .7764

13. Pepper plants watered lightly every day for a month show an average growth of 27 centimeters with a standard deviation of 8.3 centimeters, while pepper plants watered heavily once a week for a month show an average growth of 29 centimeters with a standard deviation of 7.9 centimeters. In a random sample of 60 plants, half of which are given each of the watering treatments, what is the probability that the difference in average growth between the two halves is between −3 and +3 centimeters?

(A) .3156

(B) .3240

(C) .4639

(D) .6760

(E) .6844

Answer Key

1. C	4. C	7. E	10. A	13. D
2. C	5. E	8. A	11. C	
3. D	6. A	9. D	12. B	

Answers Explained

1. **(C)** The larger the sample, the smaller the spread in the sampling distribution.

2. **(C)** Sample statistics are used to make inferences about population proportions.

3. **(D)** It is always true that the sampling distribution of $\bar{x}$ has mean μ and standard deviation $\frac{\sigma}{\sqrt{n}}$. In addition, the sampling distribution will be normal if the population is normal or if n is large.

4. **(C)** The mean of the set of sample means is equal to the mean of the population; it does not vary with the size of the samples. The variance of the set of sample means varies inversely as the size of the samples and directly as the variance of the original population.

5. **(E)** Only I is true. The sampling distribution of $\hat{p}$ has a standard deviation equal to $\sqrt{\frac{p(1-p)}{n}}$. The sampling distribution of $\hat{p}$ is considered close to normal provided that both np and $n(1-p)$ are large enough (greater than either 5 or 10 are standard guidelines).

6. **(A)** Variances can be added; standard deviations cannot.

7. **(E)** All are unbiased estimators for the corresponding population parameters; that is, the means of their sampling distributions are equal to the population parameters.

8. **(A)** The set of sample proportions is approximately normally distributed with mean .35 and standard deviation $\sigma_{\hat{p}} = \sqrt{\frac{(.35)(.65)}{100}} = .0477$. With a z-score of $\frac{.40-.35}{.0477} = 1.05$, the probability that the sample proportion exceeds 40% is $1 - .8531 = .1469$.

9. **(D)** The set of sample proportions is approximately normally distributed with mean .58 and standard deviation $\sigma_{\hat{p}} = \sqrt{\frac{(.58)(.42)}{150}} = .0403$. With z-scores of $\frac{.55-.58}{.0403} = -0.74$ and $\frac{.60-.58}{.0403} = 0.50$, the probability the sample proportion is between .55 and .60 is $.6915 - .2296 = .4619$.

10. **(A)** The set of sample means is approximately normally distributed with $\mu_{\bar{x}} = 187.50$ and $\sigma_{\bar{x}} = \frac{54.50}{\sqrt{50}} = 7.707$. The z-score of 200 is $\frac{200-187.50}{7.707} = 1.62$, and the probability that the mean outstanding bill is over \$200 is $1 - .9474 = .0526$.

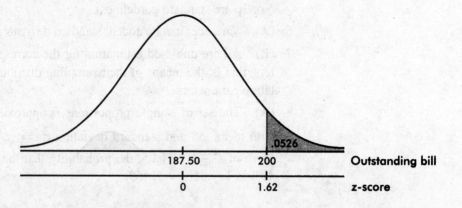

11. **(C)** The set of sample means is approximately normally distributed with $\mu_{\bar{x}} = 85$ and $\sigma_{\bar{x}} = \frac{37}{\sqrt{30}} = 6.755$. The z-scores of 75 and 95 are $\frac{75-85}{6.755} = -1.48$ and $\frac{95-85}{6.755} = 1.48$, respectively. The probability that the mean admissions in the sample are between 75 and 95 is $.9306 - .0694 = .8612$.

12. **(B)**   For the sampling distribution of $\hat{p}_1 - \hat{p}_2$, the mean is $.83 - .74 = .09$ and the standard deviation is $\sqrt{\frac{(.83)(.17)}{60} + \frac{(.74)(.26)}{50}} = .0787$. The z-score of $.15$ is $\frac{.15 - .09}{.0787} = 0.76$. Using Table A, we find $1 - .7764 = .2236$ for the probability that the difference is more than 15%.

13. **(D)**   The mean of the differences equals $27 - 29 = -2$, while the standard deviation is $\sqrt{\frac{(8.3)^2}{30} + \frac{(7.9)^2}{30}} = 2.092$. The z-scores of $+3$ and -3 are $\frac{3-(-2)}{2.092} = 2.39$ and $\frac{-3-(-2)}{2.092} = -0.48$, respectively. The probability that the difference is between these two values is $.9916 - .3156 = .6760$.

Free-Response Questions

> *Directions:* You must show all work and indicate the methods you use. You will be graded on the correctness of your methods and on the accuracy of your final answers.

Two Open-Ended Questions

1. Give an example of a population and an associated population parameter and sample statistic, and then explain what is meant by the sampling distribution.

2. Heights, weights, and like measurements tend to result in normal distributions, but normally distributed natural phenomena occur much less frequently than might be supposed. Explain why the normal curve has an importance in statistics that is independent of whether or not it appears in nature.

Answers Explained

1. The population parameter can be something like a mean μ or a proportion p, and then the sample statistic is a sample mean $\bar{x}$ or a sample proportion $\hat{p}$. For example, if the population is the set of salaries earned by adults in the United States, the population parameter is the mean of all these salaries, and the sample statistic can be the mean of the salaries in a randomly chosen sample of 100 adult salaries. The sampling distribution would then be the distribution of sample means from all possible samples of 100 adult salaries.

2. What is significant is that the results of many types of sampling experiments can be analyzed using the normal curve. For example, there is no reason to suppose that the amounts of money that different people spend in grocery stores are normally distributed. However, if every day we survey 30 people leaving a store and determine the average grocery bill, these daily averages will have a nearly normal distribution. The central limit theorem of statistics says that for any population, no matter what its distribution, if n is sufficiently large, then the set of sample means for all samples of size n will be approximately normally distributed.

Two Investigative Tasks

1. Consider a population of size $N = 5$ consisting of the elements 3, 6, 8, 10, and 18.

   a. Determine the population mean μ and the population standard deviation σ.

   b. List all possible samples of size $n = 2$ [there are $C(5, 2) = 10$ of them] and determine the mean $\bar{x}$ of each.

   c. Show that the mean of the set of ten sample means is equal to the population mean μ.

   d. Show that the standard deviation of the set of ten sample means is

$$\sigma_{\bar{x}} = \frac{\sigma}{\sqrt{n}} \sqrt{\frac{N-n}{N-1}}$$

e. More generally, what can be said about $\frac{\sigma}{\sqrt{n}}\sqrt{\frac{N-n}{N-1}}$ if the population size N is very large?

2. Suppose that, of a group of six ($N = 6$) people, A, B, C, D, E, and F, two (B and E) own their own houses. Thus the proportion of the group owning their own homes is $p = \frac{2}{6} = \frac{1}{3}$. Now consider all possible samples of size $n = 4$.

   a. List the samples [there are $C(6, 4) = 15$] and determine the proportion $\hat{p}$ of homeowners for each sample.

   b. Calculate the mean and standard deviation for this set of 15 proportions. Show that the mean is equal to p and that the standard deviation is equal to $\sqrt{\frac{p(1-p)}{n}}\sqrt{\frac{N-n}{N-1}}$.

   c. What happens to $\sqrt{\frac{p(1-p)}{n}}\sqrt{\frac{N-n}{N-1}}$ when the population size N is very large?

Answers Explained

1.   a. Using a calculator, find $\mu = 9$ and $\sigma = 5.0596$.

         b.

Sample	Mean
{3, 6}	4.5
{3, 8}	5.5
{3, 10}	6.5
{3, 18}	10.5
{6, 8}	7
{6, 10}	8
{6, 18}	12
{8, 10}	9
{8, 18}	13
{10, 18}	14

   c. $\dfrac{(4.5+5.5+6.5+10.5+7+8+12+9+13+14}{10} = 9.$

   d. Using a calculator, find $\sigma_{\bar{x}} = 3.0984$ and then note that

   $$\frac{5.0596}{\sqrt{2}}\sqrt{\frac{5-2}{5-1}} = 3.0984$$

   e. If N is very large, $\frac{N-n}{N-1}$ is approximately equal to 1 and so the expression simplifies to $\frac{\sigma}{\sqrt{n}}$.

2. *a.*

Sample	Proportion
A, B, C, D	.25
A, B, C, E	.50
A, B, C, F	.25
A, B, D, E	.50
A, B, D, F	.25
A, B, E, F	.50
A, C, D, E	.25
A, C, D, F	.00
A, C, E, F	.25
A, D, E, F	.25
B, C, D, E	.50
B, C, D, F	.25
B, C, E, F	.50
B, D, E, F	.50
C, D, E, F	.25

b. Using a calculator, find $\mu_{\hat{p}} = .333$ and $\sigma_{\hat{p}} = .149$ and note that

$$\sqrt{\frac{(.333)(.667)}{4}}\sqrt{\frac{6-4}{6-1}} = .149$$

c. If N is very large, $\frac{N-n}{N-1}$ is approximately equal to 1 and so the expression simplifies to $\sqrt{\frac{p(1-p)}{n}}$.

THEME FOUR

Statistical Inference

"I'm 100% behind you between 40% and 60% of the time."

TOPIC THIRTEEN
Confidence Intervals

Using a measurement from a sample, we are never able to say *exactly* what a population proportion or mean is; rather we always say we have a certain *confidence* that the population proportion or mean lies in a particular *interval*. The particular interval is centered around a sample proportion or mean and can be expressed as the sample estimate plus or minus an associated *margin of error*.

The Meaning of a Confidence Interval

Using what we know about sampling distributions, we are able to establish a certain confidence that a sample proportion or mean lies within a specified interval around the population proportion or mean. However, we then have the same confidence that the population proportion or mean lies within a specified interval around the sample proportion or mean (e.g., the distance from Missoula to Whitefish is the same as the distance from Whitefish to Missoula).

Typically we consider 90%, 95%, and 99% confidence interval estimates, but any percentage is possible. The percentage is the percentage of samples that would pinpoint the unknown p or μ within plus or minus a certain margin or error. We do *not* say there is a .90, .95, or .99 probability that p or μ is within a certain margin of error of a given sample proportion or mean. For a given sample proportion or mean, p or μ either is or isn't within the specified interval, and so the probability is either 1 or 0.

Large Sample Confidence Interval for a Proportion

We are interested in estimating a population proportion p by considering a single sample proportion $\hat{p}$. This sample proportion is just one of a whole universe of sample proportions, and from Topic 12 we remember the following:

1. The set of all sample proportions is approximately normally distributed.
2. The mean $\mu_{\hat{p}}$ of the set of sample proportions equals p, the population proportion.
3. The standard deviation $\sigma_{\hat{p}}$ of the set of sample proportions is approximately equal to $\sqrt{\frac{p(1-p)}{n}}$.

In finding confidence interval estimates of the population proportion p, how do we find $\sqrt{\frac{p(1-p)}{n}}$ since p is unknown? The reasonable procedure is to use the sample proportion $\hat{p}$:

$$\sigma_{\hat{p}} \approx \sqrt{\frac{\hat{p}(1-\hat{p})}{n}}$$

Example 13.1. If 64% of a sample of 550 people leaving a shopping mall claim to have spent over $25, determine a 99% confidence interval estimate for the proportion of shopping mall customers who spend over $25.

Answer: Since $\hat{p} = .64$, the standard deviation of the set of sample proportions is

$$\sigma_{\hat{p}} \approx \sqrt{\frac{(.64)(.36)}{550}} = .0205$$

From Topic 11 we know that 99% of the sample proportions should be within 2.576 standard deviations of the population mean. Equivalently, we are 99% certain that the population mean is within 2.576 standard deviations of any sample mean.[1] Thus the 99% confidence interval estimate for the population proportion is $.64 \pm 2.576(.0205) = .64 \pm .053$. We say that the *margin of error* is $\pm.053$. We are 99% certain that the proportion of shoppers spending over $25 is between .587 and .693.

Example 13.2. In a random sample of machine parts, 18 out of 225 were found to have been damaged in shipment. Establish a 95% confidence interval estimate for the proportion of machine parts that are damaged in shipment.

Answer: The sample proportion is $\hat{p} = \frac{18}{225} = .08$, and the standard deviation of the set of sample proportions is

$$\sigma_{\hat{p}} \approx \sqrt{\frac{(.08)(.92)}{225}} = .0181$$

---

[1] Note that we cannot say there is a .99 probability that the population proportion is within 2.576 standard deviations of a given sample proportion. For a given sample proportion, the population proportion either is or isn't within the specified interval, and so the probability is either 1 or 0.

The 95% confidence interval estimate for the population proportion is $.08 \pm 1.96(.0181) = .08 \pm .035$. Thus we are 95% certain that the proportion of machine parts damaged in shipment is between .045 and .115.

Suppose there are 50,000 parts in the entire shipment. We can translate from proportions to actual numbers:

$$.045(50,000) = 2250 \quad \text{and} \quad .115(50,000) = 5750$$

and so we can be 95% confident that there are between 2250 and 5750 defective parts in the whole shipment.

Example 13.3. A telephone survey of 1000 adults was taken shortly after the United States began bombing Iraq.

a. If 832 voiced their support for this action, with what confidence can it be asserted that 83.2% ± 3% of the adult U.S. population supported the decision to go to war?
Answer:

$$\hat{p} = \frac{832}{1000} = .832 \quad \text{and so} \quad \sigma_{\hat{p}} \approx \sqrt{\frac{(.832)(.168)}{1000}} = .0118$$

The relevant z-scores are $\pm\frac{.03}{.0118} = \pm 2.54$. Table A gives probabilities of .0055 and .9945, and so our answer is $.9945 - .0055 = .9890$. In other words, $83.2\% \pm 3\%$ is a 98.90% confidence interval estimate for U.S. adult support of the war decision.

b. If the adult U.S. population is 191 million, estimate the actual numerical support.
Answer: Since

$$.802(191,000,000) \approx 153,000,000$$

while

$$.862(191,000,000) \approx 165,000,000$$

we can be 98.90% confident that between 153 and 165 million adults supported the initial bombing decision.

Example 13.4.   A U.S. Department of Labor survey of 6230 unemployed adults classified people by marital status, gender, and race. The raw numbers are as follows:

| | White, 16 yr. and older | | |
	Married	Widow/Div.	Single
Men	1090	337	1168
Women	952	423	632

| | Nonwhite, 16 yr. and older | | |
	Married	Widow/Div.	Single
Men	266	135	503
Women	189	186	349

a. Find a 90% confidence interval estimate for the proportion of unemployed men who are married.

Answer: Totaling the first row across both tables, we find that there are 3499 men in the survey; $1090 + 266 = 1356$ of them are married. Therefore $\hat{p} = \frac{1356}{3499} = .3875$ and

$$\sigma_{\hat{p}} \approx \sqrt{\frac{(.3875)(.6125)}{3499}} = .008236$$

Thus the 90% confidence interval estimate is $.3875 \pm 1.645(.008236) = .3875 \pm .0135$.

b. Find a 98% confidence interval estimate of the proportion of unemployed single persons who are women.

Answer: There are $1168 + 632 + 503 + 349 = 2652$ singles in the survey. Of these, $632 + 349 = 981$ are women, so $\hat{p} = \frac{981}{2652} = .3699$ and

$$\sigma_{\hat{p}} \approx \sqrt{\frac{(.3699)(.6301)}{2652}} = .009375$$

The 98% confidence interval estimate is $.3699 \pm 2.326(.009375) = .3699 \pm .0218$.

Example 13.5.   An assembly line quality check involves the following procedure: A sample of size 50 is randomly picked, and the machinery is shut down for repairs if the percentage of defective items in the sample is c percent or more. Find the value of c that results in a 90% chance that the machinery will be stopped if, on the average, the percentage of defective items it is producing is 15%.

Answer: Since $p = .15$,

$$\sigma_{\hat{p}} \approx \sqrt{\frac{(.15)(.85)}{50}} = .0505$$

The z-score corresponding to a .90 probability is -1.282, so $c = .15 - 1.282(.0505) = .085$ or 8.5%.

One important consideration in setting up a survey is the choice of sample size. To obtain a smaller, more precise interval estimate of the population proportion, we must either decrease the degree of confidence or increase the sample size. Similarly, if we want to increase the degree of confidence, we can either accept a wider interval estimate or increase the sample size. Again, while choosing a larger sample size may seem desirable, in the real world this decision involves time and cost considerations.

In setting up a survey to obtain a confidence interval estimate of the population proportion, what should we use for $\sigma_{\hat{p}}$? To answer this question, we first must consider how large $\sqrt{p(1-p)}$ can be. We plot various values of p:

p:	.1	.2	.3	.4	.5	.6	.7	.8	.9
$\sqrt{p(1-p)}$:	.3	.4	.458	.490	.5	.490	.458	.4	.3

which gives .5 as the intuitive answer. Thus $\sqrt{\frac{p(1-p)}{n}}$ is at most $\frac{.5}{\sqrt{n}}$. We make use of this fact to determine sample sizes in problems such as Examples 13.6 and 13.7.

Example 13.6.   An Environmental Protection Agency (EPA) investigator wants to know the proportion of fish that are inedible because of chemical pollution downstream of an offending factory. If the answer must be within ±.03 at the 96% confidence level, how many fish should be in the sample tested?

Answer: We want $2.05\sigma_{\hat{p}} \leq .03$. From the above remark, $\sigma_{\hat{p}}$ is at most $\frac{.5}{\sqrt{n}}$, and so it is sufficient to consider $2.05\left(\frac{.5}{\sqrt{n}}\right) \leq .03$. Algebraically, we have $\sqrt{n} \geq \frac{2.05(.5)}{.03} = 34.17$ and $n \geq 1167.4$. Therefore, choosing a sample of 1168 fish gives the inedible proportion to within ±.03 at the 96% level.

Note that the accuracy of the estimate does *not* depend on what fraction of the whole population we have sampled. What is critical is the *absolute size* of the sample. Is some minimal value of n necessary for the procedures we are using to be meaningful? Since we are using the normal approximation to the binomial, both np and $n(1-p)$ should be at least 5 (see Topic 11).

Example 13.7. A study is undertaken to determine the proportion of industry executives who believe that workers' pay should be based on individual performance. How many executives should be interviewed if an estimate is desired at the 99% confidence level to within $\pm.06$? To within $\pm.03$? To within $\pm.02$?

Answer: Algebraically, $2.576\left(\frac{.5}{\sqrt{n}}\right) \leq .06$ gives $\sqrt{n} \geq \frac{2.576(.5)}{.06} = 21.5$, so $n \geq 462.25$. Similarly, $2.576\left(\frac{.5}{\sqrt{n}}\right) \leq .03$ gives $\sqrt{n} \geq \frac{2.576(.5)}{.03} = 42.9$, so $n \geq 1840.4$. Finally, $2.576\left(\frac{.5}{\sqrt{n}}\right) \leq .02$ gives $\sqrt{n} \geq \frac{2.576(.5)}{.02} = 64.4$, so $n \geq 4147.4$. Thus 463, 1841, or 4148 executives should be interviewed, depending on the accuracy desired.

Note that to cut the interval estimate in half (from $\pm.06$ to $\pm.03$), we would have to increase the sample size fourfold, and to cut the interval estimate to a third (from $\pm.06$ to $\pm.02$), a ninefold increase in the sample size would be required (answers are not exact because of round-off error.)

More generally, to divide the interval estimate by d without affecting the confidence level, we must increase the sample size by a multiple of d^2.

A formula for the calculations in Examples 13.6 and 13.7 is

$$n = \left[\frac{z}{2(\text{error})}\right]^2$$

Large Sample Confidence Interval for a Mean

We are interested in estimating a population mean μ by considering a single sample mean $\bar{x}$. This sample mean is just one of a whole universe of sample means, and from Topic 12 we remember that if n is sufficiently large,

1. the set of all sample means is approximately normally distributed.
2. the mean of the set of sample means equals μ, the mean of the population.
3. the standard deviation $\sigma_{\bar{x}}$ of the set of sample means is approximately equal to $\frac{\sigma}{\sqrt{n}}$, that is, equal to the standard deviation of the whole population divided by the square root of the sample size.

Frequently we do not know σ, the population standard deviation. In such cases, we must use s, the *standard deviation of the sample*, as an estimate of σ. (Note that some statisticians use t-distributions instead of the standard normal curve whenever σ is unknown, no matter what the sample size.)

Example 13.8. A bottling machine is operating with a standard deviation of 0.12 ounce. Suppose that in a sample of 36 bottles the machine inserted an average of 16.1 ounces into each bottle.

a. Estimate the mean number of ounces in all the bottles this machine fills. More specifically, give an interval within which we are 95% certain that the mean lies.

Answer: For samples of size 36, the sample means are approximately normally distributed with a standard deviation of $\sigma_{\bar{x}} = \frac{\sigma}{\sqrt{n}} = \frac{0.12}{\sqrt{36}} = 0.02$. From Topic 11 we know that 95% of the sample means should be within 1.96 standard deviations of the population mean. Equivalently, we are 95% certain that the population mean is within 1.96 standard deviations of any sample mean. In our case, $16.1 \pm 1.96(0.02) = 16.1 \pm 0.0392$, and we are 95% sure that the mean number of ounces in all bottles is between 16.0608 and 16.1392. This is called a *95% confidence interval estimate*.

b. How about a 99% confidence interval estimate?

Answer: Here, $16.1 \pm 2.576(0.02) = 16.1 \pm 0.0515$, and we are 99% sure that the mean number of ounces in all bottles is between 16.0485 and 16.1515.

Note that when we wanted a higher certainty (99% instead of 95%), we had to settle for a larger, less specific interval (± 0.0515 instead of ± 0.0392).

Example 13.9. At a certain plant, batteries are being produced with a life expectancy that has a variance of 5.76 months squared. Suppose the mean life expectancy in a sample of 64 batteries is 12.35 months.

a. Find a 90% confidence interval estimate of life expectancy for all the batteries produced at this plant.

Answer: The standard deviation of the population is $\sigma = \sqrt{5.76} = 2.4$, and the standard deviation of the sample means is $\sigma_{\bar{x}} = \frac{\sigma}{\sqrt{n}} = \frac{2.4}{\sqrt{64}} = 0.3$. The 90% confidence interval estimate for the population mean is $12.35 \pm 1.645(0.3) = 12.35 \pm 0.4935$. Thus we are 90% certain that the mean life expectancy of the batteries is between 11.8565 and 12.8435 months.

b. What would the 90% confidence interval estimate be if the sample mean of 12.35 had come from a sample of 100 batteries?

Answer: The standard deviation of the sample means would then have been $\sigma_{\bar{x}} = \frac{\sigma}{\sqrt{n}} = \frac{2.4}{\sqrt{100}} = 0.24$, and the 90% confidence interval estimate would be $12.35 \pm 1.645(0.24) = 12.35 \pm 0.3948$.

Note that when the sample size increased (from 64 to 100), the same sample mean resulted in a narrower, more specific interval (± 0.3948 versus ± 0.4935).

Example 13.10. A new drug results in lowering the heart rate by varying amounts with a standard deviation of 2.49 beats per minute.

a. Find a 95% confidence interval estimate for the mean lowering of the heart rate in all patients if a 50-person sample averages a drop of 5.32 beats per minute.

Answer: The standard deviation of sample means is $\sigma_{\bar{x}} = \frac{\sigma}{\sqrt{n}} = \frac{2.49}{\sqrt{50}} = 0.352$. We are 95% certain that the mean lowering of the heart rate is in the range $5.32 \pm 1.96(0.352) = 5.32 \pm 0.69$ or between 4.63 and 6.01 heartbeats per minute.

b. With what certainty can we assert that the new drug lowers the heart rate by a mean of 5.32 ± 0.75 beats per minute?

Answer: Converting ± 0.75 to z-scores yields $\frac{\pm 0.75}{0.352} = \pm 2.13$. From Table A, these z-scores give probabilities of .0166 and .9834, respectively, so our answer is $.9834 - .0166 = .9668$. In other words, 5.32 ± 0.75 beats per minute is a 96.68% confidence interval estimate of the mean lowering of the heart rate effected by this drug.

Example 13.11. A survey was conducted involving 250 out of 125,000 families living in a city. The average amount of income tax paid per family in the sample was $3540 with a standard deviation of $1150. Establish a 99% confidence interval estimate for the total taxes paid by all the families in the city.

Answer: We are given $\bar{x} = 3540$ and $s = 1150$. We use s as an estimate for σ and calculate the standard deviation of the sample means to be $\sigma_{\bar{x}} \approx \frac{s}{\sqrt{n}} = \frac{1150}{\sqrt{250}} = 72.73$. A 99% confidence interval estimate for the mean tax paid by each family is $3540 \pm 2.576(72.73) = 3540 \pm 187.35$. A 99% confidence interval estimate for the total taxes paid by all the families is $125,000(3540 \pm 187.35) = 442,500,000 \pm 23,400,000$ or between $419,100,000 and $465,900,000.

Statistical principles are useful not only in analyzing data but also in setting up experiments, and one important consideration is the choice of a sample size. In making interval estimates of population means, we have seen that each inference must go hand in hand with an associated confidence level statement. Generally, if we want a smaller, more precise interval estimate, we either decrease the degree of confidence or increase the sample size. Similarly, if we want to increase the degree of confidence, we either accept a wider interval estimate or increase the sample size. Thus, choosing a larger sample size always seems desirable; in the real world, however, time and cost considerations are involved.

Example 13.12.   Ball bearings are manufactured by a process that results in a standard deviation in diameter of 0.025 inch. What sample size should be chosen if we wish to be 99% sure of knowing the diameter to within ±0.01 inch?

Answer: We have

$$\sigma_{\bar{x}} = \frac{\sigma}{\sqrt{n}} = \frac{0.025}{\sqrt{n}} \quad \text{and} \quad 2.576\sigma_{\bar{x}} \leq 0.01$$

Thus

$$2.576\left(\frac{0.025}{\sqrt{n}}\right) \leq 0.01$$

Algebraically, we find that

$$\sqrt{n} \geq \frac{2.576(0.025)}{0.01} = 6.44$$

so $n \geq 41.5$. We choose a sample size of 42.

A formula for the above calculation is

$$n = \left(\frac{z\sigma}{\text{error}}\right)^2$$

which in this problem gives $n = \left[\frac{(2.576)(0.025)}{0.01}\right]^2 = 41.5$.

Example 13.13.   A government investigator plans to test for the mean quantity of a particular pollutant that a manufacturer is dumping into a river each day. She needs an estimate that is within 50 grams at the 95% confidence level. If previous measurements indicate that the variance is approximately 21,800 grams squared, how many days should she include in the sample?

Answer: We have

$$\sigma^2 = 21,800$$

so

$$\sigma = \sqrt{21,800} = 147.65$$

Then

$$\sigma_{\bar{x}} = \frac{\sigma}{\sqrt{n}} = \frac{147.65}{\sqrt{n}}$$

and

$$1.96\sigma_{\bar{x}} \leq 50$$

Thus $1.96(\frac{147.65}{\sqrt{n}}) \leq 50$, $\sqrt{n} \geq \frac{1.96(147.65)}{50} = 5.788$, and $n \geq 33.5$. The investigator should sample 34 days' dumping.

In order to cut an interval estimate in half, the sample size must be increased fourfold. To cut an estimate to a third, the sample size must be increased ninefold. More generally, if we want to divide the interval estimate by d without affecting the confidence level, we must increase the sample size by a multiple of d^2.

Large Sample Confidence Interval for a Difference of Two Proportions

From Topic 12, we have the following information about the sampling distribution of $\hat{p}_1 - \hat{p}_2$:

1. The set of all differences of sample proportions is approximately normally distributed.
2. The mean of the set of differences of sample proportions equals $p_1 - p_2$, the difference of population proportions.
3. The standard deviation σ_d of the set of differences of sample proportions is approximately equal to

$$\sqrt{\frac{p_1(1-p_1)}{n_1} + \frac{p_2(1-p_2)}{n_2}}$$

Example 13.14. Suppose that 84% of a sample of 125 nurses working 7 A.M. to 3 P.M. shifts in city hospitals express positive job satisfaction, while only 72% of a sample of 150 nurses on 11 P.M. to 7 A.M. shifts express similar fulfillment. Establish a 90% confidence interval estimate for the difference.

Answer:

$$n_1 = 125 \quad n_2 = 150$$
$$\hat{p}_1 = .84 \quad \hat{p}_2 = .72$$

$$\sigma_d \approx \sqrt{\frac{(.84)(.16)}{125} + \frac{(.72)(.28)}{150}} = .0492$$

The observed difference is $.84 - .72 = .12$, and the critical z-scores are ± 1.645. The confidence interval estimate is $.12 \pm 1.645(.0492) = .12 \pm .081$. We can be 90% certain that the proportion of satisfied nurses on 7 A.M. to 3 P.M. shifts is between .039 and .201 higher than the proportion for nurses on 11 P.M. to 7 A.M. shifts.

Example 13.15. A grocery store manager notes that in a sample of 85 people going through the express checkout line, only 10 paid with checks, whereas, in a sample of 92 customers passing through the regular line, 37 paid with checks. Find a 95% confidence interval estimate for the difference between the proportion of customers going through the two different lines who use checks.

Answer:

$$n_1 = 85 \qquad n_2 = 92$$
$$\hat{p}_1 = \frac{10}{85} = .118 \quad \hat{p}_2 = \frac{37}{92} = .402$$

$$\sigma_d \approx \sqrt{\frac{(.118)(.882)}{85} + \frac{(.402)(.598)}{92}} = .0619$$

The observed difference is $.118 - .402 = -.284$, and the critical z-scores are ± 1.96. Thus, the confidence interval estimate is $-.284 \pm 1.96(.0619) = -.284 \pm .121$. The manager can be 90% sure that the proportion of customers passing through the express line who use checks is between .163 and .405 lower than the proportion going through the regular line who use checks.

With regard to choosing a sample size, $\sqrt{p(1-p)}$ is at most .5. Thus

$$\sqrt{p(1-p)\left(\frac{1}{n_1} + \frac{1}{n_2}\right)} \le (.5)\sqrt{\frac{1}{n_1} + \frac{1}{n_2}}$$

Now, if we simplify by insisting that $n_1 = n_2 = n$, the above statement can be reduced as follows:

$$(.5)\sqrt{\frac{1}{n} + \frac{1}{n}} = (.5)\sqrt{\frac{2}{n}} = \frac{.5\sqrt{2}}{\sqrt{n}}$$

Example 13.16.   A pollster wants to determine the difference between the proportions of high-income voters and low-income voters who support a decrease in the capital gains tax. If the answer must be known to within $\pm .02$ at the 95% confidence level, what size samples should be taken?

Answer: Assuming we will pick the same size samples for the two sample proportions, we have $\sigma_d \le \frac{.5\sqrt{2}}{\sqrt{n}}$ and $1.96\sigma_d \le .02$. Thus $\frac{1.96(.5)\sqrt{2}}{\sqrt{n}} \le .02$. Algebraically we find that $\sqrt{n} \ge \frac{1.96(.5)\sqrt{2}}{.02} = 69.3$. Therefore, $n \ge 69.3^2 = 4802.5$, and the pollster should use 4803 people for each sample.

Large Sample Confidence Interval for a Difference Between Two Means

We have the following information about the sampling distribution of $\bar{x}_1 - \bar{x}_2$:

1. The set of all differences of sample means is approximately normally distributed.
2. The mean of the set of differences of sample means equals $\mu_1 - \mu_2$, the difference of population means.
3. The standard deviation $\sigma_{\bar{x}_1 - \bar{x}_2}$ of the set of differences of sample means is approximately equal to $\sqrt{\frac{\sigma_1^2}{n_1} + \frac{\sigma_2^2}{n_2}}$.

Example 13.17. A 30-month study is conducted to determine the difference in the numbers of accidents per month occurring in two departments in an assembly plant. Suppose the first department averages 12.3 accidents per month with a standard deviation of 3.5, while the second averages 7.6 accidents with a standard deviation of 3.4. Determine a 95% confidence interval estimate for the difference in the numbers of accidents per month.

Answer:

$$n_1 = 30 \qquad n_2 = 30$$
$$\bar{x}_1 = 12.3 \quad \bar{x}_2 = 7.6$$
$$s_1 = 3.5 \qquad s_2 = 3.4$$

$$\sigma_{\bar{x}_1 - \bar{x}_2} = \sqrt{\frac{\sigma_1^2}{n_1} + \frac{\sigma_2^2}{n_2}} \approx \sqrt{\frac{s_1^2}{n_1} + \frac{s_2^2}{n_2}} = \sqrt{\frac{(3.5)^2}{30} + \frac{(3.4)^2}{30}} = 0.89$$

The observed difference is $12.3 - 7.6 = 4.7$, and the critical z-scores are ± 1.96. Thus the confidence interval estimate is $4.7 \pm 1.96(0.89) = 4.7 \pm 1.74$. We are 95% confident that the first department has between 2.96 and 6.44 more accidents per month than the second department.

Example 13.18. A survey is run to determine the difference in the cost of groceries in suburban stores versus inner city stores. A preselected group of items is purchased in a sample of 45 suburban and 35 inner city stores, and the following data are obtained.

Suburban stores	Inner city stores
$n_1 = 45$	$n_2 = 35$
$\bar{x}_1 = \$36.52$	$\bar{x}_2 = \$39.40$
$s_1 = \$1.10$	$s_2 = \$1.23$

Find a 90% confidence interval estimate for the difference in the cost of groceries.

Answer:

$$\sigma_{\bar{x}_1 - \bar{x}_2} \approx \sqrt{\frac{(1.10)^2}{45} + \frac{(1.23)^2}{35}} = 0.265$$

The observed difference is $36.52 - 39.40 = -2.88$, the critical z-scores are ± 1.645, and the confidence interval estimate is $-2.88 \pm 1.645(0.265) = -2.88 \pm 0.44$. Thus we are 90% certain that the selected group of items costs between $2.44 and $3.32 *less* in suburban stores than in inner city stores.

Example 13.19. A hardware store owner wishes to determine the difference between the drying times of two brands of paint. Suppose the standard deviation between cans in each population is 2.5 minutes. How large a sample (same number) of each must the store owner use if he wishes to be 98% sure of knowing the difference to within 1 minute?

Answer:

$$\sigma_{\bar{x}_1 - \bar{x}_2} = \sqrt{\frac{(2.5)^2}{n} + \frac{(2.5)^2}{n}} = \frac{3.536}{\sqrt{n}}$$

With a critical z-score of 2.326, we have $2.326(\frac{3.536}{\sqrt{n}}) \leq 1$, so $\sqrt{n} \geq 8.22$ and $n \geq 67.6$. Thus the owner should test samples of 68 paint patches from each brand.

The analysis and procedure discussed in this section require that the two samples being compared be independent of each other. However, many experiments and tests involve comparing two populations for which the data naturally occur in pairs. In this case of *paired differences,* the proper procedure is to run a one-sample analysis on the single variable consisting of the differences from the paired data.

Example 13.20.   An SAT preparation class of 30 students produces the following improvement in scores:

Student	First Score	Second Score	Improvement
1	912	1025	113
2	1025	1085	60
3	1295	1350	55
4	1123	1202	79
5	875	982	107
6	890	950	60
7	1002	1089	87
8	998	1159	161
9	1235	1246	11
10	1045	1135	90
11	956	1005	49
12	987	1010	23
13	1028	1015	−13
14	954	1032	78
15	1152	1310	158
16	1215	1302	87
17	948	1010	62
18	1190	1235	45
19	1077	1103	26
20	1223	1200	−23
21	1100	1187	87
22	842	910	68
23	985	1049	64
24	1107	1123	16
25	847	901	54
26	987	1086	99
27	1228	1276	48
28	1005	1029	24
29	1166	1221	55
30	808	874	66

Find a 90% confidence interval estimate of the average improvement in test scores.

Answer: The two sets of test scores (before and after the course) are not independent; they are associated in matched pairs, with one pair of scores for each student. The proper procedure is to run a one-sample analysis on the single variable consisting of the set of improvements. In this case we obtain $\bar{x} = 63.2$, $s = 41.89$, $\sigma_{\bar{x}} \approx \frac{41.89}{\sqrt{30}} = 7.65$, and a 90% confidence interval estimate of $63.2 \pm 1.645(7.648) = 63.2 \pm 12.6$. We can be 90% confident that the average improvement in test scores is between 50.6 and 75.8.

Questions on Topic Thirteen: Confidence Intervals

Multiple-Choice Questions

Directions: The questions or incomplete statements that follow are each followed by five suggested answers or completions. Choose the response that best answers the question or completes the statement.

1. Changing from a 95% confidence interval estimate to a 99% confidence interval estimate, with all other things being equal,
   - (A) increases the interval size by 4%.
   - (B) decreases the interval size by 4%.
   - (C) increases the interval size by 31%.
   - (D) decreases the interval size by 31%.
   - (E) This question cannot be answered without knowing the sample size.

2. In general, how does doubling the sample size change the confidence interval size?
   - (A) Doubles the interval size
   - (B) Halves the interval size
   - (C) Multiplies the interval size by 1.414
   - (D) Divides the interval size by 1.414
   - (E) This question cannot be answered without knowing the sample size.

3. A confidence interval estimate is determined from the GPAs of a random sample of n students. Which of the following will result in a smaller margin of error?
   - I. A smaller confidence level
   - II. A smaller sample standard deviation
   - III. A smaller sample size
   - (A) I and II
   - (B) I and III
   - (C) II and III
   - (D) I, II, and III
   - (E) None of the above gives the complete set of true responses.

4. A survey was conducted to determine the percentage of high school students who planned to go to college. The results were stated as 82% with a margin of error of ± 5%. What is meant by ± 5%?

(A) Five percent of the population were not surveyed.

(B) In the sample, the percentage of students who plan to go to college was between 77% and 87%.

(C) The percentage of the entire population of students who plan to go to college is between 77% and 87%.

(D) It is unlikely that the given sample proportion result would be obtained unless the true percentage was between 77% and 87%.

(E) Between 77% and 87% of the population were surveyed.

5. One month the actual unemployment rate in France was 13.4%. If during that month you took a survey of 100 Frenchmen and constructed a confidence interval estimate of the unemployment rate, which of the following would be true?

   I. The center of the interval was 13.4.
   II. The interval contained 13.4.
   III. A 99% confidence interval estimate contained 13.4.

(A) I and II

(B) I and III

(C) II and III

(D) I, II, and III

(E) None of the above gives the complete set of true responses.

6. The margin of error in a confidence interval estimate using z-scores covers which of the following?

   I. Random sampling errors
   II. Errors due to undercoverage and nonresponse in obtaining sample surveys
   III. Errors due to using sample standard deviations as estimates for population standard deviations

(A) I only

(B) II only

(C) III only

(D) I and III

(E) None of the above gives the complete set of true responses.

7. A *USA Today* "Lifeline" column reported that in a survey of 500 people, 39% said they watch their bread while it's being toasted. Establish a 90% confidence interval estimate for the percentage of people who watch their bread being toasted.

(A) 39% ± .078%

(B) 39% ± 2.2%

(C) 39% ± 2.8%

(D) 39% ± 3.6%

(E) 39% ± 4.3%

8. In a survey funded by Burroughs-Welcome, 750 of 1000 adult Americans said they didn't believe they could come down with a sexually transmitted disease (STD). Construct a 95% confidence interval estimate of the proportion of adult Americans who don't believe they can contract an STD.

   (A) (.728, .772)
   (B) (.723, .777)
   (C) (.718, .782)
   (D) (.713, .787)
   (E) (.665, .835)

9. A 1993 *Los Angeles Times* poll of 1703 adults revealed that only 17% thought the media was doing a "very good" job. With what degree of confidence can the newspaper say that 17% ± 2% of adults believe the media is doing a "very good" job?

   (A) 72.9%
   (B) 90.0%
   (C) 95.0%
   (D) 97.2%
   (E) 98.6%

10. A politician wants to know what percentage of the voters support her position on the issue of forced busing for integration. What size voter sample should be obtained to determine with 90% confidence the support level to within 4%?

   (A) 21
   (B) 25
   (C) 423
   (D) 600
   (E) 1691

11. In a 1994 *New York Times* poll measuring a candidate's popularity, the newspaper claimed that in 19 of 20 cases its poll results should be no more than three percentage points off in either direction. What confidence level are the pollsters working with, and what size sample should they have obtained?

   (A) 3%, 20
   (B) 6%, 20
   (C) 6%, 100
   (D) 95%, 33
   (E) 95%, 1068

12. In a test for acid rain, 49 water samples showed a mean pH level of 4.4 with a standard deviation of 0.35. Find a 90% confidence interval estimate for the mean pH level.

   (A) 4.4 ± 0.01175
   (B) 4.4 ± 0.082
   (C) 4.4 ± 0.315
   (D) 4.4 ± 0.35
   (E) 4.4 ± 0.576

13. One gallon of gasoline is put in each of 30 test autos, and the resulting mileage figures are tabulated with $\bar{x} = 28.5$ and $s = 1.2$. Determine a 95% confidence interval estimate of the mean mileage.

   (A) (28.46, 28.54)
   (B) (28.4216, 28.5784)
   (C) (28.07, 28.93)
   (D) (27.36, 29.64)
   (E) (27.3, 29.7)

14. The number of accidents per day at a large factory is noted for each of 64 days with $\bar{x} = 3.58$ and $s = 1.52$. With what degree of confidence can we assert that the mean number of accidents per day at the factory is between 3.20 and 3.96?

   (A) 48%
   (B) 63%
   (C) 90%
   (D) 95%
   (E) 99%

15. A company owns 335 trucks. For a sample of 30 of these trucks, the average yearly road tax paid is $9540 with a standard deviation of $1205. What is a 99% confidence interval estimate for the total yearly road taxes paid for the 335 trucks?

   (A) $9540 \pm $103
   (B) $9540 \pm $567
   (C) $3,196,000 \pm $567
   (D) $3,196,000 \pm $35,000
   (E) $3,196,000 \pm $190,000

16. What sample size should be chosen to find the mean number of absences per month for school children to within $\pm .2$ at a 95% confidence level if it is known that the standard deviation is 1.1?

   (A) 11
   (B) 29
   (C) 82
   (D) 96
   (E) 117

17. Hospital administrators wish to learn the average length of stay of all surgical patients. A statistician determines that, for a 95% confidence level estimate of the average length of stay to within ± 0.5 days, 50 surgical patients' records will have to be examined. How many records should be looked at to obtain a 95% confidence level estimate to within ± 0.25 days?

   (A) 25
   (B) 50
   (C) 100
   (D) 150
   (E) 200

18. The National Research Council of the Philippines reported that 210 of 361 members in biology are women, but only 34 of 86 members in mathematics are women (*Science,* March 11, 1994, page 1491). Establish a 95% confidence interval estimate of the difference in proportions of women in biology and women in mathematics in the Philippines.

    (A) .187 ± .115
    (B) .187 ± .154
    (C) .395 ± .103
    (D) .543 ± .154
    (E) .582 ± .051

19. In a random sample of 300 elderly men, 65% were married, while in a similar sample of 400 elderly women, 48% were married. Determine a 99% confidence interval estimate for the difference between the percentages of elderly men and women who are married.

    (A) 17% ± 0.36%
    (B) 17% ± 9.6%
    (C) 55% ± 6.7%
    (D) 56.5% ± 6.7%
    (E) 56.5% ± 9.6%

20. A researcher plans to investigate the difference between the proportion of psychiatrists and the proportion of psychologists who believe that most emotional problems have their root causes in childhood. How large a sample should be taken (same number for each group) to be 90% certain of knowing the difference to within ±.03?

    (A) 39
    (B) 376
    (C) 752
    (D) 1504
    (E) 3007

21. In a study aimed at reducing developmental problems in low-birth-weight (under 2500 grams) babies (*Journal of the American Medical Association,* June 13, 1990, page 3040), 347 infants were exposed to a special educational curriculum while 561 did not receive any special help. After 3 years the children exposed to the special curriculum showed a mean IQ of 93.5 with a standard deviation of 19.1; the other children had a mean IQ of 84.5 with a standard deviation of 19.9. Find a 95% confidence interval estimate for the difference in mean IQs of low-birth-weight babies who receive special intervention and those who do not.

    (A) 9.0 ± 2.60
    (B) 9.0 ± 4.42
    (C) 9.0 ± 6.24
    (D) 89.0 ± 19.5
    (E) 89.0 ± 39.0

22. Does socioeconomic status relate to age at time of HIV infection? For 274 high-income HIV-positive individuals the average age of infection was 33.0 years with a standard deviation of 6.3, while for 90 low-income individuals the average age was 28.6 years with a standard deviation of 6.3 (*The Lancet,* October 22, 1994, page 1121). Find a 90% confidence interval estimate for the difference in ages of high- and low-income people at the time of HIV infection.

    (A) 4.4 ± 0.963
    (B) 4.4 ± 1.26
    (C) 4.4 ± 2.51
    (D) 30.8 ± 2.51
    (E) 30.8 ± 6.3

23. An engineer wishes to determine the difference in life expectancies of two brands of batteries. Suppose the standard deviation of each brand is 4.5 hours. How large a sample (same number) of each type of battery should be taken if the engineer wishes to be 90% certain of knowing the difference in life expectancies to within 1 hour?

    (A) 10
    (B) 55
    (C) 110
    (D) 156
    (E) 202

24. Two confidence interval estimates from the same sample are (16.4, 29.8) and (14.3, 31.9). What is the sample mean, and if one estimate is at the 95% level while the other is at the 99% level, which is which?

    (A) $\bar{x} = 23.1$; (16.4, 29.8) is the 95% level.
    (B) $\bar{x} = 23.1$; (16.4, 29.8) is the 99% level.
    (C) It is impossible to completely answer this question without knowing the sample size.
    (D) It is impossible to completely answer this question without knowing the sample standard deviation.
    (E) It is impossible to completely answer this question without knowing both the sample size and standard deviation.

25. Two 90% confidence interval estimates are obtained: I (28.5, 34.5) and II (30.3, 38.2).

    a. If the sample sizes are the same, which has the larger standard deviation?
    b. If the sample standard deviations are the same, which has the larger size?

    (A) *a.* I   *b.* I
    (B) *a.* I   *b.* II
    (C) *a.* II   *b.* I
    (D) *a.* II   *b.* II
    (E) More information is needed to answer these questions.

26. Suppose (25, 30) is a 90% confidence interval estimate for a population mean μ. Which of the following are true statements?

    I. There is a .90 probability that μ is between 25 and 30.
    II. If 100 random samples of the given size are picked and a 90% confidence interval estimate is calculated from each, then μ will be in 90 of the resulting intervals.
    III. If 90% confidence intervals are calculated from all possible samples of the given size, μ will be in 90% of these intervals.

    (A) I and II
    (B) I and III
    (C) II and III
    (D) I, II, and III
    (E) None of the above gives the complete set of true responses.

27. Under what conditions would it be meaningful to construct a confidence interval estimate when the data consist of the entire population?

    (A) If the population size is small ($n < 30$)
    (B) If the population size is large ($n \geq 30$)
    (C) If a higher level of confidence is desired
    (D) If the population is truly random
    (E) Never

Answer Key

1. **C**	7. **D**	13. **C**	19. **B**	25. **C**
2. **D**	8. **B**	14. **D**	20. **D**	26. **E**
3. **A**	9. **D**	15. **E**	21. **A**	27. **E**
4. **D**	10. **C**	16. **E**	22. **B**	
5. **E**	11. **E**	17. **E**	23. **C**	
6. **A**	12. **B**	18. **A**	24. **A**	

Answers Explained

1. **(C)** The critical z-scores will go from ± 1.96 to ± 2.576, resulting in an increase in the interval size: $\frac{2.576}{1.96} = 1.31$, or an increase of 31%.

2. **(D)** Increasing the sample size by a multiple of d divides the interval estimate by $\sqrt{d}$.

3. **(A)** The margin of error varies directly with the critical z-value and directly with the standard deviation of the sample, but inversely with the square root of the sample size.

4. **(D)** Although the sample proportion *is* between 77% and 87% (more specifically, it is 82%), this is not the meaning of $\pm 5\%$. Although the percentage of the entire population is likely to be between 77% and 87%, this is not known for certain.

5. **(E)** There is no guarantee that 13.4 is anywhere near the interval, so none of the statements are true.

6. **(A)** The margin of error has to do with measuring chance variation but has nothing to do with faulty survey design. As long as n is large, s is a reasonable

estimate of σ; however, again this is not measured by the margin of error. (With t-scores, there is a correction for using s as an estimate of σ.)

7. **(D)** $\sigma_{\hat{p}} = \sqrt{\frac{(.39)(.61)}{500}} = .0218$

$.39 \pm 1.645(.0218) = .39 \pm .036$

8. **(B)** $\sigma_{\hat{p}} = \sqrt{\frac{(.75)(.25)}{1000}} = .0137$

$.75 \pm 1.96(.0137) = .75 \pm .027$ or $(.723, .777)$

9. **(D)** $\sigma_{\hat{p}} = \sqrt{\frac{(.17)(.83)}{1703}} = .0091$

$z(.0091) = .02 \quad z = 2.20, \quad .9861 - .0139 = 97.2\%$

10. **(C)** $1.645\left(\frac{.5}{\sqrt{n}}\right) \le .04$, $\sqrt{n} \ge 20.563$, $n \ge 422.8$, so choose $n = 423$.

11. **(E)** $\frac{19}{20} = 95\%$; $1.96\left(\frac{.5}{\sqrt{n}}\right) \le .03$, $\sqrt{n} \ge 32.67$, $n \ge 1067.1$, and so the pollsters should have obtained a sample size of at least 1068. (They actually interviewed 1148 people.)

12. **(B)** $4.4 \pm 1.645\left(\frac{0.35}{\sqrt{49}}\right) = 4.4 \pm 0.082$

13. **(C)** $28.5 \pm 1.96\left(\frac{1.2}{\sqrt{30}}\right) = 28.5 \pm 0.43$

14. **(D)** $\sigma_{\bar{x}} = \frac{1.52}{\sqrt{64}} = 0.19$, $\frac{0.38}{0.19} = 2$, and $.4772 + .4772 = .9544 \approx 95\%$.

15. **(E)** $9540 \pm 2.576\left(\frac{1205}{\sqrt{30}}\right) = 9540 \pm 566.7$

$335(9540 \pm 566.7) = \$3,196,000 \pm \$190,000$

16. **(E)** $1.96\left(\frac{1.1}{\sqrt{n}}\right) \le 0.2$, $\sqrt{n} \ge 10.78$, and $n \ge 116.2$; choose $n = 117$.

17. **(E)** To divide the interval estimate by d without affecting the confidence level, multiply the sample size by a multiple of d^2. In this case, $4(50) = 200$.

18. **(A)**

$$n_1 = 361 \qquad n_2 = 86$$

$$\hat{p}_1 = \frac{210}{361} = .582 \quad \hat{p}_2 = \frac{34}{86} = .395$$

$$\sigma_d = \sqrt{\frac{(.582)(.418)}{361} + \frac{(.395)(.605)}{86}} = .0588$$

$$(.582 - .395) \pm 1.96(.0588) = .187 \pm .115$$

19. **(B)**

$$n_1 = 300 \quad n_2 = 400$$

$$\hat{p}_1 = .65 \quad \hat{p}_2 = .48$$

$$\sigma_d = \sqrt{\frac{(.65)(.35)}{300} + \frac{(.48)(.52)}{400}} = .0372$$

$$(.65 - .48) \pm 2.576(.0372) = .17 \pm .096$$

20. **(D)** $1.645\left(\frac{.5\sqrt{2}}{\sqrt{n}}\right) \le .03$, $\sqrt{n} \ge 38.77$, and $n \ge 1503.3$; the researcher should choose a sample size of at least 1504.

21. **(A)** $\sigma_{\bar{x}_1 - \bar{x}_2} = \sqrt{\frac{(19.1)^2}{347} + \frac{(19.9)^2}{561}} = 1.326$

$(93.5 - 84.5) \pm 1.96(1.326) = 9.0 \pm 2.60$

22. **(B)** $\sigma_{\bar{x}_1 - \bar{x}_2} = \sqrt{\dfrac{(6.3)^2}{274} + \dfrac{(6.3)^2}{90}} = 0.765$

$(33.0 - 28.6) \pm 1.645(0.765) = 4.4 \pm 1.26$

23. **(C)** $\sigma_{\bar{x}_1 - \bar{x}_2} = \sqrt{\dfrac{(4.5)^2}{n} + \dfrac{(4.5)^2}{n}} = \dfrac{6.364}{\sqrt{n}}$

$1.645 \left(\dfrac{6.364}{\sqrt{n}}\right) \leq 1, \sqrt{n} \geq 10.47, n \geq 109.6$; choose $n = 110$.

24. **(A)** The sample mean is at the center of the confidence interval; the lower confidence level corresponds to the narrower interval.

25. **(C)** Narrower intervals result from smaller standard deviations and from larger sample sizes.

26. **(E)** Only III is true. The 90% refers to the method; 90% of all intervals obtained by this method will capture μ. Nothing is sure about any particular set of 100 intervals. For any particular interval, the probability that it captures μ is either 1 or 0 depending on whether μ is or isn't in it.

27. **(E)** In determining confidence intervals, one uses sample statistics to estimate population parameters. If the data are actually the whole population, making an estimate has no meaning.

Free-Response Questions

> *Directions:* You must show all work and indicate the methods you use. You will be graded on the correctness of your methods and on the accuracy of your final answers.

Three Open-Ended Questions

1. A survey of 1000 voters finds that 57% believe that competence is more important than character in voting for President of the United States.

   a. Determine a 95% confidence interval estimate for the percentage of voters who believe competence is more important than character.

   b. If your parents know nothing about statistics, how would you explain to them why you can't simply say that 57% of voters believe that competence is more important.

   c. Also explain to your parents what is meant by 95% confidence.

2. Pollsters sometimes simply give a percentage result such as "40% of the voters support Candidate Smith," while at other times they express results in a form such as "40% plus or minus 5%." Comment on the missing pieces of information in such statements and on what a pollster might add so that readers can better understand the strength of such statements?

3. A sample of 40 inner city gas stations shows a mean price for regular unleaded gasoline to be $1.45 with a standard deviation of $0.05, while a sample of 120 suburban stations shows a mean of $1.38 with a standard deviation of $0.08.

   a. Construct 95% confidence interval estimates for the mean price of regular gas in inner city and in suburban stations.

b. The confidence interval for the inner city stations is wider than the interval for the suburban stations even though the standard deviation for inner city stations is less than that for suburban stations. Explain why this happened.

c. Based on your answer in part *a*, are you confident that the mean price of inner city gasoline is less than $1.50? Explain.

Answers Explained

1. *a.* $\hat{p} = .57$ and $\sigma_{\hat{p}} \approx \sqrt{\frac{(.57)(.43)}{1000}} = .0157$. The critical z-scores associated with the 95% level are ± 1.96. Thus the confidence interval estimate is $.57 \pm 1.96(.0157) = .57 \pm .031$, or between 54% and 60%.

    b. Explain to your parents that by using a measurement from a sample we are never able to say *exactly* what a population proportion is; rather we are only able to say we are confident that it is within some range of values, in this case between 54% and 60%.

    c. In 95% of all possible samples of 1000 voters, the method used gives an estimate that is within three percentage points of the true answer.

2. The first statement is close to meaningless. The reader has no idea whether 1000 voters were interviewed and 400 expressed support for the candidate or whether only 5 people were polled with 2 of them expressing support. The second statement is better; however, it is still missing a critical piece of information, the confidence level. The reader does not know if the calculation resulting in the $\pm 5\%$ figure is associated with 99%, 90%, or even 50% confidence that the resulting interval contains the actual support percentage. While the general public might not understand the term *confidence level,* they should be given something like: "In 9 out of 10 cases, our poll results are no more than five percentage points off in either direction from the true figure."

3. *a.* $1.45 \pm 1.96 \left(\frac{.05}{\sqrt{40}} \right) = 1.45 \pm .015$

    $1.38 \pm 1.96 \left(\frac{.08}{\sqrt{120}} \right) = 1.38 \pm .014$

    b. Because the sample size of inner city stations is smaller.

    c. Yes, because the standard deviation of the set of sample means is .015, and so $1.50 is more than three standard deviations away from $1.45. Thus the probability that the true mean is this far from the sample mean is extremely small.

TOPIC FOURTEEN
Tests of Significance

Closely related to the problem of estimating a population proportion or mean is the problem of testing a hypothesis about a population proportion or mean. For example, a travel agency might determine an interval estimate for the proportion of sunny days in the Virgin Islands or, alternatively, might test a tourist bureau's claim about the proportion of sunny days. A major stockholder in a construction company might ascertain an interval estimate for the proportion of successful contract bids or, alternatively, might test a company spokesperson's claim about the proportion of successful bids. A consumer protection agency might determine an interval estimate for the mean nicotine content of a particular brand of cigarettes or, alternatively, might test a manufacturer's claim about the mean nicotine content of its cigarettes. An agricultural researcher could find an interval estimate for the mean productivity gain caused by a specific fertilizer or, alternatively, might test the developer's claimed mean productivity gain. In each of these cases, the experimenter must decide whether the interest lies in an interval estimate of a population proportion or mean or in a hypothesis test of a claimed proportion or mean.

Logic of Significance Testing, Null and Alternative Hypotheses, P-Values, and One- and Two-sided Tests

The general testing procedure is to choose a specific hypothesis to be tested, called the *null hypothesis*, pick an appropriate random sample, and then use measurements from the sample to determine the likelihood of the null hypothesis. If the sample statistic is far enough away from the claimed population parameter, we say that there is sufficient evidence to reject the null hypothesis. We attempt to show that the null hypothesis is unacceptable by showing that it is improbable.

Consider the context of the population proportion. The null hypothesis H_0 is stated in the form of an equality statement about the population proportion (for example, $H_0: p = .37$). There is an *alternative hypothesis*, stated in the form of an inequality (for example, $H_a: p < .37$ or $H_a: p > .37$ or $H_a: p \neq .37$). The strength of the sample statistic $\hat{p}$ can be gauged through its associated *P-value*, which is the probability of obtaining a sample statistic as extreme as the one obtained if the null hypothesis is assumed to be true. The smaller the P-value, the more significant the difference between the null hypothesis and the sample results.

There are two types of possible errors: the error of mistakenly rejecting a true null hypothesis and the error of mistakenly failing to reject a false null hypothesis. The α-risk, also called the *significance level* of the test, is the probability of committing a *Type I error* and mistakenly rejecting a true null hypothesis. A *Type II error,* a mistaken failure to reject a false null hypothesis, has associated probability β. There is a different value of β for each possible correct value for the population parameter p.

Large Sample Test for a Proportion

We assume that we have a simple random sample of large enough size n [$n \geq 30$, and both np and $n(1-p)$ should be greater than 5].

Example 14.1.   A union spokesperson claims that 75% of union members will support a strike if their basic demands are not met. A company negotiator believes the true percentage is lower and runs a hypothesis test at the 10% significance level. What is the conclusion if 87 of 125 union members say they will strike?

Answer:

$$H_0: \quad p = .75$$
$$H_a: \quad p < .75$$

We use the claimed proportion to calculate the standard deviation of the sample proportions:

$$\sigma_{\hat{p}} = \sqrt{\frac{(.75)(.25)}{125}} = .03873$$

The observed sample proportion is $\hat{p} = \frac{87}{125} = .696$.

To measure the strength of the disagreement between the sample proportion and the claimed proportion, we calculate the P-value (also called the *attained significance level*). The z-score for .696 is $\frac{.696 - .75}{.03873} = -1.39$, with a resulting P-value of .0823. Since $.0823 < .10$, there is sufficient evidence to reject H_0 at the 10% significance level. The company negotiator should challenge the union claim at this level. Note, however, that there is not sufficient evidence to reject H_0 at the 5%, or even at the 8%, significance level because $.0823 > .05$ and $.0823 > .08$. When $.05 < P < .10$, we usually say that there is *some* evidence against H_0.

Example 14.2. A cancer research group surveys 500 women more than 40 years old to test the hypothesis that 28% of women in this age group have regularly scheduled mammograms. Should the hypothesis be rejected at the 5% significance level if 151 of the women respond affirmatively?

Answer: Since no suspicion is voiced that the 28% claim is low or high, we run a two-sided test:

$$H_0: \quad p = .28$$
$$H_a: \quad p \neq .28$$
$$\alpha = .05$$

$$\sigma_{\hat{p}} = \sqrt{\frac{(.28)(.72)}{500}} = .0201$$

The observed $\hat{p} = \frac{151}{500} = .302$. The z-score for .302 is $\frac{.302 - .28}{.0201} = 1.09$, which corresponds to a probability of $1 - .8621 = .1379$ in the tail. Doubling this value (because the test is two-sided), we obtain a *P*-value of $2(.1379) = .2758$. Since $.2758 > .05$, there is not sufficient evidence to reject H_0; that is, the cancer research group should not dispute the 28% claim. Note, for example, that the null hypothesis should not be rejected even if α is a relatively large .25. When $P > .10$, we usually say there is little or no evidence to reject H_0.

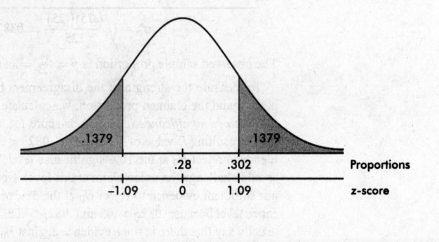

Large Sample Test for a Mean

Assume that we have a simple random sample of size $n \geq 30$.

Example 14.3. A manufacturer claims that a new brand of air-conditioning unit uses only 6.5 kilowatts of electricity per day. A consumer agency believes the true figure is higher and runs a test on a sample of size 50. If the sample mean is 7.0 kilowatts with a standard deviation of 1.4, should the manufacturer's claim be rejected at a significance level of 5%? Of 1%?

Answer:

$$H_0: \quad \mu = 6.5$$
$$H_a: \quad \mu > 6.5$$
$$\alpha = .05 \text{ or } .01$$

Here $\sigma_{\bar{x}} = \frac{\sigma}{\sqrt{n}} \approx \frac{s}{\sqrt{n}} = \frac{1.4}{\sqrt{50}} = 0.198$. The z-score of 7.0 is $\frac{7.0-6.5}{0.198} = 2.53$; using Table A, we find the P-value to be $1 - .9943 = .0057$. Since $.0057 < .05$ and $.0057 < .01$, the consumer agency should reject the manufacturer's claim at both the 5% and 1% significance levels. When $P < .01$, we usually say that there is *strong* evidence to reject H_0.

Example 14.4. A local chamber of commerce claims that the mean family income level in a city is $12,250. An economist runs a hypothesis test, using a sample of 135 families, and finds a mean of $11,500 with a standard deviation of $3180. Should the $12,250 claim be rejected at a 5% level of significance?

Answer: Note that this is a two-sided test; that is, the economist suspects that the claim may be incorrect but does not know whether it is probably too high or too low.

$$H_0: \quad \mu = 12,250$$
$$H_a: \quad \mu \neq 12,250$$
$$\alpha = .05$$

Here $\sigma_{\bar{x}} = \frac{\sigma}{\sqrt{n}} \approx \frac{s}{\sqrt{n}} = \frac{3180}{\sqrt{135}} = 273.7$. The z-score of 11,500 is equal to $\frac{11,500-12,250}{273.7} = -2.74$, and Table A gives a probability of $1 - .9969 = .0031$. Since this is a two-tailed test, where disagreement with the null hypothesis can be in either of two directions, the P-value is twice the .0031 probability, or .0062. Since $.0062 < .05$, there is sufficient evidence for the economist to reject the chamber of commerce claim. With $P < .01$, there is strong evidence to reject H_0.

Large Sample Test for a Difference Between Two Proportions

Assume that we have two simple random samples of sizes n_1 and n_2, both greater than 30.

The fact that a sample proportion from one population is greater than a sample proportion from a second population does not automatically justify a similar conclusion about the population proportions themselves. Two points need to be stressed. First, sample proportions from the same population can vary from each other. Second, what we are really comparing are confidence interval estimates, not just single points.

For many problems the null hypothesis states that the population proportions are equal or, equivalently, that their difference is 0:

$$H_0: p_1 - p_2 = 0$$

The alternative hypothesis is then

$$H_a: p_1 - p_2 < 0 \quad H_a: p_1 - p_2 > 0 \quad \text{or} \quad H_a: p_1 - p_2 \neq 0$$

where the first two possibilities lead to one-sided tests and the third possibility leads to two-sided tests.

Since the null hypothesis is that $p_1 = p_2$, we call this common value p and use it in calculating σ_d:

$$\sigma_d = \sqrt{\frac{p(1-p)}{n_1} + \frac{p(1-p)}{n_2}} = \sqrt{p(1-p)\left(\frac{1}{n_1} + \frac{1}{n_2}\right)}$$

In practice, if $\hat{p}_1 = \frac{x_1}{n_1}$ and $\hat{p}_2 = \frac{x_2}{n_2}$, we use $\hat{p} = \frac{x_1 + x_2}{n_1 + n_2}$ as an estimate of p in calculating σ_d.

Example 14.5. Suppose that early in an election campaign a telephone poll of 800 registered voters shows 460 in favor of a particular candidate. Just before election day, a second poll shows only 520 of 1000 registered voters expressing the same preference. At the 10% significance level is there sufficient evidence that the candidate's popularity has decreased?

Answer:

$$H_0: p_1 - p_2 = 0 \qquad \hat{p}_1 = \tfrac{460}{800} = .575$$

$$H_a: p_1 - p_2 > 0 \qquad \hat{p}_2 = \tfrac{520}{1000} = .520$$

$$\alpha = .10 \qquad \hat{p} = \tfrac{460+520}{800+1000} = .544$$

$$\sigma_d \approx \sqrt{(.544)(.456)\left(\frac{1}{800} + \frac{1}{1000}\right)} = .0236$$

The observed difference is $.575 - .520 = .055$. The z-score for .055 is $\frac{.055-0}{.0236} = 2.33$, and so the P-value is $1 - .9901 = .0099$. Since $.0099 < .10$, we conclude that at the 10% significance level the candidate's popularity *has* dropped. We note that $.0099 < .01$, so that the observed difference is statistically significant even at the 1% level.

Example 14.6. An automobile manufacturer tries two distinct assembly procedures. In a sample of 350 cars coming off the line using the first procedure there are 28 with major defects, while a sample of 500 autos from the second line shows 32 with defects. Is the difference significant at the 10% significance level?

Answer: Since there is no mention that one procedure is believed to be better or worse than the other, this is a two-sided test.

$$H_0: p_1 - p_2 = 0 \qquad \hat{p}_1 = \tfrac{28}{350} = .080$$

$$H_a: p_1 - p_2 \neq 0 \qquad \hat{p}_2 = \tfrac{32}{500} = .064$$

$$\alpha = .10 \qquad \hat{p} = \tfrac{28+32}{350+500} = .0706$$

$$\sigma_d \approx \sqrt{(.0706)(.9294)\left(\frac{1}{350} + \frac{1}{500}\right)} = .0179$$

The observed difference is $.080 - .064 = .016$. The z-score for $.016$ is $\frac{.016-0}{.0179} = 0.89$, which corresponds to a tail probability of $1 - .8133 = .1867$. Doubling this value because the test is two-sided results in a P-value of $2(.1867) = .3734$. Since $.3734 > .10$, we conclude that the observed difference is *not* significant at the 10% level. We note that the smallest significance level for which the observed difference is significant is a very large 37.34%. When P is so large, we can safely say that there is no evidence against H_0.

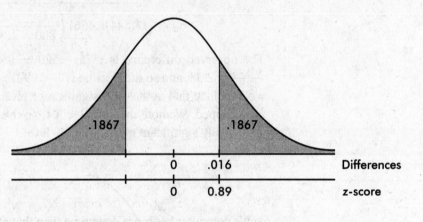

Large Sample Test for a Difference Between Two Means (Unpaired and Paired)

We assume that we have two simple random samples of sizes n_1 and n_2, both greater than 30.

In this situation the null hypothesis is usually that the means of the populations are the same or, equivalently, that their difference is 0:

$$H_0: \mu_1 - \mu_2 = 0$$

The alternative hypothesis is then

$$H_a: \mu_1 - \mu_2 < 0 \quad H_a: \mu_1 - \mu_2 > 0 \quad \text{or} \quad H_a: \mu_1 - \mu_2 \neq 0$$

The first two possibilities lead to one-sided tests, and the third possibility leads to two-sided tests.

Example 14.7. A sales representative believes that his company's computer has more average downtime per week than a similar computer sold by a competitor. Before taking this concern to his director, the sales representative gathers data and runs a hypothesis test. He determines that in a simple random sample of 40 week-long periods at different firms using his company's product, the average downtime was 125 minutes with a standard deviation of 37 minutes. However, 35 week-long periods involving the competitor's computer yield an average downtime of only 115 minutes with a standard deviation of 43 minutes. What conclusion should the sales representative draw assuming a 10% significance level?

Answer:

$$H_0: \quad \mu_1 - \mu_2 = 0$$

$$H_a: \quad \mu_1 - \mu_2 > 0$$

$$\alpha = .10$$

$$\sigma_{\bar{x}_1 - \bar{x}_2} \approx \sqrt{\frac{(37)^2}{40} + \frac{(43)^2}{35}} = 9.33$$

The difference in sample means is $125 - 115 = 10$, and the z-score is $\frac{10}{9.33} = 1.07$. Using Table A, we find the P-value to be $1 - .8577 = .1423$. Since $.1423 > .10$, the observed difference is not significant at the 10% significance level. The sales representative does not have sufficient evidence that his company's computer has more downtime. While the observed difference would be significant at, for example, the 15% level, still, with $P > .1$, we say that the evidence is weak that the salesman's company's computer has more downtime than that of the competitor's.

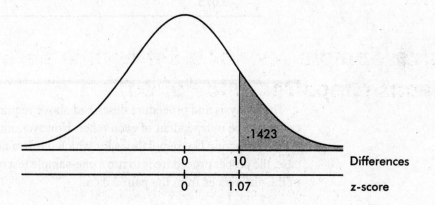

Example 14.8. A store manager wishes to determine whether there is a significant difference between two trucking firms with regard to the handling of egg cartons. In a simple random sample of 200 cartons on one firm's truck there was an average of 0.7 broken eggs per carton with a standard deviation of 0.31, while a sample of 300 cartons on the second firm's truck showed an average of 0.775 broken eggs per carton with a standard deviation of 0.42. Is the difference between the averages significant at a significance level of 5%? At a significance level of 1%?

Answer:

$$H_0: \quad \mu_1 - \mu_2 = 0$$

$$H_a: \quad \mu_1 - \mu_2 \neq 0$$

$$\alpha = .05$$

$$\sigma_{\bar{x}-\bar{y}} \approx \sqrt{\frac{(0.31)^2}{200} + \frac{(0.42)^2}{300}} = 0.0327$$

Since there is no mention that it is believed that one firm does better than the other, this is a two-sided test. The observed difference of $0.7 - 0.775 = -0.075$ has a z-score of $\frac{-0.075}{0.0327} = -2.29$. Using Table A, we find that this gives a probability of .0110. The test is two-sided, and so the P-value is $2(.0110) = .0220$. While $.0220 < .05$, we also have $.0220 > .01$, so the observed difference is statistically significant at the 5% level but not at the 1% level. With $.01 < P < .05$, we usually say that there is *moderate* evidence to reject H_0.

The analysis and procedure described above require that the two samples being compared be independent of each other. However, many experiments and tests involve comparing two populations for which the data naturally occur in pairs. In this case, the proper procedure is to run a one-sample test on a single variable consisting of the differences from the paired data.

Chi-square Test for Goodness of Fit

A critical question is often whether or not an observed pattern of data fits some given distribution. A perfect fit cannot be expected, and so we must look at discrepancies and make judgments as to the *goodness of fit*.

One approach is similar to that developed earlier. There is the null hypothesis of a good fit, that is, the hypothesis that a given theoretical distribution correctly describes the situation, problem, or activity under consideration. Our observed data consist of one possible sample from a whole universe of possible samples. We ask about the chance of obtaining a sample with the observed discrepancies if the null hypothesis is really true. Finally, if the chance is too small, we reject the null hypothesis and say that the fit is not a good one.

How do we decide about the significance of observed discrepancies? It should come as no surprise that the best information is obtained from squaring the discrepancy values, as this has been our technique for studying variances from the beginning. Furthermore, since, for example, an observed difference of 23 is more significant if the original values are 105 and 128 than if they are 10,602 and 10,625, we must appropriately *weight* each difference. Such weighting is accomplished by dividing each difference by the expected value. The sum of these weighted differences or discrepancies is called *chi-square* and is denoted as χ^2 (χ is the lowercase Greek letter chi):

$$\chi^2 = \sum \frac{(\text{obs} - \text{exp})^2}{\text{exp}}$$

The smaller the resulting χ^2-value, the better the fit. If the χ^2-value exceeds some critical value, we say there is sufficient evidence to reject the null hypothesis and to claim that the fit is poor.

To decide how large a calculated χ^2-value must be to be significant, that is, to choose a critical value, we must understand how χ^2-values are distributed. A χ^2-distribution is not symmetric and is always skewed to the right. There are distinct χ^2-distributions, each with an associated number of degrees of freedom (df). The larger the df value, the closer the χ^2-distribution to a normal distribution. Note, for example, that squaring the often-used z-scores 1.645, 1.96, and 2.576 results in 2.71, 3.84, and 6.63, respectively, which are entries found in the first row of the χ^2-distribution table.

A large χ^2-value may or may not be significant—the answer depends on which χ^2-distribution we are using. A table is given of critical χ^2-values for the more commonly used percentages or probabilities. To use the χ^2-distribution for approximations in goodness-of-fit problems, the individual expected values cannot be too small. An often-used rule of thumb is that no expected value should be less than 5.

Example 14.9.   In a recent year, at the 6 P.M. time slot, television channels 2, 3, 4, and 5 captured the entire audience with 30%, 25%, 20%, and

25%, respectively. During the first week of the next season, 500 viewers are interviewed.

a. If viewer preferences have not changed, what number of persons is expected to watch each channel?

Answer: .30(500) = 150, .25(500) = 125, .20(500) = 100, and .25(500) = 125, so we have

	Channel			
	2	3	4	5
Expected number	150	125	100	125

b. Suppose that the actual observed numbers are as follows:

	Channel			
	2	3	4	5
Observed number	139	138	112	111

Do these numbers indicate a change? Are the differences significant?

Answer: We calculate

$$\chi^2 = \sum \frac{(\text{obs} - \text{exp})^2}{\text{exp}}$$

$$= \frac{(139 - 150)^2}{150} + \frac{(138 - 125)^2}{125} + \frac{(112 - 100)^2}{100}$$

$$+ \frac{(111 - 125)^2}{125}$$

$$= 5.167$$

Is 5.167 large enough for us to reject the null hypothesis of a good fit between the observed and the expected numbers? To use Table C in the Appendix, we must decide on an α-risk and then calculate the df value. The number of degrees of freedom for this problem is $4 - 1 = 3$. (Note that, while the observed values of 139, 138, and 112 can be freely chosen, the fourth value, 111, is absolutely determined because the total must be 500; thus df = 3.)

Thus, for example, at a 10% significance level, with df = 3, the critical χ^2-value is 6.25. Since $5.167 < 6.25$, there is not sufficient evidence to reject H_0.

However, with df = 3 and a 20% significance level, the critical χ^2-value is 4.64. Since $5.167 > 4.64$, there *is* sufficient evidence to reject H_0. At the 20% level we conclude that the fit is not good and that viewer preferences have changed.

Example 14.10.   A grocery store manager wishes to determine whether a certain product will sell equally well in any of five locations in the store. Five displays are set up, one in each location, and the resulting numbers of the product sold are noted.

	Location				
	1	2	3	4	5
Actual number sold	43	29	52	34	48

Is there enough evidence that location makes a difference? Test at both the 5% and 10% significance levels.

Answer: A total of $43 + 29 + 52 + 34 + 48 = 206$ units were sold. If location doesn't matter, we would expect $\frac{206}{5} = 41.2$ units sold per location (uniform distribution).

	Location				
	1	2	3	4	5
Expected number sold	41.2	41.2	41.2	41.2	41.2

Thus

$$\chi^2 = \frac{(43-41.2)^2}{41.2} + \frac{(29-41.2)^2}{41.2} + \frac{(52-41.2)^2}{41.2}$$
$$+ \frac{(34-41.2)^2}{41.2} + \frac{(48-41.2)^2}{41.2}$$
$$= 8.903$$

The number of degrees of freedom is the number of classes minus 1; that is, df = 5 − 1 = 4.

H_0: good fit to uniform distribution

At the 5% level, with df = 4, the critical χ^2-value is 9.49, while at the 10% level the critical value is 7.78. Since 8.903 < 9.49 but 8.903 > 7.78, there is sufficient evidence to reject H_0 at the 10% level but not at the 5% level. If the grocery store manager is willing to accept a 10% chance of committing a Type I error, there is enough evidence to claim that location makes a difference.

Chi-square Test for Independence

In the goodness-of-fit problems above, a set of expectations was based on an assumption about how the distribution should turn out. We then tested whether an observed sample distribution could reasonably have come from a larger set based on the assumed distribution.

In many real-world problems we want to compare two or more observed samples without any prior assumptions about an expected distribution. In what is called a *test of independence*, we ask whether the two or more samples might reasonably have come from some larger set. For example, do nonsmokers, light smokers, and heavy smokers all have the same likelihood of being eventually diagnosed with cancer, heart disease, or emphysema?

We classify our observations in two ways and then ask whether the two ways are independent of each other. For example, we might consider several age groups and within each group ask how many employees show various levels of job satisfaction. The null hypothesis is that age and job satisfaction are independent, that is, that the proportion of employees expressing a given level of job satisfaction is the same no matter which age group is considered.

Analysis involves calculating a table of *expected* values, assuming the null hypothesis about independence is true. We then compare these expected values with the observed values and ask whether the differences are reasonable if H_0 is true. The significance of the differences is gauged by the same χ^2-value of weighted squared differences. The smaller the resulting χ^2-value, the more reasonable the null hypothesis of independence. If the χ^2-value exceeds some critical value, we can say that the evidence is sufficient to reject the null hypothesis and to claim that there *is* some relationship between the two variables or methods of classification.

In this type of problem,

$$df = (r-1)(c-1)$$

where df is the number of degrees of freedom, r is the number of rows, and c is the number of columns.

A point worth noting is that even if there is sufficient evidence to reject the null hypothesis of independence, we cannot necessarily claim any direct *causal* relationship. In other words, although we can make a statement about some link or relationship between two variables, we are *not* justified in claiming that one causes the other. For example, we may demonstrate a relationship between salary level and job satisfaction, but our methods would not show that higher salaries cause higher job satisfaction. Perhaps an employee's higher job satisfaction impresses his superiors and thus leads to larger increases in pay. Or perhaps there is a third variable, such as training, education, or personality, that has a direct causal relationship to both salary level and job satisfaction.

Example 14.11.   In a nationwide telephone poll of 1000 adults representing Democrats, Republicans, and Independents, respondents were asked if their confidence in the U.S. banking system had been shaken by the savings and loan crisis. The answers, cross-classified by party affiliation, are given in the following *contingency table*.

| | Observed | | |
	Yes	No	No opinion
Democrats	175	220	55
Republicans	150	165	35
Independents	75	105	20

Test the null hypothesis that shaken confidence in the banking system is independent of party affiliation. Use a 10% significance level.

Answer: The above table gives the observed results. To determine the expected values, we must first determine the row and column totals:

Row totals: $175 + 220 + 55 = 450$,
$150 + 165 + 35 = 350$,
$75 + 105 + 20 = 200$

Column totals: $175 + 150 + 75 = 400$,
$220 + 165 + 105 = 490$,
$55 + 35 + 20 = 110$.

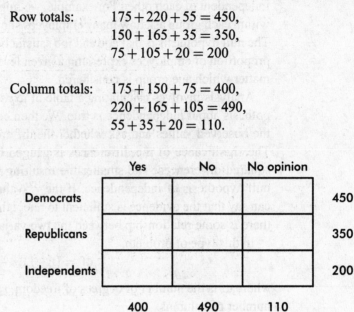

	Yes	No	No opinion	
Democrats				450
Republicans				350
Independents				200
	400	490	110	

To calculate, for example, the expected value in the upper left box, we can proceed in any of several equivalent ways. First, we could note that the proportion of Democrats is $\frac{450}{1000} = .45$; and so, if independent, the expected number of Democrat *yes* responses is $.45(400) = 180$. Instead, we could note that the proportion of *yes* responses is $\frac{400}{1000} = .4$; and so, if independent, the expected number of Democrat *yes* responses is $.4(450) = 180$. Finally, we could note that both these calculations simply involve $\frac{(450)(400)}{1000} = 180$.

In other words, *the expected value of any box can be calculated by multiplying the corresponding row total by the appropriate column total and then dividing by the grand total*. Thus, for example, the expected value for the middle box, which corresponds to Republican *no* responses, is $\frac{(350)(490)}{1000} = 171.5$.

Continuing in this manner, we fill in the table as follows:

	Expected			
	Yes	No	No opinion	
Democrats	180	220.5	49.5	450
Republicans	140	171.5	38.5	350
Independents	80	98	22	200
	400	490	110	

Next we calculate the value of chi-square:

$$\chi^2 = \frac{(175-180)^2}{180} + \frac{(220-220.5)^2}{220.5} + \frac{(55-49.5)^2}{49.5}$$
$$+\frac{(150-140)^2}{140} + \frac{(165-171.5)^2}{171.5} + \frac{(35-38.5)^2}{38.5}$$
$$+\frac{(75-80)^2}{80} + \frac{(100-98)^2}{98} + \frac{(20-22)^2}{22}$$
$$= 3.024$$

Note that, once the 180, 220.5, 140, and 171.5 boxes are calculated, the other expected values can be found by using the row and column totals. Thus the number of degrees of freedom here is 4. Or we calculate

$$df = (r-1)(c-1) = (3-1)(3-1) = 4$$

With $\alpha = .10$ and $df = 4$, the critical χ^2-value is 7.78. Since $3.024 < 7.78$, there is not sufficient evidence to reject the null hypothesis of independence. Thus, at the 10% significance level, we cannot claim a relationship between party affiliation and shaken confidence in the banking system.

Questions on Topic Fourteen: Tests of Significance

> *Directions:* The questions or incomplete statements that follow are each followed by five suggested answers or completions. Choose the response that best answers the question or completes the statement.

1. Which of the following are true statements?

   I. The *P*-value of a test is the probability of obtaining a result as extreme as the one obtained assuming the null hypothesis is true.

   II. If the *P*-value for a test is .015, the probability that the null hypothesis is true is .015.

   III. When the null hypothesis is rejected, it is because it is not true.

   (A) I only
   (B) II only
   (C) III only
   (D) I and III
   (E) None of the above gives the complete set of true responses.

2. A coffee-dispensing machine is supposed to deliver 8 ounces of liquid into each paper cup, but a consumer believes that the actual amount is less. As a test he plans to obtain a sample of 36 cups of the dispensed liquid and, if the mean content is less than 7.75 ounces, to reject the 8-ounce claim. If the machine operates with a standard deviation of 0.9 ounces, what is the probability that the consumer will mistakenly reject the 8-ounce claim even though the claim is true?

   (A) .0475
   (B) .0950
   (C) .1500
   (D) .3897
   (E) .4525

3. Which of the following are true statements?

   I. Tests of significance (hypothesis tests) are designed to measure the strength of evidence against the null hypothesis.

   II. A well-planned test of significance should result in a statement either that the null hypothesis is true or that it is false.

   III. The alternative hypothesis is one-sided if there is interest in deviations from the null hypothesis in only one direction.

   (A) I and II
   (B) I and III
   (C) II and III
   (D) I, II, and III
   (E) None of the above gives the complete set of true responses.

4. A government statistician claims that the mean monthly rainfall along the Liberian coast is 15.0 inches with a standard deviation of 12.0 inches. A meteorologist plans to test this claim with measurements over 3.5 years (42 months). If she finds a sample mean more than 2.0 inches different from the claimed 15.0 inches, she will reject the government statistician's claim. What is the probability that the meteorologist will mistakenly reject a true claim?

(A) .0675
(B) .1401
(C) .2802
(D) .4325
(E) .8650

5. Which of the following are true statements?

   I. The alternative hypothesis is stated in terms of a sample statistic.
   II. A large P-value indicates strong evidence against the null hypothesis.
   III. If a sample is large enough, the necessity for it to be a simple random sample is diminished.

(A) I only
(B) II only
(C) III only
(D) Exactly two of the above statements are true.
(E) None of the above statements are true.

6. An automotive company executive claims that a mean of 48.3 cars per dealership are being sold each month. A major stockholder believes this claim is high and runs a test by sampling 30 dealerships. What conclusion is reached if the sample mean is 45.4 cars with a standard deviation of 15.4?

(A) There is sufficient evidence to prove the executive's claim is true.
(B) There is sufficient evidence to prove the executive's claim is false.
(C) The stockholder has sufficient evidence to reject the executive's claim.
(D) The stockholder does not have sufficient evidence to reject the executive's claim.
(E) There is not sufficient data to reach any conclusion.

7. A pharmaceutical company claims that a medication will produce a desired effect for a mean time of 58.4 minutes. A government researcher runs a hypothesis test of 250 patients and calculates a mean of $\bar{x} = 59.5$ with a standard deviation of $s = 8.3$. In which of the following intervals is the P-value located?

(A) $P < .01$
(B) $.01 < P < .025$
(C) $.025 < P < .05$
(D) $.05 < P < .10$
(E) $P > .10$

8. A dentist believes that brand C toothpaste is better than brand P toothpaste. She asks 30 of her patients to use each brand and records the numbers of cavities observed over a 3-year period. She plans to reject any equality claim if the average number of cavities for brand C users is at least 1 fewer than the average for brand P users. If the standard deviation in cavities per person for

each brand is 2.3, what is the probability the dentist will mistakenly reject a correct null hypothesis of equality?

(A) .0087
(B) .0233
(C) .0465
(D) .5940
(E) There is insufficient information given to calculate this probability.

9. To test which of two fuel additives results in better gas mileage, the average miles per gallon is noted when 40 cars are run for 1 week using the first additive, and then the average miles per gallon is calculated for the same 40 cars when they are run for another week. What is the conclusion at a 10% significance level if a two-sample hypothesis test, $H_0: \mu_1 - \mu_2 = 0$, $H_a: \mu_1 - \mu_2 \neq 0$, results in a P-value of .25?

(A) The observed difference in miles per gallon is significant.
(B) The observed difference in miles per gallon is not significant.
(C) A conclusion is not possible without knowing the mean miles per gallon obtained using each additive.
(D) A conclusion is not possible without knowing both the mean and the standard deviation resulting from the use of each additive.
(E) A two-sample hypothesis test should not be used in this example.

10. A building inspector believes that the percentage of new construction with serious code violations may be even greater than the previously claimed 7%. She conducts a hypothesis test on 200 new homes and finds 23 with serious code violations. Is this strong evidence against the .07 claim?

(A) Yes, because the P-value is .0062.
(B) Yes, because the P-value is 2.5.
(C) No, because the P-value is only .0062.
(D) No, because the P-value is over 2.0.
(E) No, because the P-value is .045.

11. A survey of 1000 Canadians reveals that 585 believe that there is too much violence on television. In a survey of 1500 Americans, 780 believe that there is too much television violence. To test at the 5% significance level whether or not the data are significant evidence that the proportion of Canadians who believe that there is too much violence on television is not equal to the proportion of Americans who believe that there is too much violence on television, a student sets up the following: $H_0: p = .585$ and $H_a: p \neq .585$, where p is the proportion of Americans who believe there is too much violence on television. Which of the following is a true statement?

(A) The student has set up a correct hypothesis test.
(B) Given the sample sizes, a 1% significance level would be more appropriate.
(C) Given that $\frac{780}{1500} = .52$, $H_a: p < .585$ would be more appropriate.
(D) Given that $\frac{585+780}{1000+1500} = .546$, $H_0: p = .546$ would be more appropriate.
(E) A two-population difference in proportions hypothesis test would be more appropriate.

12. A geneticist claims that four species of fruit flies should appear in the ratio 1:3:3:9. Suppose that a sample of 4000 flies contained 226, 764, 733, and

2277 flies of each species, respectively. At the 10% significance level, is there sufficient evidence to reject the geneticist's claim?

(A) The test proves the geneticist's claim.
(B) The test proves the geneticist's claim is false.
(C) The test does not give sufficient evidence to reject the geneticist's claim.
(D) The test gives sufficient evidence to reject the geneticist's claim.
(E) The test is inconclusive.

13. A medical researcher tests 640 heart attack victims for the presence of a certain antibody in their blood and cross-classifies against the severity of the attack. The results are reported in the following table:

		Severe	Medium	Mild
Antibody test	Positive test	85	125	150
	Negative test	40	95	145

Severity of attack

Is there evidence of a relationship between presence of the antibody and severity of the heart attack? Test at the 5% significance level.

(A) There is evidence that presence of the antibody causes more severe heart attacks.
(B) There is evidence that heart attacks cause the antibody to form.
(C) There is evidence of a relationship between presence of the antibody and occurrence of a heart attack.
(D) There is evidence of a relationship between presence of the antibody and severity of the heart attack.
(E) At the 5% significance level there is not sufficient evidence of any relationship.

14. A city spokesperson claims that the mean response time for arrival of a fire truck at a fire is 12 minutes. A newspaper reporter suspects that the response time is actually longer and runs a test by examining the records of 64 fire emergency situations. What conclusion is reached if the sample mean is 13.1 minutes with a standard deviation of 6 minutes?

(A) The P-value is less than .0003, indicating very strong evidence against the 12-minute claim.
(B) The P-value is .0089, indicating strong evidence against the 12-minute claim.
(C) The P-value is .0708, indicating some evidence against the 12-minute claim.
(D) The P-value is .1838, indicating very little evidence against the 12-minute claim.
(E) The P-value is .4286, indicating no evidence against the 12-minute claim.

15. It is believed that using a new fertilizer will result in a yield of 1.6 tons per acre. A botanist carries out a two-tailed test on a field of 64 acres. Determine the P-value if the mean yield per acre in the sample is 1.72 tons with a standard deviation of 0.4. What is the conclusion at a level of significance of 10%? 5%? 1%?

 (A) $P = .0082$, and so the 1.6-ton claim should be disputed at all three of these levels.

 (B) $P = .0164$, and so the 1.6-ton claim should be disputed at the 10% and 5% levels but not at the 1% level.

 (C) $P = .0820$, and so the 1.6-ton claim should be disputed at the 10% level but not at the 5% and 1% levels.

 (D) $P = .0164$, and so the 1.6-ton claim should be disputed at the 1% level but not at the 10% and 5% levels.

 (E) $P = .0082$, and so there is not enough evidence to dispute the 1.6-ton claim at any of the three levels.

16. In an effort to curb certain diseases, especially autoimmune (AIDS), San Francisco has a program whereby drug users can exchange used needles for fresh ones. As reported in the *Journal of the American Medical Association* (January 12, 1994, p. 115), 35% of 5644 intravenous drug users in San Francisco admitted to sharing needles. Is this sufficient evidence to say that the rate of sharing needles has dropped from the pre-needle exchange rate of 66%?

 (A) $P < .001$, so this is very strong evidence that the rate has dropped.

 (B) $P = .0063$, so this is strong evidence of a drop in rate.

 (C) P is between .01 and .05, so there is moderate evidence of a drop in rate.

 (D) P is between .05 and .10, so there is some evidence of a drop in rate.

 (E) $P = .31$, so there is no real evidence of a drop in rate.

17. A recent study of health service costs for coronary angioplasty versus coronary artery bypass surgery at a London hospital (*The Lancet,* October 1, 1994, page 929) showed an average cost of £6176 with a standard deviation of £329 for 231 angioplasties and an average cost of £8164 with a standard deviation of £264 for 221 bypass surgeries. Is this sufficient evidence to say that the average cost of angioplasty is less than the average cost of bypass surgery?

 (A) $P < .001$, so this is very strong evidence that angioplasty costs less.

 (B) P is between .001 and .01, so this is strong evidence that angioplasty costs less.

 (C) P is between .01 and .05, so this is moderate evidence that angioplasty costs less.

 (D) P is between .05 and .10, so there is some evidence that angioplasty costs less.

 (E) $P > .10$, so there is little evidence that angioplasty costs less.

18. Amos Tversky and Thomas Gilovich, in their study on the "Hot Hand" in basketball (*Chance,* Winter 1989, page 20), found that in a random sample of games, Larry Bird hit a second free throw in 48 of 53 attempts after the first free throw was missed, and hit a second free throw in 251 of 285 attempts after the first free throw was made. Is there sufficient evidence to say that the probability that Bird will make a second free throw is different depending on whether or not he made the first free throw?

(A) $P < .001$, so this is very strong evidence that the probability that Bird will make a second free throw is different depending on whether he made the first.

(B) P is between .001 and .01, so this is strong evidence that the probabilities are different.

(C) P is between .01 and .05, so this is moderate evidence that the probabilities are different.

(D) P is between .05 and .10, so there is some evidence that the probabilities are different.

(E) $P > .10$, so there is little or no evidence that the probabilities are different.

19. A study of accident records at a large engineering company in England (*The Lancet,* October 22, 1994, page 1137) reported the following number of injuries on each shift for 1 year:

Shift:	Morning	Afternoon	Night
Number of injuries:	1372	1578	1686

Is there sufficient evidence to say that the number of accidents on the three shifts are not the same? Test at the .05, .01, and .001 levels.

(A) There is sufficient evidence at all three levels to say that the number of accidents on each shift are not the same.

(B) There is sufficient evidence at both the .05 and .01 levels but not at the .001 level.

(C) There is sufficient evidence at the .05 level but not at the .01 and .001 levels.

(D) There is sufficient evidence at the .001 level but not at the .01 and .05 levels.

(E) There is not sufficient evidence at any of these levels.

20. A 4-year study analyzing blood cholesterol in men more than 70 years old, reported in *The New York Times,* noted how many men with different cholesterol levels suffered a nonfatal or fatal heart attack.

	Low cholesterol	Medium cholesterol	High cholesterol
Nonfatal heart attacks	29	17	18
Fatal heart attacks	19	20	9

Is there evidence of a relationship? Does level of cholesterol seem to predict risk of heart disease for men more than 70 years old? Test at the 10% significance level.

(A) At the 10% significance level, the given data prove that level of cholesterol predicts risk of heart disease for men more than 70 years old.

(B) At the 10% significance level, the given data prove that level of cholesterol does not predict risk of heart disease for men more than 70 years old.

(C) Since $3.018 < 4.61$, there is sufficient evidence at the 10% significance level of a relationship between cholesterol level and risk of heart disease for men more than 70 years old.

(D) Since $3.018 < 4.61$, there is not sufficient evidence at the 10% significance level of a relationship between cholesterol level and risk of heart disease for men more than 70 years old.

(E) Relationship and causation give contradictory conclusions in this problem.

21. Which of the following statements are true?

    I. It is helpful to examine your data before deciding whether to use a one-sided or a two-sided hypothesis test.

    II. If the P-value is .05, the probability that the null hypothesis is correct is .05.

    III. The larger the P-value, the more evidence there is against the null hypothesis.

(A) I only

(B) II only

(C) III only

(D) II and III

(E) None of the above gives the complete set of true responses.

Answer Key

1. **A**	6. **D**	11. **E**	16. **A**	21. **E**
2. **A**	7. **C**	12. **C**	17. **A**	
3. **B**	8. **C**	13. **D**	18. **E**	
4. **C**	9. **E**	14. **C**	19. **A**	
5. **E**	10. **A**	15. **B**	20. **D**	

Answers Explained

1. **(A)** The P-value is the smallest value of the significance level α for which the null hypothesis would be rejected; or, equivalently, if the null hypothesis is assumed to be true, the P-value of a sample statistic is the probability of obtaining a result as extreme as the one obtained. The P-value does not give the probability that the null hypothesis is true. Depending on the sample we happen to choose, we may mistakenly reject a true null hypothesis, in which case we commit a Type I error.

2. **(A)** We have $H_0: \mu = 8$ and $H_a: \mu < 8$. The standard deviation of sample means is $\sigma_{\bar{x}} = \frac{\sigma}{\sqrt{n}} = \frac{0.9}{\sqrt{36}} = 0.15$. The z-score for 7.75 is $\frac{7.75-8}{0.15} = -1.67$. Using Table A, we obtain $\alpha = .0475$. Thus, if the 8-ounce claim is correct, there is a .0475 probability that the consumer will still obtain a sample mean less than 7.75 and will mistakenly reject the claim.

3. **(B)** We attempt to show that the null hypothesis is unacceptable by showing that it is improbable; however, we cannot show that it is definitely true or false.

4. **(C)** We have H_0: $\mu = 15.0$ and H_a: $\mu \neq 15.0$. This is an example of a two-sided test. The standard deviation of the sample means is $\sigma_{\bar{x}} = \frac{12.0}{\sqrt{42}} = 1.85$. The z-score for 17 is $\frac{17-15}{1.85} = 1.08$; similarly, the z-score for 13 is -1.08. From Table A, we obtain .1401, for a total probability of Type I error (mistakenly rejecting a true null hypothesis) of $.1401 + .1401 = .2802$.

5. **(E)** Both the null and alternative hypotheses are stated in terms of a population parameter, not a sample statistic. Small P-values are evidence against the null hypothesis. These hypothesis tests assume simple random samples.

6. **(D)** We have H_0: $\mu = 48.3$ and H_a: $\mu < 48.3$. Here $\sigma_{\bar{x}} = \frac{\sigma}{\sqrt{n}} \approx \frac{s}{\sqrt{n}} = \frac{15.4}{\sqrt{30}} = 2.81$. The z-score of 45.4 is $\frac{45.4-48.3}{2.81} = -1.03$, and so the P-value is .1515. With such a large P-value, there is little evidence against H_0 and the stockholder should not reject the executive's claim.

7. **(C)** We have H_0: $\mu = 58.4$, H_a: $\mu \neq 58.4$, and $\sigma_{\bar{x}} \approx \frac{s}{\sqrt{n}} = \frac{8.3}{\sqrt{250}} = 0.525$. The z-score for 59.5 is $\frac{59.5-58.4}{0.525} = 2.10$. Using Table A, we find the corresponding probability to be $1 - .9821 = .0179$. Doubling this value because the test is two-sided results in a P-value of $2(.0179) = .0358$.

8. **(C)** We have $H_0: \mu_1 - \mu_2 = 0$, $H_a: \mu_1 - \mu_2 < 0$, and $\sigma_{\bar{x}_1 - \bar{x}_2} = \sqrt{\frac{(2.3)^2}{30} + \frac{(2.3)^2}{30}}$ $= 0.594$. The z-score for -1 is $\frac{-1-0}{0.594} = -1.68$. From Table A, the resulting probability is .0465.

9. **(E)** The two-sample hypothesis test is not the proper one and should be used only when the two sets are independent. In this case, there is a clear relationship between the data, in pairs, and this relationship is completely lost in the procedure for the two-sample test. The proper procedure is to run a one-sample test on the single variable consisting of the differences from the paired data.

10. **(A)** We have $H_0: p = .07$, $H_a: p > .07$, and $\sigma_{\hat{p}} = \sqrt{\frac{(.07)(.93)}{200}} = .018$. $\hat{p} = \frac{23}{200} = .115$ with a z-score of $\frac{.115 - .07}{.018} = 2.5$. Thus the P-value is $1 - .9938 = .0062$. This low P-value is strong evidence against H_0.

11. **(E)** We are comparing two population proportions and thus the correct test involves H_0: $p_1 - p_2 = 0$ and H_a: $p_1 - p_2 \neq 0$.

12. **(C)** Since $1 + 3 + 3 + 9 = 16$, according to the geneticist the expected number of fruit flies of each species is $\frac{1}{16}(4000) = 250$, $\frac{3}{16}(4000) = 750$, $\frac{3}{16}(4000) = 750$, and $\frac{9}{16}(4000) = 2250$. We calculate chi-square:

$$\chi^2 = \frac{(226 - 250)^2}{250} + \frac{(764 - 750)^2}{750} + \frac{(733 - 750)^2}{750} + \frac{(2277 - 2250)^2}{2250} = 3.27$$

With $4 - 1 = 3$ degrees of freedom and $\alpha = .10$, the critical χ^2-value is 6.25. Since $3.27 < 6.25$, there is not sufficient evidence to reject H_0. At the 10% significance level, therefore, the geneticist's claim should not be rejected.

13. **(D)** We have H_0: independence (no relation between presence of antibody and severity of attack), H_a: dependence (severity of attack related to presence of antibody), $\alpha = .05$, and df $= (2-1)(3-1) = 2$. Totaling rows and columns yields

The expected value for each box is calculated by multiplying the row total by the column total and dividing by 640 as follows: $\frac{(360)(125)}{640} = 70.3$, $\frac{(360)(220)}{640} = 123.8$, $\frac{(360)(295)}{640} = 165.9$, $\frac{(280)(125)}{640} = 54.7$, $\frac{(280)(220)}{640} = 96.2$, and $\frac{(280)(295)}{640} = 129.1$.

	Expected			
	Severe	Medium	Mild	
Positive	70.3	123.8	165.9	360
Negative	54.7	96.2	129.1	280
	125	220	295	

Then

$$\chi^2 = \frac{(85 - 70.3)^2}{70.3} + \frac{(125 - 123.8)^2}{123.8} + \frac{(150 - 165.9)^2}{165.9}$$

$$+ \frac{(40 - 54.7)^2}{54.7} + \frac{(95 - 96.2)^2}{96.2} + \frac{(145 - 129.1)^2}{129.1}$$

$$= 10.533$$

With $\alpha = .05$ and $df = 2$, the critical χ^2-value is 5.99. Since $10.533 > 5.99$, there is sufficient evidence to reject the null hypothesis of independence. Thus, at the 5% significance level, there is evidence of a relationship between presence of antibody and severity of heart attack.

14. **(C)** We have $H_0: \mu = 12$, $H_a: \mu > 12$, and $\sigma_{\bar{x}} \approx \frac{s}{\sqrt{n}} = \frac{6}{\sqrt{64}} = 0.75$. The z-score of 13.1 is $\frac{13.1 - 12}{0.75} = 1.47$, and using Table A this gives a P-value of $1 - .9292 = .0708$, indicating some evidence against H_0.

15. **(B)** $\frac{1.72 - 1.6}{0.4/\sqrt{64}} = 2.4$, $1 - .9918 = .0082$, and because this is a two-tailed test, $P = 2(.0082) = .0164$. Since $.0164 < .10$ and $.0164 < .05$, the claim should be disputed at the 10% and 5% significance levels but not at the 1% level.

16. **(A)** $\sigma_{\bar{p}} = \sqrt{\frac{(.66)(.34)}{5644}} = .0063$

$\frac{.35 - .66}{.0063} = -49$, and the P-value is .0000.

17. **(A)** $\sigma_{\bar{x}_1 - \bar{x}_2} = \sqrt{\frac{(329)^2}{231} + \frac{(264)^2}{221}} = 28.00$

$\frac{6176 - 8164}{28.00} = -71$, and the P-value is .0000. This is very strong evidence that angioplasty costs less than bypass surgery.

18. **(E)**

$$\hat{p}_1 = \frac{48}{53} = .906$$

$$\hat{p}_2 = \frac{251}{285} = .881$$

$$\hat{p} = \frac{48+251}{53+285} = .885$$

$$\sigma_d = \sqrt{(.885)(.115)\left(\frac{1}{53} + \frac{1}{285}\right)} = .0477$$

$\frac{.906 - .881}{.0477} = 0.52$, and the P-value is either $1 - .6985 = .3015$ or $2(.3015)$ depending on whether the test is considered one- or two-sided. In either case, P is large and there is no evidence that the probability of Bird making a second free throw depends on whether he makes the first free throw.

19. **(A)** $\frac{1372 + 1578 + 1686}{3} = 1545$

$$\chi^2 = \frac{(1372 - 1545)^2}{1545} + \frac{(1578 - 1545)^2}{1545} + \frac{(1686 - 1545)^2}{1545} = 32.94$$

With df $= 3 - 1 = 2$, the critical χ^2-values for .05, .01, and .001 are 5.99, 9.21, and 13.82, respectively. Since 32.94 is greater than each of these, there is sufficient evidence at all these levels to say that the number of accidents on each shift are not the same.

20. **(D)**

	Low cholesterol	Medium cholesterol	High cholesterol	
Nonfatal heart attacks	27.4	21.1	15.5	64
Fatal heart attacks	20.6	15.9	11.5	48
	48	37	27	

$$\chi^2 = \frac{(29 - 27.4)^2}{27.4} + \frac{(17 - 21.1)^2}{21.1} + \frac{(18 - 15.5)^2}{15.5}$$
$$+ \frac{(19 - 20.6)^2}{20.6} + \frac{(20 - 15.9)^2}{15.9} + \frac{(9 - 11.5)^2}{11.5}$$
$$= 3.018$$

With df $= (2 - 1)(3 - 1) = 2$ and $\alpha = .10$, the critical χ^2-value is 4.61. Since $3.018 < 4.61$, there is not sufficient evidence at the 10% significance level of a relationship between cholesterol level and risk of heart disease for men more than 70 years old.

21. **(E)** All are false. The null and alternate hypotheses are decided on before the data come in. The *P*-value does not give the probability that the null hypothesis is true; it gives the probability of such an extreme value, assuming the null hypothesis is true. The smaller the *P*-value, the stronger the evidence against the null hypothesis.

Free-Response Questions

> *Directions:* You must show all work and indicate the methods you use. You will be graded on the correctness of your methods and on the accuracy of your final answers.

Three Open-Ended Questions

1. Three in-store surveys are taken: one before, one during, and one after a special promotion for tropical fruits. The proportions of customers expressing interest in these products are 29 out of 157, 37 out of 165, and 40 out of 152 for the surveys before, during, and after the promotion, respectively.

    a. Is the interest increase from before to during the promotion significant? From during to after the promotion? From before to after the promotion?

    b. What does the result obtained in part *a* say about the possibility that $\hat{p}_1$ and $\hat{p}_3$ are significantly different when $\hat{p}_1$ and $\hat{p}_2$ are not and when $\hat{p}_2$ and $\hat{p}_3$ are not?

2. Suppose your mathematics instructor gives as a homework assignment the problem of testing the fairness of a certain die. You are asked to roll the die 6000 times and to note how often it comes up 1, 2, 3, 4, 5, or 6. Tossing the die soon becomes tiresome, so you decide to invent some "reasonable" data. Being careful to make the total 6000, you write

	Number on die					
	1	2	3	4	5	6
Observed	988	991	1010	990	1013	1008

   Your instructor gives you an F, claiming that your results are too good to be true! Explain.

3. Suppose that your rival in the marketing department has what you consider a dumb idea. Your boss, who knows nothing about statistics, is relatively conservative but will follow up on this dumb idea if there is good evidence that more than 25% of the company's customers like it. A survey of 40 customers is taken, and 12 of them favor the idea. Your rival points out that $\frac{12}{40} = 30\%$. You know a little about statistics and perform the usual hypothesis test with H_0: $p = .25$ and H_a: $p > .25$. Write a paragraph explaining to your boss why these data are not strong evidence that more than 25% of the customers like your rival's idea.

Answers Explained

1. $\hat{p}_1 = \frac{29}{157} = .185, \hat{p}_2 = \frac{37}{165} = .224, \hat{p}_3 = \frac{40}{152} = .263.$ For $\hat{p}_1$ and $\hat{p}_2$ we calculate $\hat{p} = \frac{29+37}{157+165} = .205$ with

$$\sigma_d \approx \sqrt{(.205)(.795)\left(\frac{1}{157} + \frac{1}{165}\right)} = .0450$$

The observed difference is $.224 - .185 = .039$, and the associated z-score is $\frac{.039}{.0450} = 0.87.$ Table A gives the P-value as $1 - .8078 = .1922.$ Such a large P-value indicates that the interest increase from before to during the promotion is not significant.

For $\hat{p}_2$ and $\hat{p}_3$ we have $\hat{p} = \frac{37+40}{165+152} = .243$ with

$$\sigma_d \approx \sqrt{(.243)(.757)\left(\frac{1}{165} + \frac{1}{152}\right)} = .0482$$

The observed difference is $.263 - .224 = .039$, and the associated z-score is $\frac{.039}{.0482} = 0.81.$ Table A gives the P-value as $1 - .7910 = .2090.$ Such a large P-value indicates that the interest increase from during to after the promotion also is not significant.

For $\hat{p}_1$ and $\hat{p}_3$ we have $\hat{p} = \frac{29+40}{157+152} = .223$ with

$$\sigma_d \approx \sqrt{(.223)(.777)\left(\frac{1}{157} + \frac{1}{152}\right)} = .0474$$

The observed difference is $.263 - .185 = .078$, and the associated z-score is $\frac{.078}{.0474} = 1.65.$ Table A gives the P-value as $1 - .9505 = .0495.$ This small P-value indicates that the interest increase from before to after the promotion is significant.

Thus we see that it is possible for $\hat{p}_1$ and $\hat{p}_3$ to be significantly different when $\hat{p}_1$ and $\hat{p}_2$ are not and when $\hat{p}_2$ and $\hat{p}_3$ are not.

2. We have H_0: good fit to uniform distribution; that is, the die is fair. The expected values are all 1000, so

$$\chi^2 = \frac{12^2}{1000} + \frac{9^2}{1000} + \frac{10^2}{1000} + \frac{10^2}{1000} + \frac{13^2}{1000} + \frac{8^2}{1000} = 0.658$$

What is the conclusion if $\alpha = .01? .05? .10?$

With df $= 6 - 1 = 5$, the critical χ^2-values are 15.09, 11.07, and 9.24. Since 0.658 is less than each of these, there is not enough evidence to claim that the die is unfair. What is the conclusion if we're willing to accept $\alpha = .15? .20?$ .25? (.25 is the limit of Table C.)

These numbers give critical χ^2-values of 8.12, 7.29, and 6.63, respectively, which are all far above our χ^2-value of 0.658. Even if the die is fair, the probability of obtaining such a good-fitting sample, with $\chi^2 = 0.658$, is extremely small. Your instructor reasonably concluded that you simply made up the data. Your results were too good to be true!

3. Dear Boss:

The 40 customers surveyed represent just one possible sample out of many. Each sample has its own proportion of customers who like the idea, and these sample proportions are bunched around the true proportion. The question is whether this one sample proportion of 30% is so far away from the 25% figure that it is improbable that 25% is the true figure. I calculated a rough measure of the spread of the sample proportions to be $\sqrt{\frac{(.25)(.75)}{40}} = .0685$. Note that .30 is not even a whole one of these measurements away from .25. In fact it is only $\frac{.05}{.0685} = 0.73$ of one of these measurements of spread. Using a table that converts these figures to probabilities, I see that if the 25% figure is correct, there is more than a .23 chance of stumbling on a sample with a proportion as high as 30%. Statisticians call this .23 a P-value, and this high a P-value is no evidence that the original claim of 25% is wrong.

Four Investigative Tasks

1. An efficiency expert wishes to analyze the difference in productivity between workers exposed to two different lighting arrangements. She chooses a procedure in which the same 30 employees work under each arrangement for 1 week in turn. The outputs of each employee under the two lighting arrangements, LA1 and LA2, are summarized as follows.

Employee	1	2	3	4	5	6	7	8	9	10
LA1	15	23	18	19	27	13	22	20	20	19
LA2	12	22	18	20	24	12	20	20	19	17

Employee	11	12	13	14	15	16	17	18	19	20
LA1	25	26	15	19	19	21	20	30	24	16
LA2	26	20	14	17	15	16	22	26	24	19

Employee	21	22	23	24	25	26	27	28	29	30
LA1	15	20	19	20	17	26	12	10	23	26
LA2	19	18	19	15	20	22	14	13	20	25

a. Find the mean and standard deviation of each of the two 30-element sets corresponding to LA1 and LA2 separately.

b. Run a two-sample hypothesis test with $H_0: \mu_1 - \mu_2 = 0$, $H_a: \mu_1 - \mu_2 \neq 0$, and $\alpha = .05$.

c. Find the P-value.

d. Form the set of 30 differences (be careful with signs) and find the mean and standard deviation.

e. Run a single sample hypothesis test with $H_0: \mu = 0$, $H_a: \mu \neq 0$, and $\alpha = .05$ on this set.

f. Find the P-value.

g. Are the observed differences in lighting arrangements significant? Explain the contrasting conclusions between the two methods of analysis indicated above.

2. Suppose that a commercial is run once on television, once on the radio, and once in a newspaper. The advertising agency believes that any potential consumer has a 20% chance of seeing the ad on television, a 20% chance of

hearing it on the radio, and a 20% chance of reading it in the newpaper. In a telephone survey of 800 consumers, the numbers claiming to have been exposed to the ad 0, 1, 2, or 3 times are as follows.

	Exposures to ad			
	0	1	2	3
Observed number of people	434	329	35	2

At the 1% significance level, test the null hypothesis that the number of times any consumer saw the ad follows a binomial distribution with $\pi = .2$.

3. Suppose that in a telephone survey of 800 registered voters, the data are cross-classified both by gender of respondent and by respondent's opinion on an environmental bond issue.

	Bond issue	
	For	Against
Men	450	150
Women	160	40

  a. Determine the χ^2-value for these data.
  b. Now use the approach testing the significance of the difference between the proportions $\hat{p}_1 = \frac{450}{600} = .75$ and $\hat{p}_2 = \frac{160}{200} = .8$ and find the observed z-value.
  c. Compare the square of this z-value to the χ^2-value determined above.

  (It can be shown more generally that the χ^2-value for a two-by-two table is equal to the squared observed z-value for the difference in proportions.)

4. A survey of college students focuses on a cross-classification by year in school and positive or negative feelings about the college experience.

	Year in school			
	Freshman	Sophomore	Junior	Senior
Positive	105	100	90	125
Negative	35	50	30	25

  a. Determine the value of χ^2.

b. There are three degrees of freedom in this example. Suppose the table is split into the following three smaller tables, each having a single degree of freedom:

	Fresh-man	Soph-omore			Junior	Senior			Under-class	Upper-class
Pos.	105	100		Pos.	90	125		Pos.	205	215
Neg.	35	50		Neg.	30	25		Neg.	85	55

Determine the three χ^2-values, one from each of these tables.

c. Find a relationship between the χ^2-value of the original table and the three χ^2-values calculated above.

Answers Explained

1.   a. For LA1 we calculate $\bar{x}_1 = 19.97$ and $s_1 = 4.7086$, while for LA2 we calculate $\bar{x}_2 = 18.93$ and $s_2 = 3.9474$.

   b.

$$\sigma_{\bar{x}_1 - \bar{x}_2} \approx \sqrt{\frac{(4.7086)^2}{30} + \frac{(3.9474)^2}{30}} = 1.122$$

and the critical scores are $0 \pm 1.96(1.122) = \pm 2.20$. Since the observed difference, $19.97 - 18.93 = 1.04$, is between these scores, the observed difference is not significant.

   c. The z-score of $\frac{1.04}{1.122} = .93$ gives a probability of .1762 and a resulting p-value of $2(.1762) = .3524$.

   d. $\bar{x} = 1.03$, $s = 2.6455$

   e. $\sigma_{\bar{x}} \approx \frac{2.6455}{\sqrt{30}} = 0.483$, and the critical scores are $0 \pm 1.96(0.483) = \pm 0.95$. Since 1.03 is outside these scores, the observed difference is significant.

   f. The z-score of $\frac{1.03}{0.483} = 2.13$ gives a probability of .0166 and a resulting P-value of $2(.0166) = .0332$.

   g. The observed difference *is* significant. The reason for the apparent inconsistency is that the first test used is not the proper one. This two-sample test should be used only when the two sets are independent. In this case, there is a clear relationship between the data, in pairs, and this relationship is completely lost in the procedure for the two-sample test.

2. The complete binomial distribution with $\pi = .2$ and $n = 3$ is as follows:

$$
\begin{aligned}
P(0) &= (.8)^3 = .512 \\
P(1) &= 3(.2)(.8)^2 = .384 \\
P(2) &= 3(.2)^2(.8) = .096 \\
P(3) &= (.2)^3 = .008
\end{aligned}
$$

Multiplying each of these probabilities by 800 gives the expected number of occurrences: $.512(800) = 409.6$, $.384(800) = 307.2$, $.096(800) = 76.8$, and $.008(800) = 6.4$.

	Exposures to ad			
	0	1	2	3
Expected number of people	409.6	307.2	76.8	6.4

Thus

$$\chi^2 = \frac{(434 - 409.6)^2}{409.6} + \frac{(329 - 307.2)^2}{307.2} + \frac{(35 - 76.8)^2}{76.8} + \frac{(2 - 6.4)^2}{6.4} = 28.776$$

We have H_0: good fit to binomial distribution with $\pi = .2$. With $df = 4 - 1 = 3$ and $\alpha = .01$, the critical χ^2-value is 11.34. Since $28.776 > 11.34$, there is sufficient evidence to reject H_0 and to conclude that the number of ads seen by each consumer does not follow a binomial distribution with $\pi = .2$.

3. *a.* The table of expected values is calculated to be

	Bond issue		
	For	Against	
Men	457.5	142.5	600
Women	152.5	47.5	200
	610	190	800

$$\chi^2 = \frac{(450 - 457.5)^2}{457.5} + \frac{(150 - 142.5)^2}{142.5} + \frac{(160 - 152.5)^2}{152.5}$$
$$+ \frac{(40 - 47.5)^2}{47.5}$$
$$= 2.071$$

b. Let $\hat{p} = \frac{450 + 160}{800} = .7625$ and calculate

$$\sigma_d = \sqrt{(.7625)(.2375)\left(\frac{1}{600} + \frac{1}{200}\right)} = .0347$$

The observed z-value is $\frac{.75 - .8}{\sigma_d} = 1.439$.

c. $(1.439)^2 = 2.071$

4. *a.*

	Freshman	Sophomore	Junior	Senior	
Positive	105	112.5	90	112.5	420
Negative	35	37.5	30	37.5	140
	140	150	120	150	560

$$\chi^2 = 0 + \frac{12.5^2}{112.5} + 0 + \frac{12.5^2}{112.5} + 0 + \frac{12.5^2}{37.5} + 0 + \frac{12.5^2}{37.5} = 11.11$$

b.

	Fresh-man	Soph-omore	
Pos.	99	106	205
Neg.	41	44	85
	140	150	290

	Junior	Senior	
Pos.	95.6	119.4	215
Neg.	24.4	30.6	55
	120	150	270

	Under-class	Upper-class	
Pos.	217.5	202.5	420
Neg.	72.5	67.5	140
	290	270	560

$$\chi^2 = \frac{6^2}{99} + \frac{6^2}{106} + \frac{6^2}{41} + \frac{6^2}{44} = 2.40$$

$$\chi^2 = \frac{5.6^2}{95.6} + \frac{5.6^2}{119.4} + \frac{5.6^2}{24.4} + \frac{5.6^2}{30.6} = 2.90$$

$$\chi^2 = \frac{12.5^2}{217.5} + \frac{12.5^2}{202.5} + \frac{12.5^2}{72.5} + \frac{12.5^2}{67.5} = 5.96$$

c. Note that the first χ^2-value is equal to the sum of the other three χ^2-values (up to round-off error), illustrating the *additive property* of the χ^2-statistic.

TOPIC FIFTEEN

Special Case of Normally Distributed Data

Statisticians and other researchers would save numerous hours of work if small samples could be used instead of larger ones. In many situations, such as estimating the completion time for a certain model of nuclear reactor or determining the damage sustained by luxury cars from front-end collisions, it is prohibitively difficult or expensive to gather enough data for a large sample. In other situations, such as deciding whether to add or drop a TV series after only a few shows have been aired, there is simply not sufficient time to gather large quantities of data.

t-distribution

If we have a normal population, for n small, the set of means of all samples of size n is still normally distributed, but the set of variances is not. The modified sample variances $\frac{\sum(x-\bar{x})^2}{n-1}$ have a mean equal to the population variance σ^2, but their distribution is skewed, with more low values than high ones. Thus $\frac{\bar{x}-\mu}{s/\sqrt{n}}$ has more high values (both plus and minus) and so does not follow a normal distribution. We can no longer say, for example, that 95% of the sample means are within $1.96(s/\sqrt{n})$ of the population mean. More than 5% of the sample means lie outside these critical values.

If, however, the original population is normally distributed, there is a distribution that can be used when working with the $s/\sqrt{n}$ ratios. This *Student t-distribution* was introduced in 1908 by W. S. Gosset, a British mathematician employed by the Guiness Breweries. (When we are working with small samples from a population that is *not* nearly normal, we must use very different "nonparametric" techniques not discussed in this review book. When n is large, we use the normal distribution tables.)

Thus, for a small sample from a normally distributed population, we work with the variable

$$t = \frac{\bar{x}-\mu}{s/\sqrt{n}}$$

with a resulting t-distribution that is bell-shaped and symmetric, but lower at the mean, higher at the tails, and so more spread out than the normal distribution.

Like the binomial distribution, the t-distribution is different for different values of n. In the tables these distinct t-distributions are associated with the values for degrees of freedom (df). For this discussion the df value is equal to the sample size minus 1. The smaller the df value, the larger the dispersion in the distribution. The larger the df value, that is, the larger the sample size, the closer the distribution to the normal distribution.

Since there is a separate t-distribution for each df value, fairly complete tables would involve many pages; therefore, in Table B of the Appendix we list areas and t-values for only the more commonly used percentages or probabilities. The last row of Table B is the normal distribution, which is a special case of the t-distribution taken when n is infinite. For practical purposes, the two distributions are very close for any $n \geq 30$. However, when more accuracy is required, the Student t-distribution can be used for much larger values of n.

Note that, whereas Table A gives areas under the normal curve to the left of given z-values, Table B gives areas to the right of given positive t-values. For example, suppose the sample size is 20, and so df $= 20 - 1 = 19$. Then a probability of .05 in the tail corresponds with a t-value of 1.729, while .01 in the tail corresponds to $t = 2.539$.

Examples 15.1–15.6 involve small samples used for estimating population means, hypothesis testing on population means, and comparing two population means. *In all these examples, it is assumed that the original populations are normally distributed.* Without this stipulation, we could not use the t-distribution as explained above.

Single Sample t-procedures

Example 15.1. When ten cars of a new model were tested for gas mileage, the results showed a mean of 27.2 miles per gallon with a standard deviation of 1.8 miles per gallon. What is a 95% confidence interval estimate for the gas mileage achieved by this model?

Answer: Because the sample size is less than 30, we must use the t-distribution. The standard deviation of the sample means is $\sigma_{\bar{x}} = \frac{1.8}{\sqrt{10}} = 0.569$. With $10 - 1 = 9$ degrees of freedom and 2.5% in each tail, the appropriate t-scores are ± 2.262. Thus we can be 95% certain that the gas mileage of the new model is in the range $27.2 \pm 2.262(0.569) = 27.2 \pm 1.3$ or between 25.9 and 28.5 miles per gallon.

Example 15.2.   A new process for producing synthetic gems yielded six stones weighing 0.43, 0.52, 0.46, 0.49, 0.60, and 0.56 carats, respectively, in its first run. Find a 90% confidence interval estimate for the mean carat weight from this process.

Answer: Using the statistical package on your calculator or, much more laboriously, by hand, calculate the sample mean $\bar{x}$ and standard deviation s, and then find $\sigma_{\bar{x}}$, the standard deviation of the set of sample means:

$$\bar{x} = \frac{\Sigma x}{n} = \frac{0.43 + 0.52 + 0.46 + 0.49 + 0.60 + 0.56}{6} = \frac{3.06}{6} = 0.51$$

$$
\begin{aligned}
s &= \sqrt{\frac{\Sigma(x - \bar{x})^2}{n - 1}} \\
&= \sqrt{\frac{(0.08)^2 + (0.01)^2 + (0.05)^2 + (0.02)^2 + (0.09)^2 + (0.05)^2}{5}} \\
&= 0.0632
\end{aligned}
$$

and

$$\sigma_{\bar{x}} \approx \frac{s}{\sqrt{n}} = \frac{0.0632}{\sqrt{6}} = 0.0258$$

With df $= 6 - 1 = 5$ and 5% in each tail, the t-scores are ± 2.015. Thus we can be 90% sure that the new process will yield stones weighing $0.51 \pm 2.015(0.0258) = 0.51 \pm 0.052$ or between 0.458 and 0.562 carats.

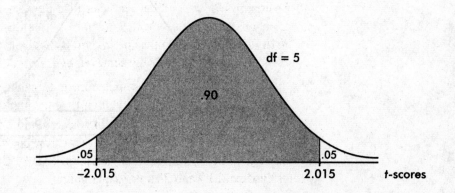

Example 15.3.   A cigarette industry spokesperson remarks that current levels of tar are no more than 5 milligrams per cigarette. A reporter does a quick check on 15 cigarettes representing a cross section of the market.

a. What conclusion is reached if the sample mean is 5.63 milligrams of tar with a standard deviation of 1.61? Assume a 10% significance level.

Answer: We have $H_0: \mu = 5$, $H_a: \mu > 5$, $\alpha = .10$, and

$$\sigma_{\bar{x}} \approx \frac{s}{\sqrt{n}} = \frac{1.61}{\sqrt{15}} = 0.42$$

With df $= 15 - 1 = 14$ and $\alpha = .10$, the critical t-score is 1.345. The critical number of milligrams of tar is $5 + 1.345(0.42) = 5.56$. Since $5.63 > 5.56$, the industry spokesperson's remarks should be rejected at the 10% significance level.

b. What is the conclusion at the 5% significance level?

Answer: In this case, the critical t-score is 1.761, the critical tar level is $5 + 1.761(0.42) = 5.74$ milligrams, and since $5.63 < 5.74$, the remarks cannot be rejected at the 5% significance level.

c. What is the P-value?

Answer: Without a software program we can't calculate the P-value exactly. However, the t-score for 5.63 is $\frac{5.63-5}{0.42} = 1.5$, and since 1.5 is between 1.345 and 1.761, we can conclude that P is between .05 and .10.

Example 15.4.   A local chamber of commerce claims that the mean sale price for homes in the city is \$90,000. A real estate salesperson notes eight recent sales of \$75,000, \$102,000, \$80,000, \$85,000, \$79,000, \$95,000, \$98,000, and \$62,000. How strong is the evidence to reject the chamber of commerce claim?

Answer:

$$H_0: \mu = 90,000 \qquad H_a: \mu \neq 90,000$$

A calculator gives $\bar{x} = 84,500$ and $s = 13,341.7$, and then one calculates $\sigma_{\bar{x}} \approx \frac{s}{\sqrt{n}} = \frac{13,341.7}{\sqrt{8}} = 4717$. The t-score of 84,500 is $\frac{84,500-90,000}{4717} = 1.17$. With df $= 8 - 1 = 7$, we note that 1.17 is between 1.119 and 1.415, corresponding to .15 and .10, respectively. Doubling these values because this is a two-sided test, we see that the P-value is between .20 and .30. With such a high P, we conclude that there is no evidence to reject the chamber of commerce claim.

Two Sample t-procedures

Many experiments and tests involve comparing two populations for which the data naturally occur in pairs. In this case of *paired differences,* the proper procedure is to run a one-sample analysis on the single variable consisting of the differences from the paired data.

In the case of independent samples, there is a procedure based on the assumption that both original populations not only are normally distributed but also have equal variances. Then for $\sigma_{\bar{x}_1 - \bar{x}_2}$ we have

$$\sigma_{\bar{x}_1 - \bar{x}_2} = \sqrt{\frac{\sigma_1^2}{n_1} + \frac{\sigma_2^2}{n_2}} = \sqrt{\frac{\sigma^2}{n_1} + \frac{\sigma^2}{n_2}} = \sigma\sqrt{\frac{1}{n_1} + \frac{1}{n_2}}$$

But what should we use for σ? The idea, motivated by

$$s^2 = \frac{\sum(x-\bar{x})^2}{n-1} \quad \text{or} \quad \sum(x-\bar{x})^2 = (n-1)s^2$$

is to use

$$\frac{\sum(x-\bar{x}_1)^2 + \sum(x-\bar{x}_2)^2}{(n_1-1) + (n_2-1)}$$

for this "pooled" s^2, where the first sum is over the first sample and the second sum is over the second sample. This quotient can be rewritten as

$$s_p^2 = \frac{(n_1-1)s_1^2 + (n_2-1)s_2^2}{n_1+n_2-2}$$

and finally we have the complex-looking equation

$$\sigma_{\bar{x}_1 - \bar{x}_2} \approx \sqrt{\frac{(n_1 - 1)s_1^2 + (n_2 - 1)s_2^2}{n_1 + n_2 - 2}} \sqrt{\frac{1}{n_1} + \frac{1}{n_2}}$$

The degrees of freedom in such a situation are

$$\text{df} = (n_1 - 1) + (n_2 - 1) = n_1 + n_2 - 2$$

Example 15.5.   Two varieties of corn are being compared as to difference in maturation time. Ten plots of the first variety reach maturity in an average of 95 days with a standard deviation of 5.3 days, while eight plots of the second variety reach maturity in an average of 74 days with a standard deviation of 4.8 days. Determine a 95% confidence interval estimate for the difference in maturation time. (Assume that the original populations are normally distributed and that their variances are equal.)

Answer:

$$
\begin{array}{ll}
n_1 = 10 & n_2 = 8 \\
x_1 = 95 & x_2 = 74 \\
s_1 = 5.3 & s_2 = 4.8
\end{array}
$$

$$\sigma_{\bar{x}_1 - \bar{x}_2} \approx \sqrt{\frac{(10 - 1)(5.3)^2 + (8 - 1)(4.8)^2}{10 + 8 - 2}} \sqrt{\frac{1}{10} + \frac{1}{8}} = 2.41$$

With df $= 10 + 8 - 2 = 16$ and .025 in each tail, the critical *t*-scores are ± 2.120. The observed difference was $95 - 74 = 21$, and so the confidence interval estimate is $21 \pm 2.120(2.41) = 21 \pm 5.1$. Thus we can be 95% certain that the first variety of corn will take between 15.9 and 26.1 more days to reach maturity than the second variety.

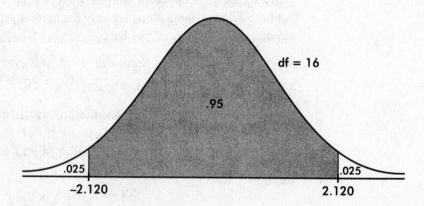

Example 15.6.   A city council member claims that male and female officers wait equal times for promotion in the police department. A women's spokesperson, however, believes women must wait longer than men. If five men waited 8, 7, 10, 5, and 7 years, respectively, for promotion while four

women waited 9, 5, 12, and 8 years, respectively, what conclusion should be drawn? (Assume that the original populations are normally distributed and that their variances are equal.)

Answer: We have $H_0: \mu_1 - \mu_2 = 0$ and $H_a: \mu_1 - \mu_2 < 0$. Using a calculator we find $\bar{x}_1 = 7.4$, $s_1 = 1.82$, $\bar{x}_2 = 8.5$, and $s_2 = 2.89$. Then

$$\sigma_{\bar{x}_1 - \bar{x}_2} \approx \sqrt{\frac{(5-1)(1.82)^2 + (4-1)(2.89)^2}{5+4-2}} \sqrt{\frac{1}{5} + \frac{1}{4}} = 1.57$$

The *t*-score of the observed difference is $\frac{7.4-8.5}{1.57} = -0.70$. With df $= 5 + 4 - 2 = 7$, we note that $0.70 < 0.711$, where 0.711 corresponds to a tail probability of .25. Thus the *P*-value is greater than .25, and we conclude there is no evidence to dispute the council member's claim.

Inference for Slope of Least Squares Line

In Topic 4 we discussed the least squares line

$$y' = \bar{y} + b_1(x - \bar{x})$$

where b_1 is the slope of the line. This slope is readily found using the statistical software on a calculator. It is an estimate of the slope β of the true regression line. A confidence interval estimate for β can be found using *t*-scores, where df $= n - 2$, and the appropriate standard deviation is

$$s_{b_1} = \frac{\sqrt{\frac{\Sigma(y_i - \hat{y}_i)^2}{n-2}}}{\sqrt{\Sigma(x_i - \bar{x})^2}}$$

where the sum in the numerator is the sum of the squared residuals (see Topic 4) and the sum in the denominator is the sum of the squared deviations from the mean. The value of s_{b_1} is found at the same time that the statistical software on your calculator finds the value of b_1. Some calculators calculate the numerator $s = \sqrt{\frac{\Sigma(y_i - \hat{y}_i)^2}{n-2}}$, and then the denominator can be calculated by $\sqrt{\Sigma(x_i - \bar{x})^2} = s_x\sqrt{n-1}$.

Example 15.7.   A random sample of 10 high school students produced the following results for number of hours of television watched per week and GPA.

TV hours:	12	21	08	20	16	16	24	0	11	18
GPA:	3.2	2.3	3.7	2.5	3.0	2.1	2.7	3.8	2.9	2.6

Determine the least squares line and give a 95% confidence interval estimate for the true slope.

Answer: Using the statistics software on a calculator gives

$$y = 3.823 - 0.06456x$$

Using, for example, the TI-83 one also obtains

$$s = 0.3461 \quad \text{and} \quad s_x = 7.074$$

Thus

$$s_{b_1} = \frac{0.3461}{7.074\sqrt{10-1}} = 0.0163$$

With 10 data points, the degrees of freedom are df $= 10 - 2 = 8$, and the critical t-values (with .025 in each tail) are ± 2.306. The 95% confidence interval of the true slope is

$$-0.06456 \pm 2.306(0.0163) = -0.06456 \pm .03759$$

We are thus 95% confident that each additional hour before the television each week is associated with between a .027 and a .102 drop in GPA. (Remember we must be careful about drawing conclusions concerning cause and effect; it is possible that students who have lower GPAs would have these averages no matter how much television they watched per week.)

In addition to finding a confidence interval for the true slope, one can also perform a hypothesis test for the value of the slope. Often one uses the null hypothesis $H_0 : \beta = 0$, that is, that there is no linear relationship between the two variables.

Example 15.8. In Example 15.7, what should be the conclusion from a hypothesis test of $H_0 : \beta = 0$ and $H_a : \beta < 0$?

Answer: Using the statistics software on your calculator, either find $t = -3.96$ or calculate

$$t = \frac{b}{s_{b_1}} = \frac{-0.06456}{0.0163} = -3.96$$

Then look across the df $= 8$ row of Table B and conclude that the P-value is between .001 and .0025. Some software immediately gives $P = .0021$. With such a small P-value, we conclude that there is strong evidence against H_0 and in support of a relationship between television hours watched and GPA.

Questions on Topic Fifteen: Special Case of Normally Distributed Data

Multiple-Choice Questions

Directions: The questions or incomplete statements that follow are each followed by five suggested answers or completions. Choose the response that best answers the question or completes the statement.

1. Which of the following statements are true?
   I. Like the normal, t-distributions are always symmetric.
   II. Like the normal, t-distributions are always mound-shaped.
   III. The t-distributions have less spread than the normal, that is, they have less probability in the tails and more in the center than the normal.

   (A) II only
   (B) I and II
   (C) I and III
   (D) II and III
   (E) I, II, and III

2. Which of the following statements about t-distributions are true?
   I. The greater the number of degrees of freedom, the narrower the tails.
   II. The smaller the number of degrees of freedom, the closer the curve is to the normal curve.
   III. Thirty degrees of freedom gives the normal curve.

   (A) I only
   (B) I and II
   (C) I and III
   (D) II and III
   (E) I, II, and III

3. Statistical analysis using the t-distributions for small samples assumes which of the following?
   I. Sample standard deviation equal to the population standard deviation
   II. Random sampling
   III. Normal population

   (A) I only
   (B) I and II
   (C) I and III
   (D) II and III
   (E) I, II, and III

4. What is the critical t-value for finding a 90% confidence interval estimate from a sample of 15 observations?
   (A) 1.341
   (B) 1.345
   (C) 1.350
   (D) 1.753
   (E) 1.761

5. In a one-sided hypothesis test for the mean, in a random sample of size 10 the t-score of the sample mean is 2.79. Is this significant at the 5% level? At the 1% level?

   (A) Significant at the 1% level but not at the 5% level
   (B) Significant at the 5% level but not at the 1% level
   (C) Significant at both the 1% and 5% levels
   (D) Significant at neither the 1% nor 5% level
   (E) Cannot be determined from the given information

6. Which of the following statements about matched pairs analysis are true?

   I. The two samples are assumed to be independent.
   II. One-sample procedures are applied to a set of differences.
   III. In a matched-pairs t-procedure, the population of differences is assumed to have a normal distribution.

   (A) I only
   (B) I and II
   (C) I and III
   (D) II and III
   (E) I, II, and III

7. In a sleep laboratory experiment, 16 volunteers sleep an average of 7.4 hours with a standard deviation of 1.3 hours. What is a 99% confidence interval estimate for the mean number of hours that people sleep at night? Assume the population has a normal distribution.

   (A) 7.4 ± 0.24
   (B) 7.4 ± 0.84
   (C) 7.4 ± 0.85
   (D) 7.4 ± 0.96
   (E) 7.4 ± 3.83

8. Acute renal graft rejection can occur years after the graft. In one study (*The Lancet*, December 24, 1994, page 1737), 21 patients showed such late acute rejection when the ages of their grafts (in years) were 9, 2, 7, 1, 4, 7, 9, 6, 2, 3, 7, 6, 2, 3, 1, 2, 3, 1, 1, 2, and 7, respectively. Establish a 90% confidence interval estimate for the ages of renal grafts that undergo late acute rejection.

   (A) 2.024 ± 0.799
   (B) 2.024 ± 1.725
   (C) 4.048 ± 0.799
   (D) 4.048 ± 1.041
   (E) 4.048 ± 1.725

9. Nine subjects, 87 to 96 years old, were given 8 weeks of progressive resistance weight training (*Journal of the American Medical Association*, June 13, 1990, page 3032). Strength before and after training for each individual was measured as maximum weight (in kilograms) lifted by left knee extension:

Before:	3	3.5	4	6	7	8	8.5	12.5	15
After:	7	17	19	12	19	22	28	20	28

   Find a 95% confidence interval estimate for the strength gain.

(A) 11.61 ± 3.03
(B) 11.61 ± 3.69
(C) 11.61 ± 3.76
(D) 19.11 ± 1.25
(E) 19.11 ± 3.69

10. An IRS representative claims that the average deduction for medical care is $1250. A taxpayer who believes that the real figure is lower samples 12 families and comes up with a mean of $934 and a standard deviation of $616. Where is the *P*-value?

   (A) Below .01
   (B) Between .01 and .025
   (C) Between .025 and .05
   (D) Between .05 and .10
   (E) Over .10

11. An auditor remarks that the accounts receivable for a company seem to average about $2000. A quick check of 20 accounts gives a mean of $2250 with a standard deviation of $600. Where is the *P*-value?

   (A) Below .01
   (B) Between .01 and .025
   (C) Between .025 and .05
   (D) Between .05 and .10
   (E) Over .10

12. Six capsules of drug A took an average of 75 seconds with a standard deviation of 1.4 seconds to dissolve, while the average time for six capsules of drug B was 71 seconds with a standard deviation of 1.7 seconds. Establish a 99% confidence interval estimate for the difference in dissolving time between the two brands.

   (A) 4 ± 1.55
   (B) 4 ± 2.48
   (C) 4 ± 2.56
   (D) 4 ± 2.85
   (E) 4 ± 3.10

13. A researcher believes a new diet should improve weight gain in laboratory mice. If ten control mice on the old diet gain an average of 4 ounces with a standard deviation of 0.3 ounces, while the average gain for ten mice on the new diet is 4.8 ounces with a standard deviation of 0.2 ounces, where is the *P*-value?

   (A) Below .01
   (B) Between .01 and .025
   (C) Between .025 and .05
   (D) Between .05 and .10
   (E) Over .10

Answer Key

1. **B**	4. **E**	7. **D**	10. **D**	13. **A**
2. **A**	5. **B**	8. **D**	11. **D**	
3. **D**	6. **D**	9. **C**	12. **D**	

Answers Explained

1. **(B)** The t-distributions are symmetric and mound-shaped, and they have more, not less, spread than the normal distribution.

2. **(A)** The larger the number of degrees of freedom, the closer the curve to the normal curve. While around the 30 level is often considered a reasonable approximation to the normal curve, it is not the normal curve.

3. **(D)** While we assume a random sample from a normal distribution, the sample standard deviation s is only an estimate of the population standard deviation σ. The larger the sample size, the better the estimate.

4. **(E)** With df $= 15 - 1 = 14$ and .05 in each tail, the critical t-value is 1.761.

5. **(B)** With df $= 10 - 1 = 9$, the critical t-scores for the .05 and .01 tail probabilities are 1.833 and 2.821, respectively. We have $2.79 > 1.833$, but $2.79 < 2.821$, and so 2.79 is significant at the 5% level but not at the 1% level.

6. **(D)** The samples are strongly dependent, for example, "before-and-after" observations on the same subject.

7. **(D)** df $= 15$, and $7.4 \pm 2.947(\frac{1.3}{\sqrt{16}}) = 7.4 \pm 0.96$.

8. **(D)** $\bar{x} = 4.048$, $s = 2.765$, df $= 20$, and $4.048 \pm 1.725(\frac{2.765}{\sqrt{21}}) = 4.048 \pm 1.041$.

9. **(C)** The confidence interval estimate of the set of nine differences is $11.61 \pm 2.306(\frac{4.891}{\sqrt{9}}) = 11.61 \pm 3.76$.

10. **(D)** $\frac{934-1250}{616/\sqrt{12}} = -1.777$. Since 1.777 is between 1.363 and 1.796, P is between .05 and .10.

11. **(D)** We have $\frac{2250-2000}{600/\sqrt{20}} = 1.863$. With df $= 20 - 1 = 19$, we note that 1.863 is between 1.729 and 2.093, which correspond to .05 and .025, respectively. This is a two-sided test, and so we double these probabilities and find the interval for the P-value to be between .10 and .05.

12. **(D)**

$$\sigma_{\bar{x}_1 - \bar{x}_2} = \sqrt{\frac{(6-1)(1.4)^2 + (6-1)(1.7)^2}{6+6-2}} \sqrt{\frac{1}{6} + \frac{1}{6}} = 0.899$$

with df $= 6 + 6 - 2 = 10$, $(75 - 71) \pm 3.169(0.899) = 4 \pm 2.85$.

13. **(A)**

$$\sigma_{\bar{x}_1 - \bar{x}_2} = \sqrt{\frac{(10-1)(0.3)^2 + (10-1)(0.2)^2}{10+10-2}} \sqrt{\frac{1}{10} + \frac{1}{10}} = 0.114$$

The t-score of the observed difference is $\frac{4-4.8}{0.114} = -7.018$. With df $= 18$, we note that $7.018 > 3.922$, and thus the P-value is less than .0005.

Free-Response Questions

> *Directions:* You must show all work and indicate the methods you use. You will be graded on the correctness of your methods as well as on the accuracy of your final answers.

Three Open-Ended Questions

1. Polychlorinated biphenyl (PCB) contamination of a river by a manufacturer is being measured by amounts of the pollutant found in fish. A company scientist claims that the fish contain only 5 parts per million, but an investigator believes the figure is higher. What is the conclusion if six fish are caught and show the following amounts of PCB (in parts per million): 6.8, 5.6, 5.2, 4.7, 6.3, and 5.4, respectively?

2. The weight of an aspirin tablet is 300 milligrams according to the bottle label. Should a Food and Drug Administration (FDA) investigator reject the label if she weighs seven tablets and obtains weights of 299, 300, 305, 302, 299, 301, and 303 milligrams, respectively?

3. An employer wishes to compare typing speeds of graduates from two different study programs. Eight graduates of the first course type at 62, 85, 59, 64, 73, 70, 75, and 72 words per minute, respectively, while six graduates of the second course have typing speeds of 75, 64, 81, 55, 69, and 58 words per minute, respectively. Should the employer conclude that one program is better than the other?

Answers Explained

1. We have H_0: $\mu = 5$ parts per million, H_a: $\mu > 5$ parts per million, $\bar{x} = 5.67$, and $s = 0.763$, and the t-value of $\bar{x}$ is $\frac{5.67-5}{0.763/\sqrt{6}} = 2.151$. With df $= 6 - 1 = 5$, we note that 2.151 is between 2.015 and 2.571. From the corresponding probabilities, we conclude that P is between .025 and .05. Thus there is moderate evidence against H_0, and, for example, at the 5% significance level there is sufficient evidence to dispute the company scientist's claim.

2. We have H_0: $\mu = 300$, H_a: $\mu \neq 300$, $\bar{x} = 301.3$, and $s = 2.21$, and the t-score of 301.3 is $\frac{301.3-300}{2.21/\sqrt{7}} = 1.556$. With df $= 7 - 1 = 6$, we note that 1.556 is between 1.440 and 1.943, corresponding to .10 and .05, respectively. Since this is a two-sided test, we double these values and conclude that P is between .10 and .20. With P this large, there is very little evidence against H_0, and the FDA does not have sufficient evidence to reject the label.

3. This is a two-sided test with H_0: $\mu_1 - \mu_2 = 0$ and H_a: $\mu_1 - \mu_2 \neq 0$. A calculator gives $\bar{x}_1 = 70, \bar{x}_2 = 67, s_1 = 8.32, s_2 = 9.98$, and

$$\sigma_{\bar{x}_1 - \bar{x}_2} = \sqrt{\frac{(8-1)(8.32)^2 + (6-1)(9.98)^2}{8+6-2}} \sqrt{\frac{1}{8} + \frac{1}{6}} = 4.89$$

The t-score of the observed differences is $\frac{70-67}{4.89} = 0.613$. With df $= 8 + 6 - 2 = 12$, we see that 0.613 is less than .695, which corresponds to a probability of .25. Since this is a two-sided test, we double this value to find that the *P*-value is greater than .50. With such a large *P*, there is no evidence that one program is better than the other.

An Investigative Task

1. An accounting firm measured the blood pressures of ten of its certified public accountants (CPAs) before and during the spring 1996 tax season. The systolic pressures for the ten individuals, designated as A through J were as follows:

	A	B	C	D	E	F	G	H	I	J
Before:	110	124	98	105	115	120	118	110	123	95
During:	115	126	97	108	115	124	119	113	121	96

Is there sufficient evidence that blood pressure rises during tax season?

a. Assuming normal populations with equal variances, perform a two-population, small-sample hypothesis test on $H_0: \mu_1 - \mu_2 = 0$, and $H_a: \mu_1 - \mu_2 < 0$. Show that this test does not indicate that the observed difference is significant even at $\alpha = .10$.

b. Which is the more appropriate test? Explain why. What conclusion can be drawn from this test?

Answers Explained

1.   a. A calculator gives $\bar{x}_1 = 111.8, \bar{x}_2 = 113.4, s_1 = 10.09, s_2 = 10.36$, and

$$\sigma_{\bar{x}_1 - \bar{x}_2} = \sqrt{\frac{(10-1)(10.09)^2 + (10-1)(10.36)^2}{10+10-2}} \sqrt{\frac{1}{10} + \frac{1}{10}} = 4.57$$

(Some calculators also give the pooled result 10.225, and then $\sigma_{\bar{x}_1 - \bar{x}_2} = 10.225\sqrt{.2} = 4.57$.) The *t*-score of the observed difference is then $\frac{111.8 - 113.4}{4.57} = -0.35$. With df = 18, we note that .35 < .688, and the *P*-value is more than .25. With such a large value of *P*, there is no evidence of a rise in blood pressure.

b. Looking at the data, however, it is apparent that a change in blood pressure occurred. The test used in part *a* does not apply the knowledge of what happened to each individual. In fact, since the before and during sets are not independent but rather are related in pairs, that test is not the proper one to use. The appropriate test is a one-population, small-sample hypothesis test on the set of differences. Forming the set of ten differences, being careful of sign, and then testing the hypotheses $H_0: \mu = 0$ and $H_a: \mu < 0$ results in $\bar{x} = -1.6, s = 2.22$, and $\sigma_{\bar{x}} = \frac{2.22}{\sqrt{10}} = 0.702$.

The *t*-score of -1.6 is $\frac{-1.6}{0.702} = -2.28$. With df = 9, we note that 2.28 is between 2.262 and 2.398, with corresponding probabilities .025 and .02, respectively. With *P* between .02 and .025 there is good evidence of a rise in blood pressure.

Practice
Examinations

Answer Sheet: Practice Examination 1

1. Ⓐ Ⓑ Ⓒ Ⓓ Ⓔ
2. Ⓐ Ⓑ Ⓒ Ⓓ Ⓔ
3. Ⓐ Ⓑ Ⓒ Ⓓ Ⓔ
4. Ⓐ Ⓑ Ⓒ Ⓓ Ⓔ
5. Ⓐ Ⓑ Ⓒ Ⓓ Ⓔ
6. Ⓐ Ⓑ Ⓒ Ⓓ Ⓔ
7. Ⓐ Ⓑ Ⓒ Ⓓ Ⓔ
8. Ⓐ Ⓑ Ⓒ Ⓓ Ⓔ
9. Ⓐ Ⓑ Ⓒ Ⓓ Ⓔ
10. Ⓐ Ⓑ Ⓒ Ⓓ Ⓔ
11. Ⓐ Ⓑ Ⓒ Ⓓ Ⓔ
12. Ⓐ Ⓑ Ⓒ Ⓓ Ⓔ

13. Ⓐ Ⓑ Ⓒ Ⓓ Ⓔ
14. Ⓐ Ⓑ Ⓒ Ⓓ Ⓔ
15. Ⓐ Ⓑ Ⓒ Ⓓ Ⓔ
16. Ⓐ Ⓑ Ⓒ Ⓓ Ⓔ
17. Ⓐ Ⓑ Ⓒ Ⓓ Ⓔ
18. Ⓐ Ⓑ Ⓒ Ⓓ Ⓔ
19. Ⓐ Ⓑ Ⓒ Ⓓ Ⓔ
20. Ⓐ Ⓑ Ⓒ Ⓓ Ⓔ
21. Ⓐ Ⓑ Ⓒ Ⓓ Ⓔ
22. Ⓐ Ⓑ Ⓒ Ⓓ Ⓔ
23. Ⓐ Ⓑ Ⓒ Ⓓ Ⓔ
24. Ⓐ Ⓑ Ⓒ Ⓓ Ⓔ

25. Ⓐ Ⓑ Ⓒ Ⓓ Ⓔ
26. Ⓐ Ⓑ Ⓒ Ⓓ Ⓔ
27. Ⓐ Ⓑ Ⓒ Ⓓ Ⓔ
28. Ⓐ Ⓑ Ⓒ Ⓓ Ⓔ
29. Ⓐ Ⓑ Ⓒ Ⓓ Ⓔ
30. Ⓐ Ⓑ Ⓒ Ⓓ Ⓔ
31. Ⓐ Ⓑ Ⓒ Ⓓ Ⓔ
32. Ⓐ Ⓑ Ⓒ Ⓓ Ⓔ
33. Ⓐ Ⓑ Ⓒ Ⓓ Ⓔ
34. Ⓐ Ⓑ Ⓒ Ⓓ Ⓔ
35. Ⓐ Ⓑ Ⓒ Ⓓ Ⓔ

Practice Examination 1
Section I
Questions 1–35

Spend 90 minutes on this part of the exam.

Directions: The questions or incomplete statements that follow are each followed by five suggested answers or completions. Choose the response that best answers the question or completes the statement.

1. Following is a histogram of home sale prices (in thousands of dollars) in one community:

Which of the following statements are true?
   I. The median price was $125,000.
   II. More homes sold for between $100,000 and $125,000 than for over $125,000.
   III. $10,000 is a reasonable estimate of the standard deviation in selling prices.
   (A) I only
   (B) II only
   (C) III only
   (D) All are true.
   (E) None is true.

2. Which of the following can stemplots show?
   I. Symmetry
   II. Gaps
   III. Clusters
   IV. Outliers
   (A) I, II, and III
   (B) I, II, and IV
   (C) I, III, and IV
   (D) II, III, and IV
   (E) I, II, III, and IV

3. The average yearly snowfall in a city is 55 inches. What is the standard deviation if 15% of the years have snowfalls above 60 inches? Assume yearly snowfalls are normally distributed.
   (A) 4.83
   (B) 5.18
   (C) 6.04
   (D) 8.93
   (E) The standard deviation cannot be computed from the information given.

4. To determine the average cost of running for a congressional seat, a random sample of 50 politicians are chosen and their records are examined. If the cost figures show a mean of $125,000 with a standard deviation of $32,000, what is the 90% confidence interval estimate for the average cost of running for office?
   (A) $125,000 ± $1053
   (B) $125,000 ± $7444
   (C) $125,000 ± $8870
   (D) $125,000 ± $32,000
   (E) $125,000 ± $52,640

GO ON TO THE NEXT PAGE ➤

5. In one study on the effect that eating meat products has on weight level, 500 subjects who admitted to eating meat at least once a day had their weights compared with those of 500 people who claimed to be vegetarians. In a second study, 500 randomly chosen subjects were served at least one meat meal per day for 6 months, while 500 others were randomly chosen to receive a strictly vegetarian diet for 6 months, with weights compared after 6 months.
   (A) The first study is a controlled experiment, while the second is an observational study.
   (B) The first study is an observational study, while the second is a controlled experiment.
   (C) Both studies are controlled experiments.
   (D) Both studies are observational studies.
   (E) Each study is part controlled experiment and part observational study.

6. A plumbing contractor obtains 60% of her boiler circulators from a company whose defect rate is 0.005, and the rest from a company whose defect rate is 0.010. What proportion of the circulators can be expected to be defective? If a circulator is defective, what is the probability that it came from the first company?
   (A) .0070, .429
   (B) .0070, .600
   (C) .0075, .500
   (D) .0075, .600
   (E) .0150, .571

7. A patient claims that he consumes only 2000 calories per day, but a dietician suspects that the actual figure is higher. The dietician plans to check his food intake for 30 days and will reject the patient's claim if the 30-day mean is more than 2100 calories. If the standard deviation (in calories per day) is 350, what is the probability that the dietician will mistakenly reject a patient's true claim?
   (A) .03
   (B) .06
   (C) .12
   (D) .28
   (E) .44

8. In the following table, what value for n results in a table showing perfect independence?

40	60
50	n

   (A) 30
   (B) 50
   (C) 70
   (D) 75
   (E) 100

9. When a random sample of 25 jars of peanut butter labeled "18 ounces" are weighed, the mean is 17.94 ounces with a standard deviation of 0.13 ounce. What is the 99% confidence interval estimate for the mean weight?
   (A) 17.94 ± 0.015 ounces
   (B) 17.94 ± 0.026 ounces
   (C) 17.94 ± 0.065 ounces
   (D) 17.94 ± 0.067 ounces
   (E) 17.94 ± 0.073 ounces

10. Given the probabilities $P(A) = .3$ and $P(B) = .2$, what is the probability of the union $P(A \cup B)$ if A and B are mutually exclusive? If A and B are independent? If B is a subset of A?
   (A) .44, .5, .2
   (B) .44, .5, .3
   (C) .5, .44, .2
   (D) .5, .44, .3
   (E) 0, .5, .3

11. A nursery owner claims that a recent drought stunted the growth of 22% of all her evergreens. A botanist tests this claim by examining 1100 trees. In which of the following intervals is the P-value located if 268 evergreens in the sample show signs of stunted growth?
   (A) $P < .01$
   (B) $.01 < P < .025$
   (C) $.025 < P < .05$
   (D) $.05 < P < .10$
   (E) $P > .10$

12. A medical research team tests for tumor reduction in a sample of patients using three different dosages of an experimental cancer drug. Which of the following is true?
    (A) There are three explanatory variables and one response variable.
    (B) There is one explanatory variable with three levels of response.
    (C) Tumor reduction is the only explanatory variable, but there are three response variables corresponding to the different dosages.
    (D) There are three levels of a single explanatory variable.
    (E) Each explanatory level has an associated level of response.

For Questions 13 and 14 consider the following: The graph below shows cumulative proportion plotted against age for a population.

13. The median is approximately what age?
    (A) 17
    (B) 30
    (C) 35
    (D) 40
    (E) 45

14. The interquartile range is approximately how many years?
    (A) 7
    (B) 17
    (C) 28
    (D) 35
    (E) 70

15. In a random sample of 300 high school students, 225 said they managed time effectively, while in a similar sample of 270 college students, only 108 felt they were effective time managers. What is a 99% confidence interval estimate for the difference between the proportions of high school and college students who think they manage time effectively?
    (A) $.35 \pm .004$
    (B) $.35 \pm .090$
    (C) $.35 \pm .100$
    (D) $.35 \pm .138$
    (E) $.35 \pm .163$

16. Which of the following are true statements?
    I. The histogram of a binomial distribution with $p = .5$ is always symmetric no matter what n, the number of trials, is.
    II. The histogram of a binomial distribution with $p = .17$ is skewed to the right.
    III. The histogram of a binomial distribution with $p = .83$ is almost symmetric if n is very large.
    (A) I and II
    (B) I and III
    (C) II and III
    (D) I, II, and III
    (E) None of the above answers gives the complete set of true responses.

GO ON TO THE NEXT PAGE ➤

17. A pet food manufacturer runs an experiment to determine whether three brands of dog food are equally preferred by dogs. In the experiment, 150 dogs are individually presented with three dishes of food, each containing a different brand, and their choices are noted. Tabulations show that 62 dogs go to brand A, 43 to brand B, and 45 to brand C. Is there sufficient evidence to say that dogs have preferences among the brands? Test at the 10% significance level.
    (A) No, with $\chi^2 = 2.09$, there is not sufficient evidence even at the 25% significance level.
    (B) No, with $\chi^2 = 4.36$, there is not sufficient evidence at the 10% level.
    (C) No, with $\chi^2 = 19.0$, there is not sufficient evidence even at the 0.1% level.
    (D) Yes, with $\chi^2 = 4.36$, there is sufficient evidence at the 10% level.
    (E) Yes, with $\chi^2 = 19.0$, there is sufficient evidence even at the 0.1% level.

18. A talk show host recently reported that in response to his on-air question, 82% of the more than 2500 e-mail messages received through his publicized address supported the death penalty for anyone convicted of selling drugs to children. What does this show?
    (A) The survey is meaningless because of voluntary response bias.
    (B) No meaningful conclusion is possible without knowing something more about the characteristics of his listeners.
    (C) The survey would have been more meaningful if he had picked a random sample of the 2500 listeners who responded.
    (D) The survey would have been more meaningful if he had used a control group.
    (E) This was a legitimate sample, randomly drawn from his listeners, and of sufficient size to be able to conclude that most of his listeners support the death penalty for such a crime.

19. A test is run to determine whether there is a difference in miles per gallon between two car models. A random sample of 40 autos of the first model and 50 of the second model are available for the test. What is the probability of mistakenly claiming there is a difference when there isn't if the cutoff difference scores are ±0.5? Assume standard deviations of 1.2 and 0.65 miles per gallon, respectively, for the two models.
    (A) .0045
    (B) .0089
    (C) .0178
    (D) .4911
    (E) .9822

20. Suppose X and Y are random variables with $E(X) = 37$, var $(X) = 5$, $E(Y) = 62$, and var $(Y) = 12$. What are the expected value and variance of the random variable $X + Y$?
    (A) $E(X+Y) = 99$, var $(X+Y) = 8.5$
    (B) $E(X+Y) = 99$, var $(X+Y) = 13$
    (C) $E(X+Y) = 99$, var $(X+Y) = 17$
    (D) $E(X+Y) = 49.5$, var $(X+Y) = 17$
    (E) There is insufficient information to answer this question.

21. Which of the following can affect the value of the correlation coefficient r?
    (A) A change in measurement units
    (B) A change in which variable is called x and which is called y
    (C) Adding the same constant to all values of the x-variable
    (D) All of the above can affect the r value.
    (E) None of the above can affect the r value.

22. The American Medical Association (AMA) wishes to determine the percentage of obstetricians who are considering leaving the profession because of the rapidly increasing number of lawsuits against obstetricians. How large a sample should be taken to find the answer to within ±3% at the 95% confidence level?
    (A) 6
    (B) 33
    (C) 534
    (D) 752
    (E) 1068

GO ON TO THE NEXT PAGE ➤

23. Following are parts of the probability distributions for the random variables X and Y.

x	$P(x)$	y	$P(y)$
1	.25	1	.3
2	?	2	.5
3	.35	3	?
4	?		

If X and Y are independent and the joint probability $P(X = 2, Y = 3) = .03$, what is $P(X = 4)$?

(A) .10
(B) .15
(C) .20
(D) .25
(E) .30

24. Which of the following sets has the smallest standard deviation? Which has the largest?

   I. 1, 2, 3, 4, 5, 6, 7
   II. 1, 1, 1, 4, 7, 7, 7
   III. 1, 4, 4, 4, 4, 4, 7

(A) I, II
(B) II, III
(C) III, I
(D) II, I
(E) III, II

25. A researcher plans a study to examine long-term confidence in the U.S. economy among the adult population. She obtains a simple random sample of 30 adults as they leave a Wall Street office building one weekday afternoon. All but two of the adults agree to participate in the survey. Which of the following are true statements?

   I. Proper use of chance as evidenced by the simple random sample makes this a well-designed survey.
   II. The high response rate makes this a well-designed survey.
   III. Selection bias makes this a poorly designed survey.

(A) I only
(B) II only
(C) III only
(D) I and II
(E) None of the statements is true.

26. Suppose that the regression line for a set of data, $y = 5x + b$, passes through the point (3, 4). If $\bar{x}$ and $\bar{y}$ are the sample means of the x- and y-values, respectively, then $\bar{y} =$

(A) $\bar{x}$.
(B) $\bar{x} - 3$.
(C) $\bar{x} + 4$.
(D) $5\bar{x}$.
(E) $5\bar{x} - 11$.

27. Consider the following three scatterplots:

What is the relationship among r_1, r_2, and r_3, the correlations associated with the first, second, and third scatterplots, respectively?

(A) $r_1 < r_2 < r_3$
(B) $r_1 < r_3 < r_2$
(C) $r_2 < r_3 < r_1$
(D) $r_3 < r_1 < r_2$
(E) $r_3 < r_2 < r_1$

28. There are two games involving flipping a coin. In the first game you win a prize if you can throw between 45% and 55% heads. In the second game you win if you can throw more than 80% heads. For each game would you rather flip the coin 30 times or 300 times?

(A) 30 times for each game
(B) 300 times for each game
(C) 30 times for the first game and 300 times for the second
(D) 300 times for the first game and 30 times for the second
(E) The outcomes of the games do not depend on the number of flips.

GO ON TO THE NEXT PAGE ➤

29. City planners are trying to decide among various parking plan options ranging from more on-street spaces to multilevel facilities to spread-out small lots. Before making a decision, they wish to test the downtown merchants' claim that shoppers park for an average of only 47 minutes in the downtown area. The planners have decided to tabulate parking durations for 225 shoppers and to reject the merchants' claim if the sample mean exceeds 50 minutes. If the merchants' claim is wrong and the true mean is 51 minutes, what is the probability that the random sample will lead to a mistaken failure to reject the merchants' claim? Assume that the standard deviation in parking durations is 27 minutes.

   (A) .0475
   (B) .2123
   (C) .2877
   (D) .7123
   (E) .9525

30. Consider the following parallel boxplots indicating the starting salaries (in thousands of dollars) for blue collar and white collar workers at a particular production plant:

   Which of the following are true statements?
   I. The ranges are the same.
   II. The interquartile ranges are the same.
   III. Because of symmetry, their medians are the same.
   (A) I only
   (B) II only
   (C) I and II
   (D) I and III
   (E) II and III

31. The mean Law School Aptitude Test (LSAT) score for applicants to a particular law school is 650 with a standard deviation of 45. Suppose that only applicants with scores above 700 are considered. What percentage of the applicants considered have scores below 740? (Assume the scores are normally distributed.)
   (A) 13.3%
   (B) 17.1%
   (C) 82.9%
   (D) 86.7%
   (E) 97.7%

32. A magazine article states that teenagers watch 2 hours of television per day. A sociologist who believes the true figure is higher interviews 18 teenagers and calculates a mean of 2.8 hours with a variance of 1.334. In what interval is the P-value found?
   (A) $P < .0025$
   (B) $.0025 < P < .005$
   (C) $.005 < P < .01$
   (D) $.01 < P < .05$
   (E) $.05 < P$

33. A researcher planning a survey of school principals in a particular state has lists of the school principals employed in each of the 125 school districts. The procedure is to obtain a random sample of principals from each of the districts rather than grouping all the lists together and obtaining a sample from the entire group. Which of the following statements about the resulting stratified sample are true?
   I. It is not a simple random sample.
   II. It is easier and less costly to obtain than a simple random sample.
   III. It gives comparative information that a simple random sample wouldn't give.
   (A) I only
   (B) I and II
   (C) I and III
   (D) II and III
   (E) I, II, and III

GO ON TO THE NEXT PAGE ➤

34. A surprising study of 1437 male hospital admissions reported in *The New York Times* (February 24, 1993, page C12) found that, of 665 patients admitted with heart attacks, 214 had vertex baldness, while of the remaining 772 non-heart-related admissions, 175 had vertex baldness. Is this evidence sufficient at the 5% significance level to say that there is a relationship between heart attacks and vertex baldness?

   (A) Yes, because $\chi^2 = 4.05$, while the critical χ^2 is 3.84.
   (B) Yes, because $\chi^2 = 16.39$, while the critical χ^2 is 3.84.
   (C) No, because $\chi^2 = 16.39$, while the critical χ^2 is 3.84.
   (D) No, because $\chi^2 = 4.05$, while the critical χ^2 is 7.81.
   (E) Yes, because $\chi^2 = 16.39$, while the critical χ^2 is 7.81.

35. Changing from a 90% confidence interval estimate to a 99% confidence interval estimate, with all other things being equal,

   (A) increases the interval size by 9%.
   (B) decreases the interval size by 9%.
   (C) increases the interval size by 57%.
   (D) decreases the interval size by 57%.
   (E) This question cannot be answered without knowing the sample size.

STOP

Section II

Part A

Questions 1–5
Spend about 65 minutes on this part of the exam.
Percentage of Section II grade—75

You must show all work and indicate the methods you use. You will be graded on the correctness
of your methods and on the accuracy of your results and explanations.

1. One hospital has 1000 live births during the summer, while a second hospital has 500 live births during
   the same time period.
   (a) Assuming there is a 50% chance for a live-born infant to be male, which hospital is more likely to
       have less than 45% male births? Explain your answer.
   (b) Suppose the first hospital has 515 male births, while the second has only 240. Is the difference
       statistically significant? Show your work.

2. Drying times y (in minutes) are tabulated for various concentrations of pigment x (in ounces per gallon)
   for a certain brand of latex paint. A linear regression model gives $y = -5.1x + 59.7$ with the following
   residual plot:

GO ON TO THE NEXT PAGE ➤

A nonlinear model gives $y = -16.81 \ln x + 59.8$ with the following residual plot:

(a) What does each model predict for the drying time when using 5 ounces of pigment per gallon?

(b) Which model is a better fit? Explain.

3. With regard to a particular gene, the percentages of genotypes *AA, Aa*, and *aa* in a particular population are, respectively, 60%, 30%, and 10%. Furthermore, the percentages of these genotypes that contract a certain disease are, respectively, 1%, 5%, and 20%.

   (a) What is the probability that a person selected at random from the population will contract the disease? Show your work.

   (b) If a person does contract the disease, what is the probability that the person is of genotype *AA*? Show your work.

4. Throughout history millions of people have used garlic to obtain a variety of perceived health benefits. A vitamin production company decides to run a scientific test to assess the value of garlic in promoting a general sense of well-being. They randomly pick 250 of their employees, and once a day for 2 months the employees fill out questionnaires about their sense of well-being that day. For the next 2 months the employees take garlic capsules daily and again fill out the same questionnaires. Finally, for 2 concluding months the employees stop taking the pills and continue to fill out the daily questionnaires. Comment on the design of this experiment.

5. A police study of 840 muggings shows the following distribution with regard to days of the week on which the crimes were committed:

Day of the week:	Mon.	Tues.	Wed.	Thur.	Fri.	Sat.	Sun.
Number of muggings:	105	121	129	115	110	134	126

At the 10% significance level, is there evidence that muggings are not evenly distributed during the week? Show your work.

GO ON TO THE NEXT PAGE ➤

Section II

Part B

Question 6
Spend about 25 minutes on this part of the exam.
Percentage of Section II grade—25

6. When Michael Jordan came up to try for a sixth free throw after having made five straight free throws, the announcer commented that the law of averages would be working against Jordan.
   (a) What did the announcer mean? Was this a correct interpretation of probability? Explain.
   (b) Jordan makes 90% of his free throws. What is the probability that he will make six straight free throws? That he will make five straight free throws and then miss the next? That he will make the next free throw given that he has made the last five in a row?
   (c) How could you set up a simulation using a random number table to analyze the situation the announcer was commenting on?
   (d) If Jordan shoots six times from the free throw line, what are the mean and standard deviation for the number of shots he is expected to make?
   (e) If Jordan makes only 35 out of 40 free throw tries during the playoffs, is this sufficient evidence that the probability of his making a free throw is really below .90? Explain.

STOP

Answer Key

Section I

1. **E**	8. **D**	15. **C**	22. **E**	29. **C**
2. **E**	9. **E**	16. **D**	23. **D**	30. **A**
3. **A**	10. **D**	17. **B**	24. **E**	31. **C**
4. **B**	11. **D**	18. **A**	25. **C**	32. **B**
5. **B**	12. **D**	19. **C**	26. **E**	33. **E**
6. **A**	13. **A**	20. **E**	27. **D**	34. **B**
7. **B**	14. **C**	21. **E**	28. **D**	35. **C**

Answers Explained

Section I

1. **(E)**   The median price would have 50% of the prices below and 50% of the prices above; however, looking at areas, it is clear that 60% of the prices are below $125,000. Area considerations also show that 30% of the prices are between $100,000 and $125,000, while 40% are above $125,000. Many values are too far from the mean for the standard deviation to be only $10,000. Between one-sixth and one-fourth of the range is a reasonable estimate for the standard deviation.

2. **(E)**   Stemplots are not used for categorical data sets and are unwieldy for use with large data sets; however, they do show symmetry, gaps, clusters, and outliers.

3. **(A)**   The critical z-score is 1.036. Thus $60 - 55 = 1.036\sigma$ and $\sigma = 4.83$.

4. **(B)** $125,000 \pm 1.645(\frac{32,000}{\sqrt{50}}) = 125,000 \pm 7444$

5. **(B)**   The first study was observational because the subjects were not chosen for treatment.

6. **(A)**

$$\begin{aligned} P(\text{def}) &= P(1\text{st} \cap \text{def}) + P(2\text{nd} \cap \text{def}) \\ &= (.6)(.005) + (.4)(.010) \\ &= .0030 + .0040 = .0070 \\ P(1\text{st}|\text{def}) &= \frac{.0030}{.0070} = .429 \end{aligned}$$

7. **(B)**   We have $H_0: \mu = 2000$ and $H_a: \mu > 2000$. The standard deviation of sample means is $\sigma_{\bar{x}} = \frac{\sigma}{\sqrt{n}} = \frac{350}{\sqrt{30}} = 63.9$. The z-score for 2100 is $\frac{2100-2000}{63.9} = 1.56$, and from Table A we obtain $1 - .9406 = .0594$. (On the TI-83 a t-test gives $P = .064$.) Thus, if the 2000-calorie claim is correct, there is approximately a .06 probability that the dietician will still obtain a sample mean greater than 2100 and mistakenly reject the patient's claim.

8. **(D)** Relative frequencies must be equal. Either looking at rows gives $\frac{40}{100} = \frac{50}{50+n}$ or looking at columns gives $\frac{40}{90} = \frac{60}{60+n}$. We could also set up a proportion $\frac{n}{50} = \frac{60}{40}$ or $\frac{n}{60} = \frac{50}{40}$. Solving any of these equations gives $n = 75$.

9. **(E)** The standard deviation $s_{\bar{x}}$ of the sample means is estimated to be $\frac{s}{\sqrt{n}} = \frac{0.13}{\sqrt{25}} = 0.026$. With $25 - 1 = 24$ degrees of freedom and 0.5% in each tail, the appropriate t-scores are ± 2.797. Thus a 99% confidence interval estimate for the mean weight is $17.94 \pm 2.797(0.026) = 17.94 \pm 0.073$ ounces.

10. **(D)** If A and B are mutually exclusive, then $P(A \cap B) = 0$, and so $P(A \cup B) = .3 + .2 - 0 = .5$. If A and B are independent, then $P(A \cap B) = P(A)P(B)$, and so $P(A \cup B) = .3 + .2 - (.3)(.2) = .44$. If B is a subset of A, then $A \cup B = A$, and so $P(A \cup B) = P(A) = .3$.

11. **(D)** We have $H_0: p = .22$, $H_a: p \neq .22$, and $\sigma_{\hat{p}} = \sqrt{\frac{(.22)(.78)}{1100}} = .0125$. $\hat{p} = \frac{268}{1100} = .244$ with a z-score of $\frac{.244 - .22}{.0125} = 1.92$ and a corresponding tail probability of $1 - .9726 = .0274$. Thus the P-value for this two-sided test is $2(.0274) = .0548$.

12. **(D)** Dosage is the only explanatory variable, and it is being tested at three levels. Tumor reduction is the single response variable.

13. **(A)** The median corresponds to a cumulative proportion of 0.5.

14. **(C)** Corresponding to cumulative proportions of 0.25 and 0.75 are $Q_1 = 7$ and $Q_3 = 35$, respectively, so the interquartile range is $Q_3 - Q_1 = 28$.

15. **(C)**

$$n_1 = 300 \qquad n_2 = 270$$

$$\hat{p}_1 = \tfrac{225}{300} = .75 \quad \hat{p}_2 = \tfrac{108}{270} = .4$$

$$\sigma_d = \sqrt{\frac{(.75)(.25)}{300} + \frac{(.4)(.6)}{270}} = .0389$$

$$(.75 - .4) \pm 2.576(.0389) = .35 \pm .100$$

16. **(D)** If $p < .5$, the more likely numbers of successes are to the left and the higher numbers of successes have small probabilities, so the histogram is skewed to the right. No matter what p is, if n is sufficiently large, the histogram will look almost symmetric.

17. **(B)** If dogs have no preferences among the three brands, we expect $\tfrac{150}{3} = 50$ dogs to go to each dish. Thus

$$\chi^2 = \frac{(62 - 50)^2}{50} + \frac{(43 - 50)^2}{50} + \frac{(45 - 50)^2}{50} = 4.36$$

With $3 - 1 = 2$ degrees of freedom and $\alpha = .10$, the critical χ^2-value is 4.61. Since $4.36 < 4.61$, there is not sufficient evidence to say that dogs have preferences among the three given brands. (Of course the company that manufactures brand A will continue to claim that more dogs prefer its food!)

18. **(A)** This is a good example of voluntary response bias, which often overrepresents strong or negative opinions. The people who chose to respond were very possibly the parents of children facing drug problems or people who had had bad experiences with drugs being sold in their neighborhoods. There is very little chance that the 2500 respondents were representative of the population. Knowing more about his listeners or taking a sample of the sample would not have helped.

19. **(C)** We have $H_0: \mu_1 - \mu_2 = 0$, $H_a: \mu_1 - \mu_2 \neq 0$, and

$$\sigma_{\bar{x}_1 - \bar{x}_2} \approx \sqrt{\frac{(1.2)^2}{40} + \frac{(0.65)^2}{50}} = 0.211$$

The z-score for 0.5 is $\frac{0.5 - 0}{0.211} = 2.37$. From Table A, each tail has a probability of $1 - .9911 = .0089$. Adding the two tails gives a probability of $.0089 + .0089 = .0178$.

20. **(E)** Without independence we cannot determine var $(X + Y)$ from the information given.

21. **(E)** The correlation coefficient r is not affected by changes in units, by which variable is called x or y, or by adding or multiplying all the values of a variable by the same constant.

22. **(E)** $1.96 \left(\frac{5}{\sqrt{n}} \right) \leq .03$ gives $\sqrt{n} \geq 32.67$ and $n \geq 1067.1$.

23. **(D)** $P(Y = 3) = 1 - (.3 + .5) = .2$. By independence, $P(X = 2, Y = 3) = P(X = 2)P(Y = 3)$, and so $.03 = P(X = 2)(.2)$ and $P(X = 2) = .15$. Then $P(X = 4) = 1 - (.25 + .15 + .35) = .25$.

24. **(E)** Note that all three sets have the same mean and the same range. The third set has most of its values concentrated right at the mean, while the second set has most of its values concentrated far from the mean.

25. **(C)** People coming out of a Wall Street office building are a very unrepresentative sample of the adult population, especially given the question under consideration. Using chance and obtaining a high response rate will not change the selection bias and make this into a well-designed survey.

26. **(E)** Since $(3, 4)$ is on the line $y = 5x + b$, we have $4 = 15 + b$ and $b = -11$. Thus the regression line is $y = 5x - 11$. The point $(\bar{x}, \bar{y})$ is always on the regression line, and so we have $\bar{y} = 5\bar{x} - 11$.

27. **(D)** The third scatterplot shows perfect negative association, so $r_3 = -1$. The first scatterplot shows strong, but not perfect, negative correlation, so $-1 < r_1 < 0$. The second scatterplot shows no correlation, so $r_2 = 0$.

28. **(D)** The probability of throwing heads is .5. By the law of large numbers,

the more times you flip the coin, the more the relative frequency tends to become closer to this probability. With fewer tosses there is more chance for wide swings in the relative frequency.

29. **(C)** $\sigma_{\bar{x}} = \frac{\sigma}{\sqrt{n}} = \frac{27}{\sqrt{225}} = 1.8$. If the true mean parking duration is 51 minutes, the normal curve should be centered at 51. The critical value of 50 has a z-score of $\frac{50-51}{1.8} = -0.56$. We use Table A to find the probability to the left of 50 to be .2877.

30. **(A)** The overall lengths (between tips of whiskers) are the same, and so the ranges are the same. The box lengths are different, and so the interquartile ranges are different. The medians are 20 and 50, respectively.

31. **(C)** Critical z-scores are $\frac{700-650}{45} = 1.11$ and $\frac{740-650}{45} = 2$ with right tail probabilities of .1335 and .0228, respectively. The percentage below 740 given that the scores are above 700 is $\frac{.1335-.0228}{.1335} = 82.9\%$.

32. **(B)** We have $H_0: \mu = 2$ and $H_a: \mu > 2$. The variance $s^2 = 1.334$, so $s = 1.155$, and $\sigma_{\bar{x}} = \frac{1.155}{\sqrt{18}} = 0.272$. Thus the t-score of 2.8 is $\frac{2.8-2}{0.272} = 2.94$. Looking at the df = 17 row in Table B, note that 2.94 is between 2.898 and 3.222, so P is between .0025 and .005.

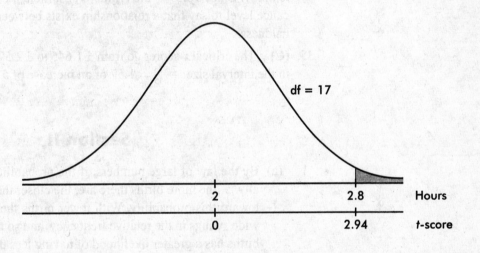

33. **(E)** This is not a simple random sample because all possible sets of the required size do not have the same chance of being picked. For example, a set of principals all from just half the school districts has no chance of being picked to be the sample. Stratified samples are often easier and less costly to obtain and also make comparative data available. In this case responses can be compared among various districts.

34. **(B)**

	Vertex baldness	No vertex baldness	
Heart attacks	214	451	665
Other admissions	175	597	772
	389	1048	1437

Expected	
180	485
209	563

$\frac{(665)(389)}{1437} = 180$, $\frac{(665)(1048)}{1437} = 485$, $\frac{(772)(389)}{1437} = 209$, and $\frac{(772)(1048)}{1437} = 563$.

$$\chi^2 = \frac{(214-180)^2}{180} + \frac{(451-485)^2}{485} + \frac{(175-209)^2}{209} + \frac{(597-563)^2}{563} = 16.39$$

(Input of the original matrix into a calculator like the TI-83 quickly gives $\chi^2 = 16.37$.) With df $= (2-1)(2-1) = 1$ and $\alpha = .05$, the critical χ^2-value is 3.841. Since $16.39 > 3.841$, there is sufficient evidence at the 5% significance level to say that a relationship exists between heart attacks and vertex baldness.

35. **(C)** The critical z-scores go from ± 1.645 to ± 2.576, resulting in an increase in the interval size: $\frac{2.576}{1.645} = 1.57$ or an increase of 57%.

Section II

1. (a) By the law of large numbers, if the probability of a male birth is actually .5, the more births there are, the closer the relative frequency tends toward this probability. With fewer births there is a greater chance for wide swings in the relative frequency, and so the hospital with only 500 births has a greater likelihood of having less than 45% male births.

   (b) We have H_0: $p_1 - p_2 = 0$ and H_a: $p_1 - p_2 \neq 0$.

$$\hat{p} = \frac{515 + 240}{1000 + 500} = .503$$

$$\sigma_d = \sqrt{(.503)(.497)} \sqrt{\frac{1}{1000} + \frac{1}{500}} = .0274$$

   The observed difference is $.515 - .48 = .035$ with a z-score of $\frac{.035}{.0274} = 1.28$, giving a tail probability of .1003. This is a two-sided test, and so the P-value is $2(.1003) = .2006$. With a P this large, there is no evidence to reject H_0.

2. (a) $y = -5.1(5) + 59.7 = 34.2$ minutes, and $y = -16.8 \ln 5 + 59.8 = 32.8$ minutes.

   (b) Model 2 is the better fit. First, the residuals are much smaller for model 2, indicating that model 2 gives values much closer to the observed values. Second, a curved residual pattern as from model 1 indicates that a nonlinear model would be better. A more uniform residual scatter as in model 2 indicates a better fit.

3. (a)

$$P\left(\begin{array}{c} \text{contract} \\ \text{disease} \end{array}\right) = .006 + .015 + .020 = .041$$

(b)

$$P\left(AA \mid \begin{array}{c} \text{contract} \\ \text{disease} \end{array}\right) = \frac{P\left(AA \cap \begin{array}{c} \text{contract} \\ \text{disease} \end{array}\right)}{P\left(\begin{array}{c} \text{contract} \\ \text{disease} \end{array}\right)} = \frac{.006}{.041} = .146$$

4. Any conclusions would probably be meaningless. There is a substantial danger of the placebo effect here; that is, real physical responses could be caused by the psychological effect of knowing the intent of the research. The experiment would be considerably strengthened by using a control group taking a look-alike capsule. Any conclusions are further suspect because of the choice of subjects. Rather than making a random selection from the intended population, the company is using a sample from its own employees, a sample almost guaranteed to have concerns, interests, and backgrounds that will confound the responses or limit their generalizability.

5. If the muggings are evenly distributed among the days of the week, the "expected" number per day is $\frac{840}{7} = 120$. The difference between the observed and expected values is measured by chi-square. We find

$$\chi^2 = \frac{15^2}{120} + \frac{1^2}{120} + \frac{9^2}{120} + \frac{5^2}{120} + \frac{10^2}{120} + \frac{14^2}{120} + \frac{6^2}{120} = 5.53$$

At the 10% significance level with df $= 7 - 1 = 6$, the critical χ^2-value from Table C is 10.64. Since $5.53 < 10.64$, there is not sufficient evidence to reject the null hypothesis of a good fit with a uniform distribution.

6. (a) The announcer meant that to maintain his tabulated free throw percentage, Jordan would have to soon miss one. This is not a correct use of probability. If Jordan makes a certain percentage of free throws, that probability applies to each throw irrespective of the previous throws. By the law of large numbers, in the long run the relative frequency tends toward the correct probability, but no conclusion is possible about any given outcome.

(b) $P(\text{six in a row}) = (.9)^6 = .531$

$P(\text{five, then a miss}) = (.9)^5(.1) = .059$

$P(\text{next}\,|\,\text{previous five}) = P(\text{next}) = .9$

(c) Let the digits 1 through 9 stand for making a free throw, while 0 stands for a miss. Look at blocks of five random numbers. If all stand for "makes" (no 0), look at the very next digit to see if it is a 0 or not. Keep a tally of how many times five makes in a row are followed by a make and how many times five makes in a row are followed by a miss.

(d) This is a binomial distribution with $n = 6$ and $p = .9$, and so the mean is $np = 6(.9) = 5.4$ while the standard deviation is $\sqrt{np(1-p)} = \sqrt{6(.9)(.1)} = .735$.

(e) We have $H_0\colon p = .9, H_a\colon p < .9$, and $\sigma_{\hat{p}} = \sqrt{\frac{(.9)(.1)}{40}} = .0474$. We have $\hat{p} = \frac{35}{40} = .875$ with a z-score of $\frac{.875-.9}{.0474} = -0.53$ and a P-value of .2981. With such a large P, there is no evidence to reject H_0. No one should conclude that Jordan's average has dropped!

Answer Sheet: Practice Examination 2

1. Ⓐ Ⓑ Ⓒ Ⓓ Ⓔ
2. Ⓐ Ⓑ Ⓒ Ⓓ Ⓔ
3. Ⓐ Ⓑ Ⓒ Ⓓ Ⓔ
4. Ⓐ Ⓑ Ⓒ Ⓓ Ⓔ
5. Ⓐ Ⓑ Ⓒ Ⓓ Ⓔ
6. Ⓐ Ⓑ Ⓒ Ⓓ Ⓔ
7. Ⓐ Ⓑ Ⓒ Ⓓ Ⓔ
8. Ⓐ Ⓑ Ⓒ Ⓓ Ⓔ
9. Ⓐ Ⓑ Ⓒ Ⓓ Ⓔ
10. Ⓐ Ⓑ Ⓒ Ⓓ Ⓔ
11. Ⓐ Ⓑ Ⓒ Ⓓ Ⓔ
12. Ⓐ Ⓑ Ⓒ Ⓓ Ⓔ

13. Ⓐ Ⓑ Ⓒ Ⓓ Ⓔ
14. Ⓐ Ⓑ Ⓒ Ⓓ Ⓔ
15. Ⓐ Ⓑ Ⓒ Ⓓ Ⓔ
16. Ⓐ Ⓑ Ⓒ Ⓓ Ⓔ
17. Ⓐ Ⓑ Ⓒ Ⓓ Ⓔ
18. Ⓐ Ⓑ Ⓒ Ⓓ Ⓔ
19. Ⓐ Ⓑ Ⓒ Ⓓ Ⓔ
20. Ⓐ Ⓑ Ⓒ Ⓓ Ⓔ
21. Ⓐ Ⓑ Ⓒ Ⓓ Ⓔ
22. Ⓐ Ⓑ Ⓒ Ⓓ Ⓔ
23. Ⓐ Ⓑ Ⓒ Ⓓ Ⓔ
24. Ⓐ Ⓑ Ⓒ Ⓓ Ⓔ

25. Ⓐ Ⓑ Ⓒ Ⓓ Ⓔ
26. Ⓐ Ⓑ Ⓒ Ⓓ Ⓔ
27. Ⓐ Ⓑ Ⓒ Ⓓ Ⓔ
28. Ⓐ Ⓑ Ⓒ Ⓓ Ⓔ
29. Ⓐ Ⓑ Ⓒ Ⓓ Ⓔ
30. Ⓐ Ⓑ Ⓒ Ⓓ Ⓔ
31. Ⓐ Ⓑ Ⓒ Ⓓ Ⓔ
32. Ⓐ Ⓑ Ⓒ Ⓓ Ⓔ
33. Ⓐ Ⓑ Ⓒ Ⓓ Ⓔ
34. Ⓐ Ⓑ Ⓒ Ⓓ Ⓔ
35. Ⓐ Ⓑ Ⓒ Ⓓ Ⓔ

Practice Examination 2

Section I

Questions 1–35

Spend 90 minutes on this part of the exam.

Directions: The questions or incomplete statements that follow are each followed by five suggested answers or completions. Choose the response that best answers the question or completes the statement.

---

1. Suppose that the regression line for a set of data, $y = mx + 3$, passes through the point (2, 7). If $\bar{x}$ and $\bar{y}$ are the sample means of the x- and y-values, respectively, then $\bar{y} =$

   (A) $\bar{x}$.
   (B) $\bar{x} - 2$.
   (C) $\bar{x} + 3$.
   (D) $2\bar{x} + 3$.
   (E) $3.5\bar{x} + 3$.

2. A study is made to determine whether more hours of academic studying leads to higher point scoring by basketball players. In surveying 50 basketball players, it is noted that the 25 who claim to study the most hours have a higher point average than the 25 who study less. Based on this study, the coach begins requiring the players to spend more time studying. Which of the following are true statements?

   I. While this study indicates a relation, it does not prove causation.
   II. There could well be a confounding variable responsible for the seeming relationship.
   III. While this is a controlled experiment, the conclusion of the coach is not justified.

   (A) I only
   (B) I and II
   (C) I and III
   (D) II and III
   (E) I, II, and III

3. The longevity of people living in a certain locality has a standard deviation of 14 years. What is the mean longevity if 30% of the people live longer than 75 years? Assume a normal distribution for life spans.

   (A) 61.00
   (B) 67.65
   (C) 74.48
   (D) 82.35
   (E) The mean cannot be computed from the information given.

4. A guidance counselor administers a vocabulary test to a random sample of high school seniors. Among 40 female students the average score is 69 with a standard deviation of 5.3, while among 48 male students the average score is 64 with a standard deviation of 5.6. What is a 90% confidence interval estimate for the difference in scores between female and male students?

   (A) 5 ± 1.16
   (B) 5 ± 1.36
   (C) 5 ± 1.92
   (D) 5 ± 2.23
   (E) 5 ± 2.46

GO ON TO THE NEXT PAGE ➤

5. Which of the following are affected by outliers?
   - I. Mean
   - II. Median
   - III. Standard deviation
   - IV. Range
   - V. Interquartile range
   - (A) I, III, and V
   - (B) II and IV
   - (C) I and V
   - (D) III and IV
   - (E) I, III, and IV

6. A manufacturer claims that a particular automobile model will get 50 miles per gallon on the highway. The researchers at a consumer-oriented magazine believe that this claim is high and plan a test with a sample of 30 cars. Assuming the standard deviation between individual cars is 2.3 miles per gallon, what should the researchers conclude if the sample mean is 49 miles per gallon?
   - (A) There is not sufficient evidence to reject the manufacturer's claim; 49 miles per gallon is too close to the claimed 50 miles per gallon.
   - (B) The manufacturer's claim should not be rejected because the P-value of .0087 is too small.
   - (C) The manufacturer's claim should be rejected because the sample mean is less than the claimed mean.
   - (D) The P-value of .0087 is sufficient evidence to reject the manufacturer's claim.
   - (E) The P-value of .0087 is sufficient evidence to prove that the manufacturer's claim is false.

7. Suppose that for a certain Caribbean island in any 3-year period the probability of a major hurricane is .25, the probability of water damage is .44, and the probability of both a hurricane and water damage is .22. What is the probability of water damage given that there is a hurricane?
   - (A) .47
   - (B) .50
   - (C) .69
   - (D) .88
   - (E) .91

8. An engineer wishes to determine the quantity of heat being generated by a particular electronic component. If she knows that the standard deviation is 2.4, how many of these components should she consider to be 99% sure of knowing the answer to within ±0.6?
   - (A) 27
   - (B) 87
   - (C) 107
   - (D) 212
   - (E) 425

GO ON TO THE NEXT PAGE ➤

9. Two possible wordings for a questionnaire on a proposed school budget increase are as follows:

 I. This school district has one of the highest per student expenditure rates in the state. This has resulted in low failure rates, high standardized test scores, and most students going on to good colleges and universities. Do you support the proposed school budget increase?

 II. This school district has one of the highest per student expenditure rates in the state. This has resulted in high property taxes, with many people on fixed incomes having to give up their homes because they cannot pay the school tax. Do you support the proposed school budget increase?

One of these questions showed that 58% of the population favor the proposed school budget increase, while the other question showed that only 13% of the population support the proposed increase. Which produced which result and why?

(A) The first showed 58% and the second 13% because of the lack of randomization as evidenced by the wording of the questions.

(B) The first showed 13% and the second 58% because of a placebo effect due to the wording of the questions.

(C) The first showed 58% and the second 13% because of the lack of a control group.

(D) The first showed 13% and the second 58% because of response bias due to the wording of the questions.

(E) The first showed 58% and the second 13% because of response bias due to the wording of the questions.

For Questions 10 and 11 consider the following: Two random samples of students are chosen, one from those taking an AP Statistics class and one from those not. The following back-to-back stemplots compare the GPAs.

AP Statistics		No AP Statistics
	1	89
97653	2	015688
98775332110	3	133344777888
1100	4	

10. Which of the following are true statements?
 I. The sample sizes are the same.
 II. The medians are the same.
 III. The means are the same.
(A) I only
(B) I and II
(C) I and III
(D) II and III
(E) I, II, and III

11. Which of the following is true about the ranges and standard deviations?
(A) The first set has both a greater range and a greater standard deviation.
(B) The first set has a greater range, while the second has a greater standard deviation.
(C) The first set has a greater standard deviation, while the second has a greater range.
(D) The second set has both a greater range and a greater standard deviation.
(E) The two sets have equal ranges and equal standard deviations.

12. A random sample of 20 batteries are tested and show a mean life expectancy of 218 hours with a standard deviation of 11 hours. Determine a 90% confidence interval estimate for this mean life expectancy.
(A) 218 ± 0.95
(B) 218 ± 3.27
(C) 218 ± 4.05
(D) 218 ± 4.25
(E) 218 ± 19.02

GO ON TO THE NEXT PAGE ➤

13. Suppose X and Y are random variables with $\mu_x = 32$, $\sigma_x = 5$, $\mu_y = 44$, and $\sigma_y = 12$. Given that X and Y are independent, what are the mean and standard deviation of the random variable $X + Y$?

(A) $\mu_{x+y} = 76$, $\sigma_{x+y} = 8.5$
(B) $\mu_{x+y} = 76$, $\sigma_{x+y} = 13$
(C) $\mu_{x+y} = 76$, $\sigma_{x+y} = 17$
(D) $\mu_{x+y} = 38$, $\sigma_{x+y} = 17$
(E) There is insufficient information to answer this question.

14. Suppose you toss a fair die three times and it comes up an even number each time. Which of the following is a true statement?

(A) By the law of large numbers, the next toss is more likely to be an odd number than another even number.
(B) Based on the properties of conditional probability the next toss is more likely to be an even number given that three in a row have been even.
(C) Dice actually do have memories, and thus the number that comes up on the next toss will be influenced by the previous tosses.
(D) The law of large numbers tells how many tosses will be necessary before the percentages of evens and odds are again in balance.
(E) The probability that the next toss will again be even is .5.

15. A college alumni office states that 20% of graduates eventually become lawyers, 25% doctors, and 35% corporate executives. The remaining 20% are spread out among a variety of professions. A new survey taken of 625 graduates turned up 110 lawyers, 140 doctors, 250 corporate executives, and 125 others. Is there sufficient evidence that the percentages quoted by the alumni office have changed? Test at the 5% significance level.

(A) No, with $\chi^2 = 2.82$ there is not sufficient evidence.
(B) No, with $\chi^2 = 5.64$ there is not sufficient evidence.
(C) No, with $\chi^2 = 7.954$ there is not sufficient evidence.
(D) Yes, with $\chi^2 = 2.82$ there is sufficient evidence.
(E) Yes, with $\chi^2 = 7.954$ there is sufficient evidence.

16. Suppose you wish to compare the AP Statistics exam results for the male and female students taking AP Statistics at your high school. Which is the most appropriate technique for gathering the needed data?

(A) Census
(B) Sample survey
(C) Experiment
(D) Observational study
(E) None of these is appropriate.

17. A local restaurant owner claims that only 15% of visiting tourists stay for more than 2 days. A chamber of commerce volunteer is sure that the real percentage is higher. He plans to survey 100 tourists and intends to speak up if at least 18 of the tourists stay longer than 2 days. What is the probability of mistakenly rejecting the restaurant owner's claim if it is true?

(A) .0357
(B) .0714
(C) .1428
(D) .2005
(E) .4010

18. Following are parts of the probability distributions for the random variables X and Y.

x	$P(x)$		y	$P(y)$
1	.1		1	?
2	?		2	?
3	?		3	.2

If X and Y are independent and two joint probabilities are $P(X = 1, Y = 1) = .025$ and $P(X = 3, Y = 3) = .08$, what is $P(X = 2, Y = 2)$?
   (A) .115
   (B) .275
   (C) .333
   (D) .725
   (E) .895

19. One medical report suggested that among a sample of 239 cesarean surgical procedures, 83 were unnecessary. What is a 99% confidence interval estimate for the proportion of cesareans that are unnecessary?
   (A) $.347 \pm .002$
   (B) $.347 \pm .060$
   (C) $.347 \pm .079$
   (D) $.347 \pm .227$
   (E) $.347 \pm .476$

20. Following is a histogram of the numbers of ties owned by bank executives.

Which of the following statements are true?
   I. The median number of ties is five.
   II. More than four executives own over eight ties.
   III. An executive is equally likely to own fewer than five ties or more than seven ties.
   (A) I only
   (B) II only
   (C) III only
   (D) I and III
   (E) I, II, and III

21. Exams I, II, and III have mean results of 67, 72, and 76, respectively, and standard deviations of 11, 8, and 5, respectively. Mary takes exam I, John takes exam II, and Sarah takes exam III. They each score 83. Rank them from lowest to highest results according to z-scores.
   (A) John, Sarah, Mary
   (B) Mary, John, Sarah
   (C) Sarah, John, Mary
   (D) John, Mary, Sarah
   (E) Mary, Sarah, John

GO ON TO THE NEXT PAGE ➤

22. Company I manufactures bomb fuses that burn an average of 50 minutes with a standard deviation of 10 minutes, while company II advertises fuses that burn an average of 55 minutes with a standard deviation of 5 minutes. Which company's fuse is more likely to last at least 1 hour? Assume normal distributions of fuse times.
    (A) Company I's, because of its greater standard deviation
    (B) Company II's, because of its greater mean
    (C) For both companies, the probability that a fuse will last at least 1 hour is 15.9%
    (D) For both companies, the probability that a fuse will last at least 1 hour is 84.1%
    (E) The problem cannot be solved from the information given.

23. Which of the following is *not* important in the design of experiments?
    (A) Control of confounding variables
    (B) Randomization in assigning subjects to different treatments
    (C) Use of a lurking variable to control the placebo effect
    (D) Replication of the experiment using sufficient numbers of subjects
    (E) All of the above are important in the design of experiments.

24. A historian believes that the average height of soldiers in World War II was greater than that of soldiers in World War I. She examines a random sample of records of 100 men in each war and notes standard deviations of 2.5 and 2.3 inches in World War I and World War II, respectively. If the average height from the sample of World War II soldiers is 1 inch greater than that from the sample of World War I soldiers, what conclusion is justified from a two-sample hypothesis test where $H_0: \mu_1 - \mu_2 = 0$ and $H_a: \mu_1 - \mu_2 > 0$?
    (A) The observed difference in average height is significant.
    (B) The observed difference in average height is not significant.
    (C) A conclusion is not possible without knowing the mean height in each sample.
    (D) A conclusion is not possible without knowing both the sample means and the two original population sizes.
    (E) A two-sample hypothesis test should not be used in this example.

25. Which of the following statements about residuals are true?
    I. The mean of the residuals is always zero.
    II. Influential scores have large residuals.
    III. A definite pattern in the residual plot is an indication that a nonlinear model should be tried.
    (A) II only
    (B) I and II
    (C) I and III
    (D) II and III
    (E) I, II, and III

26. Four pairs of data are used in determining a regression line $y = 3x + 4$. If the four values of the independent variable are 32, 24, 29, and 27, respectively, what is the mean of the four values of the dependent variable?
    (A) 68
    (B) 84
    (C) 88
    (D) 100
    (E) The mean cannot be determined from the given information.

27. According to one poll, 12% of the public favor legalizing all drugs. In a random sample of six people, what is the probability that at least one person favors legalization?
 (A) .380
 (B) .464
 (C) .536
 (D) .620
 (E) .844

28. A geologist claims that a particular rock formation will yield a mean amount of 24 pounds of a chemical per ton of excavation. His company, fearful that the true amount will be less, plans to run a test on a random sample of 50 tons. They will reject the 24 pound claim if the sample mean is less than 22. Suppose the standard deviation between tons is 5.8 pounds. If the true mean is 20 pounds of chemical, what is the probability that the test will result in a failure to reject the incorrect 24 pound claim?
 (A) .0073
 (B) .4927
 (C) .5073
 (D) .8200
 (E) .9927

29. A telephone executive instructs an associate to contact 104 customers using their service to obtain their opinions in regard to an idea for a new pricing package. The associate notes the number of customers whose names begin with A and uses a random number table to pick four of these names. She then proceeds to use the same procedure for each letter of the alphabet and combines the $4 \times 26 = 104$ results into a group to be contacted. Which of the following are true statements?
 I. Her procedure makes use of chance.
 II. Her procedure results in a simple random sample.
 III. Each customer has an equal probability of being included in the survey.
 (A) I only
 (B) I and II
 (C) I and III
 (D) II and III
 (E) I, II, and III

30. The graph below shows cumulative proportions plotted against GPAs for high school seniors.

What is the interquartile range?
 (A) 0.85
 (B) 2.25
 (C) 2.7
 (D) 2.75
 (E) 3.1

31. PCB contamination of a river by a manufacturer is being measured by amounts of the pollutant found in fish. A company scientist claims that the fish contain only 5 parts per million, but an investigator believes the figure is higher. In which of the following intervals is the P-value found if six fish are caught and show the following amounts of PCB (in parts per million): 6.8, 5.6, 5.2, 4.7, 6.3, and 5.4?
 (A) $P < .01$
 (B) $.01 < P < .025$
 (C) $.025 < P < .05$
 (D) $.05 < P < .10$
 (E) $.10 < P$

GO ON TO THE NEXT PAGE ➤

32. In a certain city 6% of teenagers are married, 25% of married teenagers have children, and 15% of unmarried teenagers have children. What is the probability that a teenager has a child? If a teenager has a child, what is the probability that the teenager is not married?
    (A) .156, .904
    (B) .200, .500
    (C) .200, .940
    (D) .400, .500
    (E) .400, .940

33. In general, how does tripling the sample size change the confidence interval size?
    (A) It triples the interval size.
    (B) It divides the interval size by 3.
    (C) It multiplies the interval size by 1.732.
    (D) It divides the interval size by 1.732.
    (E) This question cannot be answered without knowing the sample size.

34. Is hair loss pattern related to body mass index? One study on 769 men (*Journal of the American Medical Association*, February 24, 1993, page 1000) showed the following numbers:

    | | Hair loss pattern | | |
	None	Frontal	Vertex
Body mass index <25	137	22	40
25–28	218	34	67
>28	153	30	68

    The χ^2-value is 4.18. At the 5% and 10% significance levels is there a relationship between hair loss pattern and body mass index?

    (A) There is sufficient evidence of a relationship at both the 5% and 10% levels.
    (B) There is sufficient evidence of a relationship at the 5% level but not at the 10% level.
    (C) There is sufficient evidence of a relationship at the 10% level but not at the 5% level.
    (D) There is not sufficient evidence of a relationship at either the 5% or the 10% level.
    (E) There is not enough information to answer this question.

35. A study on school budget approval among people with different party affiliations resulted in the following segmented bar chart:

    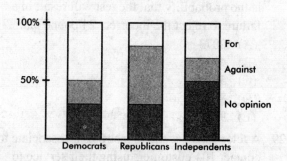

    Which of the following is greatest?
    (A) Number of Democrats who are for the proposed budget
    (B) Number of Republicans who are against the budget
    (C) Number of Independents who have no opinion on the budget
    (D) The above are all equal.
    (E) The answer is impossible to determine without additional information.

STOP

Section II

Part A

Questions 1–5
Spend about 65 minutes on this part of the exam.
Percentage of Section II grade—75

You must show all work and indicate the methods you use. You will be graded on the correctness
of your methods and on the accuracy of your results and explanations.

1. A sociologist conducts a study to determine if there is a relationship between cheating on exams and
   socioeconomic status. A random sample of 750 high school students yields the following results:

	Cheat	Don't cheat
High status	118	282
Low status	82	268

What is the conclusion about cheating and socioeconomic status at the 5% significance level?

2. The following scatterplot shows the grades for research papers for a sociology professor's class plotted against the lengths of the papers (in pages).

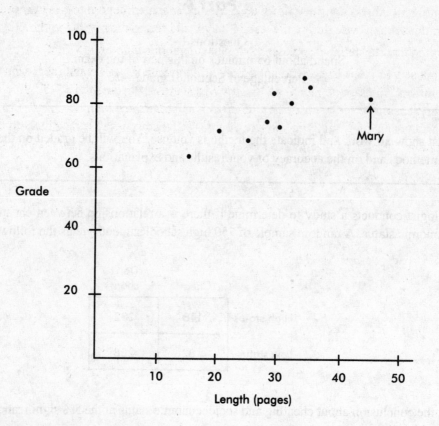

Mary turned in her paper late and was told by the professor that her grade would have been higher if she had turned it in on time. A computer printout fitting a straight line to the data (not including Mary's score) by the method of least squares gives

```
Grade = 46.51 + 1.106 Length
R-sq = 74.6%
```

(a) Find the correlation coefficient for the relationship between grade and length of paper based on these data (excluding Mary's paper).

(b) What is the slope of the regression line and what does it signify?

(c) How will the correlation coefficient change if Mary's paper is included? Explain your answer.

(d) How will the slope of the regression line change if Mary's paper is included? Explain your answer.

(e) What grade did Mary receive? Predict what she would have received if her paper had been on time.

3. A consolidated school district has regularly administered a test to all first-graders, based on which a child is labeled "exceptional" or "not exceptional." On the basis of information other than scores on this test, some of the children have been placed in a special class for the gifted. To evaluate the test, statistics have been collected and are being analyzed. They show that 80% of those who have succeeded in the special class had been labeled exceptional, that 30% of those who have not succeeded in the class had also been labeled exceptional, and that 75% of the children in the special class have been successful. What is the probability that a child labeled exceptional on the basis of the test will succeed in a special class? Show your work.

GO ON TO THE NEXT PAGE ➤

4. A new pain control procedure has been developed in which the patient uses a small battery pack to vary the intensity and duration of electric signals to electrodes surgically embedded in the afflicted area. Putting all ethical considerations aside, design an experiment to test the procedure. What ethical considerations might arise during the testing that would force an early end to the experiment?

5. It is reported that the national average cost of an automobile tune-up is $74.35.

(a) Suppose you interview a random sample of 40 people in your community who recently have had a tune-up. The sample mean is $76.72 with a standard deviation of $5.22. Find a 95% confidence interval estimate of the cost of a tune-up in your area. Show your work.

(b) What conclusion would you come to after testing the hypothesis that a tune-up costs more in your area than the national average? Explain your conclusion using a P-value calculation in your answer.

GO ON TO THE NEXT PAGE ➤

Section II

Part B

Question 6
Spend about 25 minutes on this part of the exam.
Percentage of Section II grade—25

6. If a car is stopped for speeding, the probability that the driver has illegal drugs hidden in the car is .14. A police officer manning a speed trap plans to thoroughly search cars he stops for speeding until he finds one with illegal drugs.

   (a) Use simulation to estimate the probability that illegal drugs will turn up before he stops the tenth car. Explain your work. Use the following random number table:

8417706757	1761315582	5150681435	4105092031	0644905059	5988431180
5311584469	9486857967	0581184514	7501113006	6339555041	1586606589
1311971020	8594091932	0648874987	5435552704	9035902649	4749671567
9426808844	2629464759	0898957024	9728400637	8928303514	5919507635
0330972605	2935723737	6788103668	3387635841	5286923114	1586438942

   (b) Use probability to calculate the probability that illegal drugs will be found before he stops the tenth car. Show your work.

STOP

Answer Key

Section I

1. **D**	8. **C**	15. **E**	22. **C**	29. **A**
2. **B**	9. **E**	16. **A**	23. **C**	30. **A**
3. **B**	10. **B**	17. **D**	24. **A**	31. **C**
4. **C**	11. **D**	18. **B**	25. **C**	32. **A**
5. **E**	12. **D**	19. **C**	26. **C**	33. **D**
6. **D**	13. **B**	20. **C**	27. **C**	34. **D**
7. **D**	14. **E**	21. **A**	28. **A**	35. **E**

Answers Explained

Section I

1. **(D)** Since $(2, 7)$ is on the line $y = mx + 3$, we have $7 = 2m + 3$ and $m = 2$. Thus the regression line is $y = 2x + 3$. The point $(\bar{x}, \bar{y})$ is always on the regression line, and so we have $\bar{y} = 2\bar{x} + 3$.

2. **(B)** It could well be that conscientious students are the same ones who both study and do well on the basketball court. If students could be randomly assigned to study or not study, the results would be more meaningful. Of course, ethical considerations might make it impossible to isolate the confounding variable in this way.

3. **(B)** The critical z-score is 0.525. Thus $75 - \mu = 0.525(14)$ and $\mu = 67.65$.

4. **(C)**
$$(69 - 64) \pm 1.645 \sqrt{\frac{(5.3)^2}{40} + \frac{(5.6)^2}{48}} = 5 \pm 1.92$$

5. **(E)** The median and interquartile range are specifically used when outliers are suspected of unduly influencing the mean, range, or standard deviation.

6. **(D)** We have $H_0 : \mu = 50$ and $H_a : \mu < 50$. The standard deviation of sample means is $\sigma_{\bar{x}} = \frac{2.3}{\sqrt{30}} = 0.42$. The z-score of 49 is $\frac{49 - 50}{0.42} = -2.38$. Using Table A, we determine the P-value to be .0087. With such a small P there is sufficient evidence to reject H_0. While unlikely, it is still possible that we just happened to pick an unusual sample, and so we haven't *proved* that the manufacturer is wrong.

7. **(D)**

$$P(\text{water}|\text{hurricane}) = \frac{P(\text{water} \cap \text{hurricane})}{P(\text{hurricane})} = \frac{.22}{.25} = .88$$

8. **(C)** $2.576\left(\frac{2.4}{\sqrt{n}}\right) \le 0.6$, which gives $\sqrt{n} \ge 10.304$ and $n \ge 106.2$.

9. **(E)** The wording of questions can lead to response bias. The neutral way of asking this question would simply have been, Do you support the proposed school budget increase?

10. **(B)** Both samples have 20 values, and both have 3.3 for the median.

11. **(D)** The second set has a greater range, $3.8 - 1.8 = 2.0$ as compared to $4.1 - 2.3 = 1.8$, and with its skewness it also has a greater standard deviation.

12. **(D)** df $= 19$, and $218 \pm 1.729\left(\frac{11}{\sqrt{20}}\right) = 218 \pm 4.25$.

13. **(B)** The means and the variances can be added. Thus the new variance is $5^2 + 12^2 = 169$, and the new standard deviation is 13.

14. **(E)** Dice have no memory, so the probability that the next toss will be an even number is .5 and the probability that it will be an odd number is .5. The law of large numbers says that as the number of tosses becomes larger, the proportion of even numbers tends to become closer to .5.

15. **(E)** With no changes the expected results would have been $.20(625) = 125$, $.25(625) = 156.25$, $.35(625) = 218.75$.

$$\chi^2 = \frac{(110 - 125)^2}{125} + \frac{(140 - 156.25)^2}{156.25} + \frac{(250 - 218.75)^2}{218.75} + \frac{(125 - 125)^2}{125}$$
$$= 7.954$$

With df $= 4 - 1 = 3$ and $\alpha = .05$, the critical χ^2-value is 7.815. Since $7.954 > 7.815$, there is sufficient evidence at the 5% significance level to say that the percentages have changed.

16. **(A)** Either directly or anonymously, you should be able to obtain the test results for *every* student.

17. **(D)**   We have $H_0: p = .15$ and $H_a: p > .15$. Using the claimed 15%, we calculate the standard deviation of sample proportions to be

$$\sigma_{\hat{p}} = \sqrt{\frac{(.15)(.85)}{100}} = .0357$$

The critical proportion is $c = \frac{18}{100} = .18$, and so the critical z-score is $\frac{.18-.15}{.0357} = 0.84$. This gives a probability of $1 - .7995 = .2005$. The test as set up by the volunteer has a 20.05% chance of mistakenly rejecting a true null hypothesis.

18. **(B)**   By independence, $(.1)P(Y = 1) = .025$, so $P(Y = 1) = .25$. Similarly, $P(X = 3)(.2) = .08$, so $P(X = 3) = .4$. Now $P(X = 2) = 1 - (.1 + .4) = .5$ and $P(Y = 2) = 1 - (.25 + .2) = .55$. Finally, $P(X = 2, Y = 2) = (.5)(.55) = .275$.

19. **(C)** $\hat{p} = \frac{83}{239} = .347$, and $\sigma_{\hat{p}} = \sqrt{\frac{(.347)(.653)}{239}} = .0308$. $.347 \pm 2.576(.0308) = .347 \pm .079$.

20. **(C)**   Five does not split the area in half, so 5 is not the median. Histograms such as these show relative frequencies, not actual frequencies. The area from 1.5 to 4.5 is the same as that between 7.5 and 10.5, each being about 25% of the total.

21. **(A)**   The z-scores of Mary, John, and Sarah, respectively, are $\frac{83-67}{11} = 1.455$, $\frac{83-72}{8} = 1.375$, and $\frac{83-76}{5} = 1.4$.

22. **(C)**   In both cases 1 hour is one standard deviation from the mean with a right tail probability of .1587.

23. **(C)**   Control, randomization, and replication are all important aspects of well-designed experiments. We try to control lurking variables, not to use them to control something else.

24. **(A)**

$$\sigma_{\bar{x}_1 - \bar{x}_2} \approx \sqrt{\frac{(2.5)^2}{100} + \frac{(2.3)^2}{100}} = 0.340$$

The z-score of 1 is $\frac{1-0}{0.340} = 2.94$ with a corresponding P-value of $1 - .9984 = .0016$. Such a small P is significant.

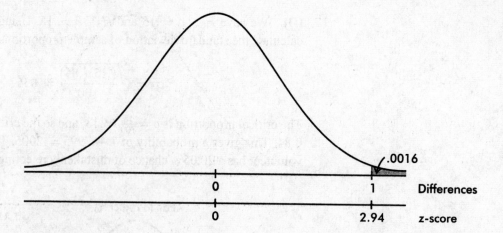

25. **(C)** The sum and thus the mean of the residuals are always zero. An influential score may have a small residual but still have a great effect on the regression line. In a good straight-line fit, the residuals show a random pattern.

26. **(C)** $\bar{x} = \frac{32+24+29+27}{4} = 28$. Since $(\bar{x}, \bar{y})$ is a point on the regression line, $\bar{y} = 3(28) + 4 = 88$.

27. **(C)** $P(\text{at least } 1) = 1 - P(\text{none}) = 1 - (.88)^6 = .536$

28. **(A)** $\sigma_{\bar{x}} = \frac{\sigma}{\sqrt{n}} = \frac{5.8}{\sqrt{50}} = 0.820$. If the true mean is 20 pounds per ton of rock, the z-score for 22 is $\frac{22-20}{0.820} = 2.44$, and so the probability is $1 - .9927 = .0073$.

29. **(A)** While the associate does use chance, each customer would have the same chance of being selected only if the same number of customers had names starting with each letter of the alphabet. This selection does not result in a simple random sample because each possible set of 104 customers does not have the same chance of being picked as part of the sample. For example, a group of customers whose names all start with A will not be chosen.

30. **(A)** Corresponding to cumulative proportions of 0.25 and 0.75 are $Q_1 = 2.25$ and $Q_3 = 3.1$, respectively, and so the interquartile range is $3.1 - 2.25 = 0.85$.

31. **(C)** We have $H_0: \mu = 5$, $H_a: \mu > 5$, $\bar{x} = 5.67$, $s = 0.763$, and $\sigma_{\bar{x}} = \frac{0.763}{\sqrt{6}} = 0.311$. The t-score of 5.67 is $\frac{5.67-5}{0.311} = 2.154$. Looking at the df = 5 row in Table B, note that 2.154 is between 2.015 and 2.571, and so P is between .025 and .05. (Note that a calculator like the TI-83 quickly gives the critical t-score as 2.139 and the P-value as .043.)

32. **(A)**

$$P(\text{child}) = P(\text{married} \cap \text{child}) + P(\text{not married} \cap \text{child})$$
$$= (.06)(.25) + (.94)(.15)$$
$$= .015 + .141 = .156$$

$$P(\text{not married}|\text{child}) = \tfrac{.141}{.156} = .904$$

33. **(D)** Increasing the sample size by a multiple of d divides the interval estimate by $\sqrt{d}$.

34. **(D)** With df $= (3-1)(3-1) = 4$, the critical χ^2-values for the 5% and 10% tail probabilities are 9.49 and 7.78, respectively. Since 4.18 is less than both these values, there is not sufficient evidence at either level of a relationship between hair loss pattern and body mass index.

35. **(E)** The given bar chart shows percentages, not actual numbers.

Section II

1. Find the row and column totals and then calculate the numbers expected if cheating and status are independent by multiplying row total by column total and dividing by 750.

106.7	293.3	400
93.3	256.7	350
200	550	

The difference between the observed and expected values is measured by chi-square:

$$\chi^2 = \frac{(118 - 106.7)^2}{106.7} + \frac{(282 - 293.3)^2}{293.3} + \frac{(82 - 93.3)^2}{93.3} + \frac{(268 - 256.7)^2}{256.7}$$
$$= 3.50$$

(A calculator such as the TI-83 quickly gives $\chi^2 = 3.52$.)

At the 5% significance level with df $= (2-1)(2-1) = 1$, the critical χ^2-value from Table C is 3.84. Since $3.52 < 3.84$, there is not sufficient evidence to reject independence and say that cheating and socioeconomic status are related.

2. (a) The correlation coefficient is $r = \sqrt{.746} = .864$. It is positive because the slope of the regression line is positive.

   (b) The slope is 1.106, signifying that each additional page raises a grade by 1.106.

   (c) Including Mary's paper will lower the correlation coefficient because her result seems far off the regression line through the other points.

   (d) Including Mary's paper will swing the regression line down and lower the value of the slope.

   (e) From the graph, Mary received an 82. From the regression line, Mary would have received $y = 46.51 + 1.106(45) = 96.3$ if she had turned in her paper on time.

3.

$$P\left(\begin{array}{c}\text{labeled}\\\text{exceptional}\end{array}\right) = .6 + .075 = .675$$

$$P\left(\begin{array}{c|c}\text{successful in}&\text{labeled}\\\text{special class}&\text{exceptional}\end{array}\right) = \frac{P\left(\begin{array}{cc}\text{successful in}&\text{labeled}\\\text{special class}\cap&\text{exceptional}\end{array}\right)}{P\left(\begin{array}{c}\text{labeled}\\\text{exceptional}\end{array}\right)}$$

$$= \frac{.6}{.675}$$

$$= .889$$

4. Ask doctors and hospitals to make known that you are looking for volunteers from among intractable pain sufferers. As the volunteers arrive, use a random number table to decide which will have the electrodes properly embedded in their pain centers and which will have the electrodes harmlessly embedded in wrong positions. For example, if the next digit in the table is odd, the volunteer receives the proper embedding, while if the next digit is even, the volunteer does not. Use double-blinding; that is, both the volunteers and their doctors should not know if the volunteers are receiving the proper

embedding. Ethical considerations will arise, for example, if the procedure is very successful. If volunteers with the wrong embeddings are in constant pain, while everyone with proper embedding is pain-free, then ethically the test should be stopped and everyone given the proper embedding. Or if most of the volunteers with proper embedding develop an unexpected side effect of the pain spreading to several nearby sites, then the test should be stopped and the procedure discontinued for everyone.

5. (a) $76.72 \pm 1.96 \left(\frac{5.22}{\sqrt{40}} \right) = 76.72 \pm 1.96(0.825) = 76.72 \pm 1.62$

   (b) We have $H_0: \mu = 74.35$ and $H_a: \mu > 74.35$. The z-score of 76.72 is $\frac{76.72 - 74.35}{0.825} = 2.87$ with a corresponding P-value of .0021. With such a small P, there is strong evidence to reject H_0 and conclude that the cost of a tune-up in your area is higher than the national average.

6. (a) Let the numbers 01 through 14 represent finding an illegal drug, while 15 through 99 and 00 represent no drugs. Read off pairs of digits from the random number table until a number representing illegal drugs is found or until nine clean cars are allowed to pass. Note whether a car with illegal drugs is found before nine clean cars pass. Repeat this procedure. Underlining numbers representing the presence of illegal drugs gives

8417706757	1761315582	5150681435	4105092031	0644905059	5988431180
5311584469	9486857967	0581184514	7501113006	6339555041	1586606589
1311971020	8594091932	0648874987	5435552704	9035902649	4749671567
9426808844	2629464759	0898957024	9728400637	8928303514	5919507635
0330972605	2935723737	6788103668	3387635841	5286923114	1586438942

   The first nine cars are clean. Then 14 is found after four clean cars, then 05 after two clean cars, then 09 before any clean cars, then 06 after two clean cars, then 11 after seven free cars, and so on. Tabulating gives

   First nine cars clean: 5
   Illegal drugs found before tenth car: 24

   The probability that illegal drugs will be found before the tenth car is estimated to be $\frac{24}{5+24} = .83$.

   (b) The probability that the first stopped car will have illegal drugs is .14. The probability that the first will be clean but that the second will have drugs is $(.86)(.14)$. The probability that two clean cars will be followed by one with drugs is $(.86)^2(.14)$. The probability that three clean ones will be followed by one with drugs is $(.86)^3(.14)$, and so on. The probability of drugs being found before the tenth car is $.14 + (.86)(.14) + (.86)^2(.14) + \cdots + (.86)^8(.14) = .744$.

1. Ⓐ Ⓑ Ⓒ Ⓓ Ⓔ
2. Ⓐ Ⓑ Ⓒ Ⓓ Ⓔ
3. Ⓐ Ⓑ Ⓒ Ⓓ Ⓔ
4. Ⓐ Ⓑ Ⓒ Ⓓ Ⓔ
5. Ⓐ Ⓑ Ⓒ Ⓓ Ⓔ
6. Ⓐ Ⓑ Ⓒ Ⓓ Ⓔ
7. Ⓐ Ⓑ Ⓒ Ⓓ Ⓔ
8. Ⓐ Ⓑ Ⓒ Ⓓ Ⓔ
9. Ⓐ Ⓑ Ⓒ Ⓓ Ⓔ
10. Ⓐ Ⓑ Ⓒ Ⓓ Ⓔ
11. Ⓐ Ⓑ Ⓒ Ⓓ Ⓔ
12. Ⓐ Ⓑ Ⓒ Ⓓ Ⓔ

13. Ⓐ Ⓑ Ⓒ Ⓓ Ⓔ
14. Ⓐ Ⓑ Ⓒ Ⓓ Ⓔ
15. Ⓐ Ⓑ Ⓒ Ⓓ Ⓔ
16. Ⓐ Ⓑ Ⓒ Ⓓ Ⓔ
17. Ⓐ Ⓑ Ⓒ Ⓓ Ⓔ
18. Ⓐ Ⓑ Ⓒ Ⓓ Ⓔ
19. Ⓐ Ⓑ Ⓒ Ⓓ Ⓔ
20. Ⓐ Ⓑ Ⓒ Ⓓ Ⓔ
21. Ⓐ Ⓑ Ⓒ Ⓓ Ⓔ
22. Ⓐ Ⓑ Ⓒ Ⓓ Ⓔ
23. Ⓐ Ⓑ Ⓒ Ⓓ Ⓔ
24. Ⓐ Ⓑ Ⓒ Ⓓ Ⓔ

25. Ⓐ Ⓑ Ⓒ Ⓓ Ⓔ
26. Ⓐ Ⓑ Ⓒ Ⓓ Ⓔ
27. Ⓐ Ⓑ Ⓒ Ⓓ Ⓔ
28. Ⓐ Ⓑ Ⓒ Ⓓ Ⓔ
29. Ⓐ Ⓑ Ⓒ Ⓓ Ⓔ
30. Ⓐ Ⓑ Ⓒ Ⓓ Ⓔ
31. Ⓐ Ⓑ Ⓒ Ⓓ Ⓔ
32. Ⓐ Ⓑ Ⓒ Ⓓ Ⓔ
33. Ⓐ Ⓑ Ⓒ Ⓓ Ⓔ
34. Ⓐ Ⓑ Ⓒ Ⓓ Ⓔ
35. Ⓐ Ⓑ Ⓒ Ⓓ Ⓔ

Practice Examination 3

Section I
Questions 1–35

Spend 90 minutes on this part of the exam.

Directions: The questions or incomplete statements that follow are each followed by five suggested answers or completions. Choose the response that best answers the question or completes the statement.

---

1. Which of the following are true statements?
   I. While properly designed experiments can strongly suggest cause-and-effect relationships, a complete census is the only way of establishing such a relationship.
   II. If properly designed, observational studies can establish cause-and-effect relationships just as strongly as properly designed experiments.
   III. Controlled experiments are often undertaken later to establish cause-and-effect relationships first suggested by observational studies.
   (A) I only
   (B) II only
   (C) III only
   (D) I and II
   (E) I, II, and III

2. Given that 10% of the nails made using a certain manufacturing process have a length less than 2.48 inches, while 5% have a length greater than 2.54 inches, what are the mean and standard deviation of the lengths of the nails? Assume that the lengths have a normal distribution.
   (A) $\mu = 2.506, \sigma = 0.0205$
   (B) $\mu = 2.506, \sigma = 0.0410$
   (C) $\mu = 2.516, \sigma = 0.0825$
   (D) $\mu = 2.516, \sigma = 0.1653$
   (E) The mean and standard deviation cannot be computed from the information given.

3. Given the probabilities $P(A) = .4$ and $P(A \cup B) = .6$, what is the probability $P(B)$ if A and B are mutually exclusive? If A and B are independent?
   (A) .2, .4
   (B) .2, .33
   (C) .33, .2
   (D) .6, .33
   (E) .6, .4

4. In a random sample of Toyota car owners, 83 out of 112 said they were satisfied with the Toyota front-wheel drive, while in a similar survey of Subaru owners, 76 out of 81 said they were satisfied with the Subaru four-wheel drive. What is a 90% confidence interval estimate for the difference in proportions between Toyota and Subaru car owners who are satisfied with their drive systems?
   (A) $-.197 \pm .004$
   (B) $-.197 \pm .049$
   (C) $-.197 \pm .081$
   (D) $-.197 \pm .097$
   (E) $-.197 \pm .162$

GO ON TO THE NEXT PAGE ➤

5. Which of the following statements about the correlation coefficient are true?

 I. The correlation coefficient and the slope of the regression line may have opposite signs.

 II. A correlation of 1 indicates a perfect cause-and-effect relationship between the variables.

 III. Correlations of $+.87$ and $-.87$ indicate the same degree of clustering around the regression line.

 (A) I only
 (B) II only
 (C) III only
 (D) I and II
 (E) I, II, and III

6. To study the relationship between car owner satisfaction and country of production, car owners were surveyed with the following results:

Level of satisfaction

	High	Medium	Low
Owners of American cars	80	100	45
Owners of Japanese cars	40	30	20
Owners of European cars	25	35	25

What percentage of those surveyed owned Japanese cars and were highly satisfied? What percentage of owners of American cars had low satisfaction?

 (A) 10%, 11%
 (B) 10%, 20%
 (C) 28%, 11%
 (D) 28%, 20%
 (E) 44%, 11%

7. In a study on the effect of music on worker productivity, employees were told that a different genre of background music would be played each day and the corresponding production outputs noted. Every change in music resulted in an increase in production. This is an example of

 (A) the effect of a treatment unit.
 (B) the placebo effect.
 (C) the control group effect.
 (D) sampling error.
 (E) voluntary response bias.

8. Suppose X and Y are random variables with $E(X) = 780$, var $(X) = 75$, $E(Y) = 430$, and var $(Y) = 25$. Given that X and Y are independent, what are the expected value and variance of the random variable $X - Y$?

 (A) $E(X - Y) = 350$, var $(X - Y) = 50$
 (B) $E(X - Y) = 350$, var $(X - Y) = 100$
 (C) $E(X - Y) = 1210$, var $(X - Y) = 50$
 (D) $E(X - Y) = 1210$, var $(X - Y) = 100$
 (E) There is insufficient information to answer this question.

9. A social scientist wishes to determine the difference between the percentage of Los Angeles marriages and the percentage of New York marriages that end in divorce in the first year. How large a sample (same for each group) should be taken to estimate the difference to within $\pm.07$ at the 94% confidence level?

 (A) 181
 (B) 361
 (C) 722
 (D) 1083
 (E) 1443

10. A study is carried out noting the numbers of cars passing through an intersection between different hours during the morning rush hour. Following is the resulting histogram:

Which of the following statements are true?
   I. The number of cars passing through before 8 A.M. is the same as the number passing through after 9 A.M.
   II. The numbers of cars passing through in any time interval can be determined by noting the area under the curve above that interval.
   III. The ratio of the number of cars passing through between 10 and 11 A.M. to the number of cars passing through between 6 and 7 A.M. is approximately $\frac{10.5}{6.5} = 1.62$.
   (A) I only
   (B) II only
   (C) III only
   (D) I and II
   (E) II and III

11. A soft drink dispenser can be adjusted to deliver any fixed number of ounces. If the machine is operating with a standard deviation in delivery equal to 0.3 ounce, what should be the mean setting so that a 12-ounce cup will overflow less than 1% of the time? Assume a normal distribution for ounces delivered.
   (A) 11.23 ounces
   (B) 11.30 ounces
   (C) 11.70 ounces
   (D) 12.70 ounces
   (E) 12.77 ounces

12. A sample of 57 laboratory rabbits fed a special carrot juice diet for a month showed an average weight loss of 242 grams with a standard deviation of 39 grams. What is a 95% confidence interval estimate for the average weight loss?
   (A) 242 ± 1.3
   (B) 242 ± 5.2
   (C) 242 ± 8.5
   (D) 242 ± 10.1
   (E) 242 ± 76.4

13. The probability that a person will show a certain gene-transmitted trait is .8 if the father shows the trait and .06 if the father doesn't show the trait. Suppose that the children in a certain community come from families in 25% of which the father shows the trait. What is the probability that a child shows the trait? Given that a child shows the trait, what is the probability that her father shows the trait?
   (A) .245, .816
   (B) .430, .250
   (C) .430, .750
   (D) .860, .250
   (E) .860, .750

14. A student handbook claims that college students study an average of 30 hours per week. A guidance counselor tests this claim, and in a simple random sample of 100 students finds that students study an average of 32 hours per week with a standard deviation of 8 hours. In which of the following intervals is the P-value located?
   (A) $P < .01$
   (B) $.01 < P < .025$
   (C) $.025 < P < .05$
   (D) $.05 < P < .10$
   (E) $P > .10$

15. If all the values of a data set are the same, all of the following must equal zero except for which one?
   (A) Mean
   (B) Standard deviation
   (C) Variance
   (D) Range
   (E) Interquartile range

GO ON TO THE NEXT PAGE ➤

16. The death rate from a particular form of cancer is 23% during the first year. When treated with an experimental drug, only 15 out of 84 patients die during the initial year. Is this strong evidence to claim that the new medication reduces the mortality rate?

    (A) Yes, because the *P*-value is .0459.
    (B) Yes, because the *P*-value is .1314.
    (C) No, because the *P*-value is only .0459.
    (D) No, because the *P*-value is above .10.
    (E) An answer cannot be given without first knowing if a placebo was also used and what the results were.

17. A company has 1000 employees evenly distributed throughout five assembly plants. A sample of 30 employees is to be chosen as follows. Each of the five managers will be asked to place the 200 time cards of their respective employees in a bag, shake them up, and randomly draw out six names. The six names from each plant will be put together to make up the sample. Will this method result in a simple random sample of the 1000 employees?

    (A) Yes, because every employee has the same chance of being selected.
    (B) Yes, because every plant is equally represented.
    (C) Yes, because this is an example of stratified sampling, which is a special case of simple random sampling.
    (D) No, because the plants are not chosen randomly.
    (E) No, because not every group of 30 employees has the same chance of being selected.

18. Following are parts of the probability distributions for the random variables *X* and *Y*.

x	*P*(*x*)		*y*	*P*(*y*)
1	?		1	?
2	?		2	?
3	?			
4	?			

    If *X* and *Y* are independent and two joint probabilities are $P(X = 3, Y = 1) = .14$ and $P(X = 3, Y = 2) = .26$, what is $P(Y = 2)$?

    (A) .35
    (B) .40
    (C) .50
    (D) .65
    (E) It cannot be determined from the given information.

19. A broker notes that the percentage gain in per share value for stock in a random sample of eight leisure time companies during a particular 1-year period was 8.2, 9.5, 4.2, 10.0, 6.7, 6.6, 9.3, and 7.9, respectively. Find a 95% confidence interval estimate for the percentage gain in per share value for leisure time company stocks for that time period.

    (A) 7.8 ± 1.33
    (B) 7.8 ± 1.60
    (C) 8.91 ± 0.57
    (D) 8.91 ± 1.33
    (E) 8.91 ± 1.60

GO ON TO THE NEXT PAGE ➤

20. Consider the following back-to-back stemplot:

	0	348
	1	01256
843	2	29
65210	3	2557
92	4	
7552	5	6
	6	1458
6	7	09
8541	8	
90	9	

Which of the following are true statements?
  I. The distributions have the same mean.
  II. The distributions have the same range.
  III. The distributions have the same standard deviation.

  (A) II only
  (B) I and II
  (C) I and III
  (D) II and III
  (E) I, II, and III

21. A highway superintendent states that five bridges into a city are used in the ratio 2:3:3:4:6 during the morning rush hour. A highway study of a random sample of 6000 cars indicates that 720, 970, 1013, 1380, and 1917 cars use the five bridges, respectively. Can the superintendent's claim be rejected at the 2.5% or 5% level of significance?

  (A) There is sufficient evidence to reject the claim at either of these two levels.
  (B) There is sufficient evidence to reject the claim at the 2.5% level but not at the 5% level.
  (C) There is sufficient evidence to reject the claim at the 5% level but not at the 2.5% level.
  (D) There is not sufficient evidence to reject the claim at either of these two levels.
  (E) There is not sufficient information to answer this question.

22. Which of the following leads to a binomial distribution?
  I. A committee of two is to be randomly selected from among seven juniors and four seniors attending an organizational meeting for a New Year's Eve dance. What are the probabilities that the committee will consist of two juniors, of two seniors, or of exactly one junior and one senior?
  II. As a basketball player continues to improve during the season, her free throw percentage rises. The coach is interested in the probability of the player sinking various numbers of free throws during the season.
  III. An inspection procedure at a chemical production plant calls for a government inspector to note each day whether the amount of pollutants being dumped into a nearby river is less than 10 kilograms, between 10 and 25 kilograms, or more than 25 kilograms.

  (A) I only
  (B) II only
  (C) III only
  (D) All of these.
  (E) None of these.

GO ON TO THE NEXT PAGE ➤

23. An educator plans to evaluate two different teaching methods by comparing the average test scores of two classes of students, each taught by one of the two techniques under study. Suppose the two classes have 35 and 38 students, respectively, with standard deviations in test scores of 24.5 and 21.2, respectively. Is an observed difference in average test scores of 2.4 significant?

    (A) The observed difference in test scores is significant.
    (B) The observed difference in test scores is not significant.
    (C) A conclusion is not possible without knowing the mean test score from each sample.
    (D) A conclusion is not possible using different size samples.
    (E) A two-sample hypothesis test should not be used in this example.

24. An inspection procedure at a manufacturing plant involves picking four items at random and accepting the whole lot if at least three of the four items are in perfect condition. If in reality 90% of the whole lot are perfect, what is the probability that the lot will be accepted?

    (A) .2916
    (B) .3439
    (C) .6561
    (D) .7084
    (E) .9477

25. A town has one high school, which buses students from urban, suburban, and rural communities. Which of the following samples is recommended in studying attitudes toward tracking of students in honors, regular, and below-grade classes?

    (A) Convenience sample
    (B) Simple random sample (SRS)
    (C) Stratified sample
    (D) Systematic sample
    (E) Voluntary response sample

26. Suppose there is a correlation of $r = 0.9$ between number of hours per day students study and GPAs. Which of the following is a reasonable conclusion?

    (A) 90% of students who study receive high grades.
    (B) 90% of students who receive high grades study a lot.
    (C) 90% of the variation in GPAs can be explained by variation in number of study hours per day.
    (D) 10% of the variation in GPAs cannot be explained by variation in number of study hours per day.
    (E) 81% of the variation in GPAs can be explained by variation in number of study hours per day.

27. To determine the average number of children living in single-family homes, a researcher picks a simple random sample of 50 such homes. However, even after one follow-up visit the interviewer is unable to make contact with anyone in 8 of these homes. Concerned about nonresponse bias, the researcher picks another simple random sample and instructs the interviewer to keep trying until contact is made with someone in a total of 50 homes. The average number of children is determined to be 1.73. Is this estimate probably too low or too high?

    (A) Too low, because of undercoverage bias.
    (B) Too low, because convenience samples overestimate average results.
    (C) Too high, because of undercoverage bias.
    (D) Too high, because convenience samples overestimate average results.
    (E) Too high, because voluntary response samples overestimate average results.

GO ON TO THE NEXT PAGE ➤

For Questions 28 and 29 consider the following: The graph below shows cumulative proportions plotted against land values (in dollars per acre) for farms on sale in a rural community.

28. What is the median land value?
    (A) $2000
    (B) $2250
    (C) $2500
    (D) $2750
    (E) $3000

29. What is the interquartile range?
    (A) $1300
    (B) $2000
    (C) $2300
    (D) $3000
    (E) $3600

30. A confidence interval estimate is determined from the monthly grocery expenditures in a random sample of n families. Which of the following will result in a smaller margin of error?
    I. A smaller confidence level
    II. A smaller sample standard deviation
    III. A smaller sample size
    (A) II only
    (B) I and II
    (C) I and III
    (D) II and III
    (E) I, II, and III

31. A medical research team claims that high vitamin C intake increases endurance. In particular, 1000 milligrams of vitamin C per day for a month should add an average of 4.3 minutes to the length of maximum physical effort that can be tolerated. Army training officers believe the claim is exaggerated and plan a test on 400 soldiers in which they will reject the medical team's claim if the sample mean is less than 4.0 minutes. Suppose the standard deviation of added minutes is 3.2. If the true mean increase is only 4.2 minutes, what is the probability that the officers will fail to reject the false claim of 4.3 minutes?
    (A) .0156
    (B) .0301
    (C) .3944
    (D) .8944
    (E) .9699

GO ON TO THE NEXT PAGE ➤

32. Suppose the regression line for a set of data, $y = -4x + b$, passes through the point $(3, 10)$. If $\bar{x}$ and $\bar{y}$ are the sample means of the x- and y-values, respectively, then $\bar{y} =$
    (A) $\bar{x}$.
    (B) $\bar{x} - 3$.
    (C) $\bar{x} + 10$.
    (D) $-4\bar{x}$.
    (E) $-4\bar{x} + 22$.

33. The weight of an aspirin tablet is 300 milligrams according to the bottle label. An FDA investigator weighs a random sample of seven tablets and obtains weights of 299, 300, 305, 302, 299, 301, and 303 milligrams, respectively. In which of the following intervals is the P-value located?
    (A) $P < .01$
    (B) $.01 < P < .025$
    (C) $.025 < P < .05$
    (D) $.05 < P < .10$
    (E) $.10 < P$

34. A teacher believes that giving her students a practice quiz every week will motivate them to study harder, leading to a greater overall understanding of the course material. She tries this technique for a year, and everyone in the class achieves a grade of at least C. Is this an experiment or an observational study?
    (A) An experiment, but with no reasonable conclusion possible about cause and effect
    (B) An experiment, thus making cause and effect a reasonable conclusion

(C) An observational study, because there was no use of a control group
(D) An observational study, but a poorly designed one because randomization was not used
(E) An observational study, and thus a reasonable conclusion of association but not of cause and effect

35. Does sea bathing lead to illness? For a sampling of 1112 bathers in four English resort areas (*The Lancet*, October 1, 1994, page 906), the following table shows exposure to varying amounts of fecal material in the water versus number of cases of gastroenteritis reported.

	Fecal streptococci per 100 ml			
	None	0–34	35–69	<70
Cases of gastroenteritis	57	34	24	17
No related illness	548	273	125	34

What is the resulting χ^2-value?
    (A) 2.74
    (B) 4.11
    (C) 5.32
    (D) 16.89
    (E) 28.31

STOP

Section II
Part A

Questions 1–5
Spend about 65 minutes on this part of the exam.
Percentage of Section II grade—75

You must show all work and indicate the methods you use. You will be graded on the correctness of your methods and on the accuracy of your results and explanations.

---

1. A mass transportation study concludes that in large cities 40% of commuters drive to work by themselves, 15% drive in car pools, 20% take trains, and 25% take buses. A city council wishes to examine whether commuters in their city follow this pattern. A random survey of 600 commuters yields the following breakdown: 263 solo drivers, 101 in car pools, 106 train riders, and 130 bus riders. What conclusion is reached at the 5% significance level? Show your work.

2. In a random sample of 30 subway cars during rush hour, the average number of riders per car was 83.5 with a standard deviation of 5.9.

    (a) Establish a 90% confidence interval estimate for the average number of riders per car during rush hour. Show your work.

    (b) Assuming the same standard deviation of 5.9, how large a sample of cars would be necessary to determine the average number of riders to within ±1 at the 90% confidence level? Show your work.

GO ON TO THE NEXT PAGE ➤

3. The following scatterplot shows the advertised prices (in thousands of dollars) plotted against ages (in years) for a random sample of Plymouth Voyagers on several dealers' lots.

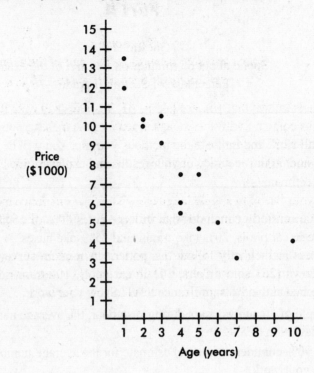

A computer printout showing the results of fitting a straight line to the data by the method of least squares gives

```
Price = 12.37 - 1.13 Age
R-sq = 75.5%
```

(a) Find the correlation coefficient for the relationship between price and age of Voyagers based on these data.

(b) What is the slope of the regression line? Interpret it in the context of these data.

(c) How will the size of the correlation coefficient change if the 10-year-old Voyager is removed from the data set? Explain your answer.

(d) How will the size of the slope of the least squares regression line change if the 10-year-old Voyager is removed from the data set?

4. A new vegetable fertilizer is to be tested at two different levels (regular concentration and double concentration). Design an experiment, including a control, for 30 test plots, half of which are in shade. Explain carefully how you will use randomization.

5. A travel agent books passages on three different tours, with half her customers choosing tour T1, one-third choosing T2, and the rest choosing T3. The agent has noted that three-quarters of those who take tour T1 return to book passage again, two-thirds of those who take T2 return, and one-half of those who take T3 return.

(a) What is the probability that a customer selected at random will return for another tour? Show your work.

(b) If a customer does return, what is the probability that the person first went on tour T2? Show your work.

GO ON TO THE NEXT PAGE ➤

Section II

Part B

Question 6
Spend about 25 minutes on this part of the exam.
Percentage of Section II grade—25

6. One of your friends knows that you are taking AP Statistics and asks for your help with her chemistry lab report. She has come up with five measurements of the melting point of a compound: 122.4, 121.8, 122.0, 123.0, and 122.3 degrees Celsius.

   (a) The lab manual asks for a 95% confidence interval estimate for the melting point. Show her how to find this estimate.

   (b) Explain to your friend in simple language what 95% confidence means.

   (c) Would a 90% confidence interval be narrower or wider than the 95% interval. Explain your answer to your friend.

   (d) The lab manual asks whether the data show sufficient evidence to call into question the established melting point of 122 degrees Celsius. State the null and alternative hypotheses and find the P-value.

   (e) Explain the meaning of the specific P-value to your friend.

STOP

Answer Key

Section I

1. **C**	8. **B**	15. **A**	22. **E**	29. **C**
2. **A**	9. **B**	16. **D**	23. **B**	30. **B**
3. **B**	10. **A**	17. **E**	24. **E**	31. **D**
4. **C**	11. **B**	18. **D**	25. **C**	32. **E**
5. **C**	12. **D**	19. **B**	26. **E**	33. **E**
6. **B**	13. **A**	20. **D**	27. **C**	34. **A**
7. **B**	14. **B**	21. **C**	28. **A**	35. **E**

Answers Explained

Section I

1. **(C)** A complete census can give much information about a population, but it doesn't necessarily establish a cause-and-effect relationship among seemingly related population parameters. While the results of well-designed observational studies might suggest relationships, it is difficult to conclude that there is cause and effect without running a well-designed experiment.

2. **(A)** The critical z-scores for 10% to the left and 5% to the right are -1.282 and 1.645, respectively. Then $\{\mu - 1.282\sigma = 2.48,\ \mu + 1.645\sigma = 2.54\}$ gives $\mu = 2.506$ and $\sigma = 0.0205$.

3. **(B)** If A and B are mutually exclusive, $P(A \cap B) = 0$. Thus $.6 = .4 + P(B) - 0$, and so $P(B) = .2$. If A and B are independent, then $P(A \cap B) = P(A)P(B)$. Thus $.6 = .4 + P(B) - .4P(B)$, and so $P(B) = \frac{1}{3}$.

4. **(C)**
$$n_1 = 112 \qquad n_2 = 81$$
$$\hat{p}_1 = \tfrac{83}{112} = .741 \quad \hat{p}_2 = \tfrac{76}{81} = .938$$
$$\sigma_d = \sqrt{\frac{(.741)(.259)}{112} + \frac{(.938)(.062)}{81}} = .0493$$
$$(.741 - .938) \pm 1.645(.0493) = -.197 \pm .081$$

5. **(C)** The slope and the correlation always have the same sign. Correlation shows association, not causation.

6. **(B)** There were 400 people surveyed, and $P(\text{Japanese} \cap \text{high}) = \frac{40}{400} = 10\%$. The conditional probability $P(\text{low}|\text{American}) = \frac{45}{225} = 20\%$.

7. **(B)** The desire of the workers for the study to be successful led to a placebo effect.

8. **(B)** If two random variables are independent, the mean of the difference of the two random variables is equal to the difference of the two individual means; however, the variance of the difference of the two random variables is equal to the *sum* of the two individual variances.

9. **(B)** $\frac{1.88(.5)\sqrt{2}}{\sqrt{n}} \le .07$ gives $\sqrt{n} \ge 18.99$ and $n \ge 360.7$.

10. **(A)** Histograms give relative frequencies, not actual frequencies, and these relative frequencies correspond to relative areas.

11. **(B)** With a right tail having probability .01, the critical z-score is 2.326. Thus $\mu + 2.326(.3) = 12$, giving $\mu = 11.3$.

12. **(D)** $242 \pm 1.96 \left(\frac{39}{\sqrt{57}} \right) = 242 \pm 10.1$

13. **(A)**

$$P\left(\begin{array}{c} \text{child} \\ \text{shows} \end{array} \right) = P\left(\begin{array}{c} \text{father} \\ \text{shows} \end{array} \cap \begin{array}{c} \text{child} \\ \text{shows} \end{array} \right) + P\left(\begin{array}{c} \text{father} \\ \text{doesn't} \end{array} \cap \begin{array}{c} \text{child} \\ \text{shows} \end{array} \right)$$

$$= (.25)(.8) + (.75)(.06)$$
$$= .200 + .045$$
$$= .245$$

$$P\left(\begin{array}{c} \text{father} \\ \text{shows} \end{array} \middle| \begin{array}{c} \text{child} \\ \text{shows} \end{array} \right) = \frac{.200}{.245} = .816$$

14. **(B)** We have $H_0 : \mu = 30$ and $H_a : \mu \ne 30$. The standard deviation of the sample means is $\sigma_{\bar{x}} = \frac{8}{\sqrt{100}} = 0.8$. The z-score of 32 is $\frac{32-30}{0.8} = 2.5$. Thus each tail has a probability of $1 - .9938 = .0062$, and the P-value for this two-sided test is $2(.0062) = .0124$.

15. **(A)** The mean equals the common value of all the data elements. The other terms all measure variability, which is zero when all the data elements are equal.

16. **(D)** We have $H_0 : p = .23$, $H_a : p < .23$, and $\sigma_{\hat{p}} = \sqrt{\frac{(.23)(.77)}{84}} = .0459$. $\hat{p} = \frac{15}{84} = .179$ with a z-score of $\frac{.179-.23}{.0459} = -1.12$. Thus the P-value is .1314. With $P > .10$, there is little evidence to reject H_0.

17. **(E)** In a simple random sample, every possible group of the given size has to be equally likely to be selected, and this is not true here. For example, with this procedure it is impossible for the employees in the final sample to all be from a single plant. This method is an example of stratified sampling, but stratified sampling does not result in simple random samples.

18. **(D)** By independence we have $P(X = 3)P(Y = 1) = .14$ and $P(X = 3)P(Y = 2) = .26$. Thus $P(X = 3) = .14 + .26 = .4$, $(.4)P(Y = 2) = .26$, and $P(Y = 2) = .65$.

19. **(B)** df $= 7$, and $7.8 \pm 2.365 \left(\frac{1.918}{\sqrt{8}} \right) = 7.8 \pm 1.60$.

20. **(D)** The two sets have different means, but they have identical shapes and thus the same variability including both range and standard deviation.

21. **(C)** We have $2 + 3 + 3 + 4 + 6 = 18$, and thus the expected numbers according to the superintendent's claim are

$$\tfrac{2}{18}(6000) = 667 \qquad \tfrac{3}{18}(6000) = 1000$$

$$\tfrac{4}{18}(6000) = 1333 \qquad \tfrac{6}{18}(6000) = 2000$$

Using chi-square to test for goodness of fit, we calculate

$$\chi^2 = \frac{(720 - 667)^2}{667} + \frac{(970 - 1000)^2}{1000} + \frac{(1013 - 1000)^2}{1000}$$
$$+ \frac{(1380 - 1333)^2}{1333} + \frac{(1917 - 2000)^2}{2000}$$
$$= 10.38$$

With df $= 5 - 1 = 4$ and tail probability .05, the critical χ^2-value is 9.49; with tail probability .025, the critical χ^2-value is 11.14. Thus there is sufficient evidence to reject the superintendent's claim at the 5% significance level but not at the 2.5% level.

22. **(E)** None of them leads to a binomial distribution. In the first, there is a lack of independence in choosing the first and second members of the committee; for example, if the first person chosen is a junior, the probability that the second will also be a junior is $\frac{6}{10}$, not $\frac{7}{11}$. In the second, p increases throughout the season. The third has three outcomes, not two.

23. **(B)** We have $H_0: \mu_1 - \mu_2 = 0$, $H_a: \mu_1 - \mu_2 \neq 0$, and

$$\sigma_{\bar{x}_1 - \bar{x}_2} \approx \sqrt{\frac{(24.5)^2}{35} + \frac{(21.2)^2}{38}} = 5.38$$

The z-score of 2.4 is $\frac{2.4}{5.38} = 0.45$, which gives .3264 in each tail and a P-value of $2(.3264) = .6528$. With such a high value of P, the observed difference is not significant.

24. **(E)** $4(.9)^3(.1) + (.9)^4 = .9477$.

25. **(C)** In stratified sampling the population is divided into representative groups, and random samples of persons from each group are chosen. In this case it might well be important to be able to consider separately the responses from each of the three groups—urban, suburban, and rural.

26. **(E)** r^2, the coefficient of determination, indicates the percentage of variation in y that is explained by variation in x.

27. **(C)** It is most likely that the homes at which the interviewer had difficulty finding someone home were homes with fewer children living in them. Replacing these homes with other randomly picked homes will most likely replace homes with fewer children with homes with more children.

28. **(A)** The median corresponds to the 0.5 cumulative proportion.

29. **(C)** The 0.25 and 0.75 cumulative proportions correspond to $Q_1 = 1300$ and $Q_3 = 3600$, respectively, and so the intermediate range is $3600 - 1300 = 2300$.

30. **(B)** The margin of error varies directly with the critical z-value and directly with the standard deviation of the sample, but inversely with the square root of the sample size.

31. **(D)** $\sigma_{\bar{x}} = \frac{3.2}{\sqrt{400}} = 0.16$. With a true mean increase of 4.2, the z-score for 4.0 is $\frac{4.0 - 4.2}{0.16} = -1.25$ and the probability to the right of 4.0 is $1 - .1056 = .8944$.

32. **(E)** Since (3, 10) is on the line $y = -4x + b$, we have $10 = -12 + b$ and $b = 22$. Thus the regression line is $y = -4x + 22$. The point $(\bar{x}, \bar{y})$ is always on the regression line, and so we have $\bar{y} = -4\bar{x} + 22$.

33. **(E)** We have $H_0: \mu = 300$, $H_a: \mu \neq 300$, $\bar{x} = 301.3$, $s = 2.21$, and $\sigma_{\bar{x}} = \frac{2.21}{\sqrt{7}} = 0.835$. The t-score of 301.3 is $\frac{301.3 - 300}{0.835} = 1.56$. Looking at the df $= 6$ row in Table B, note that 1.56 is between 1.440 and 1.943, corresponding to tail probabilities of .10 and .05, respectively. This is a two-sided test, so doubling gives a P-value above .10. (A calculator like the TI-83 quickly shows that the critical t-score is 1.54 and $P = .175$.)

34. **(A)** This study was an experiment because a treatment (weekly quizzes) was imposed on the subjects. However, it was a poorly designed experiment with no use of randomization and no control over lurking variables.

35. **(E)** Input of the original matrix into a calculator like the TI-83 (the AP exam assumes that students have calculators with statistics capabilities and are familiar with their use) quickly gives $\chi^2 = 28.67$.

Alternatively, a messy algebraic calculation gives

Expected

71.8	36.4	17.7	6.1	132
533.2	270.6	131.3	44.9	980
605	307	149	51	1112

$$\chi^2 = \frac{(57-71.8)^2}{71.8} + \frac{(34-36.4)^2}{36.4} + \frac{(24-17.7)^2}{17.7} + \frac{(17-6.1)^2}{6.1}$$
$$+ \frac{(548-533.2)^2}{533.2} + \frac{(273-270.6)^2}{270.6} + \frac{(125-131.3)^2}{131.3}$$
$$+ \frac{(34-44.9)^2}{44.9}$$
$$= 28.31$$

Section II

1. If there is a good fit with the transportation study pattern, the expected numbers are $.40(600) = 240$, $.15(600) = 90$, $.20(600) = 120$, and $.25(600) = 150$. The difference between the observed and expected values is measured by chi-square:

$$\chi^2 = \frac{(263-240)^2}{240} + \frac{(101-90)^2}{90} + \frac{(106-120)^2}{120} + \frac{(130-150)^2}{150} = 7.85$$

At the 5% significance level with df $= 4 - 1 = 3$, the critical value of χ^2 is 7.81. Since $7.85 > 7.81$, there is sufficient evidence to reject the null hypothesis of a good fit and say that the city's commuters do not follow the national pattern.

2. (a) $83.5 \pm 1.645 \left(\frac{5.9}{\sqrt{30}} \right) = 83.5 \pm 1.8$

(b) $1.645 \left(\frac{5.9}{\sqrt{n}} \right) \le 1$ gives $\sqrt{n} \ge 9.7055$, and $n \ge 94.2$, so you must choose a random sample of at least 95 subway cars.

3. (a) The correlation coefficient is the square root of .755 and has the same sign as the slope of the regression line. In this case $r = -.869$.

(b) The slope of the regression line is $-1.13(\$1000)$, signifying that a Voyager depreciates $1130 in value each additional year it ages.

(c) The 10-year-old Voyager appears to lie well off the regression line. Thus if it is removed from the data set, the correlation coefficient will increase in absolute value, or in this case be closer to -1.

(d) If the 10-year-old Voyager is removed from the data set, the line will swing downward and the slope will become more negative.

4. To achieve blocking by sunlight, first separate the sunlit and shaded plots. Label the 15 sunlit plots 01 through 15. Using a random number table, pick two digits at a time, ignoring numbers above 15 and ignoring repeats, until a group of five such numbers is obtained. These sunlit plots will receive the fertilizer at regular concentration. Relabel the remaining sunlit plots 01 through 10. Following along in the table, pick two digits at a time, ignoring numbers above 10 and ignoring repeats, until another group of five is selected. These sunlit plots will receive the fertilizer at double concentration, while the remaining sunlit plots will be a control group. Now repeat the procedure starting with labeling the shaded plots 01 through 15.

5. (a) $P(T3) = 1 - \left(\frac{1}{2} + \frac{1}{3} \right) = \frac{1}{6}$

$\frac{1}{2}$	T1 $\xrightarrow{\ \frac{3}{4}\ }$ return	$P(T1 \cap \text{return}) = \left(\frac{1}{2} \right) \left(\frac{3}{4} \right) = \frac{3}{8}$
$\frac{1}{3}$	T2 $\xrightarrow{\ \frac{2}{3}\ }$ return	$P(T2 \cap \text{return}) = \left(\frac{1}{3} \right) \left(\frac{2}{3} \right) = \frac{2}{9}$
$\frac{1}{6}$	T3 $\xrightarrow{\ \frac{1}{2}\ }$ return	$P(T3 \cap \text{return}) = \left(\frac{1}{6} \right) \left(\frac{1}{2} \right) = \frac{1}{12}$

$$P(\text{return}) = \frac{3}{8} + \frac{2}{9} + \frac{1}{12} = \frac{49}{72}$$

(b)

$$P(T2 | \text{return}) = \frac{P(T2 \cap \text{return})}{P(\text{return})} = \frac{\frac{2}{9}}{\frac{49}{72}} = \frac{16}{49}$$

6. (a) A calculator gives $\bar{x} = 122.3$ and $s = 0.458$. Then $\sigma_{\bar{x}} = \frac{0.458}{\sqrt{5}} = 0.205$. With $df = 5 - 1 = 4$, Table B gives critical t-scores of ± 2.776. Thus the 95% confidence interval is $122.3 \pm 2.776(0.205) = 122.3 \pm 0.57$ degrees Celsius.

(b) We are 95% confident that the true mean lies in the interval [121.73, 122.87]. Or, 95% of the time, intervals so constructed contain the true mean.

(c) A 90% confidence interval would be narrower than the 95% interval. If we care only about being 90% confident in our answer, we can use a tighter interval.

(d) We have H_0: $\mu = 122$, and H_a: $\mu \neq 122$, and the t-score of the observed mean of 122.3 is $\frac{122.3 - 122}{0.205} = 1.463$. In the df $= 4$ row in Table B, 1.463 lies between 1.190 and 1.533, corresponding to tail probabilities of .15 and .10, respectively. Since this is a two-sided test, we must double these probabilities and find that the P-value is between .20 and .30.

(e) If the claimed 122 value is correct, there is still a greater than .20 probability that a sample mean will be as extreme as ours. With such a large P, there is not sufficient evidence to question the 122-degree-Celsius claim.

1. Ⓐ Ⓑ Ⓒ Ⓓ Ⓔ
2. Ⓐ Ⓑ Ⓒ Ⓓ Ⓔ
3. Ⓐ Ⓑ Ⓒ Ⓓ Ⓔ
4. Ⓐ Ⓑ Ⓒ Ⓓ Ⓔ
5. Ⓐ Ⓑ Ⓒ Ⓓ Ⓔ
6. Ⓐ Ⓑ Ⓒ Ⓓ Ⓔ
7. Ⓐ Ⓑ Ⓒ Ⓓ Ⓔ
8. Ⓐ Ⓑ Ⓒ Ⓓ Ⓔ
9. Ⓐ Ⓑ Ⓒ Ⓓ Ⓔ
10. Ⓐ Ⓑ Ⓒ Ⓓ Ⓔ
11. Ⓐ Ⓑ Ⓒ Ⓓ Ⓔ
12. Ⓐ Ⓑ Ⓒ Ⓓ Ⓔ

13. Ⓐ Ⓑ Ⓒ Ⓓ Ⓔ
14. Ⓐ Ⓑ Ⓒ Ⓓ Ⓔ
15. Ⓐ Ⓑ Ⓒ Ⓓ Ⓔ
16. Ⓐ Ⓑ Ⓒ Ⓓ Ⓔ
17. Ⓐ Ⓑ Ⓒ Ⓓ Ⓔ
18. Ⓐ Ⓑ Ⓒ Ⓓ Ⓔ
19. Ⓐ Ⓑ Ⓒ Ⓓ Ⓔ
20. Ⓐ Ⓑ Ⓒ Ⓓ Ⓔ
21. Ⓐ Ⓑ Ⓒ Ⓓ Ⓔ
22. Ⓐ Ⓑ Ⓒ Ⓓ Ⓔ
23. Ⓐ Ⓑ Ⓒ Ⓓ Ⓔ
24. Ⓐ Ⓑ Ⓒ Ⓓ Ⓔ

25. Ⓐ Ⓑ Ⓒ Ⓓ Ⓔ
26. Ⓐ Ⓑ Ⓒ Ⓓ Ⓔ
27. Ⓐ Ⓑ Ⓒ Ⓓ Ⓔ
28. Ⓐ Ⓑ Ⓒ Ⓓ Ⓔ
29. Ⓐ Ⓑ Ⓒ Ⓓ Ⓔ
30. Ⓐ Ⓑ Ⓒ Ⓓ Ⓔ
31. Ⓐ Ⓑ Ⓒ Ⓓ Ⓔ
32. Ⓐ Ⓑ Ⓒ Ⓓ Ⓔ
33. Ⓐ Ⓑ Ⓒ Ⓓ Ⓔ
34. Ⓐ Ⓑ Ⓒ Ⓓ Ⓔ
35. Ⓐ Ⓑ Ⓒ Ⓓ Ⓔ

Practice Examination 4

Section I

Questions 1–35

Spend 90 minutes on this part of the exam.

Directions: The questions or incomplete statements that follow are each followed by five suggested answers or completions. Choose the response that best answers the question or completes the statement.

---

1. In a simple random survey of 89 teachers of high school AP Statistics, 73 said that it was the most satisfying, most enjoyable course they had ever taught. Establish a 98% confidence interval estimate for the proportion of all high school AP Statistics teachers who feel this way.
   (A) .820 ± .004
   (B) .820 ± .041
   (C) .820 ± .084
   (D) .820 ± .095
   (E) .820 ± .223

2. To survey the opinions of the students at your high school, a researcher plans to select every twenty-fifth student entering the school in the morning. Assuming there are no absences, will this result in a simple random sample of students attending your school?
   (A) Yes, because every student has the same chance of being selected.
   (B) Yes, but only if there is a single entrance to the school.
   (C) Yes, because the 24 out of every 25 students who are not selected will form a control group.
   (D) Yes, because this is an example of systematic sampling, which is a special case of simple random sampling.
   (E) No, because not every sample of the intended size has an equal chance of being selected.

3. One nationwide report on physical fitness claims that the proportion of midlevel managers who participate in a regular exercise program is .13. A company considering providing free health club memberships for its employees plans to survey 200 managers. The new program will be installed immediately if the proportion of exercisers is less than .10. What is the probability of proceeding too quickly when there really is no difference between managers' exercise participation and that nationwide?
   (A) .0238
   (B) .0476
   (C) .1038
   (D) .1514
   (E) .2076

4. Suppose that 60% of a particular electronic part last over 3 years, while 70% last less than 6 years. Assuming a normal distribution, what are the mean and standard deviation with regard to length of life of these parts?
   (A) $\mu = 3.677, \sigma = 3.561$
   (B) $\mu = 3.977, \sigma = 3.861$
   (C) $\mu = 4.177, \sigma = 3.561$
   (D) $\mu = 4.377, \sigma = 3.261$
   (E) The mean and standard deviation cannot be computed from the information given.

GO ON TO THE NEXT PAGE ➤

5. The graph below shows cumulative proportions plotted against numbers of employees working in mid-sized retail establishments.

What is the interquartile range?

(A) 18
(B) 35
(C) 57
(D) 68
(E) 75

6. The label on a package of cords claims that the breaking strength of a cord is 3.5 pounds, but a hardware store owner believes the real value is less. She plans to test 36 such cords; if their mean breaking strength is less than 3.25 pounds, she will reject the claim on the label. If the standard deviation for the breaking strengths of all such cords is 0.9 pounds, what is the probability of mistakenly rejecting a true claim?

(A) .05
(B) .10
(C) .15
(D) .45
(E) .94

7. Suppose X and Y are random variables with $\mu_x = 720$, $\sigma_x = 6$, $\mu_y = 240$, and $\sigma_y = 8$. Given that X and Y are independent, what are the mean and standard deviation of the random variable $X + Y$?

(A) $\mu_{x+y} = 960$, $\sigma_{x+y} = 7$
(B) $\mu_{x+y} = 960$, $\sigma_{x+y} = 10$
(C) $\mu_{x+y} = 960$, $\sigma_{x+y} = 14$
(D) $\mu_{x+y} = 480$, $\sigma_{x+y} = 14$
(E) There is insufficient information to answer this question.

8. To study the effect of alcohol on reaction time, subjects were randomly selected and given three beers to consume. Their reaction time to a simple stimulus was measured before and after drinking the alcohol. Which of the following statements are true?

 I. This study was an observational study.
 II. This study was an experiment with no controls.
 III. This study was an experiment in which the subjects were used as their own controls.
 IV. The researcher should be concerned about a placebo effect.

(A) I only
(B) II only
(C) III only
(D) II and IV
(E) III and IV

9. Suppose that the regression line for a set of data, $y = 7x + b$, passes through the point $(-2, 4)$. If $\bar{x}$ and $\bar{y}$ are the sample means of the x- and y-values, respectively, then $\bar{y} =$

(A) $\bar{x}$
(B) $\bar{x} + 2$
(C) $\bar{x} - 4$
(D) $7\bar{x}$
(E) $7\bar{x} + 18$

10. A catch of five fish of a certain species yielded the following ounces of protein per pound of fish: 3.1, 3.5, 3.2, 2.8, and 3.4. What is a 90% confidence interval estimate for ounces of protein per pound of this species of fish?

(A) 3.2 ± 0.202
(B) 3.2 ± 0.247
(C) 3.2 ± 0.261
(D) 4.0 ± 0.202
(E) 4.0 ± 0.247

GO ON TO THE NEXT PAGE ➤

11. In a sample of 39 of his decisions, one judge handed down sentences averaging 4.5 years with a standard deviation of 1.2 years, while in a sample of 46 of her decisions a second judge handed down sentences averaging 5.3 years with a standard deviation of 1.1 years. What is a 95% confidence interval estimate of the difference in average sentences handed down by the two judges?
    (A) -0.8 ± 0.063
    (B) -0.8 ± 0.251
    (C) -0.8 ± 0.414
    (D) -0.8 ± 0.493
    (E) -0.8 ± 2.083

12. Following is a histogram of ages of people applying for a particular high school teaching position.

    Which of the following statements are true?
    I. The median age is between 24 and 25.
    II. The mean age is between 22 and 23.
    III. The mean age is greater than the median age.
    (A) I only
    (B) II only
    (C) III only
    (D) All are true.
    (E) None is true.

13. To conduct a survey of which long distance carriers are used in a particular locality, a researcher opens a telephone book to a random page, closes his eyes, puts his finger down on the page, and then calls the next 75 names. Which of the following are true statements?
    I. The survey design incorporates chance.
    II. The procedure results in a simple random sample.
    III. The procedure could easily result in selection bias.
    (A) I and II
    (B) I and III
    (C) II and III
    (D) All are true.
    (E) None is true.

14. A medical researcher believes that taking 1000 milligrams of vitamin C per day will result in fewer colds than a daily intake of 500 milligrams will. In a group of 50 volunteers taking 1000 milligrams per day, the numbers of colds per individual during a winter season averaged 1.8 with a variance of 1.5. Similar tabulations from a group of 60 volunteers taking 500 milligrams per day showed an average of 2.4 with a variance of 1.6. What was the P-value of this test?
    (A) .0059
    (B) .0118
    (C) .0217
    (D) .0434
    (E) .0566

15. Suppose the probability that a person picked at random has lung cancer is .035 and the probability that the person both has lung cancer and is a heavy smoker is .014. Given that someone picked at random has lung cancer, what is the probability that the person is a heavy smoker?
    (A) .021
    (B) .049
    (C) .244
    (D) .250
    (E) .400

GO ON TO THE NEXT PAGE ➤

16. Taxi cabs in a metropolitan area are driven an average of 75,000 miles per year with a standard deviation of 12,000 miles. What is the probability that a randomly selected cab has been driven less than 100,000 miles if it is known that it has been driven over 80,000 miles? Assume a normal distribution of miles per year among cabs.

    (A) .06
    (B) .34
    (C) .66
    (D) .68
    (E) .94

17. A plant manager wishes to determine the difference in number of accidents per day between two departments. How many days' records should be examined to be 90% certain of the difference in daily averages to within 0.25 accidents per day? Assume standard deviations of 0.8 and 0.5 accidents per day in the two departments, respectively.

    (A) 39
    (B) 55
    (C) 78
    (D) 109
    (E) 155

18. Suppose the correlation between two variables is $r = .19$. What is the new correlation if .23 is added to all values of the x-variable, every value of the y-variable is doubled, and the two variables are interchanged?

    (A) .19
    (B) .42
    (C) .84
    (D) −.19
    (E) −.84

19. Five different chemical fertilizers are used, one on each of five large plots. The yield per plot in tons is

Plot:	1	2	3	4	5
Tons:	19	31	33	20	22

Is there sufficient evidence to say that the yields using the different fertilizers are not the same? Test at the 5% and 10% significance levels.

    (A) There is sufficient evidence at both levels to claim that the fertilizers result in different yields.
    (B) There is sufficient evidence to claim at the 2.5% level, but not at the 5% level, that the fertilizers result in different yields.
    (C) There is sufficient evidence to claim at the 5% level, but not at the 2.5% level, that the fertilizers result in different yields.
    (D) There is not sufficient evidence at either level to claim that the fertilizers result in different yields.
    (E) There is not sufficient information to answer this question.

20. A company has a choice of three investment schemes. Option I gives a sure $25,000 return on investment. Option II gives a 50% chance of returning $50,000 and a 50% chance of returning $10,000. Option III gives a 5% chance of returning $100,000 and a 95% chance of returning nothing. Which option should the company choose?

    (A) Option II if it wants to maximize expected return
    (B) Option I if it needs at least $20,000 to pay off an overdue loan
    (C) Option III if it needs at least $80,000 to pay off an overdue loan
    (D) All of the above answers are correct.
    (E) Because of chance, it really doesn't matter which option it chooses.

21. Suppose $P(X) = .35$ and $P(Y) = .40$. If $P(X|Y) = .28$, what is $P(Y|X)$?
    (A) .14
    (B) .32
    (C) .50
    (D) .70
    (E) .80

22. To test whether extensive exercise lowers the resting heart rate, a study is performed by randomly selecting half of a group of volunteers to exercise 1 hour each morning, while the rest are instructed to perform no exercise. Is this study an experiment or an observational study?
    (A) An experiment with a control group and blinding
    (B) An experiment with blocking
    (C) An observational study with comparison and randomization
    (D) An observational study with little if any bias
    (E) None of the above

For Questions 23 and 24 consider the following parallel boxplots of the effective durations of three over-the-counter pain relievers:

23. Which of the following are true statements?
    I. All three have the same range.
    II. All three have the same interquartile range.
    III. The difference in the medians between the first and third distributions is equal to the interquartile range of the second distribution.
    (A) I and II
    (B) I and III
    (C) II and III
    (D) I, II, and III
    (E) None of the above gives the complete set of true responses.

24. Which of the following are true statements?
    I. All three are symmetric.
    II. The first is skewed to the left, while the third is skewed to the right.
    III. The second is skewed on both sides.
    (A) I only
    (B) II only
    (C) III only
    (D) II and III
    (E) None of the above gives the complete set of true responses.

25. For their first exam, students in an AP Statistics class studied an average of 4 hours with a standard deviation of 1 hour. Almost everyone did poorly on the exam, and so for the second exam every student studied 10 hours. What is the correlation between the numbers of hours students studied for each exam?
    (A) −1
    (B) 0
    (C) .4
    (D) 1
    (E) There is not sufficient information to answer this question.

GO ON TO THE NEXT PAGE ➤

26. Suppose that 54% of the graduates from your high school go on to 4-year colleges, 20% go on to 2-year colleges, 19% find employment, and the remaining 7% search for a job. If a randomly selected student is not going on to a 2-year college, what is the probability she will be going on to a 4-year college?

    (A) .460
    (B) .540
    (C) .630
    (D) .675
    (E) .730

27. A factory manager claims that the plant's smokestacks spew forth only 350 pounds of pollution per day. A government investigator suspects that the true value is higher and plans a hypothesis test with a critical value of 375 pounds. Suppose the standard deviation in daily pollution poundage is 150 and the true mean is 385 pounds. If the sample size is 100 days, what is the probability that the investigator will mistakenly fail to reject the factory manager's false claim?

    (A) .0475
    (B) .2514
    (C) .7486
    (D) .7514
    (E) .9525

28. In the following table, what value for n results in a table showing perfect independence?

n	52
35	10

    (A) 10
    (B) 17
    (C) 27
    (D) 77
    (E) 182

29. A survey was conducted to determine the percentage of parents who would support raising the legal driving age to 18. The results were stated as 67% with a margin of error of $\pm 3\%$. What is meant by $\pm 3\%$?

    (A) Three percent of the population were not surveyed.
    (B) In the sample, the percentage of parents who would support raising the driving age is between 64% and 70%.
    (C) The percentage of the entire population of parents who would support raising the driving age is between 64% and 70%.
    (D) It is unlikely that the given sample proportion result could be obtained unless the true percentage was between 64% and 70%.
    (E) Between 64% and 70% of the population were surveyed.

30. Following are parts of the probability distributions for the random variables X and Y.

x	$P(x)$	y	$P(y)$
1	.27	1	.35
2	?	2	?
3	.53	3	.15

    If $P(X = 2, Y = 2) = .3$, is it still possible that X and Y are independent?

    (A) Yes, but only if $P(X = 1, Y = 1) = .0945$.
    (B) Yes, but only if $P(X = 3, Y = 3) = .0795$.
    (C) Yes, but only if both of the above hold.
    (D) No.
    (E) There is insufficient information to answer this question.

31. A company officer complains that the average long-distance telephone call charged to a certain department is $5.00. Wanting to defend the department, a clerk gathers data on a random sample of 10 calls. The mean is $3.95 with a standard deviation of $1.07. In which of the following intervals is the P-value located?

    (A) $P < .005$
    (B) $.005 < P < .01$
    (C) $.01 < P < .05$
    (D) $.05 < P < .10$
    (E) $.10 < P$

GO ON TO THE NEXT PAGE ➤

32. Given that the sample has a standard deviation of zero, which of the following statements are true?
   I. The standard deviation of the population is also zero.
   II. The sample mean and sample median are equal.
   III. The sample may have outliers; however, the distribution must be symmetric.
   (A) I only
   (B) II only
   (C) III only
   (D) All are true.
   (E) None is true.

33. Is there a relationship between fitness level and smoking habits? A study reported in the *New England Journal of Medicine* (February 25, 1993, page 535) cross-classified individuals in four categories of fitness and four categories of smoking habits:

	Fitness level			
	Low	Medium	High	
Never smoked	113	113	110	159
Former smokers	119	135	172	190
1 to 9 cigarettes daily	77	91	86	65
≥ 10 cigarettes daily	181	152	124	73

The χ^2-value is 87.6. Is there a relationship between fitness level and smoking habits?
   (A) The data prove that smoking causes lower fitness levels.
   (B) The data prove that lower fitness levels cause people to smoke.
   (C) There is sufficient evidence at the 0.1% significance level of a relationship between fitness level and smoking habits.
   (D) There is sufficient evidence at the 1% level, but not at the 0.1% level, of a relationship between fitness level and smoking habits.
   (E) There is sufficient evidence at the 10% level, but not at the 1% level, of a relationship between fitness level and smoking habits.

34. A poll shows that 65% of the registered voters in a county are Democrats and the rest are Republicans. Suppose that 60% of the Democrats and 50% of the Republicans support a bond issue. What is the probability that a registered voter supports the bond issue? What is the probability that a voter chosen at random who turns out to support the bond issue is a Democrat?
   (A) .535, .650
   (B) .550, .610
   (C) .550, .650
   (D) .550, .690
   (E) .565, .690

35. In one study half of a class were instructed to watch exactly 1 hour of television per day, the other half were told to watch 5 hours per day, and then their class grades were compared. In a second study students in a class responded to a questionnaire asking about their television usage and their class grades.
   (A) The first study was an experiment without a control group, while the second was an observational study.
   (B) The first study was an observational study, while the second was a controlled experiment.
   (C) Both studies were controlled experiments.
   (D) Both studies were observational studies.
   (E) Each study was part controlled experiment and part observational study.

STOP

Section II

Part A

Questions 1–5
Spend about 65 minutes on this part of the exam.
Percentage of Section II grade—75

> You must show all work and indicate the methods you use. You will be graded on the correctness of your methods and on the accuracy of your results and explanations.

---

1. Fuel economy y (in miles per gallon) is tabulated for various speeds x (in miles per hour) for a certain car model. A linear regression model gives $y = -0.16x + 34.8$ with the following residual plot:

A quadratic regression model gives $y = -0.0032x^2 + 0.26x + 23.8$ with the following residual plot:

(a) What does each model predict for fuel economy at 50 miles per hour?
(b) Which model is a better fit? Explain.

2. The Air Force receives 20% of its parachutes from company C1, 55% from company C2, and the rest from company C3. The probability that a parachute will fail to open is .0025, .002, and .0022, depending on whether it is from company C1, C2, or C3, respectively.
   (a) What is the probability that a randomly chosen parachute will fail to open? Show your work.
   (b) If a randomly chosen parachute fails to open, what is the probability that it is from company C3? Show your work.

3. Two studies are run to measure the extent to which taking zinc lozenges helps to shorten the duration of the common cold. Researchers in the first study send questionnaires to all 5000 employees of a major teaching hospital asking whether they have taken zinc lozenges to fight the common cold and what they perceive to be the benefits, if any. The response rate is 90%. The 500 people who did not respond to the first mailing receive follow-up telephone calls, and eventually responses are obtained from over 99% of the hospital employees. Researchers in the second study take a group of 100 volunteers and randomly select 50 to receive zinc lozenges while the others receive a similar-looking, similar-tasting placebo. The volunteers are not told whether they are taking the zinc lozenges, but their doctors know and are asked to accurately measure the duration of common cold symptoms experienced by the volunteers. Comment on the designs of the two studies, remarking on their good points and on possible sources of error.

4. A hospital exercise laboratory technician notes the resting pulse rates of five joggers to be 60, 58, 59, 61, and 67, respectively, while the resting pulse rates of seven nonexercisers are 83, 60, 75, 71, 91, 82, and 84, respectively.
   (a) Establish a 90% confidence interval estimate for the difference in pulse rates between joggers and nonexercisers. Show your work.
   (b) What assumptions are required for the above to be valid?

5. A restaurant owner surveys a random sample of 385 customers to determine whether customer satisfaction is related to gender and age. The numerical data are presented in the following table:

	Young male	Young female	Older male	Older female
Satisfied	25	30	135	112
Not satisfied	8	16	22	37

Is there evidence at the 5% significance level of a relationship between customer satisfaction and age and gender?

GO ON TO THE NEXT PAGE ➤

Section II

Part B

Question 6

Spend about 25 minutes on this part of the exam.

Percentage of Section II grade—25

6. A purchasing agent weighs a sample of 225 bags of rice labeled as containing 50 pounds each with the following results.

Weight (lb):	Below 49.25	49.25–49.75	49.75–50.25	50.25–50.75	Above 50.75
Observed number of bags:	25	61	70	59	10

Test the null hypothesis that the data follow a normal distribution with $\mu = 50$ and $\sigma = 0.5$. Assume a 2.5% and then a 1% significance level. Show your work.

STOP

Answer Key

Section I

1. **D**	8. **E**	15. **E**	22. **E**	29. **D**
2. **E**	9. **E**	16. **E**	23. **B**	30. **D**
3. **C**	10. **C**	17. **A**	24. **B**	31. **B**
4. **B**	11. **D**	18. **A**	25. **B**	32. **B**
5. **A**	12. **C**	19. **D**	26. **D**	33. **C**
6. **A**	13. **B**	20. **D**	27. **B**	34. **E**
7. **B**	14. **A**	21. **B**	28. **E**	35. **A**

Answers Explained

Section I

1. **(D)** $\hat{p} = \frac{73}{89} = .820$ and $\sigma_{\hat{p}} = \sqrt{\frac{(.820)(.180)}{89}} = .0407$. Then $.820 \pm 2.326(.0407) = .820 \pm .095$.

2. **(E)** For a simple random sample, every possible group of the given size has to be equally likely to be selected, and this is not true here. For example, with this procedure it will be impossible for all the early arrivals to be together in the final sample. This procedure is an example of systematic sampling, but systematic sampling does not result in simple random samples.

3. **(C)** We have $H_0: p = .13$, $H_a: p < .13$, and $\sigma_{\hat{p}} = \sqrt{\frac{(.13)(.87)}{200}} = .0238$. The z-score of .10 is $\frac{.10-.13}{.0238} = -1.26$ with a resulting tail probability of .1038.

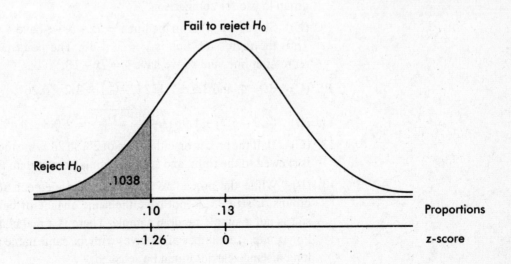

4. **(B)** The critical z-scores for 60% to the right and 70% to the left are -0.253 and 0.524, respectively. Then $\{\mu - 0.253\sigma = 3,\ \mu + 0.524\sigma = 6\}$ gives $\mu = 3.977$ and $\sigma = 3.861$.

5. **(A)**   The cumulative proportions of 0.25 and 0.75 correspond to $Q_1 = 57$ and $Q_3 = 75$, respectively, and so the interquartile range is $75 - 57 = 18$.

6. **(A)**   We have $H_0 : \mu = 3.5$ and $H_a : \mu < 3.5$. Then $\sigma_{\bar{x}} = \frac{0.9}{\sqrt{36}} = 0.15$, the z-score of 3.25 is $\frac{3.25 - 3.5}{0.15} = -1.67$, and Table A gives .0475. (A t-test on the TI-83 gives .0522.)

7. **(B)**   The means and the variances can be added. Thus the new variance is $6^2 + 8^2 = 100$ and the new standard deviation is 10.

8. **(E)**   In experiments on people, subjects can be used as their own controls, with responses noted before and after the treatment. However, with such designs there is always the danger of a placebo effect. In this case, subjects might well have slower reaction times after drinking the alcohol because they think they should. Thus the design of choice would involve a separate control group to use for comparison.

9. **(E)**   Since $(-2, 4)$ is on the line $y = 7x + b$, we have $4 = -14 + b$ and $b = 18$. Thus the regression line is $y = 7x + 18$. The point $(\bar{x}, \bar{y})$ is always on the regression line, and so we have $\bar{y} = 7\bar{x} + 18$.

10. **(C)** $df = 4$, and $3.2 \pm 2.132 \left(\frac{0.274}{\sqrt{5}} \right) = 3.2 \pm 0.261$.

11. **(D)** $(4.5 - 5.3) \pm 1.96 \sqrt{\frac{(1.2)^2}{39} + \frac{(1.1)^2}{46}} = -0.8 \pm 0.493$

12. **(C)**   Half the area is on either side of 23, so 23 is the median. The distribution is skewed to the right, and so the mean is greater than the median.

13. **(B)**   While the procedure does use some element of chance, all possible groups of size 75 do not have the same chance of being picked, so the result is not a simple random sample. There is a real chance of selection bias. For example, a number of relatives with the same name and all using the same long distance carrier might be selected.

14. **(A)**   We have $H_0 : \mu_1 - \mu_2 = 0$, $H_a : \mu_1 - \mu_2 < 0$, and

$$\sigma_{\bar{x}_1 - \bar{x}_2} \approx \sqrt{\frac{s_1^2}{50} + \frac{s_2^2}{60}} = \sqrt{\frac{1.5}{50} + \frac{1.6}{60}} = 0.238$$

The z-score of the observed difference is $\frac{1.8-2.4}{0.238} = -2.52$. From Table A, the resulting P-value is .0059.

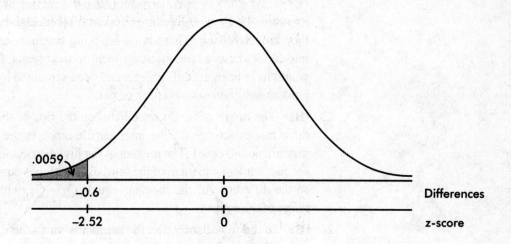

15. **(E)**

$$P(\text{smoker}|\text{cancer}) = \frac{P(\text{smoker} \cap \text{cancer})}{P(\text{cancer})} = \frac{.014}{.035} = .4$$

16. **(E)** The critical z-scores are $\frac{80,000-75,000}{12,000} = 0.42$ and $\frac{100,000-75,000}{12,000} = 2.08$, with corresponding right tail probabilities of .3372 and .0188. The probability of being less than 100,000 given that the mileage is over 80,000 is $\frac{.3372-.0188}{.3372} = .94$.

17. **(A)** $(1.645)\frac{\sqrt{(0.8)^2+(0.5)^2}}{\sqrt{n}} \le 0.25$ gives $\sqrt{n} \ge 6.208$ and $n \ge 38.5$.

18. **(A)** The correlation coefficient is not changed by adding the same number to every value of one of the variables, by multiplying every value of one of the variables by the same positive number, or by interchanging the x- and y-variables.

19. **(D)** If the yields were the same, the expected yield per plot would be

$$\frac{19+31+33+20+22}{5} = 25$$

Using chi-square to measure the difference between the expected and observed yields gives

$$\chi^2 = \frac{6^2}{25} + \frac{6^2}{25} + \frac{8^2}{25} + \frac{5^2}{25} + \frac{3^2}{25} = 6.8$$

With df $= 5 - 1 = 4$, the critical χ^2-values are 9.49 and 7.78 for the .05 and .10 tail probabilities, respectively. Since 6.8 is less than both 9.49 and 7.78, we conclude that there is not sufficient evidence at either of these levels to say that the fertilizers result in different yields.

20. **(D)** Option II gives the highest expected return: $(50,000)(.5)+(10,000)(.5) = 30,000$, which is greater than 25,000 and is also greater than $(100,000)(.05) = 5000$. Option I guarantees that the $20,000 loan will be paid off. Option III provides the only chance of paying off the $80,000 loan. The moral is that the highest expected value is not automatically the "best" answer.

21. **(B)** $P(X \cap Y) = P(X|Y)P(Y) = (.28)(.40) = .112$. Then $P(Y|X) = \frac{P(X \cap Y)}{P(X)} = \frac{.112}{.35} = .32$.

22. **(E)** This study is an experiment because a treatment (extensive exercise) is imposed. There is no blinding because subjects clearly know whether or not they are exercising. There is no blocking because subjects are not divided into blocks before random assignment to treatments. For example, blocking would have been used if subjects had been separated by gender or age before random assignment to exercise or not.

23. **(B)** The range is the distance between the tips of the two whiskers, so all three ranges are equal. The interquartile range is the length of the box, so they are not all equal. The median of the first distribution is equal to Q_3 of the second, while the median of the third distribution is equal to Q_1 of the second, so the difference of the medians equals $Q_3 - Q_1$, which is the interquartile range of the second.

24. **(B)** In the first distribution the median is far to the right, and so the scores are concentrated there, while both the lower whisker and between the median and first quartile are spread out; thus it is skewed to the left. Similarly the third distribution is skewed to the right. Only the middle distribution looks symmetric around its median. There is no such thing as being skewed to both sides.

25. **(B)** A scatterplot would be horizontal; the correlation is zero.

26. **(D)** $\frac{.54}{.54 + .19 + .07} = .675$

27. **(B)** $\sigma_{\bar{x}} = \frac{150}{\sqrt{100}} = 15.0$. With a true mean of 385, the z-score for 375 is $\frac{375 - 385}{15.0} = -0.67$ and the probability to the left of 375 is .2514.

28. **(E)** Relative frequencies must be equal. Either looking at rows gives $\frac{n}{n+52} = \frac{35}{45}$ or looking at columns gives $\frac{n}{n+35} = \frac{52}{62}$. We could also set up a proportion $\frac{n}{52} = \frac{35}{10}$ or $\frac{n}{35} = \frac{52}{10}$. Solving any of these equations gives $n = 182$.

29. **(D)** While the sample proportion is between 64% and 70% (more specifically, it is 67%), this is not the meaning of $\pm 3\%$. While the percentage of the entire population is likely to be between 64% and 70%, this is not known for certain.

30. **(D)** $P(X = 2) = 1 - (.27 + .53) = .2$
$P(Y = 2) = 1 - (.35 + .15) = .5$
$P(X = 2)P(Y = 2) = (.2)(.5) = .1 \neq P(X = 2, Y = 2)$

31. **(B)** We have $H_0: \mu = 5$, $H_a: \mu < 5$, $\bar{x} = 3.95$, $s = 1.07$, and $\sigma_{\bar{x}} = \frac{1.07}{\sqrt{10}} = 0.338$. The t-score of 3.95 is $\frac{3.95 - 5}{0.338} = -3.11$. Looking at the df = 9 row in Table B, note that 3.11 is between 2.821 and 3.250, and so P is between .005 and .01.

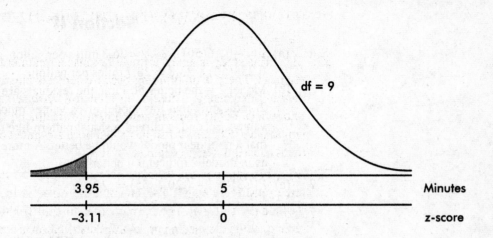

32. **(B)** If the standard deviation of a set is zero, all the values in the set are equal. The mean and median would both equal this common value and so would equal each other. If all the values are equal, there are no outliers. Just because the sample happens to have one common value, there is no reason for this to be true for the whole population.

33. **(C)** Such hypothesis tests suggest relationships but do not prove cause and effect. With $df = (4-1)(4-1) = 9$, the critical χ^2-value with .001 probability in the tail is 27.88. Since $87.6 > 27.88$, there is sufficient evidence at the 0.1% significance level of a relationship between fitness level and smoking habits.

34. **(E)**
$$
\begin{aligned}
P(\text{supports}) &= P(\text{Dem} \cap \text{supports}) + P(\text{Rep} \cap \text{supports}) \\
&= (.65)(.60) + (.35)(.50) \\
&= .390 + .175 \\
&= .565 \\
P(\text{Dem}|\text{supports}) &= \frac{.390}{.565} \\
&= .690
\end{aligned}
$$

35. **(A)** The first study is an experiment with two treatment groups and no control group. The second study is observational; the researcher did not randomly divide the subjects into groups and have each group watch a designated number of hours of television per night.

Section II

1. (a) $y = -0.16(50) + 34.8 = 26.8$ miles per gallon, and $y = -0.0032(50)^2 + 0.258(50) + 23.8 = 28.7$ miles per gallon.

   (b) Model 2 is the better fit. First, the residuals are much smaller for model 2, indicating that this model gives values much closer to the observed values. Second, a curved residual pattern like that in model 1 indicates that a nonlinear model would be better. A more uniform residual scatter as in model 2 indicates a better fit.

2. (a) $P(C3) = 1 - (.20 + .55) = .25$

   C1 —— .0025 —— fails $P(C1 \cap \text{fails}) = (.20)(.0025) = .0005$
   .20

   .55
   C2 —— .002 —— fails $P(C2 \cap \text{fails}) = (.55)(.002) = .0011$
   .25

   C3 —— .0022 —— fails $P(C3 \cap \text{fails}) = (.25)(.0022) = .00055$

   $P(\text{fails}) = .0005 + .0011 + .00055 = .00215$

   (b)
   $$P(C3|\text{fails}) = \frac{P(C3 \cap \text{fails})}{P(\text{fails})} = \frac{.00055}{.00215} = .256$$

3. The first study, an observational study, does not suffer from nonresponse bias, as do most studies involving mailed questionnaires, because the researchers made follow-up telephone calls and achieved a very high response rate. However, the first study suffers terribly from selection bias. People who work at a teaching hospital are not representative of the general population. One would expect many of them to have heard about how zinc coats the throat to hinder the propagation of viruses. The second study, a controlled experiment, used comparison between a treatment group and a control group, used randomization in selecting who went into each group, and used blinding to control for a placebo effect on the part of the volunteers. However, they did not use double-blinding; that is, the doctors knew whether their patients were receiving the zinc lozenges, and this could introduce hidden bias as the doctors make judgments about their patients' health.

4. (a) $\bar{x}_1 = 61$, $s_1 = 3.54$, $\bar{x}_2 = 78$, and $s_2 = 10.23$. If the population variances are believed to be different, use the unpooled
   $$\sigma_{\bar{x}_1 - \bar{x}_2} = \sqrt{\frac{(3.54)^2}{5} + \frac{(10.23)^2}{7}} = 4.178$$

   and let df $= 5 - 1 = 4$ (the smaller of $n_1 - 1$ and $n_2 - 1$). Then the confidence interval is $(61 - 78) \pm 2.132(4.178) = -17 \pm 8.9$.

   If the variances are believed to be the same, use the pooled
   $$\sigma_{\bar{x}_1 - \bar{x}_2} = \sqrt{\frac{4(3.54)^2 + 6(10.23)^2}{5 + 7 - 2}} \sqrt{\frac{1}{5} + \frac{1}{7}} = 4.822$$

and let $df = (5-1)+(7-1) = 10$. Then the confidence interval estimate is $(61-78) \pm 1.812(4.822) = -17 \pm 8.7$.

(b) We must assume that each population is normally distributed. In addition, to use the pooled standard deviation with the larger degrees of freedom we must assume that the variances of the two populations are equal.

5. Total the rows and columns and then find the expected numbers if customer satisfaction is independent of gender and age by multiplying row totals by column totals and dividing by 385:

25.9	36.1	123.1	116.9	302
7.1	9.9	33.9	32.1	83
33	46	157	149	385

The difference between observed and expected values is measured by chi-square:

$$\chi^2 = \frac{(25-25.9)^2}{25.9} + \frac{(34-36.1)^2}{36.1} + \frac{(129-123.1)^2}{123.1} + \frac{(112-116.9)^2}{116.9}$$
$$+ \frac{(8-7.1)^2}{7.1} + \frac{(12-9.9)^2}{9.9} + \frac{(28-33.9)^2}{33.9} + \frac{(37-32.1)^2}{32.1}$$
$$= 11.1$$

At the 5% significance level with $df = (2-1)(4-1) = 3$, the critical χ^2-value is 7.81. Since $11.1 > 7.81$, there is sufficient evidence to reject independence and conclude that customer satisfaction is related to gender and age.

6. The z-scores for 50.25 and 50.75 are, respectively, $\frac{50.25-50}{0.5} = 0.5$ and $\frac{50.75-50}{0.5} = 1.5$. Similarly, 49.75 and 49.25 have z-scores of -0.5 and -1.5, respectively. Using Table A, we find these values:

Multiplying each probability by 225 gives the expected numbers of bags for the corresponding weight ranges: $.0668(225) = 15.03$, $.2417(225) = 54.38$, $.3830(225) = 86.18$.

Weight (lb):	Below 49.25	49.25–49.75	49.75–50.25	50.25–50.75	Above 50.75
Expected number of bags:	15.03	54.38	86.18	54.38	15.03

The difference between observed and expected numbers can be measured using chi-square. Thus

$$\chi^2 = \frac{(25 - 15.03)^2}{15.03} + \frac{(61 - 54.38)^2}{54.38}$$
$$+ \frac{(70 - 86.18)^2}{86.18} + \frac{(59 - 54.38)^2}{54.38} + \frac{(10 - 15.03)^2}{15.03}$$
$$= 12.533$$

H_0: good fit to a normal distribution with $\mu = 50$ and $\sigma = 0.5$

With df $= 5 - 1 = 4$ and a tail probability of .025, the critical χ^2-value is 11.14, while a tail probability of .01 results in a critical χ^2-value of 13.28. Since $12.533 > 11.14$ and $12.533 < 13.28$, we have sufficient evidence to reject H_0 at the 2.5% significance level but not at the 1% level. Thus, if the purchasing agent is willing to accept a 2.5% risk of mistakenly rejecting a correct 50-pound claim, she should conclude that the distribution of weights of rice bags is not normal.

Answer Sheet: Practice Examination 5

1. Ⓐ Ⓑ Ⓒ Ⓓ Ⓔ
2. Ⓐ Ⓑ Ⓒ Ⓓ Ⓔ
3. Ⓐ Ⓑ Ⓒ Ⓓ Ⓔ
4. Ⓐ Ⓑ Ⓒ Ⓓ Ⓔ
5. Ⓐ Ⓑ Ⓒ Ⓓ Ⓔ
6. Ⓐ Ⓑ Ⓒ Ⓓ Ⓔ
7. Ⓐ Ⓑ Ⓒ Ⓓ Ⓔ
8. Ⓐ Ⓑ Ⓒ Ⓓ Ⓔ
9. Ⓐ Ⓑ Ⓒ Ⓓ Ⓔ
10. Ⓐ Ⓑ Ⓒ Ⓓ Ⓔ
11. Ⓐ Ⓑ Ⓒ Ⓓ Ⓔ
12. Ⓐ Ⓑ Ⓒ Ⓓ Ⓔ

13. Ⓐ Ⓑ Ⓒ Ⓓ Ⓔ
14. Ⓐ Ⓑ Ⓒ Ⓓ Ⓔ
15. Ⓐ Ⓑ Ⓒ Ⓓ Ⓔ
16. Ⓐ Ⓑ Ⓒ Ⓓ Ⓔ
17. Ⓐ Ⓑ Ⓒ Ⓓ Ⓔ
18. Ⓐ Ⓑ Ⓒ Ⓓ Ⓔ
19. Ⓐ Ⓑ Ⓒ Ⓓ Ⓔ
20. Ⓐ Ⓑ Ⓒ Ⓓ Ⓔ
21. Ⓐ Ⓑ Ⓒ Ⓓ Ⓔ
22. Ⓐ Ⓑ Ⓒ Ⓓ Ⓔ
23. Ⓐ Ⓑ Ⓒ Ⓓ Ⓔ
24. Ⓐ Ⓑ Ⓒ Ⓓ Ⓔ

25. Ⓐ Ⓑ Ⓒ Ⓓ Ⓔ
26. Ⓐ Ⓑ Ⓒ Ⓓ Ⓔ
27. Ⓐ Ⓑ Ⓒ Ⓓ Ⓔ
28. Ⓐ Ⓑ Ⓒ Ⓓ Ⓔ
29. Ⓐ Ⓑ Ⓒ Ⓓ Ⓔ
30. Ⓐ Ⓑ Ⓒ Ⓓ Ⓔ
31. Ⓐ Ⓑ Ⓒ Ⓓ Ⓔ
32. Ⓐ Ⓑ Ⓒ Ⓓ Ⓔ
33. Ⓐ Ⓑ Ⓒ Ⓓ Ⓔ
34. Ⓐ Ⓑ Ⓒ Ⓓ Ⓔ
35. Ⓐ Ⓑ Ⓒ Ⓓ Ⓔ

Practice Examination 5

Section I
Questions 1–35

Spend 90 minutes on this part of the exam.

Directions: The questions or incomplete statements that follow are each followed by five suggested answers or completions. Choose the response that best answers the question or completes the statement.

For Questions 1 and 2 consider the following:
A survey to measure job satisfaction of high school mathematics teachers was taken in 1993 and repeated 5 years later in 1998. Each year a random sample of 50 teachers rated their job satisfaction on a 1-to-100 scale with higher numbers indicating greater satisfaction. The results are given in the following back-to-back stemplot.

```
         1993          1998
                  │ 0 │
           98775  │ 1 │
           98530  │ 2 │ 1
           65210  │ 3 │ 3589
           96430  │ 4 │ 01122233455667889999
           87421  │ 5 │ 035667899
99877555322100    │ 6 │ 1344789
          976442  │ 7 │ 22689
            7511  │ 8 │ 138
               0  │ 9 │ 7
```

1. What is the trend from 1993 to 1998 with regard to the mean and median job satisfaction ratings of the two samples?
   (A) Both the mean and median increased.
   (B) The mean increased, while the median decreased.
   (C) The mean remained the same, while the median decreased.
   (D) The median increased, while the mean decreased.
   (E) Both the mean and median decreased.

2. What is the trend from 1993 to 1998 with regard to the standard deviation and range of the two samples?
   (A) Both the standard deviation and range increased.
   (B) The standard deviation increased, while the range decreased.
   (C) The range increased, while the standard deviation decreased.
   (D) Both the standard deviation and range decreased.
   (E) Both the standard deviation and range remained unchanged.

---

3. Consider the following studies being run by three different AP Statistics instructors.
   I. One rewards students every day with lollipops for relaxation, encouragement, and motivation to learn the material.
   II. One promises that all students will receive A's as long as they give their best efforts to learn the material.
   III. One is available every day after school and on weekends so that students with questions can come in and learn the material.
   (A) None of these studies use randomization.
   (B) None of these studies use control groups.
   (C) None of these studies use blinding.
   (D) Important information can be found from all these studies, but none can establish causal relationships.
   (E) All of the above.

GO ON TO THE NEXT PAGE ➤

4. The number of days it takes to build a new house has a variance of 386. A sample of 40 new homes shows an average building time of 83 days. With what confidence can we assert that the average building time for a new house is between 80 and 90 days?
   - (A) 15.4%
   - (B) 17.8%
   - (C) 20.0%
   - (D) 38.8%
   - (E) 82.2%

5. A shipment of resistors have an average resistance of 200 ohms with a standard deviation of 5 ohms, and the resistances are normally distributed. Suppose a randomly chosen resistor has a resistance under 194 ohms. What is the probability that its resistance is greater than 188 ohms?
   - (A) .07
   - (B) .12
   - (C) .50
   - (D) .93
   - (E) .97

6. Suppose 4% of the population have a certain disease. A laboratory blood test gives a positive reading for 95% of people who have the disease and for 5% of people who do not have the disease. What is the probability of testing positive? If a person tests positive, what is the probability the person has the disease?
   - (A) .086, .442
   - (B) .086, .500
   - (C) .086, .914
   - (D) .500, .950
   - (E) .914, .950

7. A service station advertises that its mechanics can change a muffler in only 15 minutes. A consumers' group doubts this claim and runs a hypothesis test using 49 cars needing new mufflers. In this sample the mean changing time is 16.25 minutes with a standard deviation of 3.5 minutes. Is this strong evidence against the 15 minute claim?
   - (A) Yes, because the P-value is .0062.
   - (B) Yes, because the P-value is 2.5.
   - (C) No, because the P-value is only .0062.
   - (D) No, because the P-value is higher than 2.0.
   - (E) No, because the P-value is .4938.

8. Suppose that the regression line for a set of data, $y = mx + 3$, passes through the point (2, 5). If $\bar{x}$ and $\bar{y}$ are the sample means of the x- and y-values, respectively, then $\bar{y} =$
   - (A) $\bar{x}$.
   - (B) $\bar{x} - 2$.
   - (C) $\bar{x} + 3$.
   - (D) $2\bar{x} + 3$.
   - (E) $3\bar{x} + 3$.

9. Which of the following are true statements?
   - I. While observational studies gather information on an already existing condition, they still often involve intentionally forcing some treatment to note the response.
   - II. In an experiment, researchers decide on the treatment but typically allow the subjects to self-select into the control group.
   - III. If properly designed, either observational studies or controlled experiments can easily be used to establish cause and effect.
   - (A) I only
   - (B) II only
   - (C) III only
   - (D) All are true.
   - (E) None is true.

GO ON TO THE NEXT PAGE ➤

10. In a random sample of 500 spectators who attend either high school football or basketball games but not both, food was purchased in the following amounts.

	Hot dogs	Popcorn	No purchase
Football	240	80	30
Basketball	50	90	10

What percentage of spectators at football games bought popcorn? What percentage of hot dog purchasers were at basketball games?
(A) 16%, 10%
(B) 16%, 17%
(C) 23%, 10%
(D) 23%, 17%
(E) 47%, 33%

11. To determine the mean cost of groceries in a certain city, an identical grocery basket of food is purchased at each store in a random sample of ten stores. If the average cost is $47.52 with a standard deviation of $1.59, find a 98% confidence interval estimate for the cost of these groceries in the city.
(A) $47.52 ± $0.449
(B) $47.52 ± $1.170
(C) $47.52 ± $1.390
(D) $47.52 ± $1.418
(E) $47.52 ± $4.485

12. A set consists of four numbers. The largest value is 200, and the range is 50. Which of the following statements is true?
(A) The mean is less than 185.
(B) The mean is greater than 165.
(C) The median is less than 195.
(D) The median is greater than 155.
(E) The median is the mean of the second and third numbers if the set is arranged in ascending order.

13. A telephone survey of 400 registered voters showed that 256 had not yet made up their minds 1 month before the election. How sure can we be that between 60% and 68% of the electorate were still undecided at that time?
(A) 2.4%
(B) 8.0%
(C) 64.0%
(D) 90.5%
(E) 95.3%

14. Suppose we have a random variable X where the probability associated with the value k is $\binom{15}{k}(.29)^k(.71)^{15-k}$ for $k = 0, \ldots, 15$. What is the mean of X?
(A) 0.29
(B) 0.71
(C) 4.35
(D) 10.65
(E) None of the above

15. A producer knows that unless a new show is watched by at least 25% of the possible audience it will be canceled. Suppose a quick survey finds that only 21 out of 100 television viewers tuned into the show. Is this sufficient evidence that the show should be canceled?
(A) Yes, because .21 < .25.
(B) Yes, because the P-value is only .0433.
(C) No, because the difference, .04, is not much.
(D) No, because the P-value is greater than .10.
(E) No, because important decisions such as this should not be based simply on a sample of a large population.

16. Suppose X and Y are random variables with $E(X) = 312$, var $(X) = 6$, $E(Y) = 307$, and var $(Y) = 8$. What are the expected value and variance of the random variable $X + Y$?
(A) $E(X+Y) = 619$, var $(X+Y) = 7$
(B) $E(X+Y) = 619$, var $(X+Y) = 10$
(C) $E(X+Y) = 619$, var $(X+Y) = 14$
(D) $E(X+Y) = 309.5$ var $(X+Y) = 14$
(E) There is insufficient information to answer this question.

GO ON TO THE NEXT PAGE ➤

17. Consider the following three events:
    I. In a survey about former drug use, an embarrassed politician deliberately gives the wrong answers.
    II. A surveyor mistakenly records answers to one question in the wrong place.
    III. Although 6% of the adult population is unemployed, in a random sample of ten adults, all are employed.

    Which of the following correctly characterizes the above?
    (A) I, response bias; II, human mistake; III, sampling error
    (B) I, nonresponse bias; II, hidden error; III, sampling error
    (C) I, voluntary sample bias; II, sampling error; III, hidden bias
    (D) I, voluntary error; II, unintentional error; III, undercoverage error
    (E) I, deliberate error; II, mistaken error; III, small sample error

18. The following histogram gives the shoe sizes of people in an elementary school building one morning.

    Which of the following statements are true?
    I. The same number of people had size 9 shoes as had size 10 shoes.
    II. The median shoe size was $7\frac{1}{2}$.
    III. The mean shoe size was less than the median shoe size.
    (A) II only
    (B) I and II
    (C) I and III
    (D) II and III
    (E) I, II, and III

19. A realtor believes that the average rent in one location exceeds the average rent in a second location by more than the published figure of $125. She runs a hypothesis test on a random sample of 30 rental units in each location and obtains averages of $480 and $330 and standard deviations of $95 and $80, respectively, for the two locations. In which of the following intervals is the P-value?
    (A) $P < .01$
    (B) $.01 < P < .025$
    (C) $.025 < P < .05$
    (D) $.05 < P < .10$
    (E) $P > .10$

20. Given a probability of .65 that interest rates will jump this year, and a probability of .72 that if interest rates jump the stock market will decline, what is the probability that interest rates will jump and the stock market will decline?
    (A) .070
    (B) .097
    (C) .468
    (D) .532
    (E) .903

GO ON TO THE NEXT PAGE ➤

21. A building inspector inspects four major construction sites every day. In a sample 100 days, the number of times each site passed inspection was

Site:	A	B	C	D
Passed:	45	33	67	83

Test the hypothesis that sites C and D pass inspection twice as often as sites A and B, that is, that the frequency of passing inspection is in the ratio 1:1:2:2.

(A) There is sufficient evidence at both the 10% and 5% significance levels that there is not a good fit with the indicated ratio.

(B) There is sufficient evidence at the 10% level, but not at the 5% level, that there is not a good fit with the indicated ratio.

(C) There is sufficient evidence at the 5% level, but not at the 10% level, that there is not a good fit with the indicated ratio.

(D) There is not sufficient evidence at either the 10% or 5% significance levels that there is not a good fit with the indicated ratio.

(E) There is not sufficient information to answer the question.

22. Suppose that the weights of trucks traveling on the interstate highway system are normally distributed. If 70% of the trucks weigh more than 12,000 pounds and 80% weigh more than 10,000 pounds, what are the mean and standard deviation for the weights of trucks traveling on the interstate system?

(A) $\mu = 14,896$; $\sigma = 6089$
(B) $\mu = 15,096$; $\sigma = 6189$
(C) $\mu = 15,296$; $\sigma = 6289$
(D) $\mu = 15,496$; $\sigma = 6389$
(E) The mean and standard deviation cannot be computed from the information given.

23. If the correlation coefficient $r = .78$, what percentage of variation in y is explained by variation in x?

(A) 22%
(B) 39%
(C) 44%
(D) 61%
(E) 78%

24. Consider the following scatterplot:

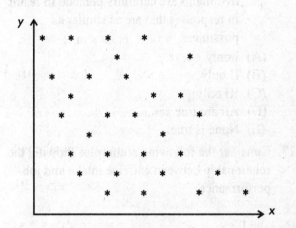

Which of the following is the best estimate of the correlation between x and y?

(A) $-.95$
(B) $-.15$
(C) 0
(D) .15
(E) .95

25. For one NBA playoff game the actual percentage of the television viewing public who watched the game was 24%. If you had taken a survey of 50 television viewers that night and constructed a confidence interval estimate of the percentage watching the game, which of the following would have been true?

I. The center of the interval would have been 24%.
II. The interval would have contained 24%.
III. A 99% confidence interval estimate would have contained 24%.

(A) I and II
(B) I and III
(C) II and III
(D) All are true.
(E) None is true.

26. Which of the following are true statements?
    I. In a well-designed, well-conducted sample survey, sampling error is effectively eliminated.
    II. In a well-designed observational study, responses are influenced through an orderly, carefully planned procedure during the collection of data.
    III. In a well-designed experiment, the treatments are carefully planned to result in responses that are as similar as possible.
    (A) I only
    (B) II only
    (C) III only
    (D) All are true.
    (E) None is true.

27. Consider the following scatterplot showing the relationship between caffeine intake and job performance.

Which of the following is a reasonable conclusion?
    (A) Low caffeine intake is associated with low job performance.
    (B) Low caffeine intake is associated with high job performance.
    (C) High caffeine intake is associated with low job performance.
    (D) High caffeine intake is associated with high job performance.
    (E) Job performance cannot be predicted from caffeine intake.

28. An author of a new book claims that anyone following his suggested diet program will lose an average of 2.8 pounds per week. A researcher believes that the true figure will be lower and plans a test involving a random sample of 36 overweight people. She will reject the author's claim if the mean weight loss in the volunteer group is less than 2.5 pounds per week. Assume that the standard deviation among individuals is 1.2 pounds per week. If the true mean value is 2.4 pounds per week, what is the probability that the researcher will mistakenly fail to reject the author's false claim of 2.8 pounds?
    (A) .0228
    (B) .3085
    (C) .6915
    (D) .8085
    (E) .9772

29. The following graph shows cumulative proportions with regard to outstanding balances on credit cards.

What is the interquartile range?
    (A) $200
    (B) $600
    (C) $1550
    (D) $1750
    (E) $2000

30. The 26 contestants in the pentathlon event of the 1992 Olympics ran the 200-meter dash in the following times (in seconds): 25.44, 24.39, 25.66, 23.93, 23.34, 25.01, 24.27, 24.54, 25.44, 24.86, 23.95, 23.31, 24.60, 23.12, 25.29, 24.40, 25.24, 24.43, 23.70, 25.20, 25.09, 24.48, 26.13, 25.28, 24.18, and 23.83 (*Journal of the American Statistical Association,* September 1994, page 1101). In testing the null hypothesis that the mean time required for pentathlon contestants to run this race is 25 seconds against the alternative hypothesis that the mean time required is less than 25 seconds, in which of the following intervals is the *P*-value located?

(A) $P < .005$
(B) $.005 < P < .01$
(C) $.01 < P < .05$
(D) $.05 < P < .10$
(E) $.10 < P$

31. A judge chosen at random reaches a just decision roughly 80% of the time. What is the probability that in randomly chosen cases at least two out of three judges reach a just decision?

(A) .384
(B) .488
(C) .512
(D) .616
(E) .896

32. A study was conducted to determine the effectiveness of varying amounts of vitamin C in reducing the number of common colds. A survey of 450 people provided the following information:

	Daily amount of vitamin C taken		
	None	500 mg	1000 mg
No colds	57	26	17
At least one cold	223	84	43

Is there evidence of a relationship between catching a cold and taking vitamin C?

(A) The data prove that vitamin C reduces the number of common colds.
(B) The data prove that vitamin C has no effect on the number of common colds.
(C) There is sufficient evidence at the 1% significance level of a relationship between taking vitamin C and catching fewer colds.
(D) There is sufficient evidence at the 10% significance level, but not at the 1% significance level, of a relationship between taking vitamin C and catching fewer colds.
(E) There is not sufficient evidence at the 10% level of a relationship between taking vitamin C and catching fewer colds.

GO ON TO THE NEXT PAGE ➤

33. What fault do all these sampling designs have in common?
    I. The Parent-Teacher Association (PTA), concerned about rising teenage pregnancy rates at a high school, randomly picks a sample of high school students and interviews them concerning unprotected sex they have engaged in during the past year.
    II. A radio talk show host asks people to phone in their views on whether the United States should keep troops in Bosnia indefinitely to enforce the ceasefire.
    III. The *Ladies Home Journal* plans to predict the winner of a national election based on a survey of its readers.
    (A) All the designs make improper use of stratification.
    (B) All the designs have errors that can lead to strong bias.
    (C) All the designs confuse association with cause and effect.
    (D) All the designs suffer from sampling error.
    (E) None of the designs makes use of chance in selecting a sample.

34. Hospital administrators wish to determine the average length of stay for all surgical patients. A statistician determines that for a 95% confidence level estimate of the average length of stay to within ±0.25 days, 100 surgical patients' records would have to be examined. How many records should be looked at for a 95% confidence level estimate to within ±0.25 days?
    (A) 25
    (B) 50
    (C) 200
    (D) 400
    (E) There is not enough information given to determine the necessary sample size.

35. Following are parts of the probability distributions for the random variables X and Y.

x	$P(x)$	y	$P(y)$
1	?	1	?
2	?	2	?
3	?	3	.1

If X and Y are independent and the joint probabilities $P(X = 1, Y = 2) = .186$, $P(X = 2, Y = 2) = .198$, and $P(X = 3, Y = 2) = .216$, what is $P(X = 1, Y = 1)$?
    (A) .031
    (B) .036
    (C) .093
    (D) .099
    (E) .108

STOP

Section II

Part A

Questions 1–5
Spend about 65 minutes on this part of the exam.
Percentage of Section II grade—75

You must show all work and indicate the methods you use. You will be graded on the correctness of your methods and on the accuracy of your results and explanations.

---

1. An article ("Undergraduate Marijuana Use and Anger" by Sue B. Stoner) in a 1988 issue of the *Journal of Psychology* (Vol. 122, p. 343) reported that in a sample of 17 marijuana users, the mean and standard deviation on an anger expression scale were $\bar{x} = 42.72$ and $s = 6.05$.

   (a) Test whether this result is significantly greater than the established mean of 41.6 for nonusers. Show your work.

   (b) What assumptions are necessary for the above test to be valid?

2. The following scatterplot shows the pulse rate drop (in beats per minute) plotted against the amount of medication (in grams) of an experimental drug being field-tested in several hospitals.

A computer printout showing the results of fitting a straight line to the data by the method of least squares gives

```
PulseRateDrop = -1.68 + 8.5 Grams
R-sq = 81.9%
```

(a) Find the correlation coefficient for the relationship between pulse rate drop and grams of medication.

(b) What is the slope of the regression line and what does it signify?

(c) Predict the pulse rate drop for a patient given 2.25 grams of medication.

(d) A patient given 5 grams of medication has his pulse rate drop to zero. Does this invalidate the regression equation? Explain.

(e) How will the size of the correlation coefficient change if the 3-gram result is removed from the data set? Explain.

(f) How will the size of the slope of the least squares regression line change if the 3-gram result is removed from the data set? Explain.

3. Five partners in a law firm brought in the following numbers of new clients during the past year:

Partner:	Jones	Smith	Brown	Allen	Cross
Number of new clients:	35	42	22	41	30

Is there sufficient evidence at the 5% or 10% significance level that the partners do not bring in equal numbers of new clients? Show your work.

4. At a certain college 10% of female students in business administration take one mathematics course, 20% take two, 30% take three, and the rest take four. Of those taking just one mathematics course, 15% successfully complete all their business courses on the first attempt, while the success rate rises to 25%, 55%, and 85%, respectively, for those taking two, three, and four mathematics courses.

(a) What is the probability that a randomly chosen female business administration major will successfully complete all her business courses on the first attempt? Show your work.

(b) If a randomly chosen female business administration student successfully completes all her business courses on the first attempt, what is the probability that she has taken at least three mathematics courses? Show your work.

5. Explain how you would design an experiment to evaluate whether praying for a hospitalized heart attack patient leads to a speedier recovery. Show how you would incorporate comparison, randomization, and blinding.

GO ON TO THE NEXT PAGE ➤

Section II

Part B

Question 6
Spend about 25 minutes on this part of the exam.
Percentage of Section II grade—25

6. As reported in *Chances: Risks and Odds in Everyday Life* by James Burke, a research team at Cornell University conducted a study in which they concluded that 10% of all businessmen who wear ties wear them so tight that they reduce blood flow to the brain, diminishing cerebral functions.

   (a) Assuming the 10% figure is correct, use simulation to determine the approximate probability that at a board meeting of ten businessmen, all of whom wear ties, at least two are wearing their ties too tight. Show your work.

8417706757	1761315582	5150681435	4105092031	0644905059	5988431180
5311584469	9486857967	0581184514	7501113006	6339555041	1586606589
1311971020	8594091932	0648874987	5435552704	9035902649	4749671567
9426808844	2629464759	0898957024	9728400637	8928303514	5919507635
0330972605	2935723737	6788103668	3387635841	5286923114	1586438942

   (b) Calculate the above probability exactly. Show your work.
   (c) Suppose you believe the Cornell University claim is too high and run a hypothesis test. If in a random sample of 200 businessmen who wear ties you find only 17 wearing them too tight, what will be your conclusion? Explain your answer.

STOP

Answer Key

Section I

1. **B**	8. **C**	15. **D**	22. **C**	29. **C**
2. **C**	9. **E**	16. **E**	23. **D**	30. **B**
3. **E**	10. **D**	17. **A**	24. **B**	31. **E**
4. **E**	11. **D**	18. **C**	25. **E**	32. **E**
5. **D**	12. **E**	19. **E**	26. **E**	33. **B**
6. **A**	13. **D**	20. **C**	27. **E**	34. **D**
7. **A**	14. **C**	21. **D**	28. **B**	35. **C**

Answers Explained

Section I

1. **(B)** The median decreased from approximately 60 to 50, while the mean actually increased (note the skewness).

2. **(C)** The range increased from $90 - 15 = 75$ to $97 - 21 = 76$, while the standard deviation decreased (note how the values are bunched together more closely in 1998).

3. **(E)** None of the studies have any controls such as randomization, a control group, or blinding, and so while they may give valuable information, they cannot establish cause and effect.

4. **(E)** $\sigma_{\bar{x}} = \frac{\sqrt{386}}{\sqrt{40}} = 3.106$. The critical z-scores are $\frac{80-83}{3.106} = -0.97$ and $\frac{90-83}{3.106} = 2.25$, resulting in a probability of $.3340 + .4878 = .8218$.

5. **(D)** The critical z-scores are $\frac{188-200}{5} = -2.4$ and $\frac{194-200}{5} = -1.2$, with corresponding left tail probabilities of .0082 and .1151, respectively. The probability of being greater than 188 given that it is less than 194 is $\frac{.1151-.0082}{.1151} = .93$.

6. **(A)**
$$
\begin{aligned}
P(\text{pos test}) &= P(\text{disease} \cap \text{pos}) + P(\text{healthy} \cap \text{pos}) \\
&= (.04)(.95) + (.96)(.05) \\
&= .038 + .048 = .086
\end{aligned}
$$
$$
P(\text{disease}|\text{pos test}) = \frac{.038}{.086} = .442
$$

7. **(A)** We have $H_0: \mu = 15$, and $H_a: \mu > 15$. Then $\sigma_{\bar{x}} = \frac{3.5}{\sqrt{49}} = 0.5$, the z-score of 16.25 is $\frac{16.25-15}{0.5} = 2.5$, and so the P-value is $1 - .9938 = .0062$. With such a small P, there *is* sufficient evidence to doubt the 15 minute claim.

8. **(C)** Since $(2, 5)$ is on the line $y = mx + 3$, we have $5 = 2m + 3$ and $m = 1$. Thus the regression line is $y = x + 3$. The point $(\bar{x}, \bar{y})$ is always on the regression line, and so we have $\bar{y} = \bar{x} + 3$.

9. **(E)** Intentionally forcing some treatment to note the response is associated with controlled experiments, not with observational studies. In experiments, the researchers decide how people are placed in different groups; self-selection is associated with observational studies. Results of observational studies may suggest cause-and-effect relationships; however, controlled studies are used to establish such relationships.

10. **(D)** $P(\text{popcorn}|\text{football}) = \frac{80}{350} = 23\%$, and $P(\text{basketball}|\text{hot dogs}) = \frac{50}{290} = 17\%$.

11. **(D)** $df = 9$, and $47.52 \pm 2.821 \left(\frac{1.59}{\sqrt{10}} \right) = 47.52 \pm 1.418$.

12. **(E)** The set could be $\{150, 150, 150, 200\}$ with mean 162.5 and median 150. It might also be $\{150, 200, 200, 200\}$ with mean 187.5 and median 200. The median of a set of four elements is the mean of the two middle elements.

13. **(D)** $\hat{p} = \frac{256}{400} = .64$, and $\sigma_{\hat{p}} = \sqrt{\frac{(.64)(.36)}{400}} = .024$. The z-scores of .60 and .68 are $\pm \frac{.04}{.024} = \pm 1.67$ for a probability of $.9525 - .0475 = .9050$.

14. **(C)** This is a binomial with $n = 15$ and $p = .29$, and so the mean is $np = 15(.29) = 4.35$.

15. **(D)** We have $H_0: p = .25$, $H_a: p < .25$, and $\sigma_{\hat{p}} = \sqrt{\frac{(.25)(.75)}{100}} = .0433$. The z-score of .21 is $\frac{.21 - .25}{.0433} = -0.92$, and thus the P-value is .1788. A high P-value like this shows very little evidence for rejecting H_0.

16. **(E)** Without independence we cannot determine var $(X+Y)$ from the information given.

17. **(A)** Embarrassing questions and resulting untruthful answers are an example of response bias. Inaccuracies and mistakes due to human error are a real concern to researchers. The natural variation in samples is called sampling error.

18. **(C)** Relative frequency is given by relative area. The distribution is skewed to the left, and so the mean is less than the median.

19. **(E)** In this problem the null hypothesis is not that the difference is 0. We have $H_0: \mu_1 - \mu_2 = 125$, $H_a: \mu_1 - \mu_2 > 125$, and

$$\sigma_{\bar{x}_1 - \bar{x}_2} \approx \sqrt{\frac{(95)^2}{30} + \frac{(80)^2}{30}} = 22.68$$

The observed difference is $480 - 330 = 150$ with z-score $\frac{150 - 125}{22.68} = 1.10$. The corresponding P-value is $1 - .8643 = .1357$.

20. **(C)**

$$P\left(\begin{matrix}\text{market}\\\text{decline}\end{matrix} \cap \begin{matrix}\text{interest}\\\text{jumps}\end{matrix}\right) = P\left(\begin{matrix}\text{market}\\\text{decline}\end{matrix} \middle| \begin{matrix}\text{interest}\\\text{jumps}\end{matrix}\right) P\left(\begin{matrix}\text{interest}\\\text{jumps}\end{matrix}\right)$$
$$= (.72)(.65)$$
$$= .468$$

21. **(D)**   We have H_0: good fit with a 1:1:2:2 ratio. Noting that $45 + 33 + 74 + 76 = 228$, $\left(\frac{1}{6}\right) 228 = 38$, and $\left(\frac{2}{6}\right) 228 = 76$, we have the following table of expected values:

Site:	A	B	C	D
Passed inspection:	38	38	76	76

The difference between the observed and expected values is measured by chi-square:

$$\chi^2 = \frac{7^2}{38} + \frac{5^2}{38} + \frac{9^2}{76} + \frac{7^2}{76} = 3.65$$

With df $= 4 - 1 = 3$, the critical χ^2-values for tail probabilities of .10 and .05 are 6.25 and 7.81, respectively. Since 3.65 is less than both of these values, there is not sufficient evidence to reject H_0 at either of these levels.

22. **(C)**   The critical z-scores for 70% to the right and 80% to the right are -0.524 and -0.842, respectively. Then $\{\mu - 0.524\sigma = 12,000, \mu - 0.842\sigma = 10,000\}$ gives $\mu = 15,296$ and $\sigma = 6289$.

23. **(D)**   The percentage of the variation in y explained by the variation in x is given by the coefficient of determination r^2. In this example, $(.78)^2 = .61$.

24. **(B)**   There is a weak negative correlation, and so $-.15$ is the only reasonable possibility among the choices given.

25. **(E)**   There is no guarantee that 24 is anywhere near the interval, and so none of the statements are true.

26. **(E)**   Sampling error relates to natural variation between samples, and it can never be eliminated. In good observational studies, responses are not influenced during the collection of data. In good experiments, treatments are compared as to the differences in responses.

27. **(E)**   The scatterplot suggests a zero correlation.

28. **(B)** $\sigma_{\bar{x}} = \frac{1.2}{\sqrt{36}} = 0.2$. The z-score of 2.5 is $\frac{2.5 - 2.4}{0.2} = 0.5$, and the probability to the right of 2.5 is $1 - .6915 = .3085$.

29. **(C)**   The cumulative proportions of 0.25 and 0.75 correspond to $Q_1 = 200$ and $Q_3 = 1750$, respectively, and so the interquartile range is 1550.

30. **(B)**   We have H_0: $\mu = 25$, H_a: $\mu < 25$, $\bar{x} = 24.581$, $s = 0.7793$, and $\sigma_{\bar{x}} = \frac{0.7793}{\sqrt{26}} = 0.153$. The t-score of 24.581 is $\frac{24.581 - 25}{0.153} = -2.74$. In looking at the df $= 25$ row in Table B, note that 2.74 is between 2.485 and 2.787, so P is

between .005 and .01. (A calculator like the TI-83 quickly gives the critical t-score as -2.74 and $P = .0056$.)

31. **(E)** $3(.8)^2(.2) + (.8)^3 = .896$

32. **(E)** The expected values are

62.2	24.4	13.3
217.8	85.6	46.7

Chi-square is calculated to measure the difference between the observed and expected values:

$$\chi^2 = \frac{(5.2)^2}{62.2} + \frac{(1.6)^2}{24.4} + \frac{(3.7)^2}{13.3} + \frac{(5.2)^2}{217.8} + \frac{(1.6)^2}{85.6} + \frac{(3.7)^2}{46.7} = 2.02$$

(*Note:* Input of the original matrix into a calculator like the TI-83 quickly gives $\chi^2 = 1.99$.) With df $= (2-1)(3-1) = 2$, the critical χ^2-value for a tail probability of .10 is 4.61. Since $2.02 < 4.61$, there is not sufficient evidence that vitamin C helps cut down on common colds.

33. **(B)** The PTA survey has strong response bias in that students may not give truthful responses to a parent or teacher about their engaging in unprotected sex. The talk show survey results in a voluntary response sample, which typically gives too much emphasis to persons with strong opinions. The *Ladies Home Journal* survey has strong selection bias; that is, people who read the *Journal* are not representative of the general population.

34. **(D)** To divide the interval estimate by d, the sample size must be increased by a multiple of d^2.

35. **(C)** $P(Y = 2) = .186 + .198 + .216 = .6$
$P(X = 1)(.6) = .186$, and so $P(X = 1) = .31$
$P(Y = 1) = 1 - (.6 + .1) = .3$
$P(X = 1, Y = 1) = (.31)(.3) = .093$

Section II

1. (a) We have H_0: $\mu = 41.6$, H_a: $\mu > 41.6$, and $\sigma_{\bar{x}} = \frac{6.05}{\sqrt{17}} = 1.47$. The t-score of 42.72 is $\frac{42.72 - 41.6}{1.47} = 0.762$. Looking across the df $= 16$ row in Table B, note that 0.762 is between .690 and .865. Thus the P-value is between .20 and .25. With such a large P, there is no evidence for rejecting H_0; that is, there is no evidence indicating that marijuana users score higher on the anger expression scale than do nonusers.

   (b) In addition to the usual assumption that we are dealing with a simple random sample, we must assume that we are also working with a normal population.

2. (a) The correlation coefficient $r = \sqrt{.819} = .905$. It is positive because the slope of the regression line is positive.

   (b) The slope is 8.5, signifying that each gram of medication lowers the pulse rate by 8.5 beats per minute.

   (c) $y = -1.68 + 8.5(2.25) = 17.4$ beats per minute.

   (d) There is always danger in using a regression line to extrapolate beyond the values of x contained in the data. In this case, the 5 grams was an overdose, the patient died, and the regression line cannot be used for such values beyond the data set.

   (e) Removing the 3-gram result from the data set will increase the correlation coefficient because the 3-gram result appears to be far off a regression line through the remaining points.

   (f) Removing the 3-gram result from the data set will swing the regression line upward so that the slope will increase.

3. If the $35 + 42 + 22 + 41 + 30 = 170$ new clients were uniformly distributed, each partner would have brought in $\frac{170}{5} = 34$ new clients. The difference between the expected and observed numbers is measured by chi-square:

$$\chi^2 = \frac{1^2}{34} + \frac{8^2}{34} + \frac{12^2}{34} + \frac{7^2}{34} + \frac{4^2}{34} = 8.06$$

With df $= 5 - 1 = 4$, the critical χ^2-values for the 5% and 10% significance levels are 9.49 and 7.78, respectively. Thus there is sufficient evidence at the 10% level, but not at the 5% level, that the partners bring in different numbers of new clients.

4. (a) $P(\text{four math classes}) = 1 - (.1 + .2 + .3) = .4$

$$P(\text{success}) = .015 + .050 + .165 + .340 = .570$$

(b)

$$= \frac{.165}{.570} + \frac{.340}{.570}$$

$$= .886$$

5. For each new heart attack patient entering the hospital, look at the next digit from a random number table. If it is odd, give the name to a group of people who will pray for the patient throughout his or her hospitalization, while if it is even, don't ask the group to pray (randomization). Don't let the patients know what is happening (blinding) and don't let the doctors know what is happening (double-blinding). Compare the lengths of hospitalization of patients who receive prayers with those of control group patients who don't receive prayers (comparison).

6. (a) Let the digit 9 represent a tie that is too tight, while the digits 0 through 8 represent ties that are not too tight. Read off groups of ten digits, checking for the number of 9s in each group. Tabulating from the table gives

> No tight ties (no 9s): 8
> One tight tie (one 9): 15
> Two tight ties (two 9s): 5
> Three tight ties (three 9s): 2.

The estimated probability of at least two tight ties among the ten businessmen is thus $\frac{5+2}{30} = .23$.

(b) $P(\text{at least } 2)$ $\begin{aligned} &= 1 - [P(0) + P(1)] \\ &= 1 - [(.9)^{10} + 10(.1)(.9)^9] \\ &= .26 \end{aligned}$

(c)   We have $H_0: p = .1$, $H_a: p < .1$, and $\sigma_{\hat{p}} = \sqrt{\frac{(.1)(.9)}{200}} = .0212$. $\hat{p} = \frac{17}{200} = .085$ with z-score $\frac{.085 - .1}{.0212} = -0.71$ with a corresponding P-value of .2389 from Table A. With such a large P, there is not sufficient evidence to dispute the Cornell University claim.

Appendix

Formulas

The following are in the form and notation as recommended by the College Board.

Descriptive Statistics

$$\bar{x} = \frac{\sum x_i}{n}$$

$$s = \sqrt{\frac{1}{n-1}\sum(x_i - \bar{x})^2}$$

$$s_p = \sqrt{\frac{(n_1 - 1)s_1^2 + (n_2 - 1)s_2^2}{(n_1 - 1) + (n_2 - 1)}}$$

$$\hat{y} = b_0 + b_1 x$$

$$b_1 = \frac{\sum(x_i - \bar{x})(y_i - \bar{y})}{\sum(x_i - \bar{x})^2}$$

$$b_0 = \bar{y} - b_1\bar{x}$$

$$r = \frac{1}{n-1}\sum\left(\frac{x_i - \bar{x}}{s_x}\right)\left(\frac{y_i - \bar{y}}{s_y}\right)$$

$$b_1 = r\frac{s_y}{s_x}$$

$$s_{b_1} = \frac{\sqrt{\frac{\sum(y_i - \hat{y}_i)^2}{n-2}}}{\sqrt{\sum(x_i - \bar{x})^2}}$$

Probability

$$P(A \cup B) = P(A) + P(B) - P(A \cap B)$$

$$P(A|B) = \frac{P(A \cap B)}{P(B)}$$

$$E(X) = \mu_x = \sum x_i p_i$$

$$\text{var}(X) = \sigma_x^2 = \sum (x_i - \mu_x)^2 p_i$$

If X has a binomial distribution with parameters n and p, then:

$$P(X = k) = \binom{n}{k} p^k (1-p)^{(n-k)}$$

$$\mu_x = np$$

$$\sigma_x = \sqrt{np(1-p)}$$

$$\mu_{\hat{p}} = p$$

$$\sigma_{\hat{p}} = \sqrt{\frac{p(1-p)}{n}}$$

If X has a normal distribution with mean μ and standard deviation σ, then:

$$\mu_{\bar{x}} = \mu$$

$$\sigma_{\bar{x}} = \frac{\sigma}{\sqrt{n}}$$

Inferential Statistics

Standardized test statistic: $\dfrac{\text{Estimate} - \text{parameter}}{\text{Standard deviation of the estimate}}$

Confidence interval:
Estimate $\pm$ (critical value) $\cdot$ (standard deviation of the estimate)

SINGLE SAMPLE

Statistic	Standard deviation
Mean	$\dfrac{\sigma}{\sqrt{n}}$
Proportion	$\sqrt{\dfrac{p(1-p)}{n}}$

TWO SAMPLE

Statistic	Standard deviation
Difference of means (unequal variances)	$\sqrt{\dfrac{\sigma_1^2}{n_1} + \dfrac{\sigma_2^2}{n_2}}$
Difference of means (equal variances)	$\sigma\sqrt{\dfrac{1}{n_1} + \dfrac{1}{n_2}}$
Difference of proportions (unequal variances)	$\sqrt{\dfrac{p_1(1-p_1)}{n_1} + \dfrac{p_2(1-p_2)}{n_2}}$
Difference of proportions (equal variances)	$\sqrt{p(1-p)}\,\sqrt{\dfrac{1}{n_1} + \dfrac{1}{n_2}}$

Chi-square statistic $= \displaystyle\sum \dfrac{(\text{observed} - \text{expected})^2}{\text{expected}}$

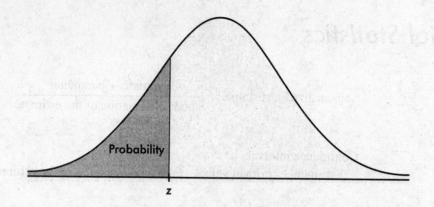

TABLE A: STANDARD NORMAL PROBABILITIES

z	.00	.01	.02	.03	.04	.05	.06	.07	.08	.09
−3.4	.0003	.0003	.0003	.0003	.0003	.0003	.0003	.0003	.0003	.0002
−3.3	.0005	.0005	.0005	.0004	.0004	.0004	.0004	.0004	.0004	.0003
−3.2	.0007	.0007	.0006	.0006	.0006	.0006	.0006	.0005	.0005	.0005
−3.1	.0010	.0009	.0009	.0009	.0008	.0008	.0008	.0008	.0007	.0007
−3.0	.0013	.0013	.0013	.0012	.0012	.0011	.0011	.0011	.0010	.0010
−2.9	.0019	.0018	.0018	.0017	.0016	.0016	.0015	.0015	.0014	.0014
−2.8	.0026	.0025	.0024	.0023	.0023	.0022	.0021	.0021	.0020	.0019
−2.7	.0035	.0034	.0033	.0032	.0031	.0030	.0029	.0028	.0027	.0026
−2.6	.0047	.0045	.0044	.0043	.0041	.0040	.0039	.0038	.0037	.0036
−2.5	.0062	.0060	.0059	.0057	.0055	.0054	.0052	.0051	.0049	.0048
−2.4	.0082	.0080	.0078	.0075	.0073	.0071	.0069	.0068	.0066	.0064
−2.3	.0107	.0104	.0102	.0099	.0096	.0094	.0091	.0089	.0087	.0084
−2.2	.0139	.0136	.0132	.0129	.0125	.0122	.0119	.0116	.0113	.0110
−2.1	.0179	.0174	.0170	.0166	.0162	.0158	.0154	.0150	.0146	.0143
−2.0	.0228	.0222	.0217	.0212	.0207	.0202	.0197	.0192	.0188	.0183
−1.9	.0287	.0281	.0274	.0268	.0262	.0256	.0250	.0244	.0239	.0233
−1.8	.0359	.0351	.0344	.0336	.0329	.0322	.0314	.0307	.0301	.0294
−1.7	.0446	.0436	.0427	.0418	.0409	.0401	.0392	.0384	.0375	.0367
−1.6	.0548	.0537	.0526	.0516	.0505	.0495	.0485	.0475	.0465	.0455
−1.5	.0668	.0655	.0643	.0630	.0618	.0606	.0594	.0582	.0571	.0559
−1.4	.0808	.0793	.0778	.0764	.0749	.0735	.0721	.0708	.0694	.0681
−1.3	.0968	.0951	.0934	.0918	.0901	.0885	.0869	.0853	.0838	.0823
−1.2	.1151	.1131	.1112	.1093	.1075	.1056	.1038	.1020	.1003	.0985
−1.1	.1357	.1335	.1314	.1292	.1271	.1251	.1230	.1210	.1190	.1170
−1.0	.1587	.1562	.1539	.1515	.1492	.1469	.1446	.1423	.1401	.1379
−0.9	.1841	.1814	.1788	.1762	.1736	.1711	.1685	.1660	.1635	.1611
−0.8	.2119	.2090	.2061	.2033	.2005	.1977	.1949	.1922	.1894	.1867
−0.7	.2420	.2389	.2358	.2327	.2296	.2266	.2236	.2206	.2177	.2148
−0.6	.2743	.2709	.2676	.2643	.2611	.2578	.2546	.2514	.2483	.2451
−0.5	.3085	.3050	.3015	.2981	.2946	.2912	.2877	.2843	.2810	.2776
−0.4	.3446	.3409	.3372	.3336	.3300	.3264	.3228	.3192	.3156	.3121
−0.3	.3821	.3783	.3745	.3707	.3669	.3632	.3594	.3557	.3520	.3483
−0.2	.4207	.4168	.4129	.4090	.4052	.4013	.3974	.3936	.3897	.3859
−0.1	.4602	.4562	.4522	.4483	.4443	.4404	.4364	.4325	.4286	.4247
−0.0	.5000	.4960	.4920	.4880	.4840	.4801	.4761	.4721	.4681	.4641

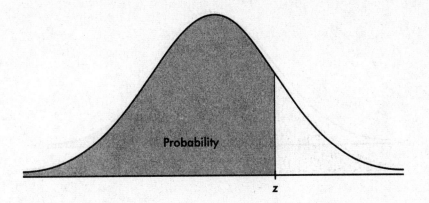

TABLE A: STANDARD NORMAL PROBABILITIES (CONTINUED)

z	.00	.01	.02	.03	.04	.05	.06	.07	.08	.09
0.0	.5000	.5040	.5080	.5120	.5160	.5199	.5239	.5279	.5319	.5359
0.1	.5398	.5438	.5478	.5517	.5557	.5596	.5636	.5675	.5714	.5753
0.2	.5793	.5832	.5871	.5910	.5948	.5987	.6026	.6064	.6103	.6141
0.3	.6179	.6217	.6255	.6293	.6331	.6368	.6406	.6443	.6480	.6517
0.4	.6554	.6591	.6628	.6664	.6700	.6736	.6772	.6808	.6844	.6879
0.5	.6915	.6950	.6985	.7019	.7054	.7088	.7123	.7157	.7190	.7224
0.6	.7257	.7291	.7324	.7357	.7389	.7422	.7454	.7486	.7517	.7549
0.7	.7580	.7611	.7642	.7673	.7704	.7734	.7764	.7794	.7823	.7852
0.8	.7881	.7910	.7939	.7967	.7995	.8023	.8051	.8078	.8106	.8133
0.9	.8159	.8186	.8212	.8238	.8264	.8289	.8315	.8340	.8365	.8389
1.0	.8413	.8438	.8461	.8485	.8508	.8531	.8554	.8577	.8599	.8621
1.1	.8643	.8665	.8686	.8708	.8729	.8749	.8770	.8790	.8810	.8830
1.2	.8849	.8869	.8888	.8907	.8925	.8944	.8962	.8980	.8997	.9015
1.3	.9032	.9049	.9066	.9082	.9099	.9115	.9131	.9147	.9162	.9177
1.4	.9192	.9207	.9222	.9236	.9251	.9265	.9279	.9292	.9306	.9319
1.5	.9332	.9345	.9357	.9370	.9382	.9394	.9406	.9418	.9429	.9441
1.6	.9452	.9463	.9474	.9484	.9495	.9505	.9515	.9525	.9535	.9545
1.7	.9554	.9564	.9573	.9582	.9591	.9599	.9608	.9616	.9625	.9633
1.8	.9641	.9649	.9656	.9664	.9671	.9678	.9686	.9693	.9699	.9706
1.9	.9713	.9719	.9726	.9732	.9738	.9744	.9750	.9756	.9761	.9767
2.0	.9772	.9778	.9783	.9788	.9793	.9798	.9803	.9808	.9812	.9817
2.1	.9821	.9826	.9830	.9834	.9838	.9842	.9846	.9850	.9854	.9857
2.2	.9861	.9864	.9868	.9871	.9875	.9878	.9881	.9884	.9887	.9890
2.3	.9893	.9896	.9898	.9901	.9904	.9906	.9909	.9911	.9913	.9916
2.4	.9918	.9920	.9922	.9925	.9927	.9929	.9931	.9932	.9934	.9936
2.5	.9938	.9940	.9941	.9943	.9945	.9946	.9948	.9949	.9951	.9952
2.6	.9953	.9955	.9956	.9957	.9959	.9960	.9961	.9962	.9963	.9964
2.7	.9965	.9966	.9967	.9968	.9969	.9970	.9971	.9972	.9973	.9974
2.8	.9974	.9975	.9976	.9977	.9977	.9978	.9979	.9979	.9980	.9981
2.9	.9981	.9982	.9982	.9983	.9984	.9984	.9985	.9985	.9986	.9986
3.0	.9987	.9987	.9987	.9988	.9988	.9989	.9989	.9989	.9990	.9990
3.1	.9990	.9991	.9991	.9991	.9992	.9992	.9992	.9992	.9993	.9993
3.2	.9993	.9993	.9994	.9994	.9994	.9994	.9994	.9995	.9995	.9995
3.3	.9995	.9995	.9995	.9996	.9996	.9996	.9996	.9996	.9996	.9997
3.4	.9997	.9997	.9997	.9997	.9997	.9997	.9997	.9997	.9997	.9998

TABLE B: *t*-DISTRIBUTION CRITICAL VALUES

df	Tail probability *p*											
	.25	.20	.15	.10	.05	.025	.02	.01	.005	.0025	.001	.0005
1	1.000	1.376	1.963	3.078	6.314	12.71	15.89	31.82	63.66	127.3	318.3	636.6
2	.816	1.061	1.386	1.886	2.920	4.303	4.849	6.965	9.925	14.09	22.33	31.60
3	.765	.978	1.250	1.638	2.353	3.182	3.482	4.541	5.841	7.453	10.21	12.92
4	.741	.941	1.190	1.533	2.132	2.776	2.999	3.747	4.604	5.598	7.173	8.610
5	.727	.920	1.156	1.476	2.015	2.571	2.757	3.365	4.032	4.773	5.893	6.869
6	.718	.906	1.134	1.440	1.943	2.447	2.612	3.143	3.707	4.317	5.208	5.959
7	.711	.896	1.119	1.415	1.895	2.365	2.517	2.998	3.499	4.029	4.785	5.408
8	.706	.889	1.108	1.397	1.860	2.306	2.449	2.896	3.355	3.833	4.501	5.041
9	.703	.883	1.100	1.383	1.833	2.262	2.398	2.821	3.250	3.690	4.297	4.781
10	.700	.879	1.093	1.372	1.812	2.228	2.359	2.764	3.169	3.581	4.144	4.587
11	.697	.876	1.088	1.363	1.796	2.201	2.328	2.718	3.106	3.497	4.025	4.437
12	.695	.873	1.083	1.356	1.782	2.179	2.303	2.681	3.055	3.428	3.930	4.318
13	.694	.870	1.079	1.350	1.771	2.160	2.282	2.650	3.012	3.372	3.852	4.221
14	.692	.868	1.076	1.345	1.761	2.145	2.264	2.624	2.977	3.326	3.787	4.140
15	.691	.866	1.074	1.341	1.753	2.131	2.249	2.602	2.947	3.286	3.733	4.073
16	.690	.865	1.071	1.337	1.746	2.120	2.235	2.583	2.921	3.252	3.686	4.015
17	.689	.863	1.069	1.333	1.740	2.110	2.224	2.567	2.898	3.222	3.646	3.965
18	.688	.862	1.067	1.330	1.734	2.101	2.214	2.552	2.878	3.197	3.611	3.922
19	.688	.861	1.066	1.328	1.729	2.093	2.205	2.539	2.861	3.174	3.579	3.883
20	.687	.860	1.064	1.325	1.725	2.086	2.197	2.528	2.845	3.153	3.552	3.850
21	.686	.859	1.063	1.323	1.721	2.080	2.189	2.518	2.831	3.135	3.527	3.819
22	.686	.858	1.061	1.321	1.717	2.074	2.183	2.508	2.819	3.119	3.505	3.792
23	.685	.858	1.060	1.319	1.714	2.069	2.177	2.500	2.807	3.104	3.485	3.768
24	.685	.857	1.059	1.318	1.711	2.064	2.172	2.492	2.797	3.091	3.467	3.745
25	.684	.856	1.058	1.316	1.708	2.060	2.167	2.485	2.787	3.078	3.450	3.725
26	.684	.856	1.058	1.315	1.706	2.056	2.162	2.479	2.779	3.067	3.435	3.707
27	.684	.855	1.057	1.314	1.703	2.052	2.158	2.473	2.771	3.057	3.421	3.690
28	.683	.855	1.056	1.313	1.701	2.048	2.154	2.467	2.763	3.047	3.408	3.674
29	.683	.854	1.055	1.311	1.699	2.045	2.150	2.462	2.756	3.038	3.396	3.659
30	.683	.854	1.055	1.310	1.697	2.042	2.147	2.457	2.750	3.030	3.385	3.646
40	.681	.851	1.050	1.303	1.684	2.021	2.123	2.423	2.704	2.971	3.307	3.551
50	.679	.849	1.047	1.299	1.676	2.009	2.109	2.403	2.678	2.937	3.261	3.496
60	.679	.848	1.045	1.296	1.671	2.000	2.099	2.390	2.660	2.915	3.232	3.460
80	.678	.846	1.043	1.292	1.664	1.990	2.088	2.374	2.639	2.887	3.195	3.416
100	.677	.845	1.042	1.290	1.660	1.984	2.081	2.364	2.626	2.871	3.174	3.390
1000	.675	.842	1.037	1.282	1.646	1.962	2.056	2.330	2.581	2.813	3.098	3.300
∞	.674	.841	1.036	1.282	1.645	1.960	2.054	2.326	2.576	2.807	3.091	3.291
	50%	60%	70%	80%	90%	95%	96%	98%	99%	99.5%	99.8%	99.9%
	Confidence level *C*											

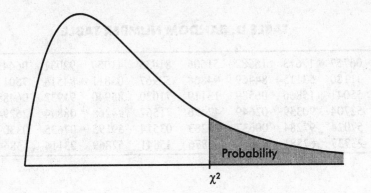

TABLE C: χ^2 **CRITICAL VALUES**

df	.25	.20	.15	.10	.05	.025	.02	.01	.005	.0025	.001
1	1.32	1.64	2.07	2.71	3.84	5.02	5.41	6.63	7.88	9.14	10.83
2	2.77	3.22	3.79	4.61	5.99	7.38	7.82	9.21	10.60	11.98	13.82
3	4.11	4.64	5.32	6.25	7.81	9.35	9.84	11.34	12.84	14.32	16.27
4	5.39	5.99	6.74	7.78	9.49	11.14	11.67	13.28	14.86	16.42	18.47
5	6.63	7.29	8.12	9.24	11.07	12.83	13.39	15.09	16.75	18.39	20.51
6	7.84	8.56	9.45	10.64	12.59	14.45	15.03	16.81	18.55	20.25	22.46
7	9.04	9.80	10.75	12.02	14.07	16.01	16.62	18.48	20.28	22.04	24.32
8	10.22	11.03	12.03	13.36	15.51	17.53	18.17	20.09	21.95	23.77	26.12
9	11.39	12.24	13.29	14.68	16.92	19.02	19.68	21.67	23.59	25.46	27.88
10	12.55	13.44	14.53	15.99	18.31	20.48	21.16	23.21	25.19	27.11	29.59
11	13.70	14.63	15.77	17.28	19.68	21.92	22.62	24.72	26.76	28.73	31.26
12	14.85	15.81	16.99	18.55	21.03	23.34	24.05	26.22	28.30	30.32	32.91
13	15.98	16.98	18.20	19.81	22.36	24.74	25.47	27.69	29.82	31.88	34.53
14	17.12	18.15	19.41	21.06	23.68	26.12	26.87	29.14	31.32	33.43	36.12
15	18.25	19.31	20.60	22.31	25.00	27.49	28.26	30.58	32.80	34.95	37.70
16	19.37	20.47	21.79	23.54	26.30	28.85	29.63	32.00	34.27	36.46	39.25
17	20.49	21.61	22.98	24.77	27.59	30.19	31.00	33.41	35.72	37.95	40.79
18	21.60	22.76	24.16	25.99	28.87	31.53	32.35	34.81	37.16	39.42	42.31
19	22.72	23.90	25.33	27.20	30.14	32.85	33.69	36.19	38.58	40.88	43.82
20	23.83	25.04	26.50	28.41	31.41	34.17	35.02	37.57	40.00	42.34	45.31
21	24.93	26.17	27.66	29.62	32.67	35.48	36.34	38.93	41.40	43.78	46.80
22	26.04	27.30	28.82	30.81	33.92	36.78	37.66	40.29	42.80	45.20	48.27
23	27.14	28.43	29.98	32.01	35.17	38.08	38.97	41.64	44.18	46.62	49.73
24	28.24	29.55	31.13	33.20	36.42	39.36	40.27	42.98	45.56	48.03	51.18
25	29.34	30.68	32.28	34.38	37.65	40.65	41.57	44.31	46.93	49.44	52.62
26	30.43	31.79	33.43	35.56	38.89	41.92	42.86	45.64	48.29	50.83	54.05
27	31.53	32.91	34.57	36.74	40.11	43.19	44.14	46.96	49.64	52.22	55.48
28	32.62	34.03	35.71	37.92	41.34	44.46	45.42	48.28	50.99	53.59	56.89
29	33.71	35.14	36.85	39.09	42.56	45.72	46.69	49.59	52.34	54.97	58.30
30	34.80	36.25	37.99	40.26	43.77	46.98	47.96	50.89	53.67	56.33	59.70
40	45.62	47.27	49.24	51.81	55.76	59.34	60.44	63.69	66.77	69.70	73.40
50	56.33	58.16	60.35	63.17	67.50	71.42	72.61	76.15	79.49	82.66	86.66
60	66.98	68.97	71.34	74.40	79.08	83.30	84.58	88.38	91.95	95.34	99.61
80	88.13	90.41	93.11	96.58	101.9	106.6	108.1	112.3	116.3	120.1	124.8
100	109.1	111.7	114.7	118.5	124.3	129.6	131.1	135.8	140.2	144.3	149.4

TABLE D: RANDOM NUMBER TABLE

84177	06757	17613	15582	51506	81435	41050	92031	06449	05059
59884	31180	53115	84469	94868	57967	05811	84514	75011	13006
63395	55041	15866	06589	13119	71020	85940	91932	06488	74987
54355	52704	90359	02649	47496	71567	94268	08844	26294	64759
08989	57024	97284	00637	89283	03514	59195	07635	03309	72605
29357	23737	67881	03668	33876	35841	52869	23114	15864	38942

Index

Parentheses indicate problem numbers